The Legacy of Edward W. Said

The Legacy of
Edward W. Said

WILLIAM V. SPANOS

University of Illinois Press

URBANA AND CHICAGO

© 2009 by William V. Spanos
All rights reserved
Manufactured in the United States of America
1 2 3 4 5 C P 5 4 3 2 1
∞ This book is printed on acid-free paper.

Library of Congress Cataloging-in-Publication Data
Spanos, William V.
The legacy of Edward W. Said / William V. Spanos.
p. cm.
Includes bibliographical references and index.
ISBN 978-0-252-03388-9 (cloth : alk. paper)
ISBN 978-0-252-07572-8 (paper : alk. paper)
1. Said, Edward W.—Influence.
2. Said, Edward W.—Political and social views.
3. Philosophy, Modern—20th century.
4. Poststructuralism. 5. Orientalism.
6. Humanism. 7. Imperialism.
8. United States—Foreign relations—Philosophy.
9. Politics and culture. 10. Mount Hermon School.
I. Title.
CB18.S25S63   2009
973.91092—dc22 [B]   2008027200

To the Memory of Edward W. Said,
In gratitude for his Presence
In a time of dearth

The nothing—what else can it be for science but an outrage and a phantasm? If science is right, then only one thing is sure: science wishes to know nothing of the nothing. Ultimately this is the scientifically rigorous conception of the nothing. We know it, the nothing, in that we wish to know nothing about it.

—Martin Heidegger, "What Is Metaphysics?"

Within its own limits, every disciple recognizes true and false propositions, but it repulses a whole teratology of learning.

—Michel Foucault, "The Discourse in Language"

To the Israelis, whose incomparable military and political power dominates us, we are at the periphery, the image that will not go away. Every assertion of our nonexistence, every attempt to spirit us away, every new effort to prove that we were never really there, simply raises the question of why so much denial of, and such energy expended on, what was not there? Could it be that even as alien outsiders we dog their military might with our obdurate moral claim, our insistence (like that of Bartleby the Scrivener) that "we would prefer not to," not to leave, not to abandon Palestine forever?

—Edward W. Said, *After the Last Sky*

Contents

Acknowledgments

As the last chapter, "Edward Said's Mount Hermon and Mine," will make amply clear, this book on Said's legacy had, in some complex and indefinable way, its origins long ago, in 1951, when, after a year at Columbia University, I came to Mount Hermon, a prep school in Bernardston, Massachusetts, to begin my errant teaching career. It was also the year when the fifteen-year-old Edward Said left Egypt and came, reluctantly, as he tells us in his memoir *Out of Place,* to this Protestant work ethic–driven school. He did not take a course with me during our two years there—alas, since I was teaching the prescribed texts against the grain, from a Kierkegaardian existentialist perspective—so I didn't come to know him at that time. But many years later, in the early 1970s, after Said had established a substantial reputation as a Conrad scholar, and I had founded *boundary 2,* he told me that he was aware of my presence at Mount Hermon because, as he put it, I and my friend Bill Burney had the reputation of being something like mysterious outsiders in that WASP environment. This was during a telephone call responding to my request for an essay for the first issue of the journal (on postmodernism); it turned out to be "Foucault as an Intellectual Imagination," which was incorporated in the penultimate chapter of *Beginnings* (1975), "*Abecedarium Culturae:* Absence, Writing, Statement, Discourse, Archeology, Structuralism." That conversation long ago, in which Edward spoke of his being "out of place" at Mount Hermon, had a great impact on me. It established a long-standing, if spatially distant, friendship and instigated in me a sense of kinship with him, not simply with his revolutionary criticism, but also, and above all, with his extraordinary humanity.

This is not to say that I became a disciple. In the years that followed, he was never sympathetic with my obsession with Heidegger's destructive ontology, nor was I entirely sympathetic with his overdetermination of politics at the expense of theory. Indeed, this difference became a constant of our all too infrequent encounters. When they did occur, he would invariably tell me jokingly, "Dear Bill, you're a good critic, but why do you weaken your originative criticism by Heideggerianizing it?" And I would respond, antiphonally, "Edward, I think you're a good critic, too, but why do you limit possibilities by not attending to Heidegger's destructive ontology?" I am not sure how seriously he took my response. What I can say about these conversations is that they instigated my career-long *Auseinandersetzung*—a critical yet collaborative dialogue—or in his own vocabulary, a "contrapuntal" relationship, with his work. It is in this spirit that I offer my book to his abiding memory.

In the process of writing it, I have, as usual, accumulated many debts to my students who have taken various courses I have given on Said and related topics over the years and to colleagues at Binghamton with whom I have discussed my work (or perhaps I should say on whom I inflicted it). With respect to the first group, I want to express my gratitude to R. Radhakrishnan, David Randall, Giovanna Covi, Jeanette McVicker, Robert Marzec, Assimina Karavanta, Michael Logan, Orac Firat, Evi Haggipavlu, Racheal Forlow, Amy Dowd, Tara Sak, and Christina Battista, who, each in his or her own way, contributed to my understanding of Said's enormously complex and finally unnameable global "vision." With respect to the second group, I want to acknowledge my debts to David Bartine, Joseph Keith, Dale Tomich, Louisa Morrera, and especially Susan Strehle, all of whom have been patient and productive collocutors in the process of my relentless, patience-exhausting obsession with Said's legacy.

A third group of people to whom I am deeply indebted is, as usual, my colleagues in the *boundary 2* editorial collective. I am particularly referring, on the one hand, to Dan O'Hara, Joseph Buttigieg, R. Radhakrishnan, and Donald Pease, who have acknowledged the viability of my perspective on Said's work, and, on the other hand, to Paul Bové, Ronald Judy, Michael Hays, Marcia Landy, and Karl Kroeber, all of whom have expressed serious reservations, especially about my poststructuralist (though not essentially antihumanist) interrogation of Said's renewed commitment to humanism, particularly at a time when the antihumanist Straussian neoconservatives who now occupy the White House are mounting an antihistorical and antidemocratic agenda that threatens the very being of the human species. Acknowledging the ominous threat from the right, I am nevertheless less certain than they seem to be that an interrogation of Said's apotheosis of humanism in his posthumously published book aids and abets the right-wing agenda. Yet I am, in the last analysis, grateful for their criticism. In pointing out the threat to humanity posed by these neoconservative antihumanist humanists, they have compelled me to modify my own, though radically different, form of antihumanism and made me more careful in what I say about Said's humanism. As with my relationship to Said's work, this book is thus in many ways undertaken in the spirit not of opposition but of intimate dialogue with my uneasy *boundary 2* colleagues.

Not least, I want to express my loving gratitude to my first three children, Maria, Aristides, and Stephania, for their care from long distance and especially to my youngest son, Adam, and his mother, Susan Strehle, both of whom have been there for me in a trying time.

Finally, I take great pleasure in expressing my gratitude to the artist and historian Nikos Stavrolakis for granting me permission to reproduce his woodcut "Palestinian Refugee" as the cover of this book. I met Nikos, a Cretan Jew, in 1969, when I was a Fulbright Professor at the University of Athens and bought a copy of this woodcut (as well as two others) in a gallery near the Fulbright offices, and it has been hanging in my living room ever since. Sometime near the end of the process of writing this book on Edward Said, it struck me with great force that this masterpiece—the epitome of silent defiance—would make the perfect cover for it. Since, however, I had not been in touch with Nikos in many years, and time had blunted my memory of the woodcut's specific provenance, I asked my dear friend and former student Assimina Karavanta, a professor of American studies at the University of Athens, to track him down in the hope of retrieving the origins of the woodcut and getting his permission to use it. Her efforts proved successful. Nikos and I renewed our acquaintanceship; he granted me the permission I sought, and he recalled for me the history of the making of this masterpiece. It is fitting, as the reader will realize in the process of reading this book about the question of representation—who is speaking for whom?—that he tell the story of the woodcut's origins and its relationship to Edward Said in his own words:

> It is I who am honoured as I had and retain a deep admiration for Said, and I suppose this is an oblique way of paying homage to a great Palestinian and scholar. As for the letter [about the circumstances of the making of the woodcut, which Nikos, on hearing of my request, had written to me but was lost when his computer crashed] I cannot find it, alas, but the gist of it was as follows: I was in Jerusalem only a few days after it was taken by the Israelis [in the Six Day War of 1967]. I was not one of the volunteers or of those who had gone out of any kind of altruism—I had an appointment at Haifa University that I felt I had to keep—so off I went in the still falling debris of war. I had good friends

in Jerusalem, and one of them . . . got me included as a "reporter artist" in a group of twelve journalists who were among the first permitted to enter the old city. It was quite a magic moment for me, and I remember so much of it as we entered through Damascus Gate and then took the street that led to the Wailing Wall—there was hardly any life about one—dark shadows moving or peering out of closed shops and houses—and the Wall was quite awesome really as the houses before it were still standing (only to be bulldozed down not long after). . . . By the time we got out through Damascus Gate there was much more movement, and I started to do sketches of the Arabs around me—of a "sous" seller and some children and others of people simply standing around, and then I caught sight of this one woman squatted down and looking terribly proud and not at all apparently fazed by what had happened—wrapped in her embroidered dress, bare footed and aloof—so there it is. And when I got back to Athens I set many of these as themes for woodcuts—hence yours. I know what readily stupid violence has been done by the European Jews in Israel—they have not only rewritten Jewish history, but their prejudices and ignorance have effected even the memory of many Arab-Jews that came from communities—Syria, Iraq, Egypt, and Yemen—who had lived for centuries in close cultural symbiosis with Muslims. . . . So much of what has transpired in Israel is a product of outdated European nationalism and more important perhaps—re: Said—"Orientalism."

I am grateful to Geoffrey Gould for reproducing Niko's woodcut; to Anita Pisani, secretary to the chair of the English Department at Binghamton University, and Ruth Stanek, assistant to the chair, for their gracious assistance in preparing my original manuscript for submission; and to the production staff of the University of Illinois Press for their efficiency in seeing this book through the publication process.

* * *

A much earlier version of chapter 2 was published as "Heidegger and Foucault: The Politics of the Gaze," in *Heidegger and Criticism: Retrieving the Cultural Politics of Destruction* (Minneapolis: University of Minnesota Press, 1993). An earlier version of chapter 6 was published as "Edward Said's Mount Hermon and Mine: A Forwarding Remembrance," in *boundary 2* 28, no. 3 (Fall 2001). I wish to thank the University of Minnesota Press and Duke University Press for granting me permission to reprint.

1. Edward W. Said and the Poststructuralists

An Introduction

> In setting up a world and setting forth the earth, the work [of art] is an instigating of this strife. This does not happen so that the work should at the same time settle and put an end to the strife in an insipid agreement, but so the strife may remain a strife. Setting up a world and setting forth the earth, the work accomplishes this strife. The work-being of the work consists in the instigation of strife between world and earth. It is because the strife arrives at its high point in the simplicity of intimacy that the unity of the work comes about in the instigation of strife. The latter is the continually self-overreaching gathering of the work's agitation. The repose of the work that rests in itself thus has its essence in the intimacy of strife.
>
> —Martin Heidegger, "The Origin of the Work of Art"

> Opposition is true friendship.
>
> —William Blake, "Proverbs of Hell"

With the untimely death of Edward W. Said in 2003 various constituencies of the academic and public intellectual community, both in the United States and abroad, have begun to reassess the writings of this powerful contemporary oppositional intellectual, seeking to determine the nature of his legacy. On the right, the Straussian neoconservatives, who have exerted inordinate influence over the policies of the George W. Bush administration, have already inaugurated a campaign that goes beyond simply discrediting Said's work as that of a subversive intent on slandering America's benign global image and undermining its global authority.[1] This initiative, for example, is epitomized by the crude testimony that the anthropologist Stanley Kurtz of the Hoover Institution gave before the House Subcommittee on Select Education (June 19, 2003). Kurtz claimed that Said's groundbreaking and extraordinarily influential critique of the ideological bias of Western scholarly and media representations of the Orient, which he first presented in *Orientalism,* had become dogma in Middle East area studies funded by the federal government under Title VI of the Higher Education Act and, in thus encouraging this kind of "extremist" and "anti-American" scholarship, had contributed massively to the undermining of the Bush administration's "war on terror," if not, as his pedagogic rhetoric insinuates, to terrorism itself:

> The ruling intellectual paradigm in academic area studies (especially Middle Eastern studies) is called "post-colonial theory." Post-colonial theory was founded by Columbia University professor of comparative literature, Edward Said. Said gained fame in 1978, with the publication of his book, *Orientalism.* In that book, Said equated professors who support American foreign policy with 19th century intellectuals who propped up racist colonial empires. The core premise of post-colonial theory is that it is immoral for a scholar to put his knowledge of foreign languages and cultures at the service of American power.
>
> In his regular columns for the Egyptian weekly *Al-Ahram,* Said has made his views about America crystal clear. Said has condemned the United States, which he calls "a stupid bully," as a nation with a "history of reducing whole peoples, countries, and even continents to ruin by nothing short of holocaust." Said has actively urged his Egyptian readers to replace their naïve belief in America as the defender of liberty and democracy with his supposedly more accurate picture of America as an habitual perpetrator of genocide.[2]

On the left, a significant number of oppositional intellectuals, claiming to be his heirs and eager to proffer an image of Said's oeuvre that would radically counter this vulgar neoconservative vilification, seem to have read his posthumously published last book, *Humanism and Democratic Criticism,* as his *apologia pro vita sua,* the culmination of the narrative history of his thought.[3] To be specific, they seek, following his directives, to offer us a Said who, in marked opposition to the "antihumanism" of the great poststructuralist thinkers who were his contemporaries—Jacques Derrida, Jean-François Lyotard, Jacques Lacan, Louis Althusser, and not least, Michel Foucault—finally and overtly identified his more or less lifelong anti-imperialist project with the Western humanist legacy these poststructuralists were committed to delegitimizing. One of the most recent—and counterproductively uncompromising—versions of this binarist left-oriented claim comes from Timothy Brennan, a former student of Said, who writes:

> With some guardedness, it is in the essays of *The World, the Text, and the Critic* that he sets out to portray a mental landscape of imperial resurgence at the dawn of Reaganism as well as a situation in which critics were cramping the scope of intellectual life. . . . Although few understood his words this way, his

target in these essays was poststructuralist "science" seen as substitute religion with its own codes of enlistment, conversion, and mystification. In this way he revisited *Orientalism*'s analysis of that thoroughly European problematic, the sublation of religion and technics, a problematic continually shadowed by the triumph of reason implicit in Europe's tireless war on a conveniently ageless and resilient Islam.[4]

Another, more palatable version of this oppositional leftist perspective that perceives *Humanism and Democratic Criticism* as Said's *Summum* and his humanism as the urgent antidote to the antihumanism of both the right and the (poststructuralist) left comes from my *boundary 2* colleague Paul Bové. It is a persuasive version, one not to be taken lightly, because of its recognition that the logic of the Straussians' dehumanizing contempt for history could fulfill its imperatives in the extinction of the human species. Nevertheless, it is also one that, in overdetermining the antihumanism of these Straussian humanists *without referring to the quite different antihumanism of the poststructuralists* (i.e., those who, in disclosing the Logos—the principle of identity, of self-presence—informing its understanding of the Self, delegitimize the tradition's interpretation of humanism and the humanities), implicitly suggests the latter's complicity with the former. Bové starkly but quite accurately asserts that neoconservative state intellectuals, indifferent to Said's Vichian historicism, "never treat history, for the simple reason that in their philosophy, history is of no matter, especially when force is available." He then writes:

> In short, the last remaining superpower is a threat to American democracy. With its end-of-history crazes and its mad impositions of "democracy" by force, it expresses its profound hatred and fear of participatory democratic possibility and has committed itself, on the foundation of capitalist commodification, to the extinction of the species as capable of thinking and living historically. It has committed itself to make the species over into something other than the human that stands at the center of high philological humanism. For if the human becomes merely the creature that consumes under the illusion that ready-made certainties and corporate totalities define reality, truth, and the limits of desire, then the very idea that the human is mind capable of understanding itself, in its own forms and those of others—the very species that lives and thinks and creates culture in that way—will no longer exist.
>
> But Said was nothing if not committed to the power of resistance and *optimism that human struggles for freedom* can be achieved.[5]

I am, of course, profoundly sympathetic to Bové's characterization of Said's humanity, to his Vichian historicist idea of the human, and to his devastating critique of the Straussian neoconservative state intellectuals who have

hijacked whatever democracy still exists in the United States. From my recalcitrant poststructuralist perspective, however, I find it ironic that in identifying Said's humanism with philological historicity, that is, the perspective
that understands humanity as radically historical—the very historicity for
which the neoconservatives have nothing but utter contempt—Bové, like Said
(at times), fails to realize that his optimistic identification of the historical
struggle for freedom and democracy with the *abstraction* "humanity" (as in
his phrase "the human struggle for freedom") seems to be indifferent to the
historically specific character of these human struggles. It would be nice to
think with Bové and Said that humanity at large has throughout history been
committed to the struggle for freedom and democracy. As poststructuralists from Nietzsche and Heidegger to Derrida and Foucault have decisively
shown, however, the overwhelming witness of history demonstrates that, on
the contrary, humans have, precisely in the name of humanity, insistently
wreaked havoc on the planet and the humanity that inhabits it. In other
words, though I am in profound solidarity with Bové's and Said's expressions
of the urgent need to attend to their Vichian historicism in the face of the
neoconservative intellectual deputies' antihumanism, the kind of optimistic
generalization of humanity's struggle to be free shared by Bové and Said is,
as I will argue in this book, simply not historical enough.

In my view, the assumption that Said's posthumously published *Humanism
and Democratic Criticism* was his last will and testament—the final statement
of his critical legacy—is a questionable one with significant implications for
the present post-9/11 occasion. I make this contention in part because such
an assumption runs counter to the open-ended and collaborative essence
of his thought and particularly to the tenor of his late lectures on the "the
late styles" of figures including composers such as Mozart, Beethoven, and
Richard Strauss; essayists such as Theodor Adorno; writers such as Lampe-
dusa and Jean Genet; and filmmakers such as Visconti. In opposition to this
assumption's unwarranted narrative orientation toward biography, Said posits
these individuals' adamant refusal of narrative closure:

> Each of us can readily supply evidence of how it is that late works crown a
> lifetime of aesthetic endeavor, Rembrandt and Matisse, Bach and Wagner. But
> what of artistic lateness not as harmony and resolution but as intransigence,
> difficulty, and unresolved contradiction? What if age and ill health don't produce
> the serenity of "ripeness is all"? . . .
>
>   It is this second type of lateness as a factor of style I find deeply interesting.
> I'd like to explore the experience of late style that involves a nonharmonious,
> nonserene tension, and above all, a sort of deliberately unproductive produc-
> tiveness going *against*. . . .[6]

Moreover, the assumption that *Humanism and Democratic Criticism* is Said's last will and testament is especially problematic because, in the process of recuperating the hegemony of humanism, Said nowhere theorizes the history of the term's usage; that is, he never attempts to specify what he means by it. Such an assumption about Said's legacy therefore permits traditional liberal humanists to dissociate themselves from the "bad" (i.e., identitarian, Eurocentric, or elitist) humanism of the "classical" humanists he excoriates as "abusers" of an authentic humanism—most notably Matthew Arnold, Irving Babbitt, Paul Elmer More, T. S. Eliot, and more recently but not least, Allan Bloom—and to identify themselves with a "good" (accommodational, i.e., tolerant) humanism that in fact smuggles a transcendental Origin, an essentialism, into its secular orbit.[7] Whatever he says *about* humanism in this posthumously published book, Said was, at least in practice, an antihumanist humanist or at any rate was engaged in thinking a humanism that was in its errancy more truly humanist than the traditional humanism (Roman, not Greek) that became hegemonic in the West in the wake of the apotheosis of Man—the anthropo-logos—in the Renaissance and especially after the Enlightenment. Indeed, he was, despite an increasing negativity toward post-structuralism, thinking a humanism that was consistent with the posthumanism (i.e., the "antihumanist humanism") that was the unsaid assumption of the so-called poststructuralists from Heidegger, through Derrida, Lyotard, Lacan, and the French feminists, to Althusser and Foucault—specifically, those postmodern thinkers whose principal project was to demonstrate the paradoxical oppressiveness of (i.e., the difficulty of achieving agency within) the hegemonic "truth discourse" of (Western) modernity. By referring to this truth discourse, I mean the discourse of "Man," whose origins lay in a totalizing metaphysical interpretation of being that spatialized, structuralized, or more precisely, territorialized temporality (the difference it always already disseminates) in the name of the transcendental principle of identity—an order tethered to an absolute Origin, the anthropologos.

The struggle over the legacy of Edward Said is not simply another debate internal to the academy; it has global consequences for oppositional thought and politics. The significance of this struggle arises not simply because, in the course of his academic career—and through his activism on behalf of the Palestinian people's right to self-determination—his thought, unlike that of most academics, especially American, achieved global visibility and influence. It also has to do with the history of humanist studies since the disintegration of the Western university, especially the American university, during the 1960s under the hammers of the civil rights, feminist, homosexual, and anti–Vietnam War movements and the rise of "theory"—a revolutionary momentum of thought that, however imperfectly, was committed to the de-struction or de-construction of the (binarist) truth discourse endemic to the West, which Heidegger called the "onto-theo-logical tradition"; Derrida, the "logocentric tradition"; and Foucault, "post-Enlightenment modernity." As the proliferation of cultural and postcolonial studies testifies, Said's work emerged to global prominence as that of the poststructuralists began to wane in influence. Given this tentative outcome of the debates over critical theory, the question that needs to be newly rethought is this: What is the relationship between poststructuralist theory and what Said calls his "historicist philology" or, alternatively, "secular criticism"? Did the latter achieve prominence as the victor of a struggle with the former? Or is it possible that Said's worldly criticism constitutes the (near) fulfillment of the unfulfilled logic of the earlier poststructuralist critique of Western metaphysical thinking, especially in its latest, "anthropological" or "humanistic" phase?

After *Orientalism* (1978), Said, as Timothy Brennan notes, insistently though not systematically represented poststructuralist theory pejoratively, as "unworldly" and even as a secular form of otherworldly "religion." This judgment has become increasingly prominent in recent years, though those Saidians who now voice it seem to claim themselves as a saving remnant. Invoking Said's legacy in a special issue of *boundary 2* entitled "Critical Secularism" and published after his death, Amir Mufti, for example, one of Said's most astute commentators, writes:

> Said's work came to the fore at a time when the world of humanistic knowledge was coming to be shaken to its core, its basic assumptions about the possibilities of knowledge seemingly washed away. In the vernacular, these complex developments in the world of thought and culture have long been collectively dubbed "postmodernism," often in the form of an epithet. Said himself of course was deeply influenced by the European thinkers—Adorno, Foucault, Derrida, and Auerbach, above all—whose work is an important element in this milieu, and he is sometimes seen as belonging fully to it. *How little it is still understood that his work was utterly at odds with this contemporary milieu and how differently he read those formative thinkers.*[8]

In a similar vein—though far more problematic in the reductiveness of his competitive possessiveness—Brennan, following Said's rather tentative identification of poststructuralist theory with Renan's "natural supernaturalism," wants to "save" Said's unique worldly political criticism from the unworldly and indeed "religious" poststructuralist (and postcolonialist) usurpers of Said's legacy after "the Heideggerian turn":

> By targeting poststructuralism, he did no more here than recall his own earlier arguments against the "science" of high humanism. He was frankly returning

to the problem described in those passages of *Orientalism* that examined the fatal methodological borrowing by the philologist Ernest Renan from the naturalist Georges Cuvier. Those passages prepare one to understand many of his emphases in *The World, the Text, and the Critic*. As described in *Orientalism*, the result of Renan's affection for Cuvier had been what Renan tellingly, and damningly for Said, called "*la science exacte des choses de l'esprit* ("an exact science of all matters of the spirit [of cultural facts]")." In ways that the American theoretical community was unprepared to fathom, Said was saying something rather subtle and unexpected: despite its assault on humanist mustiness with its arrogant Enlightenment grandeur, theory had assumed an uncomfortable resemblance to Renan. What Said in the collection repeatedly dubs the slavish attitude of American critics to their French sources had given way already (in his words) to a "secular priesthood" in the "era of scientific intelligence."[9]

In opposition to this coercive tendency to put poststructuralist theory and Saidian secular criticism in a binary opposition—and in keeping with the spirit of collaboration that, despite his criticism of poststructuralism, I take to lie at the heart of Said's work—I argue here that poststructuralist criticism is in fact radically worldly and that the kind of worldly criticism Said came to practice after *Beginnings* (1975) (which, not incidentally, by and large addresses the structuralist, not the poststructuralist, phenomenon, the latter term not yet having become prominent) was influenced far more by Foucault's poststructuralist genealogical criticism of the disciplinary society than by the Vico he celebrates at the end of that book, or rather, by the Vico Said imagined after reading Foucault's *Surveiller et punir* (1975). The Foucault he characterizes in *Beginnings* is the "archaeologist," a more structuralist than poststructuralist Foucault; there is, for example, little indication in *Beginnings* that Said was aware of the direction Foucault would take after his analysis of discourse in the *Order of Things*.

This argument will be developed at length in this book. Suffice it here to say that the Said of *Beginnings* (unlike the Said who follows) addresses the ontological question precipitated by the linguistic turn taken by the structuralists (Ferdinand de Saussure, Émile Benveniste, Claude Lévi-Strauss, Roland Barthes, and others). In this book Said, following Foucault's Nietzschean ontological critique of the Origin,[10] struggles (sometimes opaquely but always suggestively) to work out an understanding of a beginning that was neither tethered to the reductive economy of the metaphysics endemic to the West (thinking from after or above *physis*), particularly, for Said, the metaphysics of the identity, thought, and language of Man, which privileged a transcendental Origin (or enabling center), nor dependent on the postmetaphysical structuralist alternative, which, instead of thinking the condition of the lost Origin positively, opted for the willful systematization (or structuration) of (mediating) language:

The structuralists . . . do not believe in the immediacy of anything: they are content to understand and to contemplate the alphabetical order of sense as a mediating function rather than as a direct meaning. Order, they claim, is just on our human side of nothingness; it preserves us from the oblivion of unremarked duration. To perceive this order one cannot have recourse to a direct unfolding . . . of the kernel of meaning within a statement: that alternative, we recall, disappeared with the primordial Origin. We are left only with a way of perceiving how something, a sentence, or a statement—in fine, the entire world of experience conceived of as a gigantic script or musical score—works, how it hangs together. We search for structure as *Zusammenhange*, the "principle of solidarity" among parts, according to Barthes.

Structure hides the actuality of our existence because it is the nature of structure to refuse to reveal its presence directly; only language can solicit structure out of the background in which it hovers. Structure is nonrational: it is not thought thinking about anything, but thought itself as the merest possibility of activity. It can offer no rationale for its presence, once discovered, other than its primitive *thereness*. In a most important way, then, as an ensemble of interacting parts, structure replaces the Origin with the play of orderly relationships. *A univocal source has ceded to a proliferating systematic web.*[11]

In separating and privileging system over the differential temporal dynamics of being, both the metaphysical and the structuralist alternatives, according to Said, not only reduce the kinetic play of finitude and contingency to a spatialized ordered stasis but also, and above all, negate human agency, the free will that is the very essence of humanity understood as being-in-the-world:

In structuralism no real distance exists between language and any of its individual articulations, since none of the latter is under any more than token obligation to a thinking subject. There can be no tone . . . , no sense of the individual voice that is its own final authority, since for the structuralists the whole world is contained within a gigantic set of quotation marks. *Everything*, therefore, is a text—or, using the same argument, *nothing* is a text. The inherence of a structure expresses neither an intention nor any more than the barest of constitutive necessities. Communication is absorbed by the structure, since communication can never exhaust a structure or a language. The enduring power of language to signify thus almost completely collapses the beginning into the result, and the tautology completely eliminates both subject and object, and to a certain extent direct communication, too. (*B*, 338)

For Said, however, a beginning is not dependent on an end (and vice versa); that is, it is not identifiable with a creation or narrative, with a structure that resolves the play—or the anxiety-provoking ambiguity—of difference. It is the act neither of an omniscient consciousness nor of an unconscious object. It is, rather, an act of a finite human subject who, as a being-in-the-world, is both inside and outside its limits, apart from and a part of the world—Heidegger called this human condition "ek-sistent/in-sistence" or "the ontico-ontological difference,"[12] and Foucault, "the transcendental/finite double"—and therefore must, to remain human, always already begin *inter esse* (in-the-midst, interestedly) without the expectation of arrival, of coming to an end, of discovering an answer to the question of being. In the more political terms of Said's later discourse, this beginning is an act of the "secular" or, equivalently, "exilic" consciousness.

At the time Said was writing *Beginnings* and before his encounter with the poststructuralist Foucault, it was the Giambattista Vico of the *New Science* (*Scienza nuova*), the revolutionary eighteenth-century Italian philologist who bracketed God's providential Creation in favor of the idea that humans make their own world, who became the model for his antistructuralist notion of the human inquirer. Moreover, Vico's rejection of the transcendental Origin in favor of worldly beginnings became the model for his understanding of humanist inquiry. With Vico's rethinking of the Origin, Said tells us,

> a major shift in perspective and knowledge has taken place. The state of mind that is concerned with origins is, I have said, theological. By contrast, and this is the shift, beginnings are eminently secular, or gentile, continuing activities. Another difference must be noted briefly here, since in my discussions of Freud and of modern texts I have already examined one aspect of this difference in detail: a beginning intends meaning, but the continuities and methods developing from it are generally *orders* of *dispersion,* of *adjacency,* and of *complementarity* [as opposed to generic—filial, dynastic—development]. A different way of putting this is to say that whereas an origin *centrally* dominates what derives from it, the beginning (especially the modern beginning), encourages nonlinear development, a logic giving rise to the sort of multileveled coherence of dispersion we find in Freud's text, in the texts of modern writers, or in Foucault's archeological investigations. (*B,* 372–73)

If I correctly understand his laconic conclusion, Said is arguing that by rejecting the theological (or more broadly, metaphysical) concept of the Origin in favor of the human (ontico-ontological) perspective, Vico anticipated the modern (or rather postmodern) understanding of the beginning that became the point of departure for Said's secular criticism. In privileging language over the singularity of the human as a means of overcoming the dispersion of the Origin, however, Vico also unwittingly prophesied the antihumanist (structuralist) negation of this revolutionary secular humanist understanding of beginnings:

To lay this difference at Vico's feet is, if not an exaggeration, then a way of recognizing how *The New Science* prophetically suggests terms for comprehending a very modern polemic. When Vico said that *human* comes from the root *to bury,* he might not have realized that his humanistic philosophy contained in it the elements of its own negation. *To bury,* in Vico's sense, is to engender difference; and to engender difference, as Derrida has argued, is to *defer* presence, to temporize, to introduce absence. As we saw, Vico connects human history with language, the former having been made possible by the latter. What Vico only hints at, however, is that language effectively displaces human presence, just as history is engendered only by the burial (removal, displacement) of immediacy. This act of deferring can be understood as part of Vico's continuing attack upon Descartes, upon the centrality of the *cogito,* and upon geometric [structuralist] method. *When Vico speaks of a mental language common to all nations, he is, therefore, asserting the verbal community binding men together at the expense of their immediate existential presence to one another.* Such a common language—which in modern writing has appeared as Freud's unconscious, as Orwell's newspeak, as Lévi-Strauss's savage mind, as Foucault's *épistémè,* as Fanon's doctrine of imperialism—defers the human center or *cogito* in the (sometimes tyrannical) interest of universal, systematic relationships. Participation in these relationships is scarcely voluntary, only intermittently perceptible as participation in any egalitarian sense, and hardly amenable to human scrutiny.

Humanism thus engenders its own opposite. (*B,* 373)

In this "very modern polemic" that Vico anticipates, Said tentatively distinguishes between the "de-centered" discourse of Foucault (and Gilles Deleuze) and that of the the centered structuralists (including the North American Northrup Frye) that privileges the geometric method over human worldly experience. He even goes so far as to say, all too briefly, that the "philosophy of decenterment" Foucault and Deleuze espouse is positively "revolutionary," "at least in its reliance upon an intellectual who views his role within his discipline and its institutional supports as an adversary one:" "The intellectual's role is no longer to place himself 'a little to the side or a little ahead' in order to express everyone's silent truth; it is rather to fight against the forms of power wherever that role is an object and an instrument: in the order of 'knowledge,' of 'truth,' of 'consciousness,' of 'discourse'" (*B,* 378). But this encomium to the positive political possibilities inhering in Foucault's decentered perspective comes at the end of the book and is not developed. It thus seems not to be a conscious consequence of the extensive analysis of Foucault's thought Said undertakes earlier in the chapter, which, as I have noted, is basically that of Foucault the archaeologist, whose emphasis on the epistemic regime Said largely associates with the structuralists. Though he makes gestures toward distinguishing this Foucault from his fellow structuralists, he, like Foucault himself, does not yet clearly see texts such as *Madness and Civilization* and *The Birth of the Clinic* as proleptic of the genealogical/historical/political criticism—specifically, that which identifies knowledge as power, "the repressive hypothesis"—that would come to dominate Foucault's work with *Surveiller et punir.*

I mean to accomplish two goals with this brief retrieval of *Beginnings*—this effort to articulate an *antimetaphysical,* radically secular understanding of a beginning—from the oblivion to which it has been relegated by the legion of postcolonial and cultural critics who trace their genealogy back to Said.[13] First, I want to suggest that in this inaugural work, Said situates his inquiry at the site of ontology—the question of Being (*die Seinsfrage*), as Heidegger put it in *Being and Time*—as do the structuralists and the poststructuralists from whom he would eventually distance himself. Like them, Said was engaged in the revolutionary task of finding an alternative to the idea of being (the Origin), of humanity, and of inquiry, to that teleological/identitarian One that had dominated in the West since the rise of modernity in the Enlightenment, if not from the beginning of Western civilization. Second, I argue that in his crucial observation that Vico's *New Science*—particularly its announcement of a new understanding of "the beginning" that depended on neither an end nor an Origin—proleptically provided the contemporary occasion with terms that render "a very modern polemic" comprehensible, Said was also symptomatically intuiting its resolution or, at any rate, the beginning of its resolution. That is, in opposition to the traditional—disciplinary—view of this binary, he was acknowledging the belonging-togetherness of language (and deferral) and the historical world, ontology, epistemology, and politics. Like the Foucault of *Discipline and Punish,* he was in some degree intuiting the indissoluble relationality of the various sites of being—being as such, the ecos, the subject, language, gender, race, and so on—in opposition to a Western tradition that ever since Aristotle and his Roman heirs had increasingly compartmentalized them in the form of disciplines in the name of achieving more efficient knowledge of—and power over—their singularity: their living, differential, ineffable, and ungraspable force. It is precisely this symptomatic intuition into the polyvalent repressiveness of the Western teleological/disciplinary understanding of being—its tactics of divide, gain knowledge about, and conquer—and the polyvalent emancipatory dynamics of the decentering of the Origin (and the binary logic, i.e., the borders, it ultimately demands) that renders the Said of *Orientalism* the collaborative genealogical colleague, if not exactly the student of, the Foucault of *Discipline and Punish.*

In questioning Said's and especially his followers' criticism of poststructuralist theory, particularly the placement of their political orientation in a hierarchical binary opposition to the poststructuralist ontological or textual perspective, I do not want to be interpreted as apologizing for the limitations of the latter. On the contrary, I believe the poststructuralists deserve the severe criticism Said leveled against them in the great essays collected in *The World, the Text, and the Critic,* most notably "Secular Criticism," "The World, the Text, and the Critic," "Reflections on American 'Left' Literary Criticism," "Criticism between Culture and System," and "Traveling Theory," but not, as Said sometimes and his recent apostles always put it, because their theory was antihuman and antiworldly, a transcendental orientation that, on the analogy of medieval theology, was *de contemptu mundi*—about contempt for the (secular/historical) world. The prominent poststructuralists, I will argue—Heidegger, Lacan, Derrida, Lyotard, Lacoue-Labarthe, Althusser, Spivak, Deleuze, Foucault—were in varying degrees inaugurating a revolutionary effort to delegitimize the truth discourse of the Occident that culminated in "modernity." To recall what the new generation of oppositional academic critics seems to have forgotten since those early days, this was the tradition the poststructuralists identified as a geographic/cultural space in a larger world that, under the aegis of a secularized transcendental eye (I), coerced or (in its modern phase) accommodated the singular phenomena of this entire world to an unworldly (universal) principle of identity, the essence of which was the idea the West had of itself. This tradition was fundamentally and polyvalently imperial, as can clearly be seen in the metaphors (above all, center/periphery, visible/invisible [blindness], static/kinetic [play], striated/smooth, clearing/forest, maturity/adolescence, sedentary/nomadic) that poststructuralism uses in its critical rhetoric.[14] Furthermore, these early poststructuralists were, though in a less conscious or rather more symptomatic way, also inaugurating a revolutionary effort to dismantle the means of knowledge production endemic to this Occidental metaphysical tradition, developed, especially during the Enlightenment, to accomplish this totalizing imperial end: the disciplinary apparatus that rendered knowledge production and the power that knowledge commands more efficient and materially and politically economical. To put this differently, in de-structuring or de-constructing the metaphysical representation of being—I call this moment a deterritorialization in the following chapter—the early poststructuralists were initiating a momentum, however tentative, toward retrieving an understanding of being as a continuum—an indissoluble, however historically uneven, relay of "sites" of intervention—from a philosophical and cultural tradition that had spatialized, compartmentalized, territorialized, and disciplined its living force.

Evidence of this destructuring and liberatory potential can be found everywhere in the thought of the early poststructuralists, even among those who have rightly been criticized by secular critics for restricting their discourse to unworldly disciplinary sites such as ontology, language, or the subject at the expense of the more worldly sites. Let me provisionally cite the example of Martin Heidegger, the proto-poststructuralist whose thought has been utterly marginalized since the turn from theory to politics in the late 1970s. Though his inquiry was relentlessly restricted to the site of ontology, he nevertheless, especially in the *Parmenides,* quite overtly and powerfully, if not quite decisively, demonstrated the relay between, on the one hand, the reductive Western metaphysical interpretation of being—its will to power over temporality, the "nothing," the differences that time always already disseminates—inaugurated by the Romans' reduction of originative Greek thinking (*a-letheia*) to a derivative or calculative thinking (*veritas*) and, on the other hand, Western political imperialism, also inaugurated by the Romans, a continuity Heidegger epitomized in the following resonant sentences: "We still think the Greek *polis* and the 'political' in a totally un-Greek fashion. We think the 'political' as Romans, i.e., imperially. The essence of the Greek *polis* will never be grasped within the horizon of the political as understood in the Roman way."[15] This same symptomatic gesture, which aims at collapsing the constructed disciplinary boundaries between the sites of being, is evident also in the poststructuralist feminists—Hélène Cixous, Luce Irigaray, Julia Kristeva, Monique Wittig, Gayatri Spivak, and others—who perceived the indissoluble relationship between Western ontology and gender relations, between an oppressive metaphysical mode of thinking and the patriarchal symbolic order, Word and Father, Logos and Phallus, a relationship epitomized in the portmanteau term they coined to characterize the Western anthropological problematic, *phallogocentrism.*

For the purpose of understanding Edward Said's (polyvalent) emancipatory project, however, it is with the Foucault of *Surveiller et punir* that the revolutionary process of dismantling the artificial boundaries of the disciplines becomes most decidedly visible, even though too many of Foucault's recent cultural and postcolonial critics—the very ones his genealogical criticism enabled—have been blinded by their oversight to its revolutionary import.[16] This text was profoundly influenced by Nietzsche's and especially Heidegger's interrogation of the Western (ontotheological) tradition's inclusive ocular-centrism and Althusser's poststructuralist Marxist analysis of the capitalist "problematic"—his disclosure of the blindness of its "oversight."[17] I am in part referring provisionally to Foucault's disclosure of the indissoluble relationality between the spatializing/territorializing panoptics of the classical *épistémè*—the classificatory structuration of knowledge production in table form—imposed on the temporal/differential dynamics of the continuum of being by the disciplinary (imperial) imperatives of thinking *meta ta physika* in its anthropological allotrope. I am further referring, however, to the various political institutions that the overdetermination of this cartographic diagram of knowledge/power in the "classical" period of Europe spawned: the modern prison, the insane asylum, the medical clinic, the factory, the modern army, the educational classroom—and, though Foucault refers to it only tangentially (in a reference to the Roman legions and Napoléon's imperial army), the geopolitical space of empire. Though the following passage from the heart of *Discipline and Punish* is familiar, the meaning Foucault intended the term *polyvalent* to convey seems to have been entirely missed by both his admirers and his critics. I quote it here—and will return to it at length in chapter 2—to reconstellate its decisive and enabling tenor into the context of Edward Said's legacy:

> The Panopticon . . . must be understood as *a generalizable model* of functioning; a way of defining power relations in terms of the everyday life of men. . . . The fact that it should have given rise, even in our time, to so many variations, projected or realized, is evidence of the imaginary intensity that it has possessed for almost two hundred years. But the Panopticon must not be understood as a dream building: *it is the diagram* of a mechanism of power reduced to its ideal form; its functioning, abstracted from any obstacle, resistance or friction, must be represented as a pure architectural and optical system: it is in fact *a figure* of political technology that may and must be detached from any specific use.
>
> *It is polyvalent in its applications;* it serves to reform prisoners, but also to treat patients, to instruct schoolchildren, to confine the insane, to supervise workers, to put beggars and idlers to work. It is *a type* of location of bodies in space, of distribution of individuals in relation to one another, of hierarchical organization, of disposition of centres and channels of power, of definition of the instruments and modes of intervention of power, which can be implemented in hospitals, workshops, schools, prisons. Whenever one is dealing with a multiplicity of individuals on whom a task or a particular form of behaviour must be imposed, the panoptic *schema* may be used.[18]

I contend throughout this book, then, that the very real limitations Said and his late followers, especially those professing cultural and postcolonial studies, attribute to poststructuralism—its restricted disciplinary focus, its unworldliness, its indifference to history, its indifference to or disdain for the human, its paradoxical nostalgia for a religious certainty, its denial of human agency, and therefore its complicity with the dominant institutions of power[19]—do not reside in, are not essential to, the (antifoundational) principles of poststructuralist theory. Rather, they result from the failure of both its theorizers and its practitioners to fully break out of the deeply inscribed disciplinary framework they were symptomatically challenging, to perceive the full range of the continuum they were in some fundamental sense trying to retrieve by way of their de-structive or de-constructive interpretive methods. This failure—which in a certain sense was, as I will show, the inevitable consequence of a beginning that necessarily compelled the rebels to rely on the very disciplinary problematic against which they were struggling—is epitomized by the tortured historical itinerary of Jacques Derrida's deconstructive thought. At the outset—and for a very long time after that—Derrida restricted his focus to the question of being/textuality/the subject despite the specter of the broader cultural and political sites that insistently haunted his discourse. One thinks above all of the early interviews in *Positions* and the commentaries of Gayatri Spivak, in which the question of the political, particularly Marx's ghost, was tortuously ever present.[20] Eventually, however, though too late to make a difference, the pressure of this abiding haunting compelled him to perceive and thematize the political implications of deconstruction in the spirit of "a certain Marx," a thematizing that, however satisfactory, openly affirmed the continuity between a deconstructive "hauntology" and a certain Marx's political economy.[21]

Often it took writers occupying other subject positions (i.e., other than Western, white, male, and heterosexual) to perceive the adjacencies to which the early poststructuralists were blinded by their disciplinary (textual) insight: in the case of Heideggerian hermeneutics, the continuity of the critique of Being with Eurocentrism vis-à-vis Amerindia, demonstrated by Enrique Dussel and Walter Mingolo; in the case of deconstructionists such as Derrida and Paul de Man, the continuity of deconstructive ontology and textuality with feminism, Marxism, and postcoloniality, revealed by Gayatri Spivak; for the critique of the patriarchal symbolic order, works by the French feminists; for the critique of colonialism, contributions by the Subaltern Studies Group (Ranajit Guha, Partha Chatterjee, Ashis Nandy, and Dipesh Chakrabarty), Homi Bhabha, and R. Radhakrishnan; for Gramscian Marxism, writings by Ernesto Laclau and Chantal Mouffe; for black culture, works by Henry Louis Gates Jr.; in the case of Lacanian psychoanalysis, the identityless subject's continuity with gender relations, discussed by Julia Kristeva; and in the case of Foucault's genealogy, the continuity of the critique of the discourse of disciplinarity with the critique of Orientalism and, more broadly, empire in general, exposed by Edward Said. These telling examples could be easily extended in each category, but they should suffice to validate my version of the limitations of poststructuralist criticism—its vestigial adherence to the

imperatives of disciplinarity—and my argument vis-à-vis the transdisciplinary critical potential inhering in the poststructuralist ontological interrogation of the Western interpretation of being, a being that assumes that
identity or a principle of presence informs the differential dynamics of its
temporality. The "local" history of theory following its advent in the late 1960s
was characterized by the competitiveness endemic to the disciplinarity that
dominated the structure of knowledge production, the Modernist imperative
of a world that has compartmentalized being into spatialized sites. Its "global"
history, on the contrary, suggests that this local history of theory has been
symptomatically—and despite the competitive will—disclosing its vocation
as transdisciplinary, the collaborative imperative of being understood as an
indissoluble relay of sites in a kinetic and uneven historical continuum.

At the site of literary studies, this paradoxical history explains in large
part the revolutionary force of the advent of Said's *Orientalism* in American
academia, which in the early 1970s was still structured by the mechanisms
of disciplinarity, not simply literary studies that separated Anglo-American
literature from comparative literature, but, more broadly, a *studia humanitatis* that separated literature in general from the other humanist disciplines
and the social sciences, not least Middle Eastern studies. This, ironically, has
been observed by the Marxist Aijaz Ahmad, one of the most severe critics of
Said's collapsing of the traditional Marxist disciplinary base/superstructure
model:

> Apart from the unclassifiability of genre, meanwhile, *Orientalism* had been
> notable also for the sweep of its contents. So majestic was this sweep, in fact,
> that few readers initially noticed that most of Said's references in the more
> substantial parts of the book were drawn from his training in comparative
> literature and philology. This was familiar territory for people of similar back-
> ground, but those were precisely the people who were the most likely to resist
> the invitation to read this body of writing *not* as literature but as documents
> of an entirely different sort of archive, namely the *Orientalist* archive, which
> *they* had thought was none of their business. The Mid-East expert, on the
> other hand, *into* whose archive those other kinds of texts were being read, was
> equally displeased and bewildered, because this expert was being attacked, but
> with no possibility of defending himself on what he had defined as his home
> ground—the ground of libraries, the comparison of medieval texts, the labor
> of deciphering illegible manuscripts, the problems of establishing authentic
> texts and preparing the appropriate gloss, the learning of archaic languages, and
> bringing back the fruits of this labour for the enlightenment and edification of
> the public at large. He was, in his own eyes, a specialist, an innocent. As we all
> know, the effect in these fields, that of literature and of Middle Eastern studies,

was electrifying, because the book did serve to open up, despite its blunders, spaces of oppositional work in both.[22]

According to Ahmad—who failed to fully grasp the ironic contradiction between the pleasure he took from Said's radical collapsing of the institutionalized disciplinary boundaries and his own undeviating commitment to the disciplinary imperatives of the Marxist base/superstructure model—this conservative reaction to Said's transdisciplinary book was epitomized by the "Orientalist" Bernard Lewis's response to Said's *Orientalism*:

> It was the book's native amplitude which turned out to be its most enabling quality, regardless of its principal theses. Part of the pleasure of *Orientalism*— which caused anxiety in some circles, excitement in others—was its transgression of academic boundaries. Attacks on Said on this count were numerous— augmented, two years later after this prolonged orchestration, by Bernard Lewis himself, one of the doyens of Zionist historiography. His attack was unseemly on many counts, but the substantive point which Lewis raised was one of competence. What authorized Said to speak of Arab history and Orientalist disciplines? What degrees did he have? Did he know such-and-such a medieval Arabic dictionary? Did he know the meaning of such-and-such a word in the whole range of Arabic lexicography over ten centuries? Etc. (In his elegant rejoinder, Said quite rightly ignored the issue of competence and authorization, while concentrating on the issue that had gone unacknowledged in Lewis's attack: namely, that Lewis's scholarly pretense was itself a camouflage for Zionist allegiance.) (*IT*, 173)

Torn out of its local history and reconstellated into this symptomatic global history of postmodern theory, Said's groundbreaking book—and his increasingly Vichian emphasis on the worldliness or secularism of texts—could be interpreted differently than it has been recently. Against his own tendency to distance himself from Foucault and the poststructuralists and, above all, against those who have read *Humanism and Democratic Criticism* as his definitive rejection of the antihumanism of the poststructuralists, *Orientalism*'s overdetermination of the political site could be seen as something other than Said's effort to reject poststructuralist theory or, as some of his recent followers (e.g., Timothy Brennan) tacitly do, to put his worldliness in a binary opposition to the unworldliness of poststructuralist theory. Rather, it could be understood as a symptomatic, if not entirely conscious, effort to *fulfill* the differential and antidisciplinary logic of poststructuralist theory—the polyvalent logic to which the early poststructuralists were all, in some degree or other, blinded by their vestigial inscription by the imperatives of the disciplines.[23] Above all, a reconstellation such as the one I am proposing would enable us to perceive at least the possibility that Said's *Orientalism* constituted a symptomatic effort not simply to theorize the indissoluble relationship between the ontological interpretation of being privileged by the Occident—the ontology interrogated by the early poststructuralists—and the continuum of practices of political domination but also to practice its polyvalent imperatives. More specifically, I am referring to the indissoluble relationship between metaphysical knowledge production—the "truth" derived from perceiving *meta ta physika,* panoptically—and the relay of imperial practices, including the economic, ecological, cultural, racial, sexual, social, and political, that this (Occidental) truth, especially in its post-Enlightenment allotrope, has enabled by "naturalizing" or "hegemonizing" this re-presentational continuum.

The affiliative relation between Said and the poststructuralists is not limited to their interrogation of the Occidental metaphysical interpretation of being, their deconstruction of the disciplinary knowledge of the post-Enlightenment, their disclosure of the complicity of this knowledge and power, and the practical (political) polyvalency of the panoptic gaze, or rather, the spatial diagram to which metaphysical thinking reduces the temporal dynamics of being. The early poststructuralists were also symptomatically concerned with the alien and anxiety-provoking "Other" that Occidental inquiry, whatever its historical allotropes, has systematically and virtually paranoically been intent on reducing to the Same. Although they focused on critiquing metaphysics, to some degree they also sought to liberate or decolonize this "Other" from the totalized structure to which it had been reduced by the spatializing, enclosing, or structuralizing mechanics of thinking *meta ta physika.* That is, they sought to dis-close or open up to positive thought this "Other" of—*that belongs to*—the metaphysical thinking of the Occident.

This agenda is attested at the beginning of the poststructuralist era by Heidegger's identification of his antimetaphysical hermeneutics as the *Destruktion* of the ontotheological tradition. Heidegger effects this identification in *Being and Time,* whose task is both de-structive and pro-jective: not simply to critique the spatializing/structuration of radical temporality (or nothingness) and the differences it disseminates but also, and more important (as, evoking Foucauldian genealogy, he observes in his definition of his destructive project), to pro-ject into the present ("today") these spectral "Others" of that metaphysical thinking:

> If the question of Being is to have its own history made transparent, then this hardened tradition must be loosened up, and the concealments which it has brought about must be dissolved. We understand this task as one in which by taking *the question of Being as our clue,* we *destroy* the traditional content of

ancient ontology until we arrive at those primordial experiences in which we achieved our first ways of determining the nature of Being—the ways which have guided it ever since.

In thus demonstrating the origin of our basic ontological concepts . . . we have nothing to do with a vicious relativizing of ontological standpoints. But this destruction is just as far from having the *negative* sense of shaking off the ontological tradition. We must, on the contrary, stake out the positive possibilities of that tradition, and this always means keeping it within its *limits*. . . . On the negative side, this destruction does not relate itself towards the past; its criticism is aimed at "today" and at the prevalent way of treating the history of ontology, whether it is headed towards doxography, towards intellectual history, or towards a history of problems. But to bury the past in nullity [*Nichtigkeit*] is not the purpose of this destruction; its aim is *positive;* its negative function remains unexpressed and indirect.[24]

As I will show, just as Heidegger dis-closes for positive thought the noth-ing that metaphysical thinking structures into something, so the Foucault of *Discipline and Punish* dis-closes the European nation-states' domestic "Other"—the madman, the vagabond, the beggar, the schoolboy, the so-cial deviant, and so on (i.e., those who have been denied human status by the modern West's version of being)—which the disciplinary machinery of bourgeois modernity has had as its fundamental purpose to re-*form*, that is, to "normalize" or "humanize." When, as I will do at length in chapter 3, we reconstellate this "projective" aspect of poststructuralist de-struction or de-construction—which Said minimized and too many of his postcolonial disciples virtually ignore—into the Saidian context, it becomes easier to per-ceive that Said's thematization, at the end of *Culture and Imperialism,* of the globalized émigré—the vast population of "refugees, migrants, displaced persons, and exiles" precipitated "as afterthoughts" by the fulfillment and demise of the incorporative logic of colonialism[25]—is not the result of a rejection of this de-structuring methodology but rather an extension of its disclosive dynamics.

I am, then, suggesting that the question of Edward Said's relationship to poststructuralist theory, particularly in *Orientalism,* depends on which of the several Foucaults one considers in attempting an answer. Again, I be-lieve that the appropriate Foucault is the Foucault not of the archaeologies, the Foucault, that is, of Said's *Beginnings,* but the one who, shortly before Said began *Orientalism,* turned to Nietzschean genealogy after reading Heidegger. As a result, it will be necessary to undertake a detour into the relationship between Heidegger and Foucault at the outset, before offering critical readings of *Orientalism, Culture and Imperialism,* and *Humanism and Democratic Criticism,* which will constitute chapters 3, 4, and 5 of this book. In chapter 2 I will show at considerable length that in *Surveiller et punir* (the original French title emphasizes the primary role that the optics informing metaphysical thinking played in constructing the peculiar kind of power the bourgeois polity held over social-political deviance following the French Revolution), Foucault, far from dissociating his critical genealogy from Heidegger's destruction of the ontotheological (i.e., Occidental) tradition, in fact, at least in what is decisive, *extends* via Nietzsche Heidegger's ontological (i.e., antimetaphysical) critical project. First, he discloses the same relation between the knowledge production—and the (ancient) metaphorics of vision that enabled it—residing in the formation of the modern disciplinary society (or the European nation-state) that Heidegger and other early poststructuralists, such as Derrida and Lyotard, revealed in their deconstruction of the metaphysics informing the broader Occidental philosophical and cultural tradition. Second, in a related but even more important way, he thematizes the indissoluble relationship between, on the one hand, the de-viant or ab-normal—the "Other" that this modern, bourgeois Western political formation would re-form and normalize—and, on the other, the "nothingness" or "temporality" (Heidegger), the "*différance*" (Derrida), the "aporia" (de Man), the "*différend*" (Lyotard), "the Real" (Lacan), the "singular" (Deleuze), and so on that the early poststructuralists disclosed as the "Other" *of,* that *belonged to,* the being of the Occident and that now, at the "end of philosophy," as Heidegger put this paradox, had come to haunt its hegemony decisively. In pointing to this indissoluble relationship between Heidegger's destruction of the ontotheological tradition and Foucault's critical genealogy of the modern nation-state, my detour will suggest that which I will amplify in the following chapters, namely, the affiliation between their ontological or textual perspectives and Said's political one. The discussion will show, first, the indissoluble relationship between Heidegger's and Foucault's destructive or genealogical critiques of Occidental ontology and language and Said's political critique of the polyvalent discourse of Occidental Orientalism in *Orientalism.* It will also demonstrate the indissoluble continuity between the spectral "nothing"/"madness" precipitated by the fulfillment of the binary ontologic of metaphysical thinking/discourse in the "age of the world picture" (Heidegger) or, what is the same thing, the "age of panopticism" (Foucault) and the dehumanized humans precipitated by the fulfillment of the binary logic of European imperialism: the "unhoused, decentered, and exilic energies whose incarnation today is the migrant" and the "intellectual and artist in exile, the political figure between domains, between forms, between homes and between languages," who is this migrant's "consciousness," which Said thematizes at the end of *Culture and Imperialism,* the aptly titled sequel to *Orientalism* (*CI,* 332). To put it more pointedly, these exiles form the specter—the "present absentees," as the Palestinians deracinated by the Zionist momentum were called[26]— that at the end of the imperial age now haunts the Occident and calls for a rethinking of the Occidental identity in its relation to its global "Others," particularly, though not exclusively, the Orient.

In thus emphasizing the relationship between, on the one hand, the post-structuralists' (principally Foucault's) rejection of Western metaphysics—not simply the premodern allotropes of the transcendental Logos (the onto-logos of antiquity, the theo-logos of the Christian era, and the anthropo-logos of modernity)—and Said's insistent critique of Orientalism, both early and modern, as an essentialism that dehumanizes Orientals and reduces the dy-namic and various lived Orient to a fixed, reified, and inescapable identity, I am also invoking the vexed question of Said's humanism, introduced by James Clifford in his much discussed review of *Orientalism.*[27] As I observed at the beginning of this introductory chapter, this problem has been exacer-bated by his reiteration, against the supposed antihumanism of Heidegger, Foucault, and the poststructuralists, of his (re)commitment to humanism in *Humanism and Democratic Criticism.*

Chapter 5 of this book addresses this difficult question. On the basis of Said's always vague genealogy of humanism, on the one hand, and his insistent, undeviating antiessentialism, that is, his decisive reversal of the principle of metaphysical principles—that identity is the condition of the possibility of difference—on the other, I will argue that the humanism Said espoused from *Orientalism* to *Humanism and Democratic Criticism* is not the humanism that achieved hegemonic status in the West, both as an in-terpretation of being and as an institutional mode of knowledge production (the *studia humanitatis,* i.e., the humanities), between the Renaissance and the Enlightenment. Specifically, it is not the humanism that, in rejecting the arbitrary theologos of the Christian era, reoriented Western humanity toward this world but, in so doing, substituted the "rational" anthropologos for the otherworldly Logos, the Word of Man for the Word of God, that is, internalized a hitherto external transcendental principle into the new (modern) secular world. I mean, rather, to invoke Said himself, specifically his discussion in *Orientalism* of the rise of modern Orientalism as it came to be embodied in Sylvestre de Sacy and the great nineteenth-century French humanist Ernest Renan, in which, following M. H. Abrams, he underscores the reorientation that enabled rigorous scientific Orientalists to escape the anxiety of being-in-the-world, the contingency of the radically secular, by "naturalizing the supernatural": "My thesis is that the essential aspects of modern Orientalist theory and praxis (from which present-day Orientalism derives) can be understood, not as a sudden access of objective knowledge about the Orient, but as a set of structures inherited from the past, secularized, redisposed, and re-formed by such disciplines as philology, which in turn were naturalized, modernized, and laicized substitutes for (or versions of) Christian supernaturalism."[28]

I will argue, then, that the "man" to which Said refers in his pervasive Vichian reminder "that men make their own history, that what they can know is what they have made" (*O*, 5), is not the Lord of Being—Man, "the measure of all things"—as he has been understood in the hegemonic humanist tradition; he is rather *radically secular* man: the living being, who, not-at-home-in-the-world—de-centered and exilic—is not only endowed with a fragile language to name (represent) being but also, because this language is radically finite, aware of the enormous burden of his or her responsibility to the rest of being.

Conversely, I will argue that, despite the poststructuralists' inordinate overdetermination of the discursivity of discourse, their antihumanism should be understood not as the rejection of the human and of human agency, as Said and his recent followers tend to do, but as a decentering of the traditional idea of the human and of human agency that had been privileged by the essentialism or identitarianism—the natural supernaturalism—of the Enlightenment and the knowledge-producing institutions (not least the German university) of Enlightenment modernity.[29] Though the early poststructuralists, with the exception of Heidegger, never explicitly affirmed this version of the radically secular human, this, as the tentative gestures of the late Foucault testify, does not necessarily mean that it was beyond their thought.

In addressing the issue of the antihumanism of the poststructuralists and deciding its meaning, we must consider the chronological history of critical theory, especially as it pertained to the new and dislocating question of representation. That is, we must recall that what the poststructuralist revolution of the 1960s and 1970s principally disclosed in a decisive and irreversible way was the problem of (Western) language: that the signifier was not, as it had been assumed throughout the Enlightenment, transparent; that it had become separated from the signified, become thickened, as it were, a problem for knowledge production, or what in *The Order of Things* Foucault called *discourse*. More specifically, the poststructuralist revolution revealed that the naturalized supernaturalism—the logocentrism—that was concealed by the distanced visualist rhetoric of observation/objectivity or disinterestedness had become virtually totalized in the anthropological/anthropocentric discourse of the West, that it had come to saturate all the sites of being, from the ecos, the subject, language, and cultural production, through the economic and social (including race, gender, class, and ethnicity), to the political, both national and global. This, for example, is the witness of the poststructuralist antihumanist Louis Althusser in "Ideology and Ideological State Apparatuses," where, following the lead of Antonio Gramsci's concept of hegemony, he demonstrates the enormous difficulty, if not impossibly, of human agency in a secular (bourgeois capitalist) world that has naturalized—identified as the truth—the supernatural Subject, or, in his own words, in which the human subject has been "interpellated" (subjected) by a naturalized transcendental subject. (It is telling that Althusser invokes the Christian calling to characterize the interpellative operations of the secular ideological state apparatuses of modern capitalism.)

> The duplicate mirror-structure of ideology ensures simultaneity:
> 1 the interpellation of "individuals" as subjects;
> 2 their subjection to the Subject;
> 3 the mutual recognition of subjects and Subject, the subjects' recognition of each other, and finally the subject's recognition of himself;
> 4 the absolute guarantee that everything really is so, and that on condition that the subjects recognize what they are and behave accordingly, everything will be all right: Amen—*"So be it."*
>
> Result: caught in this quadruple system of interpellation as subjects, of subjection to the Subject, of universal recognition and of absolute guarantee, the subjects "work," they "work by themselves" in the vast majority of cases, with the exception of the "bad subjects" who on occasion provoke the intervention of one of the detachments of the (repressive) State apparatuses. But the vast majority of (good) subjects work all right "all by themselves," i.e., by ideology (whose concrete forms are realized in the Ideological State Apparatuses). They are inserted into practices governed by the rituals of the ISAs. They "recognize" the existing state of affairs . . . , that "it really is true that it is so and not otherwise," and that they must be obedient to God, to their conscience, to the priest, to de Gaulle, to the boss, to the engineer, thou shalt "love they neighbor as thyself," etc. Their concrete, material behaviour is simply the inscription in life of the admirable word of the prayer: *"Amen—So be it."*[30]

This inordinate difficulty of achieving agency is also the witness of Raymond Williams, whom Said everywhere acknowledges as a crucial influence, in *Marxism and Literature,* an enabling neo-Marxist book that, despite a certain shift of emphasis, is clearly indebted to Althusser, including the latter's introduction—via Quintin Hoare and Geoffrey Nowell Smith's translation of selections from Gramsci's *Prison Notebooks*—to anglophone readers.[31]

The concept of hegemony often, in practice, resembles these definitions [of ideology], but it is distinct in its refusal to equate consciousness with the articulate formal system which can be and ordinarily is abstracted as "ideology." It of course does not exclude the articulate and formal meanings, values and beliefs which a dominant class develops and propagates. But it does not equate these with consciousness, or rather it does not reduce consciousness to them. Instead it sees the relation of domination and subordination, in their forms as practical consciousness, as in effect a saturation of the whole process of living—not only of political and economic activity, nor only of manifest social activity, but of the whole substance of lived identities and relationships, to such a depth that the pressures and limits of what can ultimately be seen as a specific economic, political, and cultural system seem to most of us the pressures and limits of simple experience and common sense. Hegemony is then not only the articulate upper level of "ideology," nor are its forms of control only those ordinarily seen as "manipulation" or "indoctrination." It is a whole body of practices and expectations, over the whole of living: our senses and assignments of energy, our shaping perceptions of ourselves and our world. It is a lived system of meanings and values—constitutive and constituting—which as they are experienced as practices appear as reciprocally confirming. *It thus constitutes a sense of reality for most people in the society, a sense of absolute because experienced reality beyond which it is very difficult for most members of the society to move, in most areas of their lives.* It is, that is to say, in the strongest sense a "culture," but a culture which has also to be seen as the lived dominance and subordination of particular classes.[32]

Not incidentally, as I will show, Said, echoing Althusser and Foucault (as well as Gramsci and Williams) vis-à-vis Western discourse, bears massive and relentless witness in *Orientalism*—James Clifford refers to this as "numbingly repetitive"[33]—to the inordinate systematicity of the discourse of Orientalism and thus to its oppressive, agency-disabling power. Acknowledging his great debt to Foucault's work in the introduction of *Orientalism,* Said nevertheless goes on to say, "unlike Michel Foucault, I do believe in the determining imprint of individual writers upon the otherwise anonymous collective body of texts constituting a discursive formation like Orientalism" (*O,* 23). Despite this articulation of the variety and uniqueness of perspectives on the Orient, however, Said offers little persuasive evidence of the individual subject's alleged "determining imprint" in his analysis of the many texts he examines—travel writing, novels, autobiographies, scientific treatises—so intent is he on showing how totally and deeply the ideology of Orientalism inscribes these texts. Whatever the differences, they are always and relentlessly, as in the case of writings from the British eccentric Richard Burton, subsumed by the perennial Orientalist categories:

> The double-pronged intention of Burton's work is at the same time to use his Oriental residence for scientific observation *and* not easily to sacrifice his individuality to that end. The second of these intentions leads him inevitably to submit to the first because, as will become increasingly obvious, he is a European for whom such knowledge of Oriental society as he has is possible only for a European, with a European's self-awareness of society as a collection of rules and practices. In other words, to be a European in the Orient, and to be one knowledgeably, one must see and know the Orient as a domain ruled over by Europe. Orientalism, which is the system of European or Western knowledge about the Orient, thus becomes synonymous with European domination of the Orient, and this domination effectively overrules even the eccentricities of Burton's personal style. (*O,* 197)

Nor, as has often been observed by his commentators, does it seem that the discourse of Orientalism precipitated resistance by Orientals during the 1970s, when Said was writing *Orientalism*—specifically, that it furthered the ability of the Occident's "Others" to perceive this discourse and practice of Orientalism as oppressive and to free themselves from its soul-damaging network. This resistance—or writing back—of the colonial subject, as I will show, would become the essential project of Said's great book *Culture and Imperialism,* that is, of a much later Said.

Seen in the light of this inaugural poststructuralist moment in the history of critical theory, then, is it unreasonable to think (1) that the early poststructuralists overdetermined the question of discourse not so much because they denied the possibility of human agency but because in this moment they felt that thematizing the disabling pervasiveness of discourse for thought had priority over the issue of agency *in a world that represented itself as self-evidently democratic and humanist;* and (2) that it was both the poststructuralists' insistent, if always implicit, disclosure of the difficulty of agency in an allegedly free society and their consequent restricted disciplinary perspective on discourse that opened up the question of human agency for later critics such as Williams and Said? To use Said's language characterizing Sacy's and Renan's Orientalism, the difference between Heidegger and Foucault, on the one hand, and Said, on the other, "is the difference between inauguration and continuity" (*O,* 135). This, at any rate, is what I will argue in the last chapter, not as the final word, but as a viable possibility and in the name of the need, precipitated by the very fulfillment of the discursive logic of Western modernity, to rethink disciplinary thinking according to the imperatives of an ontology that perceives being as an indissoluble continuum, however uneven in any specific historical occasion.

2. Heidegger, Foucault, and the "Empire of the Gaze"

Thinking the Territorialization of Knowledge

> We still think the Greek *polis* and the "political" in a totally un-Greek fashion. We think the "political" as Romans, i.e., imperially. The essence of the Greek *polis* will never be grasped within the horizon of the political as understood in the Roman way.
>
> —Martin Heidegger, *Parmenides*

> The Roman reference that accompanied [the Napoleonic regime and "the form of state that was to survive it"] certainly bears with it this double index: citizens and legionaries.
>
> —Michel Foucault, *Discipline and Punish*

As I observed in the previous chapter, the difficult question of the relationship between Edward Said, above all, his critique of Orientalism, and the poststructuralists, particularly Michel Foucault, depends on which of the several Foucaults one invokes. Following a certain antipoststructuralist emphasis in Said's work after *Orientalism,* recent "secular" and often postcolonial critics, especially in the wake of Said's death, have, despite the evidence of his inaugural book, tacitly chosen the Foucault of *Les Mots et les choses* (*The Order of Things*) and *The Archaeology of Knowledge* as the one who best explains Said's (antagonistic) relationship to poststructuralist theory. This is the structuralist/archaeologist Foucault, who, in his brilliant account of the rise of discourse during the Enlightenment and his identification of this turn into modernity as a mutation from the European past, massively overemphasized the undeviating systematicity, the sheer textuality, and the totalizing structural reach of this regulative representational discourse at the expense of its authorship, its worldliness and more generally the humanity of man, and human agency. It is my contention, however, that the Foucault who is most pertinent to an understanding of the achievement of Said's

Orientalism is the Foucault of *Surveiller et punir,* which, as I have noted, was published only three years before *Orientalism.* This is Foucault the genealogist, the Foucault influenced not simply by his reading of Nietzsche as such but—and this is what I intend to contribute to the debate over Said's relation to Foucault—the Nietzsche he discovered only after reading Heidegger, presumably *Being and Time.* Because this nexus and its enabling impact on *Discipline and Punish* is not well known, it will be necessary to undertake a detour into the relationship between Heidegger, particularly his "destruction" of the Western "ontotheological" tradition (metaphysical inquiry), and Foucault's genealogy of the disciplinary society to identify this Foucault and to demonstrate his pertinence to Said's monumental analysis of the discourse of Occidental Orientalism.

* * *

Victor Farias's careless identification of Heidegger's thought with Nazism in *Heidegger et le nazisme* (1987) was enthusiastically endorsed by European and American humanist scholars who adhered to the very philosophical tradition that Heidegger's discourse sought in part to interrogate. Moreover, its scandalization of this relationship compelled many of those philosophically and politically radical poststructuralist thinkers on the Left whose thought Heidegger's had catalyzed to distance themselves from his work or to admit that its overdetermination of *die Seinsfrage* (the question of being) rendered it indifferent to history and politics or, as in the case of Jürgen Habermas, even complicit with political totalitarianism. As a consequence of this multiply situated initiative to delegitimize Heidegger's ontological approach to the question of modernity, Heidegger and Heideggerianism, which had been foundational in the discourse and practice of emancipation at least since the end of World War II, were more or less marginalized by the Left in favor of more historical and sociopolitical perspectives, more specifically, by a number of discourses—New Historicism, cultural studies, feminism, neo-Marxism, and postcolonialism—that to differing degrees had derived their problematic from a certain (disciplinary) reading of Michel Foucault. To risk an oversimplification for the sake of focalizing the question this chapter addresses, it might be said that, increasingly since the putative revelations of Farias's book, Heidegger and Foucault came to be represented by the Anglo-American Left as incommensurably opposed to each other, indeed, as a binary opposition that privileged the latter over the former. This disciplinary division, however, has obscured the relationship between Foucault's and Said's works or, more precisely, obscured the identity of the particular Foucault who influenced Said's elaboration of his genealogy of Orientalism.

This binarist representation does not simply distort the relationship between Heidegger's thought and that of Foucault; more important, it is politically disabling. This becomes especially evident when one reconstellates
Heidegger and Foucault into the post–cold war context, the era that the neoconservative deputies of the triumphant liberal capitalist/imperialist culture,
utterly indifferent to Heidegger's proleptic announcement of the fulfillment of
the (techno)logical economy of modernity in the terrible banality of the "age
of the world picture," have represented as "the end of history," that is, as the
fulfillment of the (onto)logical economy of the Western Logos.[1] Against this
tacit hierarchical binary, I argue that Heidegger's ontological destruction of
the Western philosophical tradition and Foucault's sociopolitical genealogy
of post-Enlightenment modernity belong together, not in a dialogic harmony,
but in intimate strife, that their discourses are most productively understood
if they are read in terms of Heidegger's *Auseinandersetzung,* as *polemos* that,
like Said's "contrapuntal" criticism, always already opens out (dis-closes what
is latent but in some degree invisible to each's discourse) rather than closes
down by way of a decisive victory of one over the other.[2]

This is especially the case if one thinks of this relationship in the context
of the aftermath of September 11, 2001, which is bearing witness to America's
unilateral, one is tempted to say monomaniacal, imperial will to impose the
Pax Americana on the world at large. To put it provisionally, Heidegger and
Foucault on the one hand belong together because both their discourses
begin with the recognition that the identity of the West is grounded in the
complicity of knowledge with power. More specifically, they are in some
degree attuned to the way that the West, since antiquity—for Heidegger and
perhaps Foucault, this means the Roman colonization (technologization)
of Greek thought—but especially in the post-Enlightenment period, (1) has
privileged vision in knowledge production; (2) has reified—or more precisely,
territorialized—differential and relational living processes; (3) has naturalized a socially constituted hierarchical binary logic (Being/nothing or time,
Identity/difference, the One/the many, and Truth/falsehood) *and* its corollary
metaphorics (Light/dark or shadow, Center/periphery, Clearing/wilderness,
Sedentary/nomadic, the Improved/the unimproved, Culture/savagery, and
so on); and (4) has concealed the complicity of this relay of knowledge-
producing assumptions with power over alterity in all its manifestations—that
is, has rendered its disciplinary or imperial essence invisible. On the other
hand, Heidegger and Foucault are "in strife" because their discourses remain
vestigially disciplinary. Heidegger's overdetermination of *die Seinsfrage* (and
his consequent minimization of the historically specific—or in Said's terms,
"worldly"—manifestations of the ontotheological tradition) in his confron-

tation with modernity to some degree blinded him to the sociopolitical imperatives latent in his de-structive thinking. Foucault's overdetermination of the question of sociopolitical power (and his consequent minimization, by emphasizing the uniqueness of the Enlightenment *épistémè*, of the continuity of the Western tradition) to some degree blinded him to the emancipatory ontological imperatives latent in his critical genealogical thinking.

To put it alternatively, Heidegger and Foucault belong together because they both, if only in a resonantly symptomatic way, reject the West's seductively disarming disciplinary orientation toward knowledge production (and the base/superstructure model informing it) in favor of a thinking that perceives the being into which they inquire as relational: a lateral relay or continuum of sites—from being and the subject as such all the way across to domestic and global sociopolitics—that, however unevenly developed in any historically specific moment, are quite obviously indissolubly related. They are in strife because both fail to adequately adhere to their antidisciplinary commitments to relationality and thus to perceive and to think the adjacent sites disclosed by their respective overdeterminations. Tearing Heidegger's and Foucault's discourses out of the context in which they have hitherto been embedded and reconstellating them into each other's orbit will disclose this paradoxically agonistic collaborative relationship. It will also disclose the Foucault to whom Edward Said was responding in the process of writing *Orientalism*.

Heidegger's Critique of Ontological and Epistemological Imperialism

In seeking to understand the relationship between Heidegger's thought and his politics, reconstellating his texts into Foucault's discursive orbit instigates an estrangement that enables us to consider evidence other than those sedimented and deeply worn places habitually prescribed not only by traditional Heideggerians and their humanist critics but by neo-Heideggerians, too. Indeed, the positive possibilities of Heidegger's destructive hermeneutics are evident, however minimally thought in terms of their historical specificity, at several prominent yet largely overlooked sites in his seamless texts, especially those written after his realization in 1934 that the National Socialist project to which he had committed his intellectual energies during his rectorship was itself "caught up in the consummation of nihilism."[3] These circulate above all around Heidegger's curiously neglected but insistently reiterated genealogical argument that the identity of Europe, both philosophical and political, has it origins not in ancient Greek culture (as, according to Martin Bernal's revisionary history, has been massively claimed ever since the

German Enlightenment invented "the Aryan model")[4] but in the Roman colonization of Greek thinking.

Thus, for example, in "Letter on Humanism," written after the war in 1947, Heidegger extends his ontological/epistemological genealogy of the truth of modernity found in *Being and Time*—the truth of presuppositionless or disinterested inquiry—to disclose its complicity with a coercive cultural politics. He shows how the epochal Roman translation of the Greek *a-letheia* to *veritas* gave birth to the general concept of truth that has determined knowledge production (including that of institutions of learning) in the ontotheological tradition at large, especially—and despite modern apologists who trace its origins to Greek thought—in post-Enlightenment modernity. In so doing, as I will show, Heidegger implicates the discourse of modern humanism and the sociopolitical practices of democratic/humanist states as complicit with Rome's imperial project.

According to Heidegger's genealogy of humanist (anthropo-logical) truth in essays such as "The Essence of Truth" and "The Origin of the Work of Art," which follow immediately from the existential analytic of *Being and Time,* the decisive event in the historical process of the Occident's self-representation occurred when the Romans translated the Greek understanding of truth, *a-letheia* (unconcealment), to *veritas, the adaequatio intellectus et rei,* which, whether understood as "the correspondence of the matter to knowledge" or "the correspondence of knowledge to the matter," has "continually in view a conforming to . . . and hence think[s] truth as *correctness [Richtigkeit]."*[5] The epochal turning point thus occurred when the Romans began to think temporal being, which the Greeks thought in-the-midst (interestedly; i.e., secularly), from a transcendental perspective—when, that is, they technologized the originative/existential thinking of the Greeks. "Beneath the seemingly literal and thus faithful translation," Heidegger reiterates, "there is concealed . . . a *trans*lation of Greek experience into a different way of thinking." Roman thought emphatically and insistently *"takes over the Greek words without a corresponding, equally original experience of what they say, without the Greek word. The rootlessness of Western thought begins with this translation."*[6] Henceforth, and increasingly, "the ontology which . . . has thus arisen has deteriorated to a tradition in which it gets reduced to something self-evident—merely material for reworking, as it was for Hegel." Greek ontology thus uprooted becomes "a fixed body of doctrine,"[7] a "free-floating"—and, as Heidegger's insistent emphasis on deterioration suggests, banalized—discourse that, remote from the historicity of being-in-the-world, nevertheless determines history from that remoteness.[8]

Truth as *veritas,* in other words, involves the transformation of the uncentered—originative and errant[9]—thinking of the Greeks into a secondary and
derivative—calculative—mode of inquiry in which the *ratio,* the principle that
identity is the condition for the possibility of difference, is determinative. It
is a logocentric technology that begins inquiry into the differential/relational
phenomena (objects and events) disseminated by a temporality "grounded"
in the nothing (*das Nichts*) from the distance of the end. To invoke the visual
metaphorics underlying Heidegger's differentiation between *a-letheia* and
veritas—the metaphorical relay that brings his interrogation of humanist
modernity into convergence with Foucault's various archaeologies of the
"gaze"—inquiry understood as the adequation of mind and thing proceeds
from after or above (*meta ta physika*), that is, retro-*spectively*, from a teleological or fixed transcendental vantage point—an end that is also a "center elsewhere," in Derrida's terms, "which is beyond the reach of freeplay."[10] In thus
privileging the invisible surveying eye, this all-encompassing, global mode
of knowledge production has as its ultimate purpose the coercion of difference into the circumference of the self-identical circle. The center spatializes/
reifies time in order to "comprehend" the elusive flow of the differences it
disseminates—comprehend them not simply to know them but, as the Latin
etymology suggests, "to take hold" (*prehendere*) or "to manage" (*manus*),
that is, to dominate, pacify, and utilize their force. The comportment toward
phenomena that the center elsewhere enables is thus that of the commanding
eye, or to invoke Foucault's sociopolitical vocabulary, the panoptic gaze. It is a
visual comportment that represents the force of difference as that which truth
is not—as *false* (*falsum*)—and thus as a threat to truth that must be either
exterminated or domesticated and pacified at all costs, willfully reduced to
the Same in the name of this (imperial) justice. To anticipate a metaphorics
that will become prominent (and literal) in Heidegger's later, more politically, if not historically, conscious account of the Roman origins of European
modernity, the meta-physical gaze determining knowledge production in
modernity—not unlike the scrutiny of the imperial gaze in Said's analysis of
Western Orientalism, as I will show in chapter 3—flattens out the differential
dynamics of the *being* of being into which one inquires, making it a territory
or, to anticipate Said, a visible "imaginative geography": a super-vised space
to be conquered, mapped, classified, colonized, and administered. It is, in
other words, a "disciplinary" or, more inclusively, an "imperial" gaze.

From this genealogy of the truth of humanist modernity, which both discloses its origins in the Roman translation of *a-letheia* to *veritas,* of the hermeneutic circle (repetition) to the *circulus vitiosus* (recollection), and serves to

pacify the force of that "Other" lying outside the centered circle, Heidegger proceeds to explicitly reveal how this romanized concept of truth (and its imperialist binarist logic) is tied to modern cultural production—specifically, *paedeia* (education)—and implicitly to the modern Western nation-state:

> *Humanitas,* explicitly so called, was first considered and striven for in the age of the Roman Republic. *Homo humanus* was opposed to *homo barbarus.* *Homo humanus* here means the Romans, who exalted and honored Roman *virtus* through the "embodiment" of the *paideia* taken over from the Greeks. These were the Greeks of the Hellenistic age, whose culture was acquired in the schools of philosophy. It was concerned with *eruditio et institutio in bonas artes* [scholarship and training in good conduct]. *Paideia* thus understood was translated as *humanitas.* The genuine *romanitas* of *homo romanus* consisted in such *humanitas.* We encounter the first humanism in Rome: it therefore remains in essence a specifically Roman phenomenon, which emerges from the encounter of Roman civilization with the culture of late Greek civilization. The so-called Renaissance of the fourteenth and fifteenth centuries in Italy is a *renascentia romanitatis.* Because *romanitas* is what matters, it is concerned with *humanitas* and therefore with Greek *paideia.* But Greek civilization is always seen in its later form and this itself is seen from a Roman point of view.[11]

In this decisive but largely overlooked passage, Heidegger ostensibly restricts the genealogy of modernity to the indissoluble complicity between humanist ontology and humanist pedagogy or culture production: the logocentrism (and its will to power) informing Roman *veritas* also informs the Roman *paedeia.* Truth or knowledge production and power in the anthropological tradition are, however unevenly developed, coextensive. But if Heidegger's essay is read in the historically specific context in which it was written—the catastrophe of Europe precipitated by the Third Reich—a further extension in the relay of power informing the discourse and practice of humanist modernity announces itself, one that implicates truth and knowledge production in the disciplinary politics of imperialism. Clearly, Heidegger is doing more than simply observing that the disinterested truth and the liberal humanist cultural apparatuses of the post-Enlightenment tradition have their origins in a Roman pedagogical technology designed to produce "Romans," a "manly" citizenry that, as the embodiment of a means of knowledge production that privileged Roman *virtus* (manly/powerful/good, as the etymological origins of this word make clear), would constitute a disciplined—or, in Foucault's terms, "useful and docile"—collective of individuals: subjected subjects. As the resonant binary opposition between *homo humanus* (i.e., the Romans) and *homo barbarus* makes evident, the ultimate purpose of the logocentric Roman *veritas* and its *paedeia* was the production of a disciplined, efficient, and dependable army of patriotic citizens under the aegis of a metropolitan state committed to the achievement and administration of the hegemonic empire.

To put this genealogy in terms of the metaphorics of the centered circle privileged by the humanist tradition, the self-present subject as interpellated citizen/soldier produced by the discourse of *veritas* and its *paedeia* became the structural model of the *civitas*. Just as the self-identical humanist anthropologos justifies the territorialization of knowledge and the domestication by "cultivation" of the differential "provincial" (ultimately from *pro-vincere,* "before being conquered") energies of immature and deviant youth, so the self-present metropolis justifies the colonization of the barbarian energies of provincial ("lowly") multitudes, who as "Other" threaten to turn its "civilized" space back into a savage wilderness. It is important to note that, as I have shown elsewhere, the English words *culture* and *cultivate* privileged by this humanist tradition, especially since the Enlightenment, are cognates of *colonize,* which derives from the Latin *colere* ("to cultivate or plant"), *colonus* ("tiller," "cultivator," "planter," or "settler"), or more tellingly, *agricola* ("cultivator of the *agr[i]os* or wild earth"), and that these derive their essential ideological meanings from their binary opposites: *silva* ("forest," i.e., "uncultivated wilderness") and *silvestris* ("savage," or literally, "of the forest").[12] Equally significant, these privileged yet barely visible terms have their ideological origins not in ancient Greek words referring to such agents and practices but in the Latin *circulus:* the *figure* appropriated by the Roman humanists and their Renaissance descendants from the Greek words *kyklos* ("cycle") or *kirkos* ("ring") to represent and symbolize "beauty," "truth," and "perfection."

Heidegger's genealogy of modern humanism, in sum, discloses that the Romans' ideological reduction and codification of the "errancy" and "prodigality" of originative Greek thinking—their *circumscription, cultivation,* and *colonization* of the truth as always *aletheic*—not only gave rise to their disciplinary educational project (the *studia humanitatis*) but also legitimized their imperial will to power over the peripheral and lowly—provincial— "barbarians." To put this differently, the Roman translation of Greek thinking enabled in a fundamental way the Roman *imperium sine fine* (as Virgil puts it in the *Aeneid*), which goes by the duplicitous name of the Pax Romana.

It is, according to Heidegger's genealogy, this indissoluble relay of repressions at the sites of the subject, knowledge, cultural production, the earth, and the city, a relay enabled by the *idealization* of metaphysical thinking in the image of the circle whose center is both inside and outside (above), that constitutes the origins of the discourse and practice of the modern West.[13] The circle and the affiliated "white" metaphors constelled around its center—the

polarities of Eye/appetitive senses, Light/darkness, High/low, Prelapsarian/
fallen, True/false, Beauty/ugliness, Perfection/crudity, Normality/deviance,
Plantation/wilderness, Direction/errancy, Citizen/savage, Inhabitant/nomad,
and so on—are *polyvalent* in their material applications. To put Heidegger's
Destruktion of the discourse, cultural institutions, and sociopolitical practices
of humanist modernity in terms of the legacy not of classical Greece but of
imperial Rome is to indicate that, however more generalized, it significantly
mirrors not only Michel Foucault's genealogy of the modern disciplinary society in *Surveiller et punir* but also the imperial society that Foucault did not
quite think yet made possible for Edward Said and the host of postcolonial
critics Said has influenced. By "imperial society," moreover, I mean specifically the "panoptic" society eventually precipitated by an "Enlightenment"
that, according to a certain constant in Foucault's genealogical discourse,
deliberately appropriated the Roman model (specifically, the structure of the
military camp) to articulate its disciplinary epistemology, pedagogy, cultural
agenda, and domestic and international politics.

In interpreting the historically resonant passage from "Letter on Humanism" just quoted, I have drawn a political or worldly thematic from
Heidegger's philosophical discourse that, in suggesting its affiliation with
a fundamental political motif in Foucault, no doubt exceeds what Heidegger actually says about the Roman provenance of modern humanism and
what he implies about the "disciplinary"/"imperial" character of the post–
World War II historical conjuncture his text addresses. It may be objected,
therefore, that this interpretation constitutes an apologetic reading. That the
political content I have thematized is justified by Heidegger's discourse at
this historically specific moment, indeed, with the exception of the period
of his rectorship, by his discourse at large, is further borne witness to by
the seminar on the Parmenides fragments he gave in 1942–43, significantly
after he resigned as rector of Freiburg University but considerably before he
wrote "Letter on Humanism," in fact, before Hitler and the Nazis unleashed
their genocidal project against the Jews (and the "Bolsheviks").[14] As Éliane
Escoubas puts it, this series of lectures constitutes the "*texte-charnière*" of
Heidegger's "'explication' avec"—his "reciprocal rejoinder to," as it were—
German National Socialism.[15]

This is not the occasion for a full analysis of what should be (but isn't) one
of the central texts in the debate over the relationship between Heidegger's
philosophical discourse and Nazi politics. Keeping in mind what I have said
above about Heidegger's identification of *homo romanus* with *homo humanus,*
it will suffice for my general purpose to comment on a crucial passage from
Parmenides that traces the origins of the imperial politics of Western mo-

dernity back to the Roman translation of the Greek *aletheia* as *veritas* or, more precisely, of the *pseudos,* the counterterm to *aletheia,* as *falsum,* the counterterm to *veritas.* For one thing, this synecdochic passage implicates all three sites of the indissoluble relay I have thematized: the discourse of *veritas* (the true versus the false), the *paedeia* understood as *eruditio et institutio in bonas artes* (the disciplinary pedagogy devoted to scholarship and training in good conduct), and the *imperium sine fine* (the global spatial and temporal imperial project). For another, it brings into visible play both the hidden binarist visual metaphorics encoded in these sites (the panoptic gaze, light, spatialized time, heights, directionality, and so on, which are privileged over the appetitive senses and the metaphorics to which they have given rise, such as darkness, temporality, lowness, fallenness, errancy, and the unhuman)and the indissolubly related figure of the centered circle privileged over the periphery. In so doing, as I will show, this passage constitutes a remarkable, if highly generalized, prefiguration of Foucault's genealogy of the relationship between truth and power in modernity, specifically—and most suggestively—his exposure of the "repressive hypothesis," which informs the so-called liberal discursive practices of the post-Enlightenment and enables the disciplinary society.

In the *Parmenides,* Heidegger's analysis of the Roman provenance of and the indissoluble relationship between imperial power and the modern Western understanding of truth and knowledge has its point of departure in the Roman concept of truth, which was predicated on a doctrinaire metaphysical orientation toward being. This is, again, the reduced truth—*veritas*—that the Romans, in the name of certainty, constructed and naturalized by splitting and hierarchizing the earlier, more originative—and erratic—Greek understanding of truth as *aletheia,* whose negative (*pseudos:* "dissembling") was perceived not, as was *falsum,* the Roman negative of *veritas,* as an antithetical negative but as *belonging* "positively" with the "positive": "The essence of negativity [for the Greeks] is nothing negative, but neither is it only something 'positive.' The distinction between the positive and the negative does not suffice to grasp what is essential, to which the non-essence belongs. The essence of the false is not something 'false.'"[16] In the earlier texts I have cited, Heidegger destructures the truth of metaphysics; in the *Parmenides,* however, he destructures the "false" as the counter to truth understood as the correspondence of mind and thing. But the purpose is the same: the disclosure of the will to power over alterity that informs this perennially privileged binary logic. Now, however, the destruction of the Roman reduction of *pseudos* to *falsum* will disclose the will to power informing this logic to be, literally, a polyvalent imperial will to power. What should not be overlooked in Heidegger's analysis of the Roman *falsum* is the indissolubly double register of his commentary: the fact that he is talking about knowledge production (truth) and political imperial practice at the same time (in Foucault's phrase, the "regime of truth").

In the first phase of his inquiry into the relationships among metaphysical perception, knowledge production, and imperialism, Heidegger traces the origins of the Roman *falsum* back to the Greek *sfallo* ("to overthrow, bring to a downfall, fell, make totter"). But the stem following the privative prefix (*a-*) in *aletheia* indicates that the Greeks did *not* understand the counteressence of truth in this way. By demonstrating that the Romans represented being as a domain or territory to be mastered, Heidegger suggests that this forced etymology, which enabled them to circumvent the Greek *pseudo*, a term affiliated with the *lathos* ("concealment") that constitutes the stem of *aletheia,* was intended to put the truth (of being)—and its binary opposite, the false—at the service of the *imperium.*

> The essential domain which prevails for the deployment of the Roman "*falsum*" is that of the "*imperium*" and of the "imperial." We take these words in their strict and original sense. "*Imperium*" means "command" [*Befehl*]. . . . In passing through French [a Romance language], "*befehlen*" [originally "to entrust to sheltering"] became "to command"; more precisely, it became the Roman *imperare—im-perare* = to install [*enrichten*], to take preliminary measures, that is, *prae-cipere,* to occupy in advance and by so doing to have the "possessed" as domain [*Gebiet*], to dominate over it [*darüber gebieten*]. The *imperium* is the domain that founds itself on the basis of the order [*Gebot*], and under whose dominion the others are subject. The *imperium* is the command [*Befehl*] in the sense of the disposing order. Command, thus understood, is the essential ground of domination [*Herrschaft*], not at all only its consequence, and not only a form of its exercise. . . . The gods of the Greeks are not [as the God of the Judeo-Christian tradition is] commanding gods but, rather, gods that show, that indicate. The Roman "*numen,*" by which the Roman gods are characterized, signifies by contrast "injunction" [*Geheiss*] and "will" [*Wille*] and has the character of command. The "numinous," in the strict sense, never concerns the essence of the Greek gods, that is, the gods who have their essence in the realm of *aletheia*. In the essential domain of "command" belongs the Roman "justice," *ius*. The word is attached to *jubeo:* to enjoin [*heissen*], by injunction [*Geheiss*] to have done and to determine acts and gestures. Command is the essential ground of domination and of "being in the right" and "to have the right," understood in the Roman sense. As a result *iustitia* has an altogether different essential ground than *dike,* which has its essence in *aletheia.* (P, 58 [40])

In this remarkably resonant passage, Heidegger points to the affiliation of the word *praecipere,* which possesses the same stem as the Latinate words *conceive, concept,* and *capture* (from *capere,* "to take"), with metaphysics: that is, between the epistemological act of grasping and mastering the flow that has been reified and the perception of being from the end or, equivalently, from above: panoptically, as it were. It is an affiliation that reduces being to a spatial totality, a territory "to be occupied in advance." Further, as Heidegger suggests in identifying the command with the Roman *ius/jubeo,* which he translates with the German verb *heissen,* "to enjoin, command, bid, order, or direct" but also "to name, call, or denominate," the passage constitutes a remarkable prefiguration of Althusser's analysis of ideology as the interpellation (or hailing) of the individual as (subjected) subject by an "Absolute Subject."[17] It is an analysis that, as I will show, Foucault takes over in his genealogy of the supposedly free individual celebrated by bourgeois democracy.

In keeping with this insight into the affiliation between knowledge and power, the second phase of Heidegger's analysis invokes the visual metaphorics informing metaphysical inquiry to demonstrate that the false, as a fundamental dimension of commanding, is related to *over*seeing, or, to suggest the continuity between Heidegger's thought and Foucault's, *sur*veil-lance: "To commanding as the essential foundation of sovereignty belongs 'being on high' [or "above," *Obensein*]. That is only possible through constant surmounting [*Überhohung*] in relation to others, who are thus the inferiors [*Unteren*]. In the surmounting, in turn, resides the constant ability to oversee ['super-vise and dominate,' *Übersehen-können*]. We say 'to oversee something,' which means 'to master [*beherrschen*] it'" (P, 59 [40–41]). This oversight of an absolute subject, which is also "a center elsewhere" beyond the reach of the free play of criticism, is not, as it is assumed in the prevailing discourse of Western knowledge production, a matter of the failure of attention. It is the proper form of vision understood as enframing (*Gestell*).[18] Seeing, in the ontotheological tradition, is not passive reception of that which it perceives. It is an action or discursive *praxis:* "To this commanding view, which includes surmounting, belongs a constant 'being-on-the-lookout' [*Auf-der-Lauer-liegen*]. That is the form of all action that oversees [dominates from the gaze], but that holds to itself, in Roman the *actio* of the *actus.*" And this reifying oversight, which by putting every thing/time it sees (the spatial and temporal detail) in its "proper" place constitutes an action, implicates itself essentially in the disciplinary/imperial project:

> The commanding overseeing is the dominating vision which is expressed in the often cited phrase of Caesar: *veni, vidi, vici*—I came, I *oversaw* [*übersah*], I conquered. Victory is already nothing but the consequence of the Caesarian gaze that dominates [*Obersehens*] and the seeing [*Sehens*] which has the character of *actio.* The essence of the *imperium* reposes in the *actus* of constant action.

The imperial *actio* of the constant surmounting over others implies that the others, in the case where they raise themselves to a comparable or even identical height to command, will be brought down—in Roman: *fallere* (participle: *falsum*) The "bringing-to-fall" [*das Zu-Fall-bringen*] belongs necessarily to the domain of the imperial. (*P,* 59 [41])

After establishing the literal identity of metaphysical ontology, overseeing or surveillance, and imperial domination of the inferior "Other," Heidegger goes on in the last and most resonantly contemporary—and Foucauldian (and Saidian)—phase of his meditation on the provenance of the Western idea of the false to distinguish between two kinds of imperial practice: on the one hand, a primitive and implicitly uneconomical and inefficient (i.e., politically resistible) imperialism, and on the other, a modern, fully articulated ("proper"), and as the reference to its greatness suggests, highly economical, efficient, productive, and virtually invulnerable imperialism. Significantly, this developed, polyvalent form of imperialism is deeply inscribed by the metaphorics of vision and the affiliated figure of the circle:

The "bringing-to-fall" can be accomplished in a "direct" assault [*Ansturm*] and an overthrowing [*Niederwerfen:* literally, "throwing down"]. But the other can also be brought to fall by being outflanked [*Um-gehen*] and tripped up from behind. The "bringing-to-fall" is now the way of deceptive circumvention [*Hinter-gehen*]. . . . Considered from the outside, going behind the back is a complicated, circumstantial, and thus mediate "bringing-to-fall" as opposed to an immediate overthrowing. In this way, what is brought-to-fall becomes not thereby annihilated but in a certain manner redressed within the boundaries [*in den Grenzen*] which are staked out by the dominators. (*P,* 59 [41])

In thematizing this developed imperial practice's textualization (mediation) of power—its harnessing of the truth to political domination—the distinction Heidegger articulates cannot but recall Foucault's (and, as I will show, Edward Said's) differentiation between power relations in the ancien régime and those in the Enlightenment. More specifically, it presages Foucault's enabling disclosure of the complicity of the microcosmic table or map—the advanced or modern structural model of knowledge production that develops out of the earlier and more generalized spatialization and territorialization of a recalcitrantly volatile being—with the colonization and administration of the "Other," and beyond that to Said's analysis of the imperial function of the army of savants that accompanied Napoleon's Egyptian expedition in 1798 and to the "expert" whose "blueprints" came to dominate area studies and national policy in the neoimperial age:

This "staking out" [*Abstecken*] is called in Roman: *pango*, whence the word *pax*, peace. This, thought imperially, is the firmly established condition of what has been brought to fall. In truth, the bringing-to-fall in the sense of deception and outflanking is not the mediate and derived imperial *actio* but the imperial *actio* proper. It is not in war, but in the *fallere* of deceptive outflanking [*hintergehenden Umgehens*] and its appropriation to the service of dominion that the proper and "great" trait of the imperial reveals itself. . . . In the Roman *fallere*—to bring-to-fall—as a going around resides deceit; the *falsum* is the insidiously deceptive: "the false." . . . The Greek *pseudos*, through its translation into the Roman *falsum*, is *trans*ferred [*übergesetzt*] into the imperial Roman domain of the bringing-to fall. (*P,* 60 [41])

The end of the pursuit of knowledge, according to this developed, post-Enlightenment form of imperial practice, is to produce peace. But this peace will be achieved only by the total colonization and administration of all the empire's "Others." Theory (understood as a mode of inquiry that territorializes time and privileges seeing, *theoria*) and imperial practice become coterminous. In the "age of the world picture," which constitutes the fulfillment of the spatializing/territorializing logic of Occidental enframing (*Ge-stell*), the Pax Metaphysica *is* the Pax Romana. This, finally, is what Heidegger means when, alluding to the West's claim that its origins lie in classical Greece, he says, "We today still see the Greek world with Roman eyes—and indeed not solely within historiographical research into ancient Greece but also, and this is the only decisive thing, within the historical metaphysical dialogue of the modern world with that of the ancients. . . . We think the Greek *polis* and the 'political' in a totally un-Greek fashion. We think the "political" as Romans, i.e., imperially" (*P,* 67 [43]).

The relay in this extraordinary meditation on the complicity of Roman (i.e., Western) truth (and falsehood), Roman cultural production, and Roman politics, which is determined by the "white" metaphorics of the supervisory gaze and the transcendental center, is too obvious to need further elaboration. What should not be overlooked, however, is that Heidegger's *Parmenides,* like Foucault's *Discipline and Punish,* is intended not as a history of the past as such but as a "history of the present."[19] It constitutes a genealogy of *modern* power relations. Specifically, it discloses that the "strong" discursive practices of what, in his postwar "Letter," Heidegger calls Western humanism have their origins not in Greek thought, as is generally assumed in modernity, but in the circular (anthropo)logic, the disciplinary pedagogy, and the imperial practice of Rome. Heidegger thus concludes his meditation by carefully distinguishing between two kinds of domination that nevertheless have a single (metaphysical) origin. One kind of power over the "fallen" "Other" operates directly (is "immediate") and is thus visible; the other operates by indirection or detour (*Hintergehung*)—is "distanced" and "mediate"—and is thus invisible. The "bringing-to-fall" can be accomplished by means of a direct assault (i.e., repressive conquest and exploitation), or it can be achieved by discursive practices that seem deceptively benign. The crucial issue, however, is not simply that they are both determined by a fixed center that is above or beyond the reach of the free play of criticism but also, and above all, that it is the latter—specifically, the discourse enabled by the Roman *veritas/falsum* opposition—that characterizes the developed or modern form of imperial domination. However generalized Heidegger's formulation, we are not far here from Foucault's poststructuralist interrogation of power relations in modernity, specifically, as I will show, his analysis of the "repressive hypothesis" determining the disciplinary practices of postmonarchical humanist society. Nor are we far from Edward Said's interrogation of the discourse of Orientalism: his disclosure of the complicity between the Occident's representation of the Orient and the Occident's worldly domination of the Orient.

Indeed, if we conflate the passages from Heidegger's lectures on the *Parmenides* and "Letter on Humanism" that refer to the Roman reduction of Greek thinking, we arrive at the following Foucauldian proposition: truth and power, knowledge production and repression, are not external to each other (as they are all too duplicitously assumed to be in the discursive practices of traditional humanism) but continuous and complicit with each other. To put this paradox in terms of the figure informing this relation, the circle of truth/beauty/perfection is also the circle of domination. The violence that accompanies overt imperialism is not incommensurate with, but *latent* in, the truth of European humanism. In a remarkable parallel to Foucault, Heidegger shows that the benign discursive practices that humanism substitutes for immediate overthrowing in the name of peace collectively constitute an oppressive "regime of truth."

It is true that Heidegger overdetermined the most rarified site on the indissoluble continuum of being, the ontological understood as *Technik,* in his interrogation of the dominant discourse of (Occidental) modernity. It is also true that this overdetermination blinded him to the other, more worldly sites, most notably that of contemporary European politics, where the Nazis perpetrated their murderous totalitarian practice. This failure to destructure his own historically specific sociopolitical occasion is, of course, enormously consequential and deserves the severest censure. Nevertheless, it does not invalidate the resonant sociopolitical implications of his genealogy of the modern West's representation of being:the inexorably coercive momentum of thought and language, inaugurated by the Romans, that culminated in the accommodation of the incalculable and errant differences time disseminates to the totalized, well-lighted, and normalizing circle of Being. More specifically, this is the momentum of enframing that, via the invention of the classificatory table in the Enlightenment, fulfilled its imperial binary logic in the global age of the world picture, in which being in all its manifestations (including humans) was virtually reduced to standing—that is, disposable—reserve (*Bestand*), a designation remarkably similar to, but far more sweeping than, the "useful and docile bodies" whose production Foucault attributes to the triumphant disciplinary/neoimperial society. Indeed, Heidegger's prophetic announcement of the planetary triumph of this deadly banalizing technological thinking has been borne out in the post–cold war era, even if it has not been adequately thought by oppositional intellectuals. It appears in the alleged globalization of the discourse of late capitalism, whose reifying binary logic, like the proleptic logic of the technocratic Pentagon planners of the Vietnam War (but now on a global scale), tacitly represents recalcitrant living entities wherever they appear on the global scene—Haiti, Panama, Somalia, Serbia, Afghanistan, Iraq, Iran—as nothing more than expendable obstacles in the way of History.[20]

Nor, finally, does Heidegger's overdetermination of the ontological site disable a certain destructive hermeneutics that could interrogate the representations of those more "practical," historically overdetermined sites, especially the sociopolitical, which he largely neglected, overlooked, or most crucially, misread. Indeed, such a passage from an ontological to a sociopolitical critique of Western modernity is, despite the misguided ultranationalist twist of the rectorate period, latent in Heidegger's destructive effort, beginning with *Being and Time,* to retrieve being as historicity from Being as re-presentation. This is clearly suggested, for example, in a neglected passage from "Letter on Humanism" (a text written not simply in the aftermath of the destruction of the Third Reich but also at the outset of the cold war) that, remarkably like Foucault's texts, would engage Marx in an *Auseinandersetzung.* "Because Marx by experiencing estrangement attains an essential dimension of history," Heidegger writes, "the Marxist view of history is superior to that of other historical accounts. But since neither Husserl nor—so far as I have seen till now—Sartre recognized the essential importance of the historical in being, neither phenomenology nor existentialism enters that dimension within which a productive dialogue with Marxism first becomes possible."[21]

In the specific terms of my thematization of the symptomatic political implications of Heidegger's destructive hermeneutics, the recognition that being is a lateral, however unevenly developed, continuum or field of forces makes explicit the relay between the residual humanities and the overdetermined disciplinary technologies of Western modernity, a relay that the territorialization of being and the increasingly disciplinary compartmentalization of knowledge has made invisible. More specifically, it exposes the affiliation between the negative and inactive epistemological oversight, leveling, and forgetting of difference issuing from "inquiring" *meta ta physika* and the positive and active (if largely rarefied, i.e., hegemonic) territorialization, repression, and colonization of the relay of sociopolitical "Others" enabled by the supervisory panoptic machinery of the post-Enlightenment disciplinary/ imperial society. In other words, to perceive being as an indissoluble relay of sites (or flow of forces) is to make possible—indeed, necessary in the present historical conjuncture—a productive dialogue between Heidegger's interrogation of the ontological ground of the age of the world picture and the recent, more worldly critics' interrogation of modernity's global sociopolitical practices, especially Foucault's (and Edward Said's) transdisciplinary analysis of the relationship between knowledge and power. That is, it enables a productive dialogue between Heidegger's de-struction of the ontotheological tradition at large and Foucault's genealogy not only of what he calls the modern "disciplinary society," or alternatively, the "regime of truth," but also of what Edward Said, following Foucault, refers to as the global imperial society.

In short, reconstellating Heidegger's thought into Foucault's more radical discursive orbit yields the following narrative about the course of Western history: the inaugural tendency of the grave "Romanized" metaphysical eye to "over-look" distracting or disconcerting "deviations"—what Heidegger calls the "ontological difference" and Foucault "the singular event" or "extrabeing"[22]—from the Archimedean vantage point of a transcendental signified in behalf of truth ultimately and inevitably, however erratically and unevenly, became completely internalized. In the age of the Enlightenment (which is also the "age of exploration"), it took the form of instrumental rationality's willful and indeed *mono*-maniacal and totalizing obsession to territorialize, name, classify, comprehend, administer, and control the disruptive mystery of difference. This movement, in turn, precipitated the transformation of oversight into a generalized, calculative, "reformist" cultural and sociopolitical strategy of sur-veillance or super-vision that, according to Foucault, constitutes the essence of the modern disciplinary society (and, according to Said and other postcolonial critics whom Foucault has influenced, of postcolonial colonialism). To put this territorializing narrative in the related spatial terms of geometry, the centered circle (the figure of truth/beauty/perfection theorized by the post-Socratics and, according to Heidegger, practiced by the

Romans) came to be understood and utilized in and by the modern world of liberal capitalist democracy as the *discreet and polyvalently productive* figure of not only cultural but also sociopolitical power.

This is not to say that, in overdetermining the (scientifically and techno-logically organized) sociopolitical site, the post-Enlightenment occasion has rendered Heidegger's ontological destruction of modernity irrelevant, favoring instead a Foucauldian genealogy of discipline. However uneven the distribution of power in the present historical occasion, the ontological and the sociopolitical constitute an indissoluble relay. Insofar as Heidegger's destruction emphasizes the ontological construction of modernity (its ancient philosophical ground), it is a limited agent for critical practice. Nonetheless, insofar as Foucault (along with other contemporary worldly critics, including Edward Said) emphasizes modernity's sociopolitical construction (and its "scientific/technological" ground), his genealogy, too, constitutes a limited agent for critique, especially in the post-9/11 context, which has borne witness to the United States' invocation of the ontological ground of its American exceptionalist ethos in behalf of its global imperial project. The circular/panoptic technology of power that characterizes modernity, in other words, is both ontological and sociopolitical. Moreover, it has as its calculative end the coercive re-formation, in the name of the logo-euro-centric sociopolitical Norm (the guardian eye), of "deformed" or "deviant" (or "fallen")—eccentric or erratic—forces all along the indissoluble continuum of being: temporal, linguistic, ecological, cultural, sexual, racial, ethnic, and sociopolitical. What must be emphasized provisionally is that the planetary technology of power informing the discourse and practice of Western (now American) modernity does not result solely from the rise of the Enlightenment's scientific/techno-logical *épistémè*, as Foucault's (and Said's) genealogy might suggest. Nor does it result solely from "philosophy," as Heidegger's discourse all too insistently affirms. Rather, as a reading of Heidegger with Foucault or Foucault with Heidegger suggests, it results from both. An *Auseinandersetzung* with their discourses will show that the overdetermined empirical sciences and the residual humanities—the "Two Cultures"—which the dominant culture stra-tegically represents as adversaries, a *querelle des modernes et anciens,* are in fact different but affiliated instruments of the anthropologos, the discourse of Man, and thus complicit with the late capitalist West's (neo)imperial project of planetary domination—and with its ominous banalization of terror.

Foucault's Critique of Cultural and Sociopolitical Imperialism

Michel Foucault's genealogical analysis of the theory and practice of post-Enlightenment humanist society was not explicitly intended to extend the scope of Heidegger's destructive hermeneutics to the site of sociopolitics. Indeed, Foucault apparently rejects an understanding of Western history as a continuous narrative—a progressive ontotheological tradition—in favor of one characterized by ruptures. In his last interview before his death, however, Foucault said this about his relationship to Heidegger's thought:

> For me Heidegger has always been the essential philosopher. I began by reading Hegel, then Marx, and I set out to read Heidegger in 1951 or 1952; then in 1952 or 1953 . . . I read Nietzsche. I still have here the notes that I took when I was reading Heidegger. . . . And they are much more important than the ones I took on Hegel and Marx. My entire philosophical development was determined by my reading of Heidegger. . . . My knowledge of Nietzsche certainly is better than my knowledge of Heidegger. Nevertheless, these are the two fundamental experiences I have had. . . . I had tried to read Nietzsche in the fifties but Nietzsche alone did not appeal to me—whereas Nietzsche and Heidegger: that was a philosophical shock.[23]

By itself, this statement says nothing about the specific relationship between Foucault's and Heidegger's discourses. If it is remembered, however, that the "very small article on Nietzsche" to which Foucault refers elsewhere in the interview was his "Nietzsche, Genealogy, History" (1971),[24] this teasing aside in his discussion of Heidegger's hitherto unacknowledged influence on his thought activates a resonance that demands but has not received adequate attention.[25] Unlike Foucault's earlier work, which underscores his antihumanism, his pivotal essay locates the enabling source of Nietzsche's critique of modern Western historiography, culture, and sociopolitics at precisely the site where Heidegger's does: the distanced visualist (i.e., "meta-physical") perspective from which secular humanist historiography is enabled to accommodate and reduce the differential dynamics of historicity to the subsuming principle of identity:

> Nietzsche's criticism, beginning with the second of the *Untimely Meditations*, always questions the form of history that reintroduces (and always assumes) a suprahistorical perspective: a history whose function is to compose the finally reduced diversity of time into a totality fully closed upon itself; a history that always encourages subjective recognitions and attributes a form of reconciliation to all the displacements of the past; a history whose perspective on all that

precedes it implies the end of time, a completed development. The historian's history finds its support outside of time and pretends to base its judgments on an apocalyptic objectivity. This is only possible, however, because of its belief in eternal truth, the immortality of the soul, and the nature of consciousness as always identical to itself. Once the historical sense is mastered by a suprahistorical perspective, metaphysics can bend it to its own purpose and, by aligning it to the demands of objective science, it can impose its own "Egyptianism."[26]

In focusing on Nietzsche's exposure of the Egyptianism of a modern secularism that in fact constitutes a "naturalized supernaturalism"—that is, the will to power over difference inscribed in the suprahistorical perspective of humanist historiography—Foucault's essay also enables his epoch-making genealogy of modern knowledge/power relations, the aptly titled *Surveiller et punir* (1975),[27] which discloses the origins of Western modernity's disciplinary/hegemonic "microphysics of power" in the panoptic technology precipitated by the Enlightenment's obsessive quest for enlightenment.

Reconstellating Foucault's *Surveiller et punir* (and the much earlier texts it restructures, especially *Madness and Civilization* and *The Birth of the Clinic*) into Heidegger's disclosure of the founding metaphorics informing and determining the truth achieved by the Western tradition's discourse of knowledge production will go far to establish the affiliation between Heidegger's destruction of the philosophical discourse of the ontotheological tradition and Foucault's genealogy of the discursive practices of the Enlightenment—and, as I will show later, Edward Said's genealogy of the discourse of Orientalism. Again, these metaphorics involve the spatialization or territorialization of being that precipitates the Light/darkness opposition or, equivalently, the Centered Circle/periphery binary, which privileges the first term as the symbol of beauty, perfection, and civilization and thus justifies the "conquest," "occupation," and "colonization" of the "inferior" second. More important, such a reconstellation will also suggest a theory of knowledge/power relations that overcomes the disabling disciplinary tendencies of each discourse, a theory that is more adequate than either for a critique of modernity at large. By modernity, I do not mean simply Foucault's "regime of truth" (and Gramsci's "hegemony"), the discursive practice that has internalized visible manifestations of state power by putting the truth (identity) of disinterested inquiry in a binary, adversarial opposition to the false (difference). Following the directive suggested by Heidegger's *Parmenides* lectures, I also mean the global regime of truth (increasingly called the Pax Americana by postcolonial critics such as Edward Said, Gayatri Spivak, R. Radhakrishan, and the Subaltern Studies Group) that has internalized the visible manifestations of imperial power by putting the white, civilized, technologically developed

West in a binary, adversarial opposition to various elements in the so-called Third World: the colored, barbarian, errant, "undeveloped," and "strife-riven" East and South.

Taking Foucault's critique of the concept of progress as their point of departure, his early commentators represented the origins of the disciplinary society as lying in the epistemic rupture that precipitated the Enlightenment. They took as axiomatic what is, as Foucault observed, only an emphasis in his genealogy: "This business about discontinuity has always rather bewildered me. . . . My problem was not at all to say, 'Voilà, long live discontinuity, we are in the discontinuous and a good thing too,' but to pose the question, 'How is it that at certain moments and in certain orders of knowledge, there are sudden take-offs, these hastenings of evolution, these transformations which fail to correspond to the calm, continuist image that is normally accredited?'"[28] In thus interpreting Foucault's apparent rejection of the continuist understanding of Western history (i.e., the ontotheological tradition) as an affirmation of historical discontinuity, his commentators went far to crystallize as dogma a corollary tendency in his discourse: the separation of traditional philosophy (i.e., the truth discourse of classical humanism) and the post-Enlightenment empirical sciences. As a result of this disciplinary partitioning, they overlooked, among other things, the symptoms that point to the affinities between Foucault's genealogy of the disciplinary society and Heidegger's destruction of the ontotheological tradition.

To retrieve these critically resonant affinities, therefore, it will be necessary to extricate *Surveiller et punir* from the interpretive matrix in which it has hitherto been embedded and to reconstellate it into the Heideggerian context, focusing especially on what has necessarily been overlooked by commentary grounded on the assumption that modernity begins with an epistemic break occurring in the eighteenth century. I am referring to those marginal but insistently recurrent occasions where Foucault's text refers to a history of the figuration of being (the "site" of knowledge production) as a conquerable territory, specifically, as a centered circle presided over by the panoptic gaze (and the will to power over difference inscribed in these metaphorics), that long precedes its consummation and overdetermination in the Enlightenment and after. These occasions suggest the affiliative relationship between Heidegger's and Foucault's discourses; they also implicate the "Two Cultures" in the establishment, legitimation, and reproduction of the disciplinary society and its global allotrope, the global empire.[29] Foucault is remarkably persuasive in suggesting that the supervisory schema emerging as something resembling an epistemic break in the Enlightenment, if not constituting one, has determined and continues increasingly to invest every facet of life in the modern West, from the everyday lives of ordinary men and women (what Heidegger calls *das Man*), through pedagogy and cultural and material production, to the history-making agendas of those who administer civil and political societies. By thinking Foucault's historically specific discourse within the larger framework of Heidegger's interrogation of philosophy (the ontotheological tradition at large), however, I am suggesting that this practically polyvalent schema long precedes the historical conjuncture in which Foucault apparently locates it. It is, as the affiliation of Foucault's and Heidegger's "Nietzschean" rhetoric suggests, a latent possibility of the suprahistorical metaphysical mode of inquiry: of the circle that has its center—the *ratio*—elsewhere, of the binary Light/darkness opposition inaugurated by post-Socratic Greek philosophy (Plato, for example, in the "Allegory of the Cave") and decisively codified by the official intellectuals of republican and imperial Rome. By attending to what Heidegger left unsaid, I am also suggesting that this disciplinary supervisory schema came to be theorized and practiced, however experimentally or underdeveloped in execution, considerably earlier than the Enlightenment.

This schema can be seen to operate in the utopian discourses of the Renaissance, in Tommaso Campanella's *City of the Sun* (1623), for example.[30] The circular and radial geometry of this ideal humanist—Platonic/Roman/ Christian—city was theoretically intended not simply to re-present in visual microcosmic form the self-identical beauty, the harmony, the integration, and the permanence of a heliocentric macrocosm supervised by a transcendental deity or Being but also to produce a private and collective form of life that reflected this ideal: an *urbis* mirroring the *orbis*. The supervisory/circular schema, however, was not restricted to the utopian discourses of Renaissance "poetic" humanists. The rediscovery and mediation of Vitruvius's *Ten Books of Architecture* (a Roman text contemporary with and ideologically harnessed to Augustus Caesar's imperial project) in the fifteenth century inaugurated an architectural and city-planning tradition in Europe that put the aesthetic and political imperatives of the circle into practice. Taking as its point of departure an ideological principle in Vitruvius's first book—namely, that Rome was the metropolitan center of the *orbis terrarum*—this tradition posited a radially organized circularity as the ideal design not only for defense but for the corporeal and spiritual health of its citizens.[31] This architectural initiative led inevitably, however unevenly, from the circular city modeled on the Christian/ humanist figure of beauty, order, perfection (Filarete [1400–1469], Giocondo [ca. 1435–1515], Cerceau the Elder [1500–1584], Daniel Speckle [1536–89], etc.) through the circular fortress cities of the seventeenth and eighteenth centuries (Sardi, Errard de Bar-le-Duc [1554–1610], and above all, Vauban [1633–1707]) to the overdetermined manufactory (Claude-Nicholas Ledoux's Arc-et-Senans [1775–79]) and city (Chaux). These last, according to Foucault, are the immediate predecessors of Jeremy Bentham's Panopticon.[32]

This synecdochic architectural history thematizes a process in which the humanist trope of beauty par excellence gradually and inexorably, however unevenly, manifested the practical potential for political domination latent in it—a process paralleling at the site of architectural design that which occurs at the sites of philosophy, education, and culture. It thus suggests a significant modification of the received understanding of Foucault's genealogy of the disciplinary society, which, according to his emphasis, was given its enabling impetus by the "sudden take-offs" of the empirical sciences (most notably, "biology, political economy, psychiatry, medicine, etc.") and the technological apparatuses developed in the Enlightenment. There is, I suggest, an affiliative relationship, however occluded by the rapid historical accretion of and attention to detail in the eighteenth century, between the panoptic polis of the post-Enlightenment and the circular cities of the Renaissance humanists. The latter, moreover, were secular cities that drew their inspiration not only from Vitruvius's text on architecture but also from the medieval theo-logians (St. Augustine, *The City of God*) and from the onto-logians of late classical antiquity (Plato, *The Laws*), whose texts provide the focus for Heidegger's interrogation of the metaphysical circle. The microphysical technologies of power that, according to Foucault, were enabled by the panoptic schema's development into the classificatory table of the Enlightenment are more "scientific," more "objective," more detailed and complex, more ordinary, more pervasive, more economical, more productive, and above all, *less visible* than the obviously arbitrary and crude mathematical techniques of supervision and discipline enabled, for example, by the poetic humanist Campanella's circular/cosmic City of the Sun. Moreover, the disciplinary effects of power—the uniform life of docile and useful bodies—produced by the spatial geometry of a technologized panopticism are far more differentiated and muted than is the monochromatic uniformity of social life envisaged by the geometry of Campanella's Platonic/Christian heliocentrism. Nonetheless, both are enabled by re-presentation: an interpretation of the knowledge of being that territorializes its differential flow. Both, more specifically, are inscribed in a fundamental way by the polyvalent diagram of the centered circle and, as the passages on genetics in *City of the Sun* make clear, by the supervisory procedures and disciplinary end that this perennially ideal trope is intended to produce.[33]

This retrieval of the history of the disciplinary uses to which the figure of the circle was put in architecture and urban planning, whose origins Foucault's emphasis places far more recently, in Claude-Nicholas Ledoux's construction of the salt plant at Arc-et-Senans, near Besançon, has therefore important consequences for the question of the relationship between Heidegger's and Foucault's—and, as I will argue in the next chapter, Said's—thought. On the one hand, it enables us to see that Heidegger's overdetermination of the ontological site of the continuum of being precludes an adequate (worldly) perception of the possibility of a *sociopolitical* critique of the modern technological/imperial city. On the other, it allows us to see that Foucault's overdetermination of sociopolitical power precludes an adequate perception of the possibility of an *ontological* critique of the disciplinary/imperial society: the degree to which the model of the circle as beauty (perfection and civilization)/power has been already inscribed in the discursive practices of the "disinterested" humanitarian reformers (and the Old World proponents of planting the New World wilderness). These practices, of course, are the classificatory discourses of the Enlightenment (Linnaeus, Buffon, Cuvier, Sauvage, etc.), which culminate in Jeremy Bentham's *Panopticon; or Inspection House* (and analogously in the newly invented Eurocentric map of the world enabled by Gerardus Mercator's geometric projections).

To locate the emergence of the supervisory schema in the Enlightenment as such, as Foucault tends to do, is to suggest that the repressive ideology informing its ostensibly benign purposes coincides with the emergence of instrumental reason, empirical science, the classificatory table, modern cartography, applied technology, the bourgeois class, and capitalism. It is, as the so-called Two Cultures debate in the 1960s bears witness, a context from which liberal humanists can all too easily disengage their poetic anthropology from complicity in the production of the disciplinary society and the colonial empire. This distinction collapses, however, when it is seen that the fulfilled supervisory schema can be traced back through the idealized circular cities of the Renaissance to the generalized polyvalent image of beauty/perfection privileged by Augustine, and before that by Vitruvius and Plato, and that, as I have suggested in discussing Heidegger's "Letter on Humanism" and *Parmenides,* was harnessed politically in the form of the opposition between center and periphery, metropolis and provinces, *homo romanus* and *homo barbarus,* to the Roman pursuit of the *imperium sine fine:* the global empire. In other words, to recognize with Heidegger the always reconstituted "continuity" of this schema is not simply to realize the profound degree to which the relationship between the spatial perception of temporal difference and sociopolitical power is inscribed in the Occidental consciousness at large. It is also to suggest the continuing complicity of the two cultures: modern humanism—its classical mode of disinterested inquiry, the philosophical and literary texts it privileges, its institutions of knowledge production, and its cultural apparatuses—with the instrumental mode of putatively objective inquiry and its disciplinary/imperial technology that Foucault (along with other sociopolitical thinkers, such as Althusser, Adorno, and Said) overdetermines in his critique of modernity.

According to Foucault's emphasis, then, the relationship between the spatializing eye—"the disciplinary gaze" (*DP*, 170)[34]—and power, supervision and discipline, assumes overt theoretical articulation and practical implementation during the Enlightenment, or *Aufklärung*. This theoretical and practical reality became increasingly prominent thereafter: when the "universal" (Occidental) possibilities of humanistic (i.e., disinterested and liberal) cultural practices began to become manifest.[35] The reformers of the spectacularly brutal aristocratic punitive machinery were not essentially committed to humanitarian principles. Their real intention was to formulate and elaborate a more efficient penal system, one that overcame the economic limitations and political vulnerability of penal practices in the ancien régime:

> The true objective of the reform movement, even in its most general formulations, was not so much to establish a new "right" to punish based on more equitable principles, as to set up a new "economy" of power to punish, to assure its better distribution, so that it should be neither too concentrated at certain privileged points, nor too divided between opposing authorities; so that it should be distributed in homogeneous circuits capable of operating everywhere, in a continuous way, down to the finest grain of the social body. The reform of criminal law must be read as a strategy for the rearrangement of the power to punish, according to modalities that render it more regular, more effective, more constant and more detailed in its effects; in short, which increase its effects while diminishing its economic cost . . . and its political cost. (*DP*, 80–81)

Ultimately, then, the early bourgeois reformers of the Enlightenment were not searching for a penal system that reformed the arbitrary brutality of punishment in the ancien régime by acknowledging the otherness of the antisocial "Others." Rather, they sought a system that would diminish the economic wastefulness of the indiscriminate irregularities and, equally important, the political visibility of the earlier, arbitrary (overt) use of power, a biopolitical system that would internalize, distribute, and saturate power in and throughout the body politic both to increase productivity of "knowledge" (cultural capital) and capital goods and to decrease the threat of revolt to which an identifiable power—a visible sovereign center—is necessarily exposed. They were, in short, seeking a *generalized and generalizable system*— a microcosm, a table, a map, as it were—capable of annulling the force of the alienated "Other" and producing the peace of docile and useful bodies, namely, what Heidegger, in invoking the dynamics of enframement, refers to as "disposable reserve." As Foucault puts the fully developed agenda of the post-Enlightenment:

> The historical moment of the disciplines was a moment when an art of the human body was born, which was directed not only at the growth of its skills, nor at the intensification of its subjection, but at the formation of a relation that in the mechanism itself makes it more obedient as it becomes more useful, and conversely. . . . This discipline produces subjected and practiced bodies, "docile" bodies. Discipline increases the forces of the body (in economic terms of utility) and diminishes these same forces (in political terms of obedience). In short, it dissociates power from the body; on the one hand, it turns it into an "aptitude," a "capacity," which it seeks to increase; on the other hand, it reverses the course of the energy, the power that might result from it, and turns it into a relation of strict subjection. If economic exploitation separates the force and the products of labor, let us say that disciplinary coercion established in the body the constricting link between an increased aptitude and an increased domination. (*DP,* 138)

In their search for such a "new 'economy' of the power to punish," the reformers were inevitably guided by the photological semiotic network developed and privileged by the Enlightenment. The *épistémè*'s overdetermined valorization of the eye and its light and the discriminating technology of optics to which it gave rise ("the telescope, the lens and the light beam, which were an integral part of the new physics and cosmology" [*DP,* 170]) made these reformers increasingly aware of the relationship between enlightenment—making visible, particular, knowable, and measurable the obscure, fluid, amorphous, and always wasteful and threatening "Other"—and power. They thus sought a sophisticated design/apparatus whose economy could organize and apply visible space so as to give them optimal disciplinary supervision of and productivity from the individualized multiplicity enclosed within this space's well-lighted and pacified parameters.

There is no doubt, as Foucault remarks, that the "obscure art of light and visibility was preparing a new knowledge of man" that was to culminate in the disciplinary society (*DP,* 170–71).[36] Nonetheless, the historically specific density of Foucault's genealogy—especially its emphasis on the new science of optics and its technology—should not obscure the legacy these secular humanist reformers inherited from the ontotheological tradition, above all, that variation of optics inscribed in the theology of Calvinist Protestantism. It is no coincidence that the "reformatories"—from the Rasphuis of Amsterdam

(1596) through the penitentiary at Gloucester (England) to the Walnut Street
Prison (in Philadelphia, 1790), all of which provided architectural models for
the disciplinary prison (as well as the analogous insane asylum and medical
clinic) that culminated in Bentham's Panopticon—were largely Protestant in
origin (the Walnut Street Prison instituted "under the direct influence of the
Quakers") (*DP*, 124). Despite Foucault's minimization of significant reference,
it is quite clear that, however overdetermined, the Enlightenment's war of reason (the *ratio*) against "wastefulness" (and deviance, errancy, or irregularity)
in behalf of sociopolitical and economic economy (duty and utility) coincides
with the Calvinist/Protestant work ethic, which according to Max Weber gave
rise, especially in America, to the "spirit of Capitalism." This was the ethic
rationalized and enabled by the circular doctrine of predestination—that is, by
the austere pro*vide*ntial history that, as the etymology suggests, was the project of the absolutely hidden, inscrutable, and supervisory eye of the Calvinist
God. In Weber's telling words, it was the "transcendental being," "beyond the
reach of human understanding," who by his "quite incomprehensible decrees
has decided the fate of every individual and regulated the tiniest details of
the cosmos from eternity."[37] Foucault, in fact, alludes to this resonant continuity between the eye of the Calvinist theologos, which, in accounting for
even the fall of a sparrow, makes *every singular thing and event accountable,*
and the later anthropologos, which, in the accommodation and surveillance
of detail (difference) via the invention of the table and the map, makes the
detail serve the hegemonic purposes of the dominant culture (identity). The
Enlightenment did not inaugurate the "utilitarian rationalization of detail in
moral accountability and political control."

> Rather it accelerated it, changed its scale, gave it precise instruments, and per-
> haps found some echoes for it in the calculation of the infinitely small or in
> the description of the most detailed characteristics of natural beings. In any
> case, "detail" had long been a category of theology and asceticism: every detail
> is important since in the sight of God no immensity is greater than a detail, all
> minutiae of Christian education, of scholastic or military pedagogy, all forms
> of "training" found their place easily enough. For the disciplined man, as for
> the true believer, no detail is unimportant, but not so much for the meaning
> that it conceals within it as for the hold it provides for the power that wished
> to seize it. (*DP*, 140)[38]

What lay more immediately at hand as architectural/methodological models for these "observatories" were, significantly, the insane asylum, the medical
clinic, the workshop, the elementary classroom, and above all, the military
camp. In these spaces, as in the medieval plague town (*DP*, 147), time was

territorialized, enclosed, partitioned, serialized, functionalized, and thus immobilized or frozen in space. It was, that is, arranged to achieve optimal supervision under "the scrupulously 'classificatory' eye of the master" (*DP,* 17)[39] of a prolific and proliferating differential temporal world assumed to be naturally deviant—or on another level, "prodigal" or "fallen" and "dispersed." It was a spatializing economy, in short, designed to eliminate confusion and waste by rechanneling the irregular force of living bodies from the vantage point of a preestablished judgmental Norm: a regularizing Logos or center elsewhere, as it were.[40] In the perfect military camp (the model was, not accidentally, that of the Roman imperial legion)

> power would be exercised solely through exact observation; each gaze would form a part of the overall functioning of power. . . . the geometry of paths, the number and distribution of tents, the orientation of their entrance, the disposition of files and ranks were exactly defined; the network of gazes that supervised one another was laid down. . . . The camp is the *diagram of a power* that acts by means of *general visibility.* For a long time this model of the camp *or at least its underlying principle* was found in urban development in the construction of working-class housing estates, hospitals, asylums, prisons, schools: the spatial "nesting" of hierarchical surveillance. (*DP,* 171–72; emphasis added)

Thus, a whole new spatial problematic emerges: that of an architecture that would ensure the pacifying ends of discipline by rendering those errant or nomadic "deviants" on whom power acted visible to the supervisory gaze. It was to be "an architecture . . . no longer built simply to be seen (as with the ostentation of palaces), or to observe the external space (cf., the geometry of fortresses)."[41] Its spatial economy was designed, rather, "to permit an internal, articulated, and detailed control—to render visible those who are inside it." More generally, it was "an architecture that would operate to transform individuals: to act on those it shelters, to provide a hold on their conduct, to carry the effects of power right to them, to make it possible to know them, to alter them. Stones can make people docile and knowable" (*DP,* 172).

"The [Roman] camp is a *diagram* of power": I provisionally emphasize the spatial abstraction, from which Foucault's rhetorical focus on the effects of the military camp's structure might deflect attention. Reconstellated into the context of Heidegger's thematization of the will to power that informs the perennially privileged but naturalized metaphors of vision and the centered circle, Foucault's account of the origin of such modern disciplinary architectural experiments undergoes a telling metamorphosis. It discloses, in fact, how deeply the affiliation between spatial or (in Foucault's Nietzschean terms) "suprahistorical" perception—perception *meta ta physika*—and power, Being and time, Center and periphery, was inscribed as an "underlying principle" of Western thinking by the time of the Enlightenment. In Great Britain, it should be remarked, this historical conjuncture was characterized by the politically troubling dislocation and unhoming of the traditional peasantry as their commons were privatized by the enclosure movement, the geopolitical equivalent of the classificatory table. It was thus inevitable, however ironic, that in seeking such a functional economy of space—a productive economy that would serve as agency of both surveillance and correction (reformation and pacification) according to the anthropological Norm—the efforts made by this demographically volatile age's emergent bourgeois culture would culminate at the end of the century in an architectural model of the ideal prison that, vis-à-vis the differences temporality disseminates, epitomized *in practice* the operation and effects of the territorializing gaze of logocentric thinking. That gaze is precisely the distancing/reifying panoramic one that, according to Heidegger's story, informs the ontotheological philosophical tradition at large: its ontology (metaphysics), its epistemology (truth as *adaequatio intellectus et rei*), its pedagogy (*eruditio et institutio in bonas artes*), its affiliated symbolic figurations (the centered circle and the commanding gaze), and not least, its end: the imperial *pax*. It was inevitable, in other words, that the Enlightenment, as its very name suggests, should "discover" an architectural model for reforming and normalizing sociopolitical deviants in which military surveillance becomes sur-veillance, supervision, super-vision.

Nor is it coincidental that this particular structural model should have been inferred from the Western philosophical tradition by a bourgeois humanist of the English Enlightenment who, in the context of the social dislocations produced by the enclosure movement's deterritorializing/reterritorializing effects on the peasantry,[42] contributed significantly not only to the advance of technology, industrialization, and capitalism but also to the detemporalizing and reifying cultural momentum that culminated in what Heidegger tellingly calls the "age of the world picture" and the consequent reduction of being in all its manifestations to "disposable reserve." It was inevitable, to put it alternatively, that this specific architectural trope should have been developed by a thinker who brought the tradition beginning with the Romans' institutionalization of the gaze (*veritas:* the adequation of mind and thing), the re-collective memory, and by extension, the binary spatial logic of the hierarchized polis to its fulfillment—and, according to Heidegger, its end. This figure, of course, was the utilitarian philosopher Jeremy Bentham, whose Panopticon, or "Inspection House," laid the foundations for the production of the disciplinary (and colonialist) society. This centered/circular architectural structure drew the territorializing/disciplinary machinery of knowledge production into absolute symmetry with the political super-vision that re-formed and "normalized" errancy, that is, with the policing enabled by the binary metaphorics that privileged light over darkness and space over time. It was the dedifferentiating differentiating structure that brought into affiliation the panoptic gaze and the microcosmic figure of the centered circle—now, with the rise of empirical science, differentiated into the "taxonomic table"—with the "'evolutive' time of genesis," the "examination," and so on and the partitioned spatial economy of the presiding public institutions articulated during the eighteenth century (the hospital, the insane asylum, the workhouse, the military camp, the classroom, the factory, and so on).

Since Foucault's account of the Panopticon has become well known by this time, there is no need to rehearse its description here. It will suffice to say that his analysis of its circular structural economy is intended to foreground Bentham's "guiding principle": "that power should be visible and unverifiable" (*DP*, 201). "The Panopticon," Foucault writes, "is a machine for dissociating the seeing/being seen dyad: in the peripheric ring, one is totally seen, without ever seeing; in the central tower, one sees everything without ever being seen" (*DP*, 201–2). As its primary effect, it would induce in the errant inmates

> a state of conscious and permanent visibility that assures the automatic functioning of power. So to arrange things that the surveillance is permanent in its effects, even if it is discontinuous in its action; that the perfection of power should tend to render its actual exercise unnecessary; that this architectural apparatus should be a machine for creating and sustaining a power relation *independent of the person who exercises it;* in short, that the inmates should be caught up in a power situation of which they are themselves the bearers. (*DP*, 201; emphasis added)

In other words, the totalizing geometric structure of Bentham's Panopticon was designed to transform or re-collect the threatening force of any amorphous and errant constituency of the nation into unitary conformity and predictable regularity. Its end was to produce a collective of discrete and thus knowable individuals who would eventually take their proper place in the identical and self-present national whole—would, that is, become subjected (or colonized) subjects. Like Heidegger's ventriloquized *das Man* in *Being and Time*—the collective "they" whose speech and acts are determined by "the way things are publicly interpreted"—Bentham's deviants would themselves become the ventriloquized transmitters of the normative power that renders them docile and useful instruments of the dominant cultural and sociopolitical orders. Behind this particular post-Enlightenment disciplinary practice, it should now be evident (even though Foucault does not overtly refer to them), lies what Heidegger's destruction of the ontotheological tradition discloses to be the enabling and perennial principle and figurative corollaries of Western metaphysical thinking at large: (1) the ontological principle that identity is the condition for the possibility of difference and not the other way around; (2) the transcendental/imperial Eye (and its light), which this founding principle must necessarily privilege; and (3) the metaphorics of the centered circle, which it precipitates to do its discreetly colonizing and pacifying work.

In thus reconstellating Foucault's *Surveiller et punir* into the matrix of Heidegger's interrogation of the ontotheological tradition, then, I am suggesting that Bentham's Panopticon does not constitute a historical rupture. Rather, it both brings to momentary fulfillment in a particular practice the coercive potential always already latent in the "oversight" of the metaphysical thinking that constitutes the foundation of the identity of Europe and, through this identifiable excess, makes explicit (visible) the coercive disciplinary genealogy of the supposedly disinterested or objective discursive practices of modern liberal democratic (humanist) societies.

A reading of Foucault's text that is indifferent to the *Seinsfrage* might raise the objection that Bentham's Panopticon represents a historically specific institution: the reformatory prison that emerges to prominence at the beginning of the nineteenth century. But such an interpretation is clearly what Foucault's genealogy fundamentally resists. This is suggested by several previously quoted passages from *Surveiller et punir* that disclose (often inadvertently) the degree to which the generalized disciplinary model—the figure of the centered circle—had been inscribed, long before Bentham's historical occasion, in the knowledge-producing, social, and political institutions of the West. As I have provisionally remarked, it is further suggested by Foucault's insistent, however muted, reference to the principle underlying the concrete architectural instance; the Roman military camp, recall, is a "diagram of a power that acts by means of general visibility." But this essential affiliation between Bentham's Panopticon and the metaphysical tradition at large is most decisively thematized in Foucault's analysis of the Panopticon itself. There, he shows that Bentham himself conceived of his historically specific inspection house as a *generalized* structural model that was separable from any concrete and particular practice:

> [The Panopticon] is the *diagram of a mechanism of power reduced to its ideal form; its functioning, abstracted from any obstacle, resistance or friction, must be represented in a pure architectural and optical system*: it is in fact a *figure* of political technology that may and must be *detached* from any specific use.

It is polyvalent in its application; it serves to reform prisoners, but also to treat patients, to instruct school children, to confine the insane, to supervise workers, to put beggars and idlers to work. . . . Whenever one is dealing with a multiplicity of individuals on whom a task or a particular form of behaviour must be imposed, the *panoptic schema* may be used. It is—necessary modifications apart—applicable "to all establishments whatsoever, in which, within a space not too large to be covered or commanded by buildings, a number of persons are meant to be kept under inspection." (*DP*, 205–6; emphasis added)[43]

Bentham's Panopticon, in other words, is not the historically specific effect of an epistemic rupture that bears witness to the sudden emergence of the positivist scientific worldview as such. It represents, rather, an overdetermined and highly developed (i.e., modern) instance of the multiple practical uses to which the traditional polyvalent panoptic diagram enabled by metaphysics—and mediated by the imperial Roman prototype's inscription into the culture of the revolutionary age[44]—was put in the post-Enlightenment, when the transcendental eye/center was compelled to descend to the secular world in the form of the empirical or objective gaze of Man, when, that is, the earlier generalized and empty space it projected was transformed into the gridded and individuated table. The prominence that Foucault gives to the panoptic penal institution should not obscure the fact that this ancient diagram, now differentiated to accommodate the smallest detail in the world of modernity, was simultaneously although unevenly being applied to other institutional discourses and practices as diverse as medicine, psychiatry, economics, hermeneutics, education, literature, literary criticism, and other modes of cultural production. Not least, though Foucault does not refer to it overtly in *Discipline and Punish,* it was being applied to the discourse and practice of cartography (Mercator's projection), so crucial to the purposes of colonizing the New World and the old worlds, such as the Arab countries, India, and China, whose civilizations had "degenerated." I invoke this globalization of Foucault's genealogy of the disciplinary society not simply to recall Heidegger's location of the origins of Europe in ancient Rome and his identification of the Roman metropolis's (metaphysical territorializing) mind with modern Western imperialism but also to anticipate my reading of Edward Said's *Orientalism* in the next chapter: his brilliant extension of Foucault's analysis of the "polyvalent" Panopticon—"the diagram of a mechanism of power reduced to its ideal form," which gave birth to the modern Western, "democratic" nation-state—to include the European nation-states' "orientalist/imperialist" project.[45]

In the end, given the compelling seductiveness of its totalizing binarist logical economy, this polyvalent diagram would utterly obscure all the material signs of its genealogy and power—the "inventory of its traces," in Gramsci's (and Said's) phrase—to become the naturalized, all-encompassing, and comprehensive "truth of being," the truth of the free subject of liberal democracy that concealed the hegemonic panopticism of the (secular) disciplinary society: "The movement from a schema of exceptional discipline [the Panopticon] to one of generalized surveillance [panopticism] rests in a historical transformation." This was "the gradual extension of the mechanisms of discipline throughout the seventeenth and eighteenth centuries, their spread throughout the whole social body." The result of this totalizing extension and internalization of the panoptic gaze was not only "the formation of what might be called in general the disciplinary society" (*DP*, 209) but also, as Heidegger's theoretical discourse maintains and, as I will show, Said's postcolonial discourse powerfully attests, the creation of the imperial society.

Reconstellated into the Heideggerian matrix, the usual "political" reading of Foucault's genealogical analysis of the modern disciplinary society undergoes a sea change. The post-Enlightenment historical process that, according to Foucault, bears witness to the internalization of the panoptic technological mechanism and the centered circle in the "soul" of the body politic suddenly appears remarkably like Heidegger's genealogy of modern Western thought, the logical economy of which begins with the Roman reduction of an originative Greek truth to a derivative/calculative truth—Roman expertise, as it were—and comes to its end in the planetary triumph of technological thought and practice: the age of the world picture. This, it will be recalled, is the age in which anthropo-logical re-presentation in its instrumentalist modality comes to traverse the entire lateral continuum of being, from the representation of being itself, through language and cultural production, to national and international political formations. In the end, Foucault's primary concern is less the panoptic prison, the hospital, the asylum, the classroom, and the factory as such than it is the discreetly repressive polyvalent panoptic *schema* that, masquerading as the objective pursuit of knowledge, informs these practical institutions and that has become totalized in the present age as the panopticism of the disciplinary/imperial society. That is, it is the totalized *regime* of truth, the end of whose logical economy is the reduction—or better, the colonization—of the force of human being, the "actual intensities . . . of life,"[46] to the "useful and docile body." It is this insight into the dominion of the *ratio*, largely activated by the ubiquity during the French Enlightenment of what Foucault calls "the Roman reference" (*DP*, 169), this recognition of the indissoluble relation between Western thought and practice (truth and power), that affiliates Foucault's genealogy of the disciplinary society with Heidegger's genealogy of the age of the world picture. In speaking of this latter genealogy I mean specifically the truth of enframement (*Ge-stell*) that has as its inevitable end the reduction of the singular force of being in its totality, including human being, to a regulated mindlessness, to "disposable reserve." It will not be an exaggeration, especially if we are attuned to the operations of Enlightenment thinking in both the domestic and the international spheres, to say that the emergent bourgeois reformers ultimately sought to bring the *pax* of this world picture into being, but in such a way as to conceal the fact that this peace, like the Pax Romana (or the Pax Britannica, or the Pax Americana), has as its essential purpose the colonization, administration, and exploitation of the "Other" all across the continuum of being, from thinking itself to the practices of nationhood and colonialism.

In short, then, the reconstellation of Foucault's thought into the context of Heidegger's unexpectedly reveals that Foucault's intent is to disclose not just the painful effects of a repressive political power but also something that is more focal in Heidegger's discourse, namely, the apparently irreversible global momentum, undertaken in the name of a triumphant objective reason and its "freedom," toward the colonization of the human mind. Both thinkers, that is, disclose modern reason's reduction to a calculative instrument that, in territorializing being—in seeing and occupying being in advance (meta-physically)—for the purpose of comprehending and utilizing "it," must eventually become utterly indifferent to the differential singularity of life that is not seeable and speakable. At the risk of censure in the anti-Heideggerian climate of the present, post-Farias intellectual occasion, I will at this point recall Hannah Arendt's profound but still to be understood invocation of the synecdochic modern mind of Adolf Eichmann—for whom human beings (Jews) and trucks were identical entities—to explain why she undertook her last great labor in behalf of the making of a viable polis. In *The Life of the Mind,* her unfinished meditation on the history of Western thought, she offers both a disclosure of the hardening of reason into a pervasive instrumentalism and a powerful argument for rethinking this thoughtless thinking that is its deadly legacy (a legacy of which Edward Said is profoundly aware, as his unrelenting emphasis on the inhumanity of the discourse of the modern policy expert testifies):

> The immediate impulse [behind "my preoccupation with mental activities"] came from my attending the Eichmann trial in Jerusalem. In my report of it I spoke of "the banality of evil." Behind that phrase, I held no thesis or doctrine, although I was dimly aware of the fact that it went counter to our tradition of thought . . . about the phenomenon of evil. Evil, we have learned, is something demonic. . . . However, what I was confronted with was utterly different and

still undeniably factual. . . . The deeds were monstrous, but the doer . . . was quite ordinary, commonplace, and neither demonic nor monstrous. There was no sign in him of firm ideological convictions or of specific evil motives, and the only characteristic one could detect in his past behavior as well as in his behavior during the trial and throughout the pre-trial police examination was something entirely negative: it was not stupidity but *thoughtlessness.*[47]

This massive Western momentum toward the banalization of thinking—a thinking that, according to Heidegger and Foucault, reduces being to disposable reserve or docile and useful body in behalf of a productive peace—is that to which both Foucault's genealogy of the modern panoptic disciplinary society and Heidegger's destruction of the modern age of the world picture point. If so, then it is also their awareness of the imminent global triumph of this thoughtless Western thinking, which results in the routinization of practical violence, that instigates their recognition of the urgency of rethinking this thinking and its legacy of violence. More specifically, it is their awareness of the pending total colonization and pacification of the mind by this calculative and leveling instrumentalism that provides the directive of this project: the radical difference/contradiction precipitated by the totalization, that is, the fulfillment—the coming to its end—in humanist modernity of the visualist/territorializing logical economy of the West's metaphysical/panoptic thought. It is a directive to which Edward Said, as I will show, was acutely attuned.

Certainly Heidegger inaugurated this "antihumanist" project (however adequately he executed it) in "What Is Metaphysics?" when, compelled by his meditation in *Being and Time* on the dictatorship of "the way things are publicly interpreted" (i.e., the ungraspable and unsayable "essence" of time disclosed by philosophy's coming to its end), the self-evidence and certainty of metaphysics had become an urgent question. To put it more specifically, Heidegger inaugurated this project when, urged by the spectacle of the banality of an instrumentalist Pax Metaphysica—the utter reduction of the living force, the singularity, of being to a "stock pile"[48]—he asked the question of "the nothing" (*das Nichts*), which, he realized, belongs to and haunts modern science's triumphant territorializing logic of enframing. This is the nothing, reflected symptomatically in the spectral "silences" of Hölderlin, Nietzsche, and Trakl, for example, that this triumphalist science can represent only as "an outrage and a phantasm" and, therefore, "wants to know nothing about":

> What is remarkable is that, precisely in the way scientific man secures to himself what is most properly his, *he speaks of something different.* What should be examined [according to the scientific problematic] are beings only, and

besides that—nothing; beings alone, and further—nothing; solely beings, and beyond that nothing.

What about this nothing? Is it an accident that we talk this way so automatically?[49]

It is also the nothing that, thought positively, becomes the directive of the *Abgeschiedene* in the age of the world picture. The *Abgeschiedene* is the estranged poet or thinker "who is apart,"[50] who, cast as "mad" according to the imperatives of the inexorable binary logic of instrumental reason and exiled[51] from his or her intellectual homeland by the triumph of its banal peace, wanders ghostlike in the interregnum between the "the No-more of the gods that have fled and the Not-yet of the god that is to come."[52] Like the phantasmic nothing itself, the *Abgeschiedene* is not only the errant specter that haunts the plenary peace of metaphysics by bearing witness to its deadly banality—as "a time of dearth"—and *by refusing to be answerable to* its truth[53] but also the symptom of a lack in the imperial discourse of the West that, in its refusal to be accommodated, demands to be thought anew.

Is it an exaggeration to claim that Foucault, in his own, far more practico-historical way, inaugurated this same project against the hardened (anthropological) "discourse of Man" at the disclosive close of *Madness and Civilization*, his carnivalesque genealogy of the "triumph" of reason in modernity? He invokes there the symptomatic errant voices of the "madmen," including Hölderlin, Nerval, Nietzsche, and Artaud, whose "irreducible" "unreason," in refusing to be answerable to the imperial (normative) narrative logic of instrumental reason, haunts the deadly peace of the synecdochic disciplinary asylum presided over by the total gaze (*le regard total*) of a triumphant "liberatory" positivist psychiatry of the *ratio*.[54] Is it insignificant that two of these "madmen"—Hölderlin and Nietzsche—figure in an essential way in Heidegger's effort to think the spectral nonbeing of modernity's imperialist representation of being? "Since the end of the eighteenth century, the life of unreason no longer manifests itself except in the lightning-flash of works such as those of Hölderlin, of Nerval, of Nietzsche, or of Artaud—forever irreducible to those alienations that can be cured, resisting by their own strength that gigantic moral imprisonment which we are in the habit of calling, doubtless by antiphrasis, the liberation of the insane by Pinel and Tuke."[55]

This, it should be emphasized, is not to say that Foucault, any more than Heidegger, was positing madness against the "gigantic moral imprisonment" incumbent on the triumph of instrumental rationality in modernity. It is to say, rather, that he, like Heidegger vis-à-vis Hölderlin, Nietzsche, Trakl, and van Gogh, understood these "madmen" as *Abgeschiedene*—err-ant or nomadic and unaccommodatable specters that the fulfillment of panopticism's positive territorializing logic had precipitated as its symptomatic and delegitimizing contradictions. This is Heidegger's witness in his encounter with the "rift (*der Riss*) between world and earth" precipitated by the madman Vincent van Gogh's painting of a pair of peasant's shoes.[56] This, too, is the witness of Foucault in his encounter with the accusatory silence of the works of Hölderlin, Nietzsche, Nerval, Artaud (and, not surprisingly, of van Gogh):

> This does not mean that madness is the only language common to the work of art and the modern world . . . ; but it means that, through madness, a work that seems to drown in the world, to reveal there its non-sense, and to transfigure itself with the features of pathology alone, actually engages within itself the world's time, masters it, and leads it; *by the madness which interrupts it, a work of art opens a void, a moment of silence, a question without answer, provokes a breach without reconciliation where the world is forced to question itself.* What is necessarily a *profanation* in the world of art returns to that point, and, in the time of that work swamped in madness, the world is made aware of its guilt.[57]

It is also to say that Foucault, like Heidegger before him, understood the unspeakable silence, or "profanation," of the "lightning-flash" of the work of these "madmen" as symptomatic of the creative potential for both thought and praxis inhering in the multiple allotropes of the nothing with which the plenary and banalizing discursive practices of "the world" produced by the Cogito (i.e., the disciplinary society) would have nothing to do.

In the light of this second, positive phase of Heidegger's and Foucault's destructuring projects, can we see a continuation of their respective onto-logical and sociopolitical projects in the increasing urgency of Edward Said's post-*Orientalism* focus on the migrant and the exilic intellectual deracinated from his or her homeland and rendered "stateless" by the fulfillment of im-perialism's totalizing logic? For Heidegger, the nothing that is an "outrage" to a triumphant modern science manifests itself when "philosophy comes to its end" in the age of the world picture. For Foucault, "madness" manifests itself when the logic of Enlightenment Man fulfills itself in a universal panopticism. In other words, the nothing of Western metaphysics and its practical corol-lary, the madman of the Western bourgeois nation-state, not only come into threatening visibility but demand to be thought positively when the related logical economies of the former self-destruct. So, I suggest, for Edward Said, the "Other"—"the nobodies" or "nonhuman"—of the Occident's "humanity" manifests itself when the logical economy of Western imperialism comes to its end. Said's extension of Heidegger's and Foucault's (or, rather, the Heideg-gerian Foucault's) thematization of the specter that haunts the West becomes prominent after *Orientalism,* after, that is, Said has persuasively shown the inordinate degree to which the discourse of Orientalism has come to saturate late modernity.

To amplify my suggestion concerning Said's momentous political extension of Heidegger's destruction and Foucault's genealogy will be the burden of chapter 4, my reading of *Culture and Imperialism.* Here, for the sake of orientation, I will simply call attention to this relationship by quoting and briefly commenting on the conclusion of that great book, in which Said, following the directives of Paul Virilio and Gilles Deleuze and Félix Guattari (poststructuralists, not incidentally), thematizes the paradoxical global legacy of Euro-American imperialism: the spectral presence of the vast, indeed numberless and diverse members of the human community who, previously denied human being, have been deracinated and rendered homeless (in the multiple senses of this now, in the age of globalization, resonant word) by the practical fulfillment of imperialism's relentlessly exclusionary or accommodational binary logic:

> Surely it is one of the unhappiest characteristics of the age to have produced more refugees, migrants, displaced persons, and exiles then ever before in history, most of them an accompaniment to and, ironically enough, *as afterthoughts of great post-colonial and imperial conflicts.* As the struggle for independence produced new states and new boundaries, it also produced homeless wanderers, nomads, and vagrants, unassimilated to the emerging structures of institutional powers, rejected by the established order for their intransigence and obdurate rebelliousness. And in so far as these people exist between the old and the new, between the old empire and the new state, their condition articulates the tensions, irresolutions, and contradictions in the overlapping territories shown on the cultural map of imperialism.
>
> There is a great difference, however, between the optimistic mobility, the intellectual *liveliness,* and "the logic of daring" described by the various theoreticians on whose work I have drawn, and the massive dislocations, waste, misery, and horrors endured in our century's migrations and mutilated lives. *Yet it is no exaggeration to say that liberation as an intellectual mission, born in the resistance and opposition to the confinements and ravages of imperialism, has now shifted from the settled, established, and domesticated dynamics of culture to its unhoused, decentered and exilic energies, energies whose incarnation today is the migrant, and whose consciousness is that of the intellectual and artist in exile, the political figure between domains, between forms, between homes, and between languages.* . . . And while it would be the rankest Panglossian dishonesty to say that the bravura performances of the intellectual exile and the miseries of the displaced person are the same, it is possible, I think, to regard the intellectual as first distilling then articulating the predicaments that disfigure modernity—

mass deportation, imprisonment, population transfer, collective dispossession, and immigration. (*CI*, 332; emphasis added)

As in the case of Heidegger's and Foucault's thematization of the nothing that belongs to being as understood by the West (one could also invoke Derrida's "*différance,*" Lacan's "lack," Lyotard's "*différend,*" de Man's "aporia," Deleuze and Guattari's "rhizome," and Bhabha's "minus in the one," among others) and the madness that belongs to bourgeois disciplinary society, Said's thematization of the unhomed migrant/exile is intended not simply to evoke pity or resistance (and certainly not, as the afterword of *Orientalism* makes emphatically clear, a nationalist will) but also to urge thinking these "damaged lives" positively: to instigate the rethinking of the human community (if not the human) as it was formulated under the aegis of the principle of identity.

What I point out provisionally in thus emphasizing these apparently different precipitates of Heidegger's, Foucault's, and Said's respective counter-mnemonic ontological, social, and global political projects is more than just the indissoluble affiliative relationship among the nothing, madness, and the nomadic life of the migrant disclosed by the post-modern—the coming to their ends of metaphysics, the bourgeois nation-state, and imperialism. I want to suggest in addition that these "Others," along with other phenomena of being that have been traditionally deemed to be devoid of being, have now assumed the status of specters who haunt the very essence and thus the hegemony of Western civilization, that is, who demand to be thought positively. This is especially the case in an intellectual environment that unaccountably has been blind to the theoretical and practical directives, vis-à-vis disciplinary knowledge production (biopower), of the corrosive dynamics of postmodernity, that is, the age of globalization.

Heidegger, Foucault, and the Repressive Hypothesis

Let me summarize Foucault's historically specific analysis of the transformation of power relations that took place between the period of the ancien régime and the post-Enlightenment, using the rhetoric Foucault introduces in *The History of Sexuality, Vol. I,* which follows immediately after *Discipline and Punish.* The bourgeois humanist "reformers" of the Enlightenment seized the opportunity afforded by the delegitimation of monarchical uses of power—the arbitrary, overt, visible employment of force by a sovereign agent that was economically wasteful and politically vulnerable (in the sense that its visibility—we might say with Arendt, its easy identifiability with the traditional concept of evil—made it resistible)—to elaborate in the name of justice a far more subtle system of coercion grounded in the repressive hypothesis. This "new" view of power relations, according to Foucault, represented power in essentially negational terms, as "prohibition, censorship and denial": "repression" pure and simple.[58] In so doing, the new sovereignty authorized and instigated, rather than restricted, the proliferation of the discourse of truth (the will to knowledge). Indeed, it rendered (the production of) truth (its pacifying light) the essential agency of deliverance from power's negative (evil) effects (its strife-riven darkness).[59] Reconstellated into the Heideggerian matrix, this post-Enlightenment version of power became the privileged means of bringing universal peace (the Pax Romana, as it were) to a volatile world, a world that the dominant culture represented as being, otherwise, in perpetual strife.

Foucault's point, of course, is that the "repressive hypothesis" on which the relation between truth and power in modernity rests is a seductive *deception*—a strategic construction of the dominant culture and sociopolitical order that is endowed with the tempting semblance of being naturally derived—and that this deception must be exposed. In representing power as purely negative, external, and essentially in opposition to truth, post-Enlightenment humanists also represented the discourse of truth (and justice) as essentially benign: disinterested and thus "liberal," "emancipatory," "ameliorative," and not least, "irenic." In fact, this bourgeois humanist truth discourse is, precisely in its ability to produce detailed knowledge (of the "Other"), complicit with power. It is a compelling ruse by the dominant bourgeois culture that, in Gramsci's phrase (amplified by Said in *Orientalism*), is intended to evoke "spontaneous consent" from those differential constituencies on which power is practiced: "We must cease once and for all to describe the effects of power in negative terms. . . . In fact, power produces; it produces reality; it produces domains of objects and rituals of truth. The individual and the knowledge that may be gained of him belong to this production" (*DP*, 194). And again: "the notion of repression is quite inadequate for capturing what is precisely the productive aspect of power. . . . If power were never anything but repressive, if it never did anything but say no, do you really think one would be brought to obey it?"[60]

Despite Foucault's overdetermination of the rhetoric of "rupture," "break," and "mutation," his analysis of the repressive hypothesis in fact suggests that the transition from the ancien régime to the disciplinary society of liberal capitalist democracy accomplished by the Enlightenment humanists was not a radical departure. Rather, to invoke Heidegger's tripartite division of the history of Western philosophy, the onto-theo-logical tradition, it entailed the substitution of one center for another.[61] In the age of monarchs (this is true of modern totalitarian regimes, too), the determining and repressive center elsewhere, or "eye of power" (the theologos that sanctioned the sovereign king's direct use of spectacular force to punish or discourage deviation—and to conquer, colonize, and exploit the "new worlds"), was visible, identifiable, and thus vulnerable to critique or insurrection (as the French Revolution bears witness). In the post-Enlightenment, however, the commanding/supervisory gaze (the anthropologos) of the bourgeois humanist reformers (and their colonialist counterparts) became increasingly *invisible* (internalized) as the objectifying and banalizing effects of its power spread throughout the capillary network of the social body. Put alternatively, the center of the ancien régime was not abandoned; it was *mediated.* In Edward Said's words, it became a "textual attitude" (*O*, 92–93). The immediate and visible center, that is, was rendered a center elsewhere that at the same time operated invisibly *in* the secular—ever-expanding circumferential—world, reducing being to territory, the mind to calculative instrument, and the body to useful and docile mechanism. This difference-in-continuity is, in fact, the enabling thesis of Foucault's genealogy of truth/power relations inscribed in the related site of modernity's discursive practices of sexuality: "At bottom, despite the differences in epochs and objectives, this representation of power has remained under the spell of monarchy. In political thought and analysis, we still have not cut off the head of the king."[62]

Revealing in this way the affiliated naturalized tropes (what Derrida calls the white metaphors) of the centered circle and the supervisory gaze, which according to Foucault inform the humanist "ruse of the repressive hypothesis" and its leveling peace, one may well recall Heidegger's neglected genealogy of truth/power relations as these have been increasingly elaborated in and by Western civilization. This genealogy includes, first, his disclosure of the origins of the modern humanist discourse of truth in the Romans' epochal reduction of the Greeks' originative thinking (*aletheia/pseudos*) to a derivative thinking (*veritas/falsum*) and the origins of the humanist *studia humanitatis* in the Romans' reduction of the Greeks' radically dialogic *paideia* (*polemos: Auseinandersetzung*) to *eruditio et institutio in bonas artes,* both of which modes of knowledge production, according to Heidegger, were undertaken to facilitate the Roman imperial project by lightening its effects. More important, it further includes the distinction Heidegger makes by theorizing how this Roman secularization of the transcendental center (i.e., the territorialization of the knowledge of being) relates to knowledge/power, namely, the distinction between the older, "immediate" Western imperialism, which applied force against the "Other" directly, and its developed, fulfilled, and proper form, a mediate/discursive or "neo"-imperialism, which accomplished the hegemonic end—the global *pax*—of empire through the ruse of the discourse of truth understood as *adaequatio intellectus et rei*. "The bringing-to-fall," the reader should recall,

> can be accomplished in a "direct" assault [*Ansturm*] and an overthrowing [*Nie-derwerfen*]. But the other can also be brought-to-fall by being outflanked and tripped from behind. . . . Considered from the outside, going behind the back is a complicated, circumstantial, and thus mediate "bringing-to-fall" as opposed to an immediate overthrowing. In this way, what is brought-to-fall becomes not thereby annihilated but in a certain manner redressed within the boundaries which are staked out by the dominators. This "staking out" [*Abstecken*] is called in Roman: *pango*, whence the word *pax*, peace. . . . In truth the bringing-to-fall in the sense of deception and outflanking is not the mediate and derived imperial *actio*, but the imperial *actio* proper. It is not in war, but in the *fallere* of deceptive outflanking [*hintergehenden Umgehens*] and its appropriation to the service of dominion that the proper and "great" trait of the imperial reveals itself. (*P,* 59 [41])

Furthermore, it should be recalled, this "mediate" *hintergehenden Um-gehens*—the ruse enabled by "naturalizing" or "secularizing" the transcendental imperial center and the invisible commanding gaze (the *Übersehen-können*) in the truth discourse of humanist modernity—is what, according to Heidegger, has facilitated both the "Europeanization of the planet"[63] in the technocratic age of the world picture and the establishment of the Pax Europa/Americana that ensues from the total transformation of the temporality of being (the differences that time disseminates) to a territorialized and "staked-out" spatial totality in which things and events have been reduced to expendable stockpile.

Despite Heidegger's generalization of its sociopolitical implications, this *hintergehenden Umgehens* clearly bears a striking resemblance to Foucault's analysis of the ruse of the repressive hypothesis, which was enabled not simply by the Enlightenment's rendering of the visible center as elsewhere or the sovereign king's panoptic gaze as invisible but also by its ontologically prior spatialization of being, that is, *by its reduction of knowledge to a material and gridded space* to be "conquered" and "settled." This is precisely the point Heidegger makes in the *Parmenides* when he implicates the Romans' epochal reduction of the Greek *pseudos* to *falsum* in behalf of their imperial/colonial project with their indissolubly related reduction of the Greek *gea* to *terra*: "For the Romans . . . the earth, *tellus, terra*, is dry, the land as distinct from the sea; this distinction differentiates that upon which construction, settlement, and installation are possible from those places where they are impossible. *Terra* becomes *territorium,* land of settlement as realm of command. In the Roman *terra* [which refers to both the literal earth and the knowledge of being] can be heard an imperial accent, completely foreign to the Greek *gea* and *ge*" (*P,* 88 [60]).

This point, too, especially if it is thought in terms of the pervasiveness of the "Roman reference" in his genealogy of the modern disciplinary society, is the one Foucault makes in an important but neglected interview conducted by the Marxist editors of the journal *Hérodote,* who wanted to apply his analysis of modern knowledge/power relations to the unduly neglected discourse of geography. To their suggestion that this discourse "grew up in the shadow of the military" and is thus informed by naturalized "spatial metaphors [that] are equally geographical and strategic"—"The *region* of the geographers is the military region (from *regere,* to command), a *province* is a conquered territory (from *vincere)*"—Foucault responds in a way that, as I will show, anticipates Edward Said's emphasis on the role "imaginative geography" played in the West's domination of the Orient:

> Once knowledge can be analyzed in terms of region, domain, implantation, displacement, transposition [i.e., notions pertaining to planting colonies], one is able to capture the process by which knowledge functions as a form of power and disseminates the effects of power. There is an administration of knowledge, a politics of knowledge, relations of power which pass via knowledge and which, if one tries to transcribe them, lead one to consider forms of domination designated by such notions of field, region and territory. *And the politico-strategic term is an indication of how the military and the administration actually come to inscribe themselves both on a material soil and within forms of discourse.*[64]

The end of the logical economy of this double inscription is the same as that of the epochal spatialization/territorialization of being that, according to Heidegger's genealogy of the truth discourse of modernity at large, enabled the Romans to put knowledge production (their truth) in the service of their imperial project: the pax that, in representing itself as the benign light of the truth, deflects attention away from the repressive darkness that belongs to it.

In invoking this dark end of the light of truth, I am referring first to the total colonization of the "Other" of Being in all its particular manifestations—the reduction of its differential force to useful and docile body or to disposable reserve. Following Heidegger's version of this reduction, however, I am referring also to its necessarily de-ethicized concomitant: the banalization of thought and the leveling and standardization of violence against whatever, in its refusal to be accommodated, presents itself as an obstacle to this deadly, "benignly productive" logic. In both Heidegger and Foucault, the peace that constitutes the ultimate end of the binarist logic of instrumental reason is a living death.

Let us return, after this long detour, to the question of Edward Said's relationship to Michel Foucault. Against a growing consensus that would put Said's "worldly criticism" in a binary opposition to poststructuralist theory, I have been suggesting that it is the Heideggerian Foucault I have retrieved in this chapter that lies behind *Orientalism* and the works that followed, *The Question of Palestine, Covering Islam,* and not least, *Culture and Imperialism.* This is not to say that Said was conversant with Heidegger's thought, to say nothing about being influenced by it. It is to say, rather, that the Foucault of Said's *Orientalism* was the Foucault who had discovered Nietzsche the genealogist through reading Heidegger, the Foucault who, via Heidegger's antimetaphysical and antihistoricist Nietzsche, came to realize the political limitations of his earlier "archaeological" project or, at any rate, the critical political, if not emancipatory, implications to which his "structuralist" leanings had blinded him. It was, as I will argue in the following chapters, this poststructuralist Foucault—this Heideggerian/Nietzschean genealogist of *Surveiller et punir*—who, in the context of an elitist Anglo-American academic establishment still given to apotheosizing the unworldly (i.e., autotelic) text or celebrating the "literary canon," provided Said with directives for elaborating his antifilial or antidynastic (i.e., antimetaphysical) concept of "beginnings" into a polyvalent and transdisciplinary mode of "worldly" or "secular" criticism that he would later call "contrapuntal analysis." Through this elaboration of Foucault's genealogy, Said discovered a powerful vehicle not simply for the critique of Orientalism and other discursive practices vis-à-vis the Occident's "Others" but also for the reclamation of the very human being that "we" have from the beginning of "our" history denied "them."

3. Orientalism

Foucault, Genealogy, History

The purpose of history, guided by genealogy, is not to discover
the roots of our identity but to commit itself to its dissipation.
It does not seek to define our unique threshold of emergence, the
homeland to which metaphysicians promise a return; it seeks
to make visible all of those discontinuities that cross us. . . .
If genealogy in its own right gives rise to questions concerning
our native land, native language, or the laws that govern us, its
intention is to reveal the heterogeneous systems which, masked
by the self, inhibit the formation of any form of identity
—Michel Foucault, "Nietzsche, Genealogy, History"

The state of mind that is concerned with origins is . . . theological.
By contrast, and this is the shift, beginnings are eminently secular,
a gentile [Vico] continuing activity.
—Edward Said, *Beginnings*

As I observed in the previous chapter, the Michel Foucault who influenced
Said in framing the question Orientalism poses about Western knowledge
production is the Foucault not of Said's *Beginnings*—Foucault the archaeolo-
gist/structuralist—but the Foucault of *Surveiller et punir*. More specifically,
it was the Foucault not of *Folie et déraison* (1961; *Madness and Civilization*),
Naissance de la clinique (1963; *The Birth of the Clinic*), *Les Mots et les choses*
(1966; *The Order of Things*), *L'Archéolgie du savoir* (1969; *The Archaeology of
Knowledge*), and "L'Ordre du discours" (1971; "The Discourse of Language")
but of *Surveiller et punir* (1975; published in English in 1977)—the Foucault
who had, through "a concrete experience that [he] had with prisons, starting
in 1971–2,"[1] discovered what had eluded him as an archaeologist/structural-
ist in the earlier texts: *the relationality* between knowledge production—the
truth discourse of the Enlightenment *épistémè*—and the social institutions
of power and discipline that had emerged in the wake of the French Revolution, that is, with the collapse of the ancien régime and the rise of the

"democratic" bourgeoisie. Commenting retrospectively on precisely this in-between moment in his thought (and on the discursive turn in the period of the Enlightenment), Foucault said in response to his interlocutors' question about his opposition to structuralism:

> In short, there is a problem of the regime, the politics of the scientific statement. At this level it's not so much a matter of knowing what external power imposes itself on science, as of what effects of power circulate among scientific statements, what constitutes, as it were, their internal regime of power, and how and why at certain moments that regime undergoes a global modification.
>
> It was these different regimes that I tried to identify and describe in *The Order of Things,* all the while making it clear that I wasn't trying for the moment to explain them, and that it would be necessary to try and do this in a subsequent work. But what was lacking here [in his archaeological phase] was this problem of the "discursive regime," of the effects of power peculiar to the play of statements. I confused this too much with systematicity, theoretical form, or something like a paradigm. This same problem of power, which at that time I had not yet properly isolated, emerges in two very different aspects at the point of juncture of *Madness and Civilization* and *The Order of Things.*[2]

To be more specific, this Foucault is the one who had discovered the Nietzsche of *The Genealogy of Morals,* or to put it according to my argument in chapter 2, the Nietzsche whom Foucault came to understand for the first time only after reading Heidegger, presumably *Being and Time,* which, elaborating Nietzsche's antimetaphysical will to retrieve the contingency of being from Being, absence from Presence, and the Dionysian from Apollonian in the name of historicity, inaugurates Heidegger's de-struction (*Destruktion*) of the Western (onto-theo-logical) philosophical tradition. Again, this was the philosophical tradition that, under the aegis of metaphysical inquiry (thinking *meta ta physika*: after or above *physis*) interpreted the be-*ing* of being as Being, as a *summum ens,* a total thing or picture), thus betraying the will to power over the nothingness of being (temporality, difference, singularity) inhering in its binary logic. Closer, but not alien to the concerns of Said's *Orientalism,* this was also the interpretation of being that founded the (official) Occident—that set off the known and domesticated world (the *oikoumene;* Latin, *orbis terrarium*) in a binary opposition to *terra incognita* (the unknown and uncharted rest of the world), the "evening land" (the "Occident," from the Latin *occidere,* "to go down, to set"; a correlate of *cadere,* "to fall," "to perish," and *occasus,* "the setting of the sun") from the Orient (from *oriens,* participle of *oriori,* "rising," "rising sun," "east") to justify ontologically the former's conquest and exploitation of the latter's space.[3]

To begin establishing the relationship between Said's *Orientalism* and the Foucault of *Disciple and Punish,* it could be said that, via Heidegger's de-struction, the latter found in Nietzsche's genealogical historiography the following eight interrelated and fundamental methodological propositions, which, as I will show, seem to be fundamental to Said's discourse on the West's representation of the East.

(1) The Occident was produced in the mid-Mediterranean area with the advent of thinking being *meta ta physika* (I emphasize the etymology to highlight the eye and its vision, which was privileged over the other, appetitive senses, and the [pan]optics and the spatializing/structuring of temporality that inform this kind of thinking from above).[4]

(2) The truth discourse of this metaphysical thinking is a *construction,* a fiction that eventually becomes internalized and assimilated, that is, "natu-ralized."

(3) This thinking is informed by a binary logic that privileges identity over difference (temporality), that, in other words, spatializes and accommodates the differential temporality of being to its unmoving center.

(4) The primary role of such inquiry is informed by an imperial will to power over whatever resisted such accommodation. (As Foucault put this proposition in his essay on Nietzsche, "once the historical sense is mastered by a suprahistorical perspective, metaphysics can bend it to its own purpose and, by aligning it to the demands of objective science, it can impose its own 'Egyptianism.'")[5]

(5) This imperial ontological interpretation of being is polyvalent in its application; in other words, this Occidental ontology understands being not simply as a philosophical category, a discipline of inquiry, but in some degree as an indissoluble continuum extending from the interpretation of being as such to the subject, the ecos, gender, culture, and sociopolitical formations—in short, from what has conventionally come to be called "theory" to the multiple sites of practice.[6]

(6) The counter-mnemonic thinking of this (de-structive) genealogical project was not simply the exposure of the constructedness of truth and the polyvalent imperialism of its binary logic but also, at least symptomatically, an act of emancipation—the release, liberation, or decolonization of the temporality/nothingness/difference that the spatializing, territorializing, or more precisely, structuralizing of being endemic to metaphysical thinking reduced, pacified, and domesticated to predictable, measurable, graspable (comprehendible) *object.*

(7) The project of criticizing the Western tradition is not historicist—not a disinterested corrective of the historiography of the past from a universal,

teleological, or suprahistorical (unworldly) perspective—but *interested* (from *inter esse,* "in the midst," "worldly"), that is, de-structive or genealogical: a "history of the present" (*DP*, 31).

(8) Finally, this interested historian of the present must be a part of yet apart from the world, an *Abgeschiedene* (as Heidegger called Trakl), a de-viant (Foucault), an exile (Said).

* * *

Not unlike the genealogy of the modern disciplinary society in Foucault's *Discipline and Punish,* Said's genealogy of Orientalism is structured in terms of an apparently sharp contrast between the power relations of a premodern past and those of modernity. Foucault offers the starker contrast in his effort to dramatize the suddenness of the transformation from a monarchical polity that, from the perspective of sovereignty, employed power arbitrarily and overtly—spectacularly—to intimidate potential transgressors of the king's law, to one in which knowledge production and power became mutually complicit in the wake of the French Revolution and the triumph of the bourgeoisie. Nonetheless, as I have shown through his pervasive invocation of the "Roman reference" to characterize this emergent bourgeois polity, this should not obscure the fact that in tracing the formation of this "democratic" polity Foucault assigns a significant role to Western antiquity, particularly the alliance between calculative thinking and the Roman legions, that is, the use of *eruditio et institutio in bonas artes* to discipline a dependable Roman citizenry in behalf of metropolitan Rome's imperial project. Like Foucault, Said focuses primarily on the period of Enlightenment modernity. He is, however, more overt in demonstrating the continuity between classical antiquity (for Said, as I have noted, it is Greece, not Rome, that constituted the origins of Western civilization) and European modernity vis-à-vis this transformation of power relations and in articulating its phases. At the risk of oversimplification, the "structure" of *Orientalism* could be said to involve four broad and loosely overlapping stages: (1) the period from Greek antiquity to the medieval era, which, in founding the Occidental ontological perspective, also founded the "Orient" as its (barbarian) "Other"; (2) the period of the Napoleonic era (particularly the Egyptian expedition of 1798), which witnessed the beginnings of the conscious identification of scientific knowledge about the Orient and political domination of its space, though these remained subordinated to military conquest; (3) the period of the rise of modernity, when the previous generations' general "textual attitude" toward the Orient became Orientalism, the object of the scientific gaze, as in the case of Sylvestre de Sacy, Ernest Renan, Edward William Lane, H. A. R.

Gibb, and Louis Massignon, and came to supersede military conquest as the agency of domination; and (4) the period when scientific Orientalism became, especially in America, managerial expertise serving the ideological purposes of the nation-state, as in the case of Gustave von Grunebaum, Bernard Lewis, P. J. Vatikiotis, and many others.

Later on, I will discuss the significance of this four-part structure of *Orientalism* in terms of transformations in the relationship between knowledge and power (the repressive hypothesis). Here, I want to engage the issue of Said's commitment to the worldliness of criticism against the alleged unworldly textual analysis of the early poststructuralists, a worldliness that many of Said's followers and the vast majority of the postcolonial critics he influenced have put into a binary opposition to the supposed unworldliness of critical theory on the basis of the latter's tendency to restrict the study of texts to the ontological/linguistic site at the expense of the political. I will do this not to exonerate these early poststructuralists, who indeed tended to overlook the transdisciplinary imperatives of their radical interrogation of the European (logocentric) tradition—its metaphysical ontology, its territorializing language, and its self-identical subject—but to suggest that Said, somewhat like the Nietzschean Foucault I have retrieved, is symptomatically fulfilling these transdisciplinary (and collaborative) imperatives rather than rejecting the poststructuralist turn.

Like Foucault in *Discipline and Punish,* and unlike Heidegger and Nietzsche, Said overdetermines cultural/political discourse—its Eurocentrism—in *Orientalism.* This emphasis was clearly intended to counter the deconstructionists' overdetermination of textuality—their dissociation of representation from the world, from history, from human agency—as exemplified by Jacques Derrida's notorious assertion in *On Grammatology* that "il n'y a pas de hors-texte" (there is nothing outside the text). It should not be overlooked, however, as it all too often has been, that Said's overdetermination of the Enlightenment imperial/colonial agenda is not undertaken at the expense of the Western ontological interpretation of being. Like Foucault in *Discipline and Punish,* Said in *Orientalism* is writing a "history of the present,"[7] specifically, a genealogy of a truth discourse that posits the Oriental as ontologically as well as racially inferior to Western Man. Both Foucault's rejection of the negativity of power (the repressive hypothesis) in favor of its productivity—that is, his focus on the relationship between knowledge production and disciplinary power—and Said's focus on the relationship between cultural production and imperialism—*the allotrope of metaphysical thinking*—were instigated by the self-destruction of the (theo)logical economy of the ancien régime (divine right) and the emergence of Enlightenment empiricism, science, and the bourgeoisie following the French Revolution. That is, they both rest on the moment in Western history when the *visible* Logos (the principle of the absolute origin or identity) that had hitherto been the means of coercing difference (the "Other") into taking its proper place in the larger whole was internalized by the new humanist/democratic polity into the sociopolitical body by means of the truth of empirical science. More specifically, this was the moment of modernity when the imperial mechanisms of the binary logic of the Logos in knowledge/power relations were rendered infinitely more efficient (economically and politically) by the compartmentalization of being into the classificatory table or *tableau vivant,* that is, by the establishment of the disciplines, the mode of knowledge production, so prominent in Foucault's analysis of the Panopticon and its assimilation into the everyday life of Western humanity as panopticism, that enabled the dynamics of divide and conquer.

As I noted in chapter 2 by emphasizing his invocation of the Roman references, however, just as Foucault (as opposed to "the Foucauldians") understood this historical transformation not as a mutation but as a development, however abrupt, of Western metaphysical knowledge production, so Said understood the rise of the political (disciplinary) character of Orientalism in Enlightenment modernity not as a sudden irruption but as an extension of the ancient metaphysical *épistémè.* I will return to this continuous historical divide later. Here I stress it to show that, like Foucault, Said perceives, in some degree at least, the indissoluble continuity between the ontology—the metaphysics—that differentiates Europe from and privileges it over the Orient and political (imperialist) power. The difference between Foucault and Said is that the former locates his analysis of knowledge/power at the site of the European nation (not necessarily the state), whereas Said, in a gesture that could be said to fulfill the transdisciplinary imperative of the logic of the continuum of being, overdetermines the site of Western imperialism.

In emphasizing the transdisciplinarity of Said's critical genealogical perspective, I do not want to suggest that this attunement to the polyvalency of the West's representation of the Orient constitutes a regression to the notion of the general or universal intellectual, whom Michel Foucault, with the orthodox Marxist in mind (though it could also include the classical humanist), condemns for pontificating the agenda of various constituencies of the oppressed from a transcendental perspective. On the contrary, I am suggesting that Said, like Foucault, is committed to the idea of the "specific" or, in Gramsci's phrase, "organic" intellectual. This is the worldly intellectual who emerges from one of the historically specific constituencies—the working class, women, homosexuals, racial or ethnic minorities, and so on—as an alienated (exilic) identity and who, for that reason, is more capable than the general or universal intellectual of understanding the particularity of his or her oppression. *He is also the intellectual who is always attuned to all the sites of the continuum of being represented by the truth discourse of the dominant culture—to, that is, the alienated identities of those other indissolubly related constituencies its system of power produces, with the view to establishing "alliances" or, in Gramsci's phrase, "a historical bloc" to resist it.*[8]

This continuity within difference is clearly and emphatically demonstrated in the general structure of *Orientalism,* which traces the genealogy of modern Orientalism—in its developed scientific disciplinary mode—back to (as Said questionably takes it) the origins of the Occident in Greece: the era between Homer's *Iliad* and Aeschylus's play *The Persians* and Euripides' *Bacchae,* when the Occident identifies itself as such against the "Oriental world."

> Almost from earliest times in Europe the Orient was something more than what was empirically known about it. As least until the early eighteenth century . . . European understanding of one kind of Oriental culture, the Islamic, was ignorant but complex. For certain associations with the East—not quite ignorant, not quite informed—always seem to have gathered around the notion of an Orient. Consider first the *demarcation* [emphasis added] between Orient and West. It already seems bold by the time of the *Iliad.* Two of the most profoundly influential qualities associated with the East appear in Aeschylus's *The Persians,* the earliest Athenian play extant, and in *The Bacchae* of Euripides, the very last one extant. . . .
>
> The two aspects of the Orient that set it off from the West in this pair of plays will remain essential motifs of European imaginative geography. A line is drawn between two continents. Europe is powerful and articulate; Asia is defeated and distant. Aeschylus *represents* Asia, makes her speak in the person of the aged Persian queen, Xerxes' mother. It is Europe that articulates the Orient; this articulation is the prerogative, not of a puppet master, but of a genuine creator, whose life-giving power represents, animates, constitutes the otherwise silent and dangerous space beyond familiar boundaries. There is an analogy between Aeschylus's orchestra [the chorus of Persian women who have learned of the Greeks' destruction of the Persian army], which contains the Asiatic world as the playwright conceives it, and the learned envelope of Orientalist scholarship, which also will hold in the vast, amorphous Asiatic sprawl for sometimes sympathetic but always dominating scrutiny. Second, there is the motif of the Orient as insinuating danger. Rationality is undermined by Eastern excesses, those mysteriously attractive opposites to what seem to be normal values. The difference separating East from West is symbolized by the sternness with which, at first, Pentheus rejects the hysterical bacchantes. When later he himself becomes a bacchant, he is destroyed not so much for having given in to Dionysus as for having incorrectly assessed Dionysus's menace in

the first place. . . . Hereafter Oriental mysteries will be taken seriously, not least because they challenge the rational Western mind to new exercises of its enduring ambition and power. (*O*, 55–57)

Said generally represents this inaugural and inaugurating hierarchical demarcation between West and East in spatial terms—as an "imaginative geography." He does this, as I have noted, because of his commitment to the political in the face of a critical discourse that seemed indifferent to it. Prior to this dominant register of his discourse, however, as it is to the territorialization of being that Foucault overdetermines, is the *ontology* that enables it. Though the following summary passage about the scope and continuity of Orientalism precedes that quoted previously, it is clear from the reference to Aeschylus that for Said, this divide was inaugurated when the Greeks (allegedly) began to think being (its temporality) metaphysically, as a space informed by a principle of presence:

> Orientalism is a style of thought based upon an ontological and epistemological distinction made between "the Orient" and (most of the time) "the Occident." Thus a very large mass of writers, among whom are poets, novelists, philosophers, political theorists, economics, and imperial administrators, have accepted the basic distinction between East and West as the starting point for elaborate theories, epics, novels, social descriptions, and political accounts concerning the Orient, its people, customs, "mind," destiny, and so on. *This* [essentialized] Orient can accommodate Aeschylus, say, and Victor Hugo, Dante and Karl Marx. (*O*, 2–3)

Henceforth in *Orientalism,* as I have noted, Said rarely refers to Western knowledge production as ontological, preferring from his subject position to increasingly privilege the rhetoric of cultural and political domination. Nevertheless, the operations of metaphysical inquiry—thinking *meta ta physika*—saturate the genealogical rhetoric he employs to expose the Occident's perennial cultural and political domination of the Orient, a fact overlooked by virtually all his critics, both critical and sympathetic, including the legion of postcolonial critics he has influenced. This saturation appears especially in the metaphorics of vision that, as I have shown in chapter 2, is utterly intrinsic to the practice of metaphysical thinking. Such thinking, more specifically, employs a *pan*-optics that, in *re-presenting* time, in *placing* "it" before the eye, spatializes (and fixes) its flux or, to put it alternatively, reifies the nothingness of temporality to render it graspable by the mind's transcendental, omnipresent, and totalizing eye or, closely related to this, territorializes being—reduces its contingency to center and periphery—to render its threatening mystery knowable, conquerable, and colonizable.[9]

This system of allotropes endemic to metaphysical inquiry, as in the case of Foucault's *Discipline and Punish,* pervades Said's analysis of the discourse of Orientalism, from his reading of the Greek dramatists and the early European travelers to the Orient; through that of the early students of the Orient such as D'Herbelot and Anquetil-Duperron and the more "scientific" scholars such as Sylvestre de Sacy, Ernest Renan, William Jones, Edward Lane, and Hamilton Gibb; to that of the administrators of European empires such as Lord Evelyn Baring Cromer and Robert Curzon, exponents of imperialism such as Arthur Balfour, and the "area studies experts" who now, following the United States' rise to superpower status, dominate the production of knowledge about the Orient. I could invoke virtually any of Said's many readings of these Orientalist discourses to show his acute awareness of the ontological ground on which the West's cultural/political practice regarding the Orient was founded and on which it continues to rest, but I will confine myself to his inaugural example from the first page of *Orientalism,* that of Lord Arthur Balfour's speech to the British House of Commons, delivered on June 13, 1910, on "the problems with which we have to deal in Egypt." Said quotes what he takes to be at the heart of Balfour's speech: a question posed to him by a colleague, J. M. Robertson, of his right "to take up these airs of superiority with regard to people whom you choose to call Oriental." This is what Balfour said:

> I take up no attitude of superiority. But I ask [anyone] . . . who has even the most superficial knowledge of history, if they will look in the face the facts with which a British statesman has to deal when he is put in a position of supremacy over great races like the inhabitants of Egypt and countries in the East. We know the civilization of Egypt better than we know the civilization of any other country. We know it further back; we know it intimately; we know more about it. It goes far beyond the petty span of the history of our race, which is lost in the prehistoric period at a time when the Egyptian civilization had already passed its prime. Look at all the oriental countries. Do not talk about superiority or inferiority. (*O,* 32)

Said interprets Balfour's response in a way that might be surprising were it not for the ontological register he is attempting to establish as the ground of cultural and political analysis of Western Orientalism in general:

> Two great themes dominate his remarks here and in what will follow: knowledge and power, the Baconian themes. As Balfour justifies the necessity for British occupation of Egypt, supremacy in his mind is associated with "our knowledge" of Egypt and not principally with military or economic power. Knowledge to Balfour means *surveying* a civilization from its origins to its prime to its

decline—and of course, it means *being able to do that.* Knowledge means *rising above immediacy, beyond* self, into the foreign and *distant.* The *object* of such knowledge is inherently vulnerable to *scrutiny*; this *object is a "fact"* which, if it develops, changes, or otherwise transforms itself in the way that civilizations frequently do, nevertheless is *fundamentally, even ontologically stable.* To have such knowledge of such a *thing* is to dominate it, to have *authority over it.* And authority here means for "us" to deny authority to "it"—the Oriental country— since we know it and it exists, in a sense, *as* we know it. British knowledge of Egypt *is* Egypt for Balfour, and the burdens of knowledge make such questions as inferiority and superiority seem petty ones. Balfour nowhere denies British superiority and Egyptian inferiority; he takes them for granted as he describes the consequences of knowledge. (*O,* 32; emphasis added, except in the first and last two cases)

This introductory passage in Said's history of the West's representation of the East—a history that begins with Homer, Aeschylus, and Euripides, that is, with the founding of the identity of the West, and culminates in the American pundit—casts the Orientalist as endowed above all with "vision" ("Empirical data about the Orient or about any of its parts count for very little; what matters and is decisive is what I have been calling the Orientalist vision, a vision by no means confined to the professional scholar, but rather the common possession of all who have thought about the Orient in the West" [*O,* 69]). This vision, to use Said's language, enables the spatially removed "spectator"[10]—this "light-emanating center" (*O,* 241)—to "survey," "scrutinize," "watch," "view," "see," "observe," "oversee," "encompass," "circumscribe," and "focus on" the Orient, that is, to "shape," "place," "structure," "restructure," "emplot" (*O,* 95, 151), "construct," "fabricate," "produce" (bring forth into the light), "archivalize," "contain," "fix in a visionary cosmology" (*O,* 70), and "grasp" the Orient, which is then understood as "eccentric," "silent," "obscure," "unknown," "alien," "mysterious," "elusive," "threatening," lasciviously, sensually "female" (*O,* 182), "decadent," and on and on. Analogously, the Orientalist represents the historical Orient as a (theatrical) "stage," a "geography," a "field," an "area," a "grid," "a picture," and not least, reminding us of its central importance in Foucault's genealogy of knowledge/power relations in the disciplinary society, a classificatory "table" or "*tableau vivant*" (*O,* 103, 125, 126–27)[11] that theoretically enables him or her to reduce the complex historical diversity of the East to an "eternal," "unchanging" "essentialist" presence under its "commanding" gaze, or, alternatively, to see all at once, objectify, and classify the living dynamics of Oriental life for the purpose of "compelling" or "accommodating" its multitudinous differences into their *proper* place in the larger and inclusive European "picture" or "comprehensive vision."

Invoking the "defeat of narrative [the corrosive force of temporality and history] by vision" in T. E. Lawrence's *Seven Pillars of Wisdom*,[12] Said, epitomizing this allotropic system inhering in Western metaphysical thinking, writes summarily:

> The Orientalist surveys the Orient from above, with the aim of getting hold of the whole sprawling panorama before him—culture, religion, mind, history, society. To do this he must see every detail through the device of a set of reductive categories (the Semite, the Muslim mind, the Orient, and so forth). Since these categories are primarily schematic and efficient ones, and since it is more or less assumed that no Oriental can know himself the way an Orientalist can, any vision of the Orient ultimately comes to rely for its coherence and force on the person, institution, or discourse whose property it is. Any comprehensive vision is fundamentally conservative, and we have noted how in the history of ideas about the Near Orient in the West these ideas have maintained themselves regardless of any evidence disputing them. (Indeed, we can argue that these ideas produce evidence that proves their validity.) (*O*, 239)

Clearly, if always implicitly, in all this, Said understands "theory" (from the Greek *theoros*, "spectator") not as a free-floating manifestation of an ahistorical subject but as a consequential worldly practice.

It is, finally, this subtly coercive Occidental ontology—this (worldly) will to power over difference—inhering in thinking *meta ta physika* that, as in Foucault's understanding of "discourse," lies behind Said's inordinate emphasis on the role that the textual attitude has played (e.g., in Napoleon's Egyptian project) and continues to play in the West's representation and domination of the Orient:

> It may appear strange to speak about something or someone holding a *textual attitude,* but a student of literature will understand the phrase more easily if he will recall the kind of view attacked by Voltaire in *Candide,* or even the attitude to reality satirized by Cervantes in *Don Quixote.* What seems unexceptionable good sense to these writers is that it is a fallacy to assume that the swarming, unpredictable, and problematic mess in which human beings live can be understood on the basis of what books—texts—say; to apply what one learns out of a book literally to reality is to risk folly or ruin. One would no more think of using *Amadis of Gaul* to understand sixteenth-century (or present-day) Spain than one would use the Bible to understand, say, the House of Commons. But clearly people have tried and do try to use texts in so simple-minded a way, for otherwise *Candide* and *Don Quixote* would not still have the appeal for readers that they do today. It seems a common human failing to prefer the schematic authority of a text to the disorientations of direct encounter with the human. (*O*, 92–93)

Given his emphasis on the essential characteristics of Occidental representation in what has preceded and what follows, the problem with this otherwise profoundly suggestive analysis of the textual attitude is that, as the last sentence suggests, Said attributes it to human nature in general. This attribution is no doubt generally valid. Nonetheless, in *Orientalism* Said insistently identifies everything he says about the textual attitude specifically with the collective *Western* mind, a mind whose overdetermined textual attitude was eventually naturalized by metaphysical/spatializing thinking. Indeed, Said makes this identification clear when, at the end of his discussion on the way a textual attitude achieves commanding authority, he draws an implicit analogy between the truth-producing systems Cervantes and Voltaire attack in satirizing their protagonists' textual attitudes and both the *idées reçues* Flaubert attacks in *Bouvard et Pécuchet* and the discourse Foucault thematizes as the basic determinant of the truth in the (modern) West, the two most prominent accounts in Said's book of the operative characteristics of the Western mind:

> A text purporting to contain knowledge about something actual, and arising out of circumstances similar to the ones I have just described, is not easily dismissed. Expertise is attributed to it. The authority of academics, institutions, and governments can accrue to it, surrounding it with still greater prestige than its practical successes warrant. Most important, such texts can *create* not only knowledge but also the very reality they appear to describe. In time such knowledge and reality produce a tradition, or what Michel Foucault calls a discourse, whose material presence or weight, not the originality of a given author, is really responsible for the texts produced out of it. This kind of text is composed out of those preexisting units of information deposited by Flaubert in the catalogue of *idées reçues*. (*O,* 94)

In the context of the argument I am pursuing, the first important aspect of Said's analysis of the textual attitude is that the two examples of its critique he cites, Cervantes's and Voltaire's, identify the textual attitude of their foolish or ruined protagonists with the (Western) "meta-physical" interpretations of being: Cervantes, with the theo-logy of the Inquisition (masked as the universal logic of the romances); Voltaire, with the anthropo-logy of the early Enlightenment, Leibniz's optimistic notion that the dreadful contingencies of being are a coherent part of a larger preestablished cosmic harmony, or as Alexander Pope put it in his "Essay on Man," "Whatever is, is right." It thus follows that Said's understanding of the textual attitude, like Cervantes's, Voltaire's, Flaubert's, and Foucault's, involves a sleight of hand that conceals the static spatial image or picture lying behind the temporality of words. The one who holds the textual attitude, whether Don Quixote, Pangloss, Orientalists such as Napoleon and his army of savants, Renan, T. E. Lawrence, or Bernard Lewis, holds a *pre*-conceived (i.e., preseen and -grasped) image or picture of the heterogeneous reality he or she encounters. That is, such individuals re-*present* this existential reality—place "it" before their eyes or under their gazes—in the *form* of what is desired beforehand. In other words, the commanding panoptic distance that such a territorialization of existential being enables allows those who hold the textual attitude, like those who adhere to the truth of metaphysics, not simply to reduce the singularity of immediacy and the anxiety it instigates to an abstract and tranquilizing timeless and unchanging spatial image or picture but also to endow their representations with the particular traits—*an imagined geography*—that will justify and facilitate its domination. As in the case of Foucault's understanding of discourse, it is this metaphysical interpretation of being and the allotropes of vision endemic to it that inform Said's understanding of the textual attitude and explain its methodological importance for his political critique of the discourse of Orientalism and the astonishing richness of insight this critique has produced.

However blinded he was by his hostility to the remarkably productive possibilities for a critical understanding of the West's perennial dominance over the world, the Marxist Aijaz Ahmad, Said's most severe critic on the left, is correct to identify the Said of *Orientalism* with the poststructuralists of the era that witnessed the rise of "a world supervised by Reagan and Thatcher," particularly with the Foucault of *Discipline and Punish,* and to claim that his discourse "essentialized" the West and East on "ontological" grounds, if we understand these terms, as Ahmad may not have done, as the eventual naturalization of the West's founding construction of itself and its Oriental "Other" on the basis of the metaphysical truth discourse endemic to it:

> Alongside these large theoretical and political shifts [away from Marxist critique] was a matter of a certain transhistoricity which, in claiming that Europe establishes its own Identity by establishing the *Difference* of the Orient, and that Europe has possessed, since the days of Athenian drama, a unitary will to inferiorize and vanquish non-Europe, made it possible for Said to assert that *all* European knowledges of non-Europe are bad knowledges because they are already contaminated with this aggressive Identity-formation. [The reference is primarily to Said's criticism of the "Orientalism" of Marx's writing on India.] This, indeed, was a novel idea. Numerous writers had previously demonstrated the complicity of European cultural productions in the colonial enterprise, but only the most obscurantist indigenists and cultural nationalists had previously argued—surely, no writer with any sense of intellectual responsibility had ever

accepted—that Europeans were *ontologically* incapable of producing any true knowledge about non-Europe. But Said was emphatic on this point, and mobilized all sorts of eclectic procedures to establish it.[13]

Ahmad's representation of Said's putatively transhistorical characterization of the history of the West vis-à-vis the Orient as monolithic is an exaggeration that enables him to interpret the difference between Said's inaugural account of the Orientalism of the ancient Greeks and his account of "modern Orientalism"—the Orientalism complicit with colonialism—as a contradiction: "Now, if there really is only this seamless and incremental history of 'Orientalist Discourse' from Aeschylus to Dante to Marx to Bernard Lewis," he writes,

> then in what sense could one take the eighteenth century "as a roughly defined starting point"? In other words, one does not really know whether "Orientalist Discourse" begins in the post-Enlightenment period or at the dawn of European civilization. . . . This, then, raises the question of the relationship between Orientalism and colonialism. In one sort of reading, where post-Enlightenment Europe is emphasized, Orientalism appears to be an ideological corollary of colonialism. But so insistent is Said in identifying its origins in European Antiquity and its increasing elaboration throughout the European Middle Ages that it seems to be the *constituting element,* transhistorically, of what he calls "the European imagination." (*IT,* 181)

Like Foucault, though unlike Derrida and especially the textual deconstructionists he influenced in the United States, Said takes pains throughout *Orientalism* to register the diversity of this Western representational history, particularly at the rise of colonialism. Nonetheless, as is forcefully underscored by the preceding thematization of the systemic optical metaphorics underlying Said's analysis of this history from the Greeks to the present, a continuity subsumes these differences, however historically important they may be. This continuity, analogous to the itinerary of Foucault's genealogy of the disciplinary society, begins with a metaphysical mode of inquiry that constructs the political identities of the West and its "Other" and culminates in modernity with the naturalization of this construction and the application of its truth to the European cultural/political colonial project. Demonstrating this analogy and this continuity in difference will be the burden of the next section of this chapter.

* * *

As I argued in chapter 2, the Foucault of *Discipline and Punish* locates the most historically consequential transformation of Europe's civilizational identity in the Enlightenment—what came to be called modernity—that culminated in the French Revolution with the collapse of the ancien régime and the rise to dominance of the "disciplinary society." This was the period that witnessed the apotheosis of Man: the displacement of the theologos by the anthropologos, the supernatural interpretation of the phenomena of being (above all, the exegetical system of correspondences endemic to the theological notion of the great chain of being) by the empirical (especially the natural) scientific disciplines, of the aristocracy by the merchant class, mercantilism by capitalism, and the monarchy by constitutional democracy. For Foucault, it was also and above all the period that witnessed a revolutionary transformation of power relations: the displacement of a spectacular form of punishment by the microtechnologies of discipline or, to put it alternatively, the appropriation of knowledge production by the new constitutional polity in behalf of power, despite this polity's affirmation of their radical opposition (what Foucault called the repressive hypothesis). However dramatic and far reaching in its worldly effects, this remarkable transformation did not, as I emphasized in chapter 2, constitute a historical mutation. Under the aegis of this new "regime of truth," the transcendental Logos (and its panoptic eye), which from European antiquity to the ancien régime had justified the coercion of difference into identity, the many into the one, was not annulled; it was secularized, brought down into the world of history. In the language of M. H. Abrams, the prestigious humanist whom Said cites to characterize the "science" of Ernest Renan, the new bourgeois humanist polity naturalized the supernatural. The new polity did this, as Foucault reiterates, not so much to improve the execrable condition of the lowly under the sovereign gaze of the monarch as to secure its hegemony against insurrection. In the premodern period, the transcendental Logos and the will to power over deviance—the policing—it justified was visible to those on whom it was applied and thus vulnerable to resistance. As I argued previously, by naturalizing the Logos (and the internalization of the panoptic eye), the new "democratic" polity rendered it invisible, a disciplinary instrument for normalizing "deviant" or "abnormal" behavior, that is, for efficiently producing not only useful but also docile bodies:

> The historical moment of the disciplines was the moment when an art of the human body was born, which was directed not only at the growth of its skills, nor at the intensification of its subjection, but at the formation of a relationship that in the mechanism itself makes it more obedient as it becomes more useful, and conversely. What was then being formed was a policy of coercions that act upon the body, a calculated manipulation of its elements, its gestures,

its behavior. The human body was entering a machinery of power that explores it, breaks it down and rearranges it. A "political anatomy," which was also a "mechanics of power," was being born; it defined how one may have a hold over others' bodies, not only so that they may do what one wishes, but so that they may operate as one wishes, with the techniques, the speed and efficiency that one determines. Thus discipline produces subjected and practiced bodies, "docile" bodies. Discipline increases the forces of the body (in economic terms of utility) and diminishes these same forces (in political term of obedience). In short, it dissociates power from the body; on the one hand, it turns it into an "aptitude," a "capacity," which it seeks to increase; on the other hand, it reverses the course of the energy, the power that might result from it, and turns it into a relation of strict subjection. If economic exploitation separates the force and the product of labor, let us say that disciplinary coercion establishes in the body the constricting link between an increased aptitude and an increased domination. (*DP*, 138–39)

Said's genealogy of Orientalism is far less systematic than Foucault's genealogy of the disciplinary society, and his representation of the transition from the premodern to the modern is less sudden. As I have noted, his history of the Occident's ontological, cultural, and political comportment to the Orient is articulated in terms of four broad and overlapping phases: (1) the period from Greek antiquity through the Middles Ages, (2) the period before and during Napoleon's Egyptian expedition of 1798, (3) the period when Orientalism emerged as a (social) scientific academic discipline, and (4) the period when Orientalism became a matter of managerial expertise under the global hegemony of the United States. Nevertheless, Said's apparently more continuous analysis of the transformation of power relations vis-à-vis the Orient is largely analogous to and betrays the influence of Foucault's analysis, in *Discipline and Punish,* of the transformation of power relations vis-à-vis the European polity that occurred with the advent of modernity.

For reasons I take to be strategic, this relationship, like the ontological register of his discourse, is not immediately visible in Said's elaboration of the metamorphosis that Orientalist discourse underwent between Greek antiquity and modernity. To show that Said's elaboration of this metamorphosis is nevertheless analogous to the distinction Foucault makes between the premodern and the modern forms of the relationship between knowledge and power, I will have to make a detour, invoking the second of the two epigraphs that inaugurate the last chapter of *Orientalism,* "Orientalism Now," in which Said amplifies the interpretation of modern Orientalism he has introduced in the previous chapter. This epigraph is appropriately from the early, defining pages of Joseph Conrad's *Heart of Darkness* (written in the interregnum between modernity and postmodernity, administrative or disciplinary colonialism and postcolonialism), in which Marlow, speaking to his attentive British companions, meditates aloud about the perennial philosophy and practice of European imperialism: "The conquest of the earth, which mostly means the taking it away from those who have a different complexion or slightly flatter noses than ourselves, is not a pretty thing when you look into it too much. What redeems it is the idea only. An idea at the back of it; not a sentimental pretence but an idea; and an unselfish belief in the idea—something you can set up, and bow down before, and offer a sacrifice to. . . ." What Said leaves out of Marlow's resonant insight into European imperialism—and what, as I will underscore in the next chapter, he will tellingly include in returning to this same crucial, indeed, enabling, passage at the beginning of *Culture and Imperialism*—is the following, which immediately precedes the lines he chooses to quote. I quote at length to focalize the distinction Marlow is making between two kinds of imperialism, at which Said's epigraph only faintly hints:

> Mind, none of us would feel exactly like this. What saves us is efficiency—the devotion to efficiency. But these chaps [the Romans who conquered Britain when it, too, was a "heart of darkness"] were not much account, really. They were no colonists; their administration was merely a squeeze, and nothing more, I suspect. They were conquerors, and for that you want only brute force— nothing to boast of, when you have it, since your strength is just an accident arising from the weakness of others. They grabbed what they could get for the sake of what was to be got. It was just robbery with violence, aggravated murder on a great scale, and men going at it blind—as is very proper for those who tackle a darkness.[14]

Taken together with these lines, the passage Said quotes as his epigraph to "Orientalism Now" and that he will expand in *Culture and Imperialism* constitutes in essence the distinction I am suggesting he is making—symptomatically or indirectly—in *Orientalism* between premodern and modern Orientalism. And in a general but quite recognizable way, it is Foucauldian. What distinguishes British imperialism from that of the Romans (and all those modern European nations, such as King Leopold's Belgium, that have not become modern) is, as in the case of premodern and modern power relations in Foucault, essentially a matter of (economic and political) economy. The Romans were interested only in exploiting those who had "a different complexion or slightly flatter noses" than themselves and used brute force (overt power) to achieve their immediate selfish ends. Motivated by this narrow selfishness— the lack of a large, redeeming "idea"—their imperial project thus inevitably manifested itself in waste (became economically uneconomical); furthermore, by wasting the lives of the colonized in the process, they opened themselves to moral condemnation and, implicitly, political resistance (became politically uneconomical). The modernized British, however, perceive and represent their imperial project as fundamentally benign, reciprocally beneficial to colonist and colonizer. Their imperial project is motivated and redeemed, in other words, by "a devotion to efficiency," to "an unselfish belief in the idea—something you can set up, and bow down to, and offer a sacrifice to," that is, by the truth discourse of modernity. As a result of the economy of this textual attitude, their imperialism escapes the economic and political consequences of the inefficiency of brutal and greedy selfishness. This is more or less how Said puts this distinction between premodern and modern imperialism in *Culture and Imperialism* when he demonstrates the decisive role that cultural production has played in the modern history of European imperialism: "Thus Conrad encapsulates two quite different but intimately related aspects of imperialism: the idea that is based on the power to take over territory, an idea utterly clear [visible] in its force and unmistakable consequences; and the practice that essentially disguises or obscures this [renders it invisible] by developing a justificatory regime [of truth] of self-aggrandizing, self-originating authority interposed between the victim of imperialism and its perpetrator."[15]

Returning to the first phase of the four-part structure of *Orientalism,* which covers the period from Greek antiquity to the medieval era, Said, it may be recalled, overdetermines the metaphysical ground of early Europe's hierarchical binarist representation of the Orient. Though he does not elaborate this historically inaugural ontological first principle (an omission, I have argued, that was more a symptom of his having assimilated the antiessentialist philosophical discourse of the poststructuralists than a rejection of it), the fact is that, again, Said's critical rhetoric is saturated with the poststructuralist understanding of the binary (now "white") metaphorics that Western metaphysics, in establishing its sovereignty over thinking, had inscribed into European perception, thought, and language, had rendered hegemonic, or in Said's phrase, made into a "textual attitude." I am referring once again and above all to the vision/blindness, light/darkness opposition and its corollaries, space (territory) and time (flux), the comprehendible (graspable) and the mysterious (ungraspable), and the center and periphery, the binaries that Heidegger, Derrida, Lyotard, Lacan, Althusser, and Foucault and the early poststructuralists thematized by de-structuring or deconstructing the binary logic of the ontotheological or logocentric tradition.

These binaries of the (onto)logic of premodern Orientalism, as Said shows with great persuasive force, determined the Occident's self-image with respect to the Orient—its racial, cultural, and political superiority over it.

Throughout this long period from the Trojan War through the Crusades to the various European (mainly British and French) military conquests of Eastern lands, however, these imperial cultures did not use the general knowledge of the Orient that these binaries enabled in any decisive way to facilitate and render efficient—politically and economically economical—the political domination of the Orient. Rather, the discourse of Orientalism was primarily used for self-aggrandizement, for enhancing the West's sense of superiority over the Orient. In other words, the transcendental and sovereign Logos presiding over these binaries, like the ontologos of the Romans and Belgians in Conrad's novel, seems merely to have justified the various and intermittent brute-force plunderings of the Orient, plunderings that, as in the case of the spectacular divinely authorized violence of the king in the ancien régime, were simply as wasteful and finally counterproductive as were the temporary, erratic, and adventurous plunderings of the early conquests (for example, Alexander the Great's invasion of the East or the European Crusaders' assaults on the "Holy Lands").

It was only with the rise of modernity—the creation of the nation-state, the displacement of sacred by secular or scientific knowledge, the deemphasizing of the whole in favor of the detail, the subordination of theory to practice (i.e., the secularizing of the visibly transcendental theologos)—that the earlier, premodern discourse of Orientalism began to show signs of a transformation, its crude understanding of the relationship between knowledge production of and political power over the Orient developing into one that turned the prior opposition into a productive continuity. This, the second of Said's four phases, was the interregnum leading up to and culminating in Napoleon's expedition to Egypt, when, armed by the textual attitude (the *image* of the Orient he had assimilated from his adolescent reading of texts such as Marigny's *Histoire des Arabes,* the Greek classics, and those trumpeting Alexander's conquest of the Orient), he invaded that Oriental space with two armies, one of soldiers and the other of French savants. The function of the first was, of course, military conquest, but that of the second was to temper, if not to render invisible, the use of force. Like the prison overseers, psychiatrists, physicians, teachers, and factory bosses vis-à-vis their subjects in Foucault's genealogy of the disciplinary society, it was meant not so much to ameliorate what the French world took to be the degraded conditions of the Egyptian people as to totally encode Egyptian space: to develop an encyclopedic knowledge of this Arab world—languages, familial and social habits, religious beliefs and practices, political formations, and so on—the more efficiently to control its various and destabilizing manifestations.

Said inaugurates his brilliant analysis of Napoleon's expedition in such a way as to point to its transitional and ultimately contradictory character with respect to the transformation of knowledge/power relations accompanying the modernization of Europe. On the one hand, Napoleon's motive was glory and the aggrandizement of the French Empire at the expense of his rival, the British: "[His] military successes that had culminated in the Treaty of Campo Formio left him no other place to turn for additional glory than the East. Moreover, Talleyrand had recently animadverted on 'les avantages à retirer des colonies nouvelles dans les circonstances présentes,' and this notion, along with the appealing prospect of hurting, Britain drew him eastwards" (*O*, 80). On the other hand, Said perceives Napoleon's expedition according to the directives of an emergent transformation of premodern power relations that would, thanks to the harnessing of knowledge production to power, ensure that France's empire would not suffer the fate of the empires of the past:

> Napoleon considered Egypt a likely project precisely because he knew it tactically, strategically, historically, and—not to be underestimated—textually, that is, as something one read about and knew through the writings of recent as well as classical European authorities. The point in all this is that for Napoleon Egypt was a project that acquired reality in his mind, and later in his preparations for its conquest, through experiences that belong to the realm of ideas and myths culled from texts [most notably the Comte de Volney's *Voyage en Égypte et en Syrie* (1787)], not empirical reality. His plans for Egypt therefore became the first in a long series of European encounters with the Orient in which the Orientalist's special expertise was put directly to functional colonial use; for at the crucial instance when an Orientalist had to decide whether his loyalties and sympathies lay with the Orient or with the conquering West, he always chose the latter, from Napoleon's time on. As for the emperor himself, he saw the Orient only as it had been encoded first by classical texts and then by Orientalist experts, whose vision, based on classical texts, seemed a useful substitute for any actual encounter with the real Orient. (*O*, 80)

Despite the emphasis here on the resonant relationships among vision, preconception (knowledge), and the territorialization of the Orient enabling Napoleon to know and to occupy it "tactically, strategically, historically," this way of putting things does not quite shift the emphasis from the brute force of Western premodern imperial practice to domination by the internalization of power in the bodies of the subjects of domination. The shift, however— and the analogy with Foucault's genealogy of modern knowledge/power relations—becomes more patent a little later in a telling anticipation of the previously quoted epigraph from Conrad's *Heart of Darkness*. Following

Volney's directives, Said writes, Napoleon minimized the use of force in his relations with the Egyptians:

> From the first moment that the Armée d'Égypte appeared on the Egyptian horizon, every effort was made to convince the Muslims that "nous sommes les vrais musulmans" [a tactical locution, not incidentally, that anticipates John F. Kennedy's famous "Ich bin ein Berliner" during the crisis of the Berlin Wall], as Bonaparte's proclamation of July 2, 1798, put it to the people of Alexandria. . . . What more than anything impressed the first Arab chronicler of the Expedition, Abd-al-Rahman al-Jabarti, was Napoleon's use of scholars to manage his contacts with the natives—that and the impact of watching a modern European intellectual establishment at close quarters. Napoleon tried everywhere to prove that he was fighting *for* Islam; everything he said was translated into Koranic Arabic, just as the French army was urged by its command always to remember the Islamic sensibility. (*Compare, in this regard, Napoleon's tactics in Egypt with the tactics of the* Requerimiento, *a document drawn up in 1513—in Spanish—by the Spaniards to be read aloud to the Indians: "We shall take you and your wives and your children, and shall make slaves of them, and as such sell and dispose of them as their Highnesses [the king and queen of Spain] may command, and we shall take away your goods, and shall do you all the mischief and damage that we can, as to vassals who do not obey," etc, etc.*) When it seemed obvious to Napoleon that his force was too small to impose itself on the Egyptians, he then tried to make the local imams, cadis, muftis, and ulemas interpret the Koran in favor of the Grande Armée. . . . This worked, and soon the population of Cairo seemed to have lost its distrust of the occupiers. Napoleon later gave his deputy Kleber strict instructions after he left always to administer Egypt through the Orientalists and the religious Islamic leaders whom they could win over; *any other politics was too expensive and foolish* [politically and economically uneconomical]. (*O,* 82; emphasis added)

This emergent distinction between premodern and modern power relations is brilliantly articulated by Said in his sustained summary of the inexorably schematic structure and function of the *Description de l'Égypte,* the encyclopedic text collectively written by the Orientalists who accompanied Napoleon's army to Egypt and "published in twenty-three enormous volumes between 1809 and 1828":

> To restore a region from its present barbarism to its former classical greatness; to instruct (for its own benefit) the Orient in the ways of the modern West; to subordinate or underplay military power in order to aggrandize the project of glorious knowledge acquired in the process of political domination of the Orient; to formulate the Orient, to give it shape, identity, definition with full recognition of its place in memory, its importance to imperial strategy, and its

"natural" role as an appendage to Europe; to dignify all the knowledge collected during colonial occupation with the title "contribution to modern learning" when the natives had neither been consulted nor treated as anything except as pretexts for a text whose usefulness was not to the natives; to feel oneself as a European in command, almost at will, of Oriental history, time, and geography; to institute new areas of specialization; to establish new disciplines; to divide, deploy, schematize, tabulate, index, and record everything in sight (and out of sight); to make out of every observable detail a generalization and out of every generalization an immutable law about the Oriental nature, temperament, mentality, custom, or type; and above all, to transmute living reality into the stuff of texts, to possess (or think one possesses) actuality mainly because nothing in the Orient seems to resist one's powers: these are the features of Orientalist projection entirely realized in the *Description de l'Égypte,* itself enabled and reinforced by Napoleon's wholly Orientalist engulfment of Egypt by the instruments of Western knowledge and power. (*O,* 86)

Besides its clear connection with Foucault's rejection of the repressive hypothesis—that power in modernity is negative: "it 'excludes,' it 'represses,' it 'censors,' it 'abstracts,' it 'masks,' it 'conceals'" (*DP,* 194)—in favor of power's productivity, Said's forcefully succinct account of the relation between knowledge and power that was emerging in the Napoleonic era makes relatively obvious what I have called the relation's ontologically induced territorialization of the actualities of Oriental life. What should not be overlooked, however, is that Said articulates this territorialization of lived experience in such a way as to emphasize, as does Foucault, the infinitely more efficient and productive character it was to achieve in modernity through the transformation of the earlier emphasis on a general spatialization to an emphasis on the tactical and strategic potential inhering in the territorialization of the historicity of human life. This was, in other words, the moment in Western history that, simultaneous with the expanding geographical horizon of the Eurocentric gaze, witnessed the compartmentalization of the knowledge of being into disciplines and the consequent reduction of its be-*ing* to "fields," "domains," or "maps" and further classifications and tabulations of its living details—that is, the development of knowledge/power relations that, according to Said, came to characterize the next (third) phase of the history of Orientalist discourse.

In this third phase, represented by Orientalists such as Sylvestre de Sacy and Ernest Renan in France and William Edward Lane and Sir Hamilton Gibb in Britain, Orientalism, according to Said, became an ostensibly empirical science that, analogous to Foucault's account of the domestic function of knowledge with respect to power, was institutionalized by the imperial nations. That is, it became a "disinterested" mode of inquiry into alien cultures whose research results were represented as the objective truth of the Orient but that in fact were complicit with the will to political domination, thus rendering invisible the still-visible power in the Orientalism of the Napoleonic era. More important, Said's articulation of the third phase's history is remarkably analogous to Foucault's insight that in modernity the earlier, inefficient spatialization of being becomes a productive tactics of territorialization.

In the interview with the geographers of *Hérodote* (1976), it may be recalled, Foucault's interlocutors, profoundly influenced by his analysis of the panoptics of modernity, open the discussion by suggesting that his insistent use of spatial metaphors to characterize his notion of discourse—"territory," "field," "displacements," "region," "horizon"—was pertinent to their work as oppositional geographers. "The point that needs to be emphasized here," they said, echoing Nietzsche's famous depiction of the truth of language as "a mobile army of metaphors, metonyms, and anthropomorphisms," "is that certain spatial metaphors *are equally geographical and strategic, which is only natural since geography grew up in the shadow of the military.* A circulation of notions can be observed between geographical and strategic discourse. The *region* of the geographers is a military region (from *regere*, to command), a *province* is a conquered space (from *vincere*). *Field* evokes the battlefield."[16] At the end of the lively discussion precipitated by this resonant suggestion, Foucault concludes:

> The longer I continue, the more it seems to me that the formation of discourses and the genealogy of knowledge need to be analyzed, not in term of types of consciousness, modes of perception and forms of ideology, but in terms of tactics and strategies of power. Tactics and strategies deployed though implantations, distributions, demarcations, control of territories and organizations of domains which could well make up a sort of geopolitics where my preoccupations would link up with your methods. One theme I would like to study in the next few years is that of the army as a matrix of organization and knowledge; one would need to study the history of the fortress, the "campaign," the "movement," the colony, the territory. Geography must indeed necessarily lie at the heart of my concerns.[17]

Said's primary source for his "imaginary geography" is clearly, as he has reiterated, Antonio Gramsci. Nonetheless, this attribution should not deflect attention from the remarkable similarity between his understanding of the imaginative geography underlying modern Orientalism and the poststructuralists' understanding of the modern West's spatialization or territorialization of the knowledge of being articulated in chapter 2. This is particularly true of Deleuze and Guattari's distinction between "striated" and "smooth" space in

A Thousand Plateaus and of Foucault's emphasis on the ideological implications of the classificatory table, especially if this discussion of geography with the editors of *Hérodote* is kept in mind.

This affiliation between Said's imaginative geography and Foucault's territorialized temporality is strongly, if symptomatically, suggested in a *boundary 2* interview with Said conducted by Paul Bové and Joseph Buttigieg on *Culture and Imperialism*. Taking up the "intriguing question of geography" in the context of his own experience as a colonized subject, Buttigieg observes to Said that, in having as its goal the mastery of "the techniques of reading" that would get one a scholarship to study in England and become "as good as the English," colonial education induces in the colonized subject a sense that geography has, "sort of, collapsed—and you could be in Cairo or Malta, or wherever, but in fact you might as well be in a classroom in England." Echoing Foucault in emphasizing the constructedness of this hegemonic geography, Said responds:

> Well, I don't think it's as collapsed as that. I think one becomes aware of [its imaginative character] only when (a) one begins to move [has retrieved one's temporality], and when (b) the British finally leave—or the French, for that matter, in the case of Algeria. I mean, at the time of colonialism, that setting, *that geographical locale that we're talking about is naturalized; you accept it.* I try to say this [that the geography the colonized inhabit is a naturalized fabrication of the colonizer] over and over again: that you really believe because they want you to believe, that it is [therefore] the destiny of these inferior people to be held by the British, for example, or by the French. . . . Now, it's always different in the various colonies, *but I would say that we accept it* [this imagined geography and destiny] *as natural because it is "natural" geography under those circumstances. By natural, I mean because they're there. In our generation, we didn't see them coming; they were already there. They were there when we were born. So, they're part of the landscape. And you think the world is ordered by the British, or white man, or the West; you think that and it isn't until you move and it isn't until you travel, until there is decolonization, until there's nationalism (all of which somebody of my generation actually lived through), that you begin to see it* [i.e., that the geography that hitherto seemed natural is a strategically imagined construct.][18]

Having thus disclosed both the colonizers' representation of the *lived* experience of the colonized in *spatial* rather than temporal terms and the naturalization of this construction by schooling, Said goes on to attribute geography's importance for him to Gramsci:

> I say this is the single most important thing that I took from Gramsci . . . , the idea that everything, including civil society to begin with, but really the whole

world, is organized according to geography. He thought in geographical terms, and the *Prison Notebooks* are a kind of *map of modernity*. They're not a history of modernity, but his notes really try to *place* everything, *like a military map; I means that there was always some struggle going on over territory. I think this is his single, most powerful idea.* (CI, 194–95; emphasis added, except *place*)

Said again attributes his understanding of imaginative geography to Gramsci, this time more fully, in the essay "History, Literature, and Geography," doing so to distinguish Gramsci's orientation toward being from those of his contemporaries, such as Lukacs, who were influenced by the Hegelian perspective, which overdetermined the language of temporality.[19] In an essay entitled "Foucault and the Imagination of Power," however, Said tellingly characterizes Foucault's theoretical/critical perspective in virtually the same terms he uses to characterize Gramsci's. Invoking the previously mentioned interview with the geographers of *Hérodote,* Said writes:

Thus Foucault's view of things was, as he implied to the journal *Hérodote* in 1976, spatial, which makes it somewhat easier to understand his predilection for the analysis of discontinuous but actual spaces, territories, domains, and sites—libraries, schools, hospitals, prisons—rather than, as one would expect in a historian, a tendency to talk principally about continuities, temporalities, and absences. It is probable that Foucault's admirably un-nostalgic view of history and the almost total lack in it of metaphysical yearning, such as one finds in heirs to the Hegelian tradition, are both ascribable to his geographical bent.[20]

Having brought out this similarity between Said's extraordinarily productive notion of imaginative geography and Foucault's strategic territorialization of the being of knowledge, I should add that in both the *boundary 2* interview and "History, Literature, and Geography," Said is not quite clear as to whether the Gramsci (or Foucault, for that matter) he is privileging is referring (as I think Foucault quite clearly is) to an imperial Western metaphysical perspective that reduces the differential temporal dynamics of being (and the finally undecidable knowledge of being) to a territory to be mastered or unwittingly representing being according to the imperatives of the metaphysical thinking he abhors. This ambiguity manifests itself in what Said goes on to say in the previously quoted interview:

All these things coalesce in Gramsci, and he gave them a quite startling formation, especially if you compare him with his contemporaries in Europe at the time, such as Lukacs and others [in "Literature, History, and Geography," these others include Erich Auerbach], who are in the Hegelian tradition, which is organized around a temporal scheme. The geographical, or spatial, scheme is quite a different one; the spatial is much more material. And Gramsci, you know better than anyone Joe, is really not interested in mediating, transmuting, overcoming and all those other Hegelian processes by which antinomies are somehow resolved, but he's really interested in actually working them out as discrepant realities physically, on the ground, where territory is the place you do it. (CI, 195; see also LH, 464–68)

Is the spatial orientation vis-à-vis the be-ing of being that Said attributes to Gramsci (and Foucault) the latter's own interpretation? Or is it his ironic recognition that the Hegelian tradition, which is "organized around a temporal scheme," in fact *obscures* its imperial spatialization/territorialization of temporality, its will to power over the differences of historicity? Is Gramsci's (and Foucault's) imaginative geography, that is, simply a reversal that, however critical of the imperial territorializing of Hegelian temporal metaphysics, nevertheless leaves it and the will to power it authorizes intact? Or is Gramsci, like Nietzsche and Foucault, in the manner of genealogy in the parodic mode, pushing the Hegelian territorializing logic informing his concept of temporality to the point where it self-destructs?

In "History, Literature, and Geography" Said comes closer to identifying Gramsci's geography with Foucault's Nietzschean exposure of the spatializing or territorializing of differential time concealed by the Hegelian overdetermination of the language of temporality. "We must remember," he says, "that most of Gramsci's terminology—hegemony, social territory, ensembles of relationship, intellectuals, civil and political society, emergent and traditional classes, territories, regions, domains, historical blocks—is what I would call a critical and geographical rather than an encyclopedic or totalizing nominative or systematic terminology" (HLG, 467). Above all, Said thinks that "Gramsci is interested in using terms for thinking about society and culture as productive activities occurring territorially, rather than as repositories of goods, ideas, traditions, institutions to be incorporated and reconcile correspondences" in the manner of the spatializing Hegelian temporal dialectic (HGL, 467). Gramsci's terms, he continues, "always depart from oppositions—mind vs matter, rulers vs ruled, theory vs praxis, intellectuals vs workers—*which are then contextualized, that is, they remain within contextual control, not the control of some hypostatized, outside force like identity or temporality which supposedly gives them their meaning by incorporating their differences into a larger identity*" (HGL 467; emphasis added; note that identity and temporality are contradictory categories if the latter is understood as ontological prior to a transcendental Origin]). Indeed, Said goes on to identify this anti-Hegelian Gramsci with Foucault: "Like Foucault after him Gramsci is interested in hegemony and power." Typically, however, he distinguishes them by attributing greater agency to Gramsci:

> But it is a much more subtle understanding [Gramsci] has of power than Foucault because it is never abstracted, or even discussed as abstracted from a particular social totality; unlike Foucault's, Gramsci's notion of power is neither occult nor irresistible and finally one-directional. The basic social contest for Gramsci is the one over hegemony, that is, the control of essentially heterogeneous, discontinuous, nonidentical, and *unequal* geographies of human habitation and effort. There is no redemption in Gramsci's world, which . . . is profoundly secular. (HLG, 467–68)

It should not be overlooked that, despite his initial affiliation of Gramsci and Foucault, Said in these last two sentences silently, and no doubt inadvertently, incorporates Foucault's thought—his fundamental commitment to the singularity of the event—into the Hegelian dialectic.

The issue at stake in all this is far too complicated to be dealt with in this limited space. Suffice it here to say this: the overdetermination of temporality in the discourse of the Hegelian tradition conceals *its fundamentally spatializing/territorializing function*—that it is the (metaphysical) Hegelian view of being that has represented time and the differences it disseminates (history) in the imaginary geographical terms in which modernity perceives it. To put this alternatively, Gramsci's overdetermination of spatial terms (geography) was intended to use this Hegelian "imagined geography," as Gramsci did with "Cuvier's little bones,"[21] against itself; that is, it was meant to expose the will to power over singularity (the "heterogeneous, discontinuous, nonidentitarian, and *unequal* geographies of human habitation and effort") that is endemic to this metaphysical view of being. In keeping with my argument in this book, then, I conclude that had Said clearly perceived the duplicity of this Hegelian temporal dialectic, he would have seen more consciously that Gramsci is not so much a counter to Foucault as a collaborative ally. Foucault emphasizes the pole of theory, whereas Gramsci emphasizes the pole of praxis, but they are both committed to the struggle against Hegelianism ("Lorianism" in Gramsci's terms) in its reduction of singularity to the same—that is, the struggle to think mind and matter, ruler and a rule, theory and praxis, and intellectual and worker not as binary opposites that eventually become reconciled in a higher (unworldly) synthesis but as always already belonging together in (productive) strife and therefore as worldly, open-ended.

In *Orientalism*, then, it is this version of anti-Hegelianism, common to both Gramsci and Foucault—this recognition that the Hegelian overdetermination of temporality constitutes an accommodation of its corrosive singularity to a transcendental, now projected in the more efficient economy of the classificatory table (or map)—that Said employs to characterize the third (modern) phase of the Orientalist vision of the Orient.

Early in *Orientalism*, Said, in keeping with the ontological/visual metaphorics informing the Western interpretation of being, refers in general to the spatialization of the Orient by the discourse of Orientalists as an imaginative geography and, more specifically, as a "field of study based on a geographical, cultural, linguistic, and ethnic unit called the Orient," emphasizing that "fields. . . are made. They acquire coherence and integrity in time because scholars devote themselves in different ways to what seems to be a commonly agreed-upon subject matter." To refer to scholarly specialization as a "geographical 'field,'" he writes,

> is, in the case of Orientalism, fairly revealing since no one is likely to imagine a field symmetrical to it called Occidentalism. Already the special, perhaps even eccentric attitude of Orientalism becomes apparent. For although many learned disciplines imply a position taken towards, say, *human* material (a historian deals with the human past from a special vantage point in the present), there is no real analogy for taking a fixed, more or less total geographical position towards a wide variety of social, linguistic, political, and historical realities. . . . But Orientalism is a field with considerable geographical ambition. And since Orientalists have traditionally occupied themselves with things Oriental . . . , we must learn to accept enormous, indiscriminate size plus an almost infinite capacity for subdivision as one of the chief characteristics of Orientalism—one that is evidenced in its confusing amalgam of imperial vagueness and precise detail. (*O,* 50)

In discussing the point when Orientalism becomes modern, however, a human science, as in the cases of the scholarship of Sacy, Renan, Massignon, Lane, Jones, and Gibb, Said uses a more specific language to characterize this imaginative geography, a language that, in its appeal to the structuring (territorializing) principles of the natural sciences—the attention to the smallest detail, comparison, classification, tabulation, and so on—is remarkably reminiscent of the language of tactics and strategy Foucault (and the geographers of *Hérodote*) uses to characterize the modern—and more economically and politically efficient—turn that the premodern spatialization of being takes.

Said inaugurates this crucial turning point in his text by distinguishing the Orientalism of the Christian medieval and Renaissance periods, "for which Islam was the essential Orient" (i.e., an Orientalism whose truth and judgments of the "Other" were determined by the visible theologos), from the broader, more inclusive "scientific" or "secular" Orientalism that was to come in the nineteenth century. In a manner reminiscent of Foucault's reference to the emergence of the disciplinary society in the Enlightenment in terms of a sudden take off, a hastening of evolution, a transformation that failed "to correspond to the calm, continuist image that is normally accredited," Said draws this distinction by invoking four major eighteenth-century momenta of modernization. The first of these initiatives lay in the opening out of the Orient "considerably beyond the Islamic lands" by way of "European exploration of the rest of the world (*O*, 117). The second emerged in the rise of comparative historiography, which, unlike earlier historiography that "judged the Orient inflexibly as an enemy," addressed "the Orient's peculiarities with some detachment and with some attempt at dealing directly with Oriental source material" (ibid.). The third momentum involved the rise of historicism, which, under the aegis of an emergent philology, a "veritable science of humanity" (*O*, 133) (exemplified by Vico, Herder, and Hamann) that enabled "objects" to "speak," i.e., disclose the *Logos* informing their differences (*O*, 140), exceeded "comparative study, and its judicious survey of mankind . . . by sympathetic identification" (*Einfühlung*) (*O*, 118). Finally, the fourth lay in the sudden emergence of the "impulse to classify nature and man into types":

> The greatest names are, of course, Linnaeus and Buffon, but the intellectual process by which bodily (and soon moral, intellectual, and spiritual) extension—the typical materiality of an object—could be transformed from a mere spectacle to the precise measurement of characteristic elements was widespread. . . . In natural history, in anthropology, in cultural generalization, a type had a particular *character* which provided the observer with a designation and, as Foucault says, "a controlled derivation." These types and characters belonged to a system, a network, of related generalizations. (*O*, 119)

These four historical initiatives of modernity—"expansion, historical confrontation, sympathy, classification"—Said goes on, "are the currents in eighteenth-century thought on whose presence the specific intellectual and institutional structures of modern Orientalism depend." Above all, they were secularizing currents that, like those Foucault invokes to demonstrate the obsolescence of the ancien régime's power relations, "had the effect of releasing the Orient in general and Islam in particular from the narrowly religious scrutiny by which it had hitherto been examined (and judged) by the Christian West" (*O*, 120). The geographic and historical extension of the Orient to include India, China, and Japan "temporally loosened, even dissolved, the Biblical framework considerably." The philological/historicist initiative enabled perceiving a non-European and non-Judeo-Christian cul-

ture "historically (and not reductively, as a topic of ecclesiastical politics."
The new willingness to (selectively) identify other "regions and cultures not
one's own wore down the obduracy of self and identity, which had been po-
larized into a community of embattled believers facing barbarian hordes."
Finally, the classificatory initiative "systematically multiplied" and "refined"
"the possibilities of designation and derivation" of humankind far beyond
the prior reductive categories endemic to the older theological perspective:
"race, color, origin, temperament, character, and types [now] overwhelmed
the distinction between Christians and everyone else" (*O*, 120).

This momentous shift of the Orientalist vision from heaven to earth,
from the Word of the priest (the spokesperson of God) to the Word of the
scientist (the spokesperson for Man)—and the accompanying emphasis
on accounting for the minutest details of the phenomena of the Orient—
resulted, of course, in the attribution of objectivity and disinterestedness to
the new Orientalism and its findings. Despite this increasingly differentiated
and differentiating secularizing momentum, however, Said (and this takes
us back to my argument about the enormous, if subdued, importance of the
ontological register of his genealogical critique) emphatically shows that the
new, modern Orientalist scholarship of Sacy, Renan, Lane, Jones, Gibb, and
the others whose texts he analyzes remained tethered to a transcendental
(and panoptic) principle. Just as Foucault had argued that we moderns
who would be free from the constraints of power "need to cut off the King's
head; in political theory that has still to be done,"[22] so Said insistently reminds us that modernity's secularization of the West's perspective on the
Orient was not a radical break with the metaphysical or providential view
of history. Rather, he says that despite appearances, this secular humanism
remained a determinative otherworldly worldly practice, what, borrowing
from M. H. Abrams's sympathetic interpretation of the Romantic period,
he calls a "natural supernaturalism":

> But if these interconnected elements represent a secularizing tendency, this is
> not to say that old religious patterns of human history and destiny and "the
> existential paradigms" were simply removed. Far from it: they were resitu-
> ated, redeployed, redistributed in the secular frameworks just enumerated.
> For anyone who studied the Orient a secular vocabulary in keeping with these
> frameworks was required. Yet if Orientalism provided the vocabulary, the con-
> ceptual repertoire, the techniques—for this is what, from the end of the eigh-
> teenth century, Orientalism *did* and what Orientalism *was*—it also retained,
> as an undislodged current in its discourse, a reconstructed religious impulse,
> a natural supernaturalism. (*O*, 120–21)

To put it in the Foucauldian terms I used in chapter 1 to demonstrate the continuity in difference of the Christian and modern periods—the eras of the theologos and the anthropologos—Orientalism as a field of knowledge became, with the advent of modernity, a highly sophisticated *anthropology* that rendered its premodern counterpart obsolete. In securalizing the Word of God and then, with the prosthetic instruments that the disciplinary technology of the empirical sciences enabled, internalizing and distributing this centralized Logos throughout the world's body, this anthropology was enabled to transform the visible and thus politically uneconomical negatively oriented will to power of premodern Orientalism into a "productive" ("creative") instrument of (invisible) power:

> The modern Orientalist was, in his view, a hero rescuing the Orient from the obscurity, alienation, and strangeness which he himself had properly distinguished. His research reconstructed the Orient's lost languages, mores, even mentalities, as Champollion reconstructed Egyptian hieroglyphics out of the Rosetta Stone. The specific Orientalist techniques—lexicography, grammar, translation, cultural decoding—restored, fleshed out, reasserted the values both of an ancient, classical Orient and of the traditional disciplines of philology, history, rhetoric, and doctrinal polemic. But in the process, the Orient and Orientalist disciplines changed dialectically, *for they could not survive in their original form.* The Orient, even in the "classic" form which the Orientalist usually studied, was modernized, restored to the present; the traditional disciplines too were brought into contemporary culture. *Yet both bore the traces of* power—*power to have resurrected, indeed, created, the Orient,* power that dwelt in the new, scientifically advanced techniques of philology and of anthropological generalization. In short, having transported the Orient into modernity, the Orientalist could celebrate his method, and his position, as that of a secular creator, a man who made new worlds as God had made the old. As for carrying on such methods and such positions beyond the life-span of any individual Orientalist, there would be a secular tradition of continuity, a lay order of disciplined methodologists, whose brotherhood would be based, not on blood lineage, but upon a common discourse, a praxis, a library, a set of received ideas, in short, a doxology common to everyone who entered the ranks. (*O,* 121; emphasis added)

As Said goes on to show in his brilliant readings of a number of modern Orientalists, this highly differentiated and "constantly refined" (*O,* 215) natural supernaturalism—this anthropology that accommodates difference to the larger whole, or in Foucault's version, territorializes being, renders everything and every time in the world accountable to the invisible Word of Man—pervades more than just the fixed and conservative "latent" Orientalism of writers such as T. E. Lawrence and imperialist administrators such as Curzon and Cromer.[23] It pervades as well the more progressive, explorative and productive—"manifest"—Orientalism of the scholarly guild (Sacy, Renan, Lane, etc.) that, in addressing the realities of the Orient from a secular, empirical scientific perspective, codified and institutionalized Orientalism as an academic discipline. This highly differentiated, efficient, and productive natural supernaturalism—and its affiliation with Foucault's genealogy of the modern disciplinary society—is especially evident, as I have noted in passing, in Said's analysis of what he appropriately calls the "rational anthropology" (*O*, 123) of the scholarly Orientalist discourse of Sylvestre de Sacy, one of the founders of modern Orientalism. Said's analysis highlights the dominant role that the spatializing, comparativist classificatory system of the emergent natural sciences played in territorializing the various and dynamic lives of the people of the Orient, that is, in both the discursive and political occupation of the living Orient. I am referring particularly to the notion of the tableau vivant, the schema that, from an internalized transcendental perspective, coerces the differential phenomena of being into taking their "proper place" in a sealed off, totalized field. Summarizing the essential characteristics of Sacy's *Chrestomathy arabe* (published in three volumes between 1806 and 1827) by way of its influence on Joseph Daciers's report, *Tableau historique de l'érudition française,* on "the state and progress of the arts and sciences since 1789," commissioned by Napoleon, Said writes:

The importance of the *Tableau historique* for an understanding of [modern] Orientalism's inaugural phase is that it exteriorizes the form of Orientalist knowledge and its features, as it also describes the Orientalist's relationship to his subject matter. In Sacy's pages on Orientalism—as elsewhere in his writing— he speaks of his own work as having *uncovered, brought to light, rescued* a vast amount of obscure matter. Why? In order *to place it before* the student. For like all his learned contemporaries Sacy considered a learned work a positive addition to an edifice that all scholars erected together. Knowledge was essentially the *making visible* of material, and the aim of a tableau was the construction of a sort of Benthamite Panopticon. Scholarly discipline was therefore a specific technology of power: it gained for its use (and his students) tools and knowledge which (if he was a historian) had hitherto been lost.

. . . Like his colleagues in other fields [the Hellenists and Latinists "working on the Institut team"] he believed that knowledge is seeing—pan-optically, so to speak—but unlike them he not only had to identify the knowledge, he had to decipher it, interpret it, and most difficult, make it available. *Sacy's achievement was to have produced a whole field. As a European he ransacked the Orientalist archives, and he could do so without leaving France.* What texts he isolated, he then brought back; he doctored them; then he annotated, codified, arranged, and commented on them. In time, the Orient as such became less important than what the Orientalist made of it; thus, drawn by Sacy into this sealed discursive space of a pedagogical tableau, the Orientalist's Orient was thereafter reluctant to emerge into reality. (*O*, 127–28; emphasis added in second paragraph)

Much more could be said about Said's analysis of this highly differentiated and (politically) productive natural supernatural initiative of the modern Orientalist. For the sake of economy, however, I will bring my analysis of this third phase of Orientalism's historical itinerary to a close by briefly invoking Said's brilliant critical reading of the great French humanist Ernest Renan, who from his "laboratory" brought Sacy's archival Orientalism to its fulfillment through a secular philology harnessed to the structuralizing or territorializing imperatives of "objective" science. In inaugurating his account of Renan's Orientalism—he focuses his scathing criticism on *Histoire générale et système comparé des langues sémitiques*—Said stresses Renan's typically nineteenth-century loss of faith in the Christian Logos as a means of interpreting human history and his consequent adoption in 1845 of a "life of scholarship," namely, "his initiation into philology," that is, a secular, scientific perspective. Said also observes, however, that "in his life [Renan] determined to be as Christian as he once was, only now without Christianity and with what he called 'la science laïque' (lay science) of philology." What Renan meant by this philological lay science was, according to Said, made manifest in the former's lecture at the Sorbonne in 1878, "On the Services Rendered by Philology to the Historical Sciences," where Renan represented philology as a mode of inquiry that, "like religion, teaches us about the origins of humanity, civilization, and language," but as "a comparative discipline," doing so in a manner "far less coherent, less knitted together and positive" (more attentive to the differential complexities of these origins) than was Christian exegesis (*O*, 134–35):

> Since Renan was irremediably historical . . . , it stood to reason that the only way in which . . . he could move out of religion into philological scholarship was to retain in the new lay science the historical world-view he had gained from religion. Hence, "one occupation alone seemed to me to be worthy of filling my life; and that was to pursue my critical research into Christianity [an allusion to Renan's major scholarly project on the origins and history of Christianity] using those far ampler means offered me by lay science." Renan had assimilated himself to philology according to his own post-Christian fashion. (*O*, 135)

According to Said, by speaking of this secular philology, Renan, it is important to emphasize, was referring to a "new" human science that emerged with the rise of a secularized modernity and the delegitimation of the earlier interpretation of history, whose Origin and authorization lay in the transcendental Christian Logos. More specifically, he was referring to the linguistic allotrope of the emergent comparativist method of inquiry and the spatializing classificatory system it enabled. "Whenever 'philology' is spoken of around the end of the eighteenth century and the beginning of the nineteenth," Said writes, "we are to understand the *new* philology, whose major successes include comparative grammar, the reclassification of languages into families, and the final rejection of the divine origins of language" in favor of "a view that held language to be an entirely human phenomenon." Said then adds, "what [Foucault] called the discovery of language was therefore a secular event that displaced a religious conception of how God delivered language to man in Eden. Indeed, one of the consequences of this change, by which an etymological, dynastic notion of linguistic filiation was pushed aside by the view of language [of such diverse figures as William Jones and Franz Bopp] as a domain all of its own held together with jagged internal structures and coherences, is the dramatic subsidence of interest in the problem of the origins of language" (*O*, 135).

Said observes that the legacy of these early modern philologists, especially its pertinence to the origins and history of language, was far more important to Renan than was Sacy's legacy. First, this "new" comparativist philology allowed Renan to displace the Christian Logos, for the West's expanding horizons meant that the Logos, which ordered and hierarchized the world in a crude binary opposition between the Christian West and Islamic East, could no longer maintain its authority. Further, in naturalizing the supernatural—in assuming, in other words, that an Origin or principle of presence *inheres in the secular world* (a protolanguage, "Sanskrit in its earliest Indo-European form" [*O*, 137]), as opposed to God's all too visibly reductive transcendental Word (Hebrew)—this modern, anthropological science of philology also enabled Renan to achieve the same perennially desired end—the West's domination of the Orient—but with far more authority and efficiency than its visibly reductive earlier theological counterpart could wield. More specifically, the new comparative and hierarchical philology, which in Foucauldian fashion Said insistently identifies with the "comparative philosophical anatomy" of Cuvier and Geoffroy Saint-Hilaire (*O*, 142), permitted Renan both to take into account the great variety of human languages and cultures in the name of scientific objectivity and, via the discriminating technology of classification, to privilege the "vital" and "organic" languages and cultures of Europe against the "decadent" and "inorganic" Semitic languages and cultures of the Orient—and do this without rendering his discourse, unlike the premodern Christian binary, vulnerable to accusations of religious and racist prejudice. Paralleling Foucault in *The Order of Things,* where he uses his "analytic of finitude" to show that anthropological Man recuperates the Origin he rejects, Said sees Renan's secular philological strategy as "a return to the Origin"—to, in Foucault's word in "Nietzsche, Genealogy, History," a "suprahistorical" ontology—in the very process of rejecting it. Reading his "productive" philological strategy (Said calls it "creative") against the grain, Said discloses not only Renan's utter indifference to the existential realities of the languages and cultures he would bring to presence in his "laboratory"— that is, his complete reliance for his evidence on the European Orientalist archive—but also the arrogant racism and imperial will to power that lie behind his supposedly objective conclusions:

> Thus for Renan Semitic is a phenomenon of arrested development in comparison with the mature languages and cultures of the Indo-European group, and even with the other Semitic Oriental languages. The paradox that Renan sustains, however, is that even as he encourages us to see languages as in some way corresponding to "êtres vivants de la nature [living beings of nature]," he is everywhere else proving that his Orientalist languages, the Semitic languages, are inorganic, arrested, totally ossified, incapable of self-regeneration; in other words, he proves that Semitic is not a live language, and for that matter, neither are Semites live creatures. Moreover, Indo-European language and culture are alive and organic *because* of the laboratory, not despite it. But far from being a marginal issue in Renan's work, this paradox stands, I believe, at the center of his entire work, his style, and his archival existence in the culture of his time, a culture to which . . . he was a very important contributor. To be able to sustain a vision that incorporates and holds together life and quasi-living creatures (Indo-European, European culture) as well as quasi-monstrous, parallel inorganic phenomena (Semitic, Oriental culture) is precisely the achievement of the European scientist in his laboratory. He *constructs,* and the very act of construction is a sign of imperial power over recalcitrant phenomena, as well as a confirmation of the dominating culture and its "naturalization." Indeed, it is not too much to say that Renan's philological laboratory is the actual locale of his European ethnocentrism; but what needs emphasis here is that the philological laboratory has no existence outside the discourse, the writing by which it is constantly produced and experienced. Thus even the culture he calls organic and alive—Europe's—is also a *creature being created* in the laboratory of philology. (*O*, 145–46)[24]

In this reading of the third phase of Said's history of the Orientalism, I have emphasized, against far too many commentaries on *Orientalism,* his insistently made distinction between, on the one hand, an earlier mode of knowledge production about the Orient that in being tethered to the Origin, the reductive transcendental—and visible—theologos, was rendered vulnerable to criticism or resistance and, on the other, a later, modern Orientalism that in secularizing the transcendental Logos enabled it to appear as the disinterested truth and thus minimized the possibility of criticism or resistance. My intention has been to show that Said's reading of this third, post-Napoleonic phase of the history of Orientalism is remarkably analogous to Foucault's reading of the transformation of knowledge/power relations that occurred with the advent of modernity. It reveals the territorializing logic of Orientalism not only as arriving at its penultimate stage of development but also as manifesting itself as a mode of knowledge production about the Orient that—just as, according to Foucault, knowledge production in the disciplinary society did in replacing that of the ancien régime—reverses the original subordination of knowledge to power (as in the case of the relationship between Napoleon's occupying military army and his army of savants). This Orientalism, that is, renders power invisible and thus (theoretically) invulnerable to criticism or resistance.

In the fourth phase of his genealogy, in which America replaces Europe as the arbiter of knowledge concerning global space, Said ostensibly intends to characterize Orientalism in terms of the fulfillment of it imperial logic. I find this to be the least satisfactory aspect of his book, not simply because it generally lacks the coherence of his analysis of the first three phases, but also because it is informed by two apparently conflicting initiatives, one, as noted, intent on characterizing the completion of the Orientalist project and the other pointing to a crisis that threatens its hegemony, that is, that symptomatically intuits its self-destruction and the collapse of the Orientalist edifice. I will begin by commenting on the first and then turn to the second to suggest a reading of this intuition of crisis that renders it the prelude to the thematics of *Culture and Imperialism.*

Under the aegis of American "realism," the period of this final phase in Said's genealogy witnessed the "rigorous" philological science of erudite European Orientalists transformed into crude expertise, a calculative mode of late modern (or postmodern?) knowledge production about America's "Others" that is deliberately deployed to "authorize" and "manage" preconceived state-sponsored ideological scenarios about particular (local) crises of imperial command in the "Third World," for example, the Arab-Israeli war of 1967 or the oil boycott of 1973–74. The function of the Orientalist as an adviser to imperial governments was, according to Said, always an aspect of modern philological Orientalism. Now, however, following the rise to global hegemony of a pragmatic democratic (i.e., exceptionalist, though Said does not use the word) America—and the globalization of the American media—it has become a matter of strategy (*O,* 295). Whereas the science of the great European Orientalist scholars who advised imperial nations was characterized by an awesome erudition and scientific rigor—a philological erudition and rigor given to close "disinterested" examination of the details of near and remote literary, cultural, linguistic, theological, and political documents—the weightiness of which obscured these nations' imperial, racist, and disciplinary projects, the "science" of American Orientalists became a matter of "factuality" (*O,* 291): a facile discipline, intellectually narrow in scope, non-philological, instrumentalist, indeed, "propagandist," the strategic instrument of "some policy objective" (*O,* 295). In other words, the putative objectivity and disinterestedness of the American Orientalist were authorized not by erudite scholarship but by the "self-evident" worth of "American democracy." Said discusses this immediately following his demonstration of the relationship between the vulgar popular American view of the Arab disseminated for the media (journalism, cinema, television) following the United States' rise to superpower status after World War II and the view of American academia as evidenced in the report "produced in 1967 at the behest of the Department of Health, Education, and Welfare by Morroe Berger, a professor of sociology and Near Eastern Studies at Princeton and president of the Middle East Studies Association.":

> I mention Berger as an instance of the academic attitude towards the Islamic Orient, an instance of how a learned perspective can support the caricatures propagated in the popular culture. Yet Berger stands also for the most current transformation overtaking Orientalism: its conversion from a fundamentally philological discipline and a vaguely general apprehension of the Orient into a social science specialty. No longer does an Orientalist try first to master the esoteric languages of the Orient; he begins instead as a trained social scientist and "applies" his science to the Orient or anywhere elsewhere. This is the specifically American contribution to the history of Orientalism, and it can be dated roughly from the period immediately following World War II, when the United States found itself in the position recently vacated by Britain and France. . . . [Earlier] there was no deeply invested tradition of Orientalism, and consequently in the United States knowledge of the Orient never passed through the refining and reticulating and reconstructive processes, whose beginning was in philological study, that it went through in Europe. Furthermore, the imaginative investment was never made either, perhaps because the American frontier, the one that counted, was the westward one. Immediately after World War II, then, the Orient became, not a broad catholic issue as it had been for centuries in Europe, *but an administrative one, a matter of policy. Enter the social*

scientist and the expert, on whose somewhat narrower shoulders was to fall the
mantle of Orientalism. (O, 290; emphasis added)

With the postwar rise of the national security state, then, this Orientalism
of the expert came to preside over the "entire vast apparatus for research on
the Middle East," which at the same time retained "in most of its general
as well as its detailed functioning, the traditional outlook which had been
developed in Europe" (*O*, 295). It informed the research ethos of the Middle
East Institute, which was "founded in 1946 in Washington under the aegis of,
if not entirely within or by, the federal government." This institution, "both
in its frankly strategic attitude and in its sensitivity to public security and
policy (not, as is often postured, to pure scholarship)," became the model of
Orientalist research in America: "Out of such organizations grew the Middle
East Studies Association, the powerful support of the Ford and other foundations, the various federal programs of support to universities, the various
federal research projects, research projects carried out by such entities as the
Defense Department, the RAND Corporation, the Hudson Institute, and the
consultative and lobbying efforts of banks, oil companies, multinationals, and
the like" (*O*, 295). It is this facile yet, thanks to the American "culture industry,"
powerfully persuasive Orientalism of the expert in all its permutations, from
the hard to the soft, from Gustave von Grunebaum and Bernard Lewis to
Leonard Binder, Henry Kissinger, and Samuel P. Huntington, that Said was to
brilliantly excoriate in his books, following *Orientalism*, devoted to America's
representation of the Orient, most notably *Covering Islam* (1981; rev. ed., 1997),
After the Last Sky (1986), and *The End of the Peace Process* (2000).[25]

In all this, Said tends to overdetermine the aspect of Orientalism that
justifies the West's superiority over the Orient rather than, as in the case of
the third phase, its disciplinary function, which is Foucault's focus. At the
same time, as I have noted, his account of this "latest [American] phase" of
Orientalism appears to be contaminated by a second motif that strangely
contradicts the affirmations about the first disciplinary momentum: the intuition that this discourse of expertise faces a crisis threatening its authority.
This symptomatic recognition is evident in Said's insistent reference to the
"new eccentricity in Orientalism," pointing out that his "use of the word itself
is anomalous. For there is little in what academic experts on the Near East
do now that resembles traditional Orientalism of the sort that ended with
Gibb and Massignon; the main things that are reproduced are . . . a certain
cultural hostility and a sense based not so much on philology as on 'expertise'" (*O*, 291). It is further evident, Said adds, in the last phase's crude facility:
its reduction of modern Orientalism's resonant philological perspective and

consequent persuasive force to the discourse of facticity (*O*, 291); of scholarly erudition and its "disinterested" research to a monolithic instrument of state ideology; and of global scope to the management of practical local crises (*O*, 324). In other words, Said's genealogy of Orientalism seems to culminate in an irresolvable ambivalence. On the one hand, he speaks of the fulfillment of the "productive" logic of Orientalism, and on the other, he points to the symptoms of its demise, that is, to a weightlessness that renders visible the power that was previously embedded in and thus theoretically invulnerable to resistance by minds that the earlier Orientalism had hitherto colonized.

If, however, we think this ambivalence on the analogy of Heidegger's resonant Nietzschean paradox, which, in opposition to Hegel's dialectics of the *Aufhebung,* announces "the end of philosophy" at the end of modernity, we can entertain a perspective that reconciles this ambivalence. As I discussed in chapter 2, in speaking of the end of history Heidegger is referring to an epochal paradox: at the moment when the binary logic of metaphysics achieves its fulfillment, when Western ocularcentric thought has transformed the differential dynamics of temporality into a totalized spatial/territorialized "age of the world picture," it self–de-structs, comes to its end in the sense of reaching its demise. For it is when this metaphysical view achieves its fulfillment as strategic world picture that it discloses, brings to visibility (against itself), the ineffable and unpresentable nothing (*das Nichts*) that belongs to and has always haunted this tradition's anxious obsession to reduce difference to identity, the nothing to something, the many to the one. To put this epochal disclosure in terms of Althusser's retrieval of the antimetaphysical Marx from the Hegelian tradition in the late 1960s, what occurs at this culminating moment—at this limit situation—is a "change of terrain" that estranges the world territorialized and naturalized by the panoptic eye, transforms the homeland into a not-at-home, *die unheimliche Welt.*

This self–de-struction of the humanist perspective's "oversight," moreover, along with the changed terrain it precipitated in late modernity, was not restricted to the Western philosophical tradition. Concomitantly and significantly, the adjacent field of literary production witnessed the emergence of a postmodern literature that, in response to this collapse, rejected the Western model established by Aristotle's privileging of narrative, the circular/spatializing structure of beginning, middle, end. Indeed, this antimetaphysical postmodern writing may well have inaugurated the revolution in German thought that came to be called "Continental theory"—Heidegger, Jaspers, the Frankfurt school (especially Horkheimer and Adorno), Benjamin, Lukacs, Kojève, and Arendt—which in turn, especially through the Heidegger of *Being and Time,* instigated the poststructuralist momentum in France: Derrida, Lacan, Lyotard, Althusser, Foucault, and Kristeva. This postmodern literary witness to the changed terrain, it is worth noting, was epitomized, though on a different tonal register, by Samuel Beckett in his great novel *Watt* when, early in this antinarrative, his antiheroic protagonist experiences a decentering estrangement of the familiar world—an unhoming, as it were—that would henceforth render the absent nothing a haunting, unspeakable presence, especially after he enters the appropriately named house of Knott:

> Where was I? The change. In what did it consist? It is hard to say. Something slipped. There I was, warm and bright, smoking my tobacco-pipe, watching the warm bright wall, when suddenly somewhere some little thing slipped, some little tiny thing. Gliss—iss—iss—STOP! I trust I make myself clear. . . . It was a slip like that I felt, that Tuesday afternoon, millions of little things moving all together out of their old place, into a new one nearby, and furtively, as though it were forbidden. And I have little doubt that I was the only person living to discover them. To conclude from this that the incident was internal would, I think, be rash. For my—how shall I say?— my personal system was so distended at the period of which I speak that the distinction between what was inside it and what was outside it was not at all easy to draw. Everything that happened happened inside it, and at the same time everything that happened happened outside it. I trust I make myself plain. I did not, need I add, see the thing happen, nor hear it, but I perceived it with a perception so sensuous that in comparison the impressions of a man buried alive in Lisbon on Lisbon's great day seem a frigid and artificial construction of the understanding. The sun on the wall, since I was looking at the sun on the wall at the time, underwent an instantaneous and I venture to say radical change of appearance. It was the same sun and the same wall, or so little older that the difference may safely be disregarded, but so changed that I felt I had been transported, without my having remarked it, to some quite different yard, and to some quite different season, in an unfamiliar country. At the same time my tobacco-pipe, since I was not eating a banana, ceased so completely from the solace to which I was inured, that I took it out of my mouth to make sure it was not a thermometer, or an epileptic's dental wedge. . . . But in what did the change *consist*? What was changed, and how? What was changed, if my information is correct, was the sentiment that a change, other than a change of degree, had taken place. What was changed was existence off the ladder. Do not come down the ladder, Ifor, I haf taken it away. This I am happy to inform you is the reversed metamorphosis. The Laurel into Daphne.[26]

I have quoted Beckett at length not simply to convey the aura of the changed terrain precipitated by the self-destruction of the metaphysical/visualist logic of the West in late modernity but also to recall what too many of Said's recent commentators, especially those postcolonial critics who have identified him and his criticism with Arab nationalism, have forgotten: the deterritorialized terrain—in which he (like those of us in the Western world who, in the 1960s and early 1970s, had crossed over the Modernist boundary into the new terra incognita) found himself at the time he was writing *Orientalism*. In worrying the *aporia*—"the eccentricity"—disclosed by the fulfillment of Orientalism's logic in American expertise, Said, like postmodern writers such as Samuel Beckett and thinkers such as Heidegger, the German Continental theorists, and the French poststructuralists, is symptomatically intuiting the self-destruction of the West's founding binarist logic and the implications of this epochal event: the estrangement of the world territorialized by the metaphysical eye—the changed terrain—on the one hand and, on the other, the potential release of the Oriental "Other" from the bondage of Western discursive and political domination.

In *Orientalism,* as many of his commentators have observed, Said overdetermines the discourse of Orientalism and the discursive/political domination it enabled. Indeed, he says almost nothing about the history of resistance to Western domination, whether theoretical or practical, by the indigenous people of the East (the "writing back" of Albert Memmi, George Antonius, S. H. Atalas, Mohandas Gandhi, and Ranajit Guha, for example) or Africa (Frantz Fanon, C. L. R. James, George Padmore, and Aimé Césaire) or the tremendous significance of the Sepoy Rebellion of 1859 in India, the Algerian Revolution of 1954–62, and the South African antiapartheid movement in the last decades of twentieth century, to invoke the most obvious of many instances. Nor does he refer to his exilic (unhomed) predicament that, soon after *Orientalism,* would become a fundamental factor of his oppositional persona. These "lacks" could be interpreted, as Said himself has done on occasion, as his testament to the inordinately effective power of the discourse of Orientalism or as his refusal to posit a "real" Orient (or Occident) beyond his assertion of the variety and plurality of cultures that resist easy fixation. What I am suggesting, however, is that at this early stage in his rethinking of the Western representation of the Orient, Said had not arrived at the point where he thought of himself consciously as an exile—a Palestinian émigré— and, more broadly, of the ways in which the fulfillment and self-destruction of Orientalist discourse might affect resistance to the Occident's cultural and political domination.[27] Instigated in part by poststructuralist thinkers such as Gilles Deleuze, Félix Guattari, and Paul Virilio, as well as his awakening to his exilic condition in the wake of the Arab-Israeli War of 1967, a recognition of this possibility, which flickers in the corner of his eye, will come into focus in the fifteen-year interval between *Orientalism* and *Culture and Imperialism*. As I will show in the next chapter, it then became the supreme theme of his future forays into the indirect ravages of Western and especially American neocolonialism—and the untraditional discursive and political opposition that the fulfillment of Orientalism's logic enabled.

4. *Culture and Imperialism*

The Specter of Empire

It is therefore, a source of great virtue for the practiced mind to learn, bit by bit, first to change about in visible and transitory things, so that afterwards it may be able to leave them behind altogether. The person who finds his homeland sweet is still a tender beginner; he to whom every soil is as his native one is already strong; but he is perfect to whom the entire world is as a foreign place. The tender soul has fixed his love on one spot in the world; the strong person has extended his love to all places; the perfect man has extinguished his.

—Hugo of St. Victor (qtd. in Edward Said, *Culture and Imperialism*)

Il n'est point vrai que l'oeuvre de l'homme est finie
que nous n'avons rien à faire au monde
que nous parasitons le monde
qu'il suffit que nous nous mettions au pas du monde
mais l'oeuvre de l'homme vient seulment de commencer
et il reste à l'homme a conquérir toute interdiction
immobilisée aux coins de sa ferveur et aucune race
ne possède le monopole de la beauté, de l'intelligence, de la force

et il est place pour tous au rendez-vous de la conquête

—Aimé Césaire, *Cahier d'un retour*

He wrote a long tract about it presently, called *On Preterition*. It was published in England, and is among the first books to've been not only banned but also ceremoniously burned in Boston. Nobody wanted to hear about all the Preterite, the many God passes over when he chooses a few for salvation. William argued holiness for these "second Sheep," without whom there'd be no elect. You can bet the Elect in Boston were pissed off about that. . . . Could he have been the fork in the road America never took, the singular point she jumped the wrong way from? Suppose the Slothropite heresy had had time to consolidate and prosper? . . . It seemed to Tyrone Slothrop that there might be a route back—maybe that anarchist he met in Zurich was right, maybe for a little while all the fences are down, one road as good as another,

the whole space of the Zone cleared, depolarized, and somewhere
inside the waste of it a single set of coordinates from which to
proceed, without elect, without preterite, without even nationality
to fuck it up.
—Thomas Pynchon, *Gravity's Rainbow*

Strangely, Edward Said's magisterial book *Culture and Imperialism* has not
received even remotely the kind of attention that *Orientalism* has had ever
since its publication in 1978. This is in part, no doubt, because *Orientalism* was
a groundbreaking book that, in its powerful de-struction of the Occident's
polyvalent truth discourse about the Orient, rendered it no longer possible for
Westerners—scholars, intellectuals, public officials, and ordinary people—to
perceive the Orient according to the representational imperatives of the binarist logic that, as I have shown, is intrinsic to the very idea of the Occident.
Since its publication, *Orientalism* has instigated a revolution in literary and
cultural studies and the production of an archive called postcolonialism,
whose texts, whether sympathetic to or critical of their origin, bear (paradoxical) witness to its virtually scriptural status. Coming in the aftermath of
the critical revolution, *Culture and Imperialism* has implicitly been seen as at
best simply a development and refinement of its predecessor's argument, one
that, responding to the criticism of the scholars and critics Said had enabled,
made up in some degree for his "failure" in *Orientalism* to attend to the voices
of the very world he was retrieving from the Orientalist gaze.

I suggest, however, not against this too obvious interpretation of the reception of *Culture and Imperialism* but in marked addition to it, that the
primary reason many of the book's commentators viewed it as secondary to
Orientalism concerns Said's *apparent* indifference to narrative: *Culture and
Imperialism* displays a more or less episodic, often digressive, and even erratic
structure, in marked contrast to the undeviatingly sustained story Said tells
about the history of the Occident's relationship to the Orient in *Orientalism*.
This is not so much a consciously articulated judgment as a symptomatic one
in that, as far as I can tell, there has been no sustained analysis of the book in
its entirety; rather, we have a multitude of commentaries—often very percep-
tive ones—that focus, on the one hand, on specific episodes such as Said's
brilliant critical studies of Joseph Conrad's *Heart of Darkness,* Jane Austen's
Mansfield Park, Giuseppi Verdi's *Aïda,* Rudyard Kipling's *Kim,* E. M. Forster's
Passage to India, and Camus's *L'Étranger* and, on the other, on his positive
analysis of works by postcolonial critics of imperialism such as Frantz Fanon,
C. L. R. James, George Antonius, S. H. Alatas, and Ranajit Guha. None of
these connections attends in any substantial way to the relationship between
these episodes and the structure of *Culture and Imperialism* as a whole.

In this chapter I examine the apparently errant structure of *Culture and Imperialism*; in so doing I suggest, against the implicit indifference to its formal characteristics and the negative judgment this indifference perhaps implies, not simply that it is a carefully structured book but also, and more important, that its deep structure, which Said characterizes as "contrapuntal," on the analogy with Bach's polyphonic compositions, *enacts* its very content. Following the directives of counterpoint as applied to secular history—that not just one (the West's) but "many voices" produce history[1]—the structure of *Culture and Imperialism* discloses two momenta in particular. First, it reveals the process wherein the "Other" of (i.e., that belongs to) empire gradually and inevitably impinges—initially as an idea and then in the form of living bodies—on the collective consciousness of the imperial metropolitan culture, becoming a dislocating spectral anxiety to the colonizing power, which in its prime understood the colonial project and its distant victims as the natural consequences of being Western (especially British). Second, it uncovers the analogous gradual but inevitable emergence of the exilic, migrant, or nomadic intellectual as the positive organic consciousness of the deracinated and destabilizing multitude precipitated by imperialism's own (onto)logical economy and political practice—its Eurocentrism.

∗ ∗ ∗

To undertake the itinerary of this contrapuntal structure economically—and at the risk of oversimplification—I will focus primarily on Said's interrogations of the canonical and synecdochic British novels (and other European texts, such as Verdi's *Aïda*) that follow his preparatory discussion of "narrative and social space" in Joseph Conrad's *Heart of Darkness* (to which I will return later).[2] These interrogations constitute the first phase of the deep structure of *Culture and Imperialism*, which extends from Jane Austen's "insular" *Mansfield Park* (1814) to Rudyard Kipling's more globally oriented *Kim* (1901), and reflect the historical momentum of British imperialism from its inaugural stage, epitomized by distanced plantations in the West Indies, to its most "mature phase" (*CI*, 133), epitomized by its immediate administrative rule over India, "the greatest, most durable, and most profitable of all British, perhaps even European, colonial possessions" (*CI*, 133).

Again, Said's intervention takes the form of a sustained contrapuntal reading of these novels—more specifically, of the "structure of attitudes" or "structures of reference"[3] informing their rhetoric about geographical space and historical time. Said reads this cultural history from the perspective of one of imperialism's victims, the outside insider who has educated himself in the history and culture of his adopted Western "homeland." By using this sustained inside/outside contrapuntal perspective—his a-partness, as it were—Said intends to demonstrate more than, as he has been commonly assumed to have done, merely the general complicity of the British novel with the British imperial project or the development of this complicity from an unconscious and invisible one (as in the case of Jane Austen) to a conscious and visible one (as in the case of Kipling). He further intends—and this is, above all, what the commentaries on *Cultural Imperialism* have missed—to disclose the incredible *remoteness*, both spatial and psychological, that separates the human victims of the imperial project from the consciousnesses of these otherwise sensitive and discriminating creative artists, which in turn allows him to reveal the utter indifference to the violence perpetrated on the subjected peoples—the unending bodily suffering, the mental anguish— that was the necessary malignant imperative and consequence of what the dominant imperial culture represented as the great achievement of British civilization. In other words, it is also Said's intention, to invoke Hannah Arendt's apt phrase, to foreground the banality of the evil of the thinking and practice of Western imperialism.

Deeply inscribed by a national hegemonic discourse that privileged the virtues of at-homeness, order, rationality, economy, administrative efficiency, and so on, Jane Austen, writing at the beginning of the nineteenth century, during the early stages of British imperial history, naturally—without consciousness—understood Antigua, in the West Indies, as a distant place whose proper role was to enable the good life of Mansfield Park. As Said puts this remoteness in his reading of *Mansfield Park,*

> Take . . . the casual references to Antigua, the ease with which Sir Thomas's needs in England are met by a Caribbean sojourn, the uninflected, unreflective citations of Antigua (or Mediterranean, or India, which is where Lady Bertram, in a fit of distracted impatience, requires that William should go "that I may have a shawl. I think I will have two shawls"). They stand for a significance "out there" that frames the genuinely important action *here,* but not for a great significance. Yet these signs of "abroad" include, even as they repress, a rich and complex history, which has since achieved a status that the Bertrams, the Prices, and Austen herself would not, could not recognize. To call this "the Third World" begins to deal with the realities but by no means exhausts the political or cultural history. (*CI,* 93)

Said's emphasis on Austen's representative cultural perspective on Britain's remote colonies at the beginning of the nineteenth century—their raison d'être in the collective British mind—has been amply registered by commentators on his book. Left underremarked, however, are the implications that his analysis of this hegemonic attitude bears for the identity of the colonial peoples upon whom the British relied for their "civilized" way of life and national identities. What Said's contrapuntal reading of Austen's *Mansfield Park* discloses, above all, is that even for such a sophisticated, knowledgeable, and sensitive—worldly—intelligence, the humanity inhabiting the remote world of Antigua has *no existence.* To put it in the ontological terms that, as I have shown in chapter 3, underlie Said's representation and critique of the British imperial gaze, the native and enslaved inhabitants of the remote world of Antigua—the world peripheral to the British metropolis—are *nonbeings,* manifestations of the nothing on which the West has, in an increasingly silent way, relied to establish its metaphysical interpretation of the phenomena of being as the truth about being. As Enrique Dussel observes about Europe's imperial perception of the natives of Latin America, "*The center is; the periphery is not.* Where [metaphysically understood] Being reigns, there reign and control the armies of Caesar, the emperor. *Being is; beings are what are seen and controlled.*"[4] It is primarily this disclosure—that Austen is virtually unconscious of the historical fact that there *is a humanity,* indeed, a suffering humanity, in the Antigua that enables the plenary being of Mansfield Park—that Said's contrapuntal analysis of her novel enables. To put it positively and more precisely, Said's analysis of the hegemonically inscribed "structures of attitude and reference" that saturate Austen's narrative enables him to force the British "Other" from the remote margins of Austen's consciousness to center stage. In short, Said's analysis of Austen's novel compels his readers to recognize not simply the inexorable reality of her novel's Britain, namely, its status as an imperial nation, but also, by retrieving the Eurocentric global history that this novel of domestic manners dims down—the immense suffering the nation inflicts on the inhabitants of the other worlds it dominates—the historical reality (meticulously detailed by Said) of these inhabitants, which the exigencies of her domestic narrative have reduced to nonbeings.

This first phase in the structure of *Culture an Imperialism* culminates, after a discussion of Camus's Eurocentrism, in Said's brilliant commentary on Rudyard Kipling's *Kim.* Since Said's inaugural reading of Kipling's masterpiece is now well known, I will not rehearse its content. Instead, I will briefly focus on the aspect of it that most commentators, especially those postcolonial critics who have drawn heavily on Said, have either ignored or marginalized in treating the novel independently—in, that is, overlooking its relation to what precedes (and what follows) it. I am referring, above all, to Said's sustained effort, similar to that undertaken in his analysis of *Mansfield Park,* to infer Kipling's fundamental attitude toward the various Indian populations subjected by the British colonial project, the degree to which he was aware of the singularity of their being.

Reconstellated into this historical-structural context, *Kim* comes to be seen as a synecdochic text that constitutes not simply the culmination of British imperialist practice but also the fulfillment of the imperial sensibility, which expresses itself in terms of "structures of attitude and references." For Austen, writing at the beginning of British imperialism, Antigua (the British colonies) and the inhuman slavery on which Mansfield Park unconsciously depends are geographically and psychologically *remote* from the Britain she inhabits; for Kipling, however, writing about a century later, at the apogee of British imperialism, the distance between Britain and India has been reduced to a virtual presence. What has changed dramatically in the historical interval between them is the British national culture's greater awareness of the relationship between Britain and its colonies, the dependency of the latter on the former. But this awareness does not emerge as a sense of intrusion by the Indian "Other." Rather, it manifests itself as a sense of triumphalist vindication, as the confirmation of the *natural* rightness of Britain's imperial presence in India and of the perennial Orientalist binary logic—the "us" against "them"—that justified this destined presence, an assumed rightness that Said reiteratively foregrounds by centralizing Kipling's marginalization, if not obliteration, of the actual history of Indian resistance (the Great Mutiny of 1857, for example), a marginalization taking the subtle form of ventriloquizing the native, rendering him the spokesperson of British truth. Referring to events subsequent to the mutiny, he writes:

> In such a situation of nationalist and self-justifying inflammation, to be an Indian would have meant to feel natural solidarity with the victims of British reprisal. To be British meant to feel repugnance and injury—to say nothing of righteous vindication—given the terrible displays of cruelty by "natives," who fulfilled the role of savages cast for them. For an Indian, *not* to have had those feelings would have been to belong to a very small minority. It is therefore highly significant that Kipling's choice of an Indian to speak about the Mutiny is a loyalist soldier who views his countrymen's revolt as an act of madness. Not surprisingly, this man is respected by British "Deputy Commissioners" who, Kipling tells us, "turned aside from the main road to visit him." What Kipling eliminates is the likelihood that his compatriots regard him as (at the very least) a traitor to his people. And when, a few pages later, the old veteran tells the lama and Kim about the Mutiny, his version of the events is highly charged with the British rationale for what happened:
>
> > "A madness ate into all the Army, and they turned against their officers. That was the first evil, but not past remedy if they had then held their hands. But they chose to kill the Sahibs' wives and children. Then came the Sahibs from over the sea and called them to most strict account" (*CI*, 147).

What Said's contrapuntal reading of the structures of attitude and reference permeating this turn-of-the-century text insistently emphasizes—as it recalls the preceding discussion of Austen's *Mansfield Park* and anticipates what is to follow—is Kipling's confidence in the British imperial vision at the height of its global sway, indeed, the pleasure in the "Great Game" that derives from this confidence. Commenting on the classic readings of *Kim* by Mark Kinkead-Weekes, who claims that the novel reconciles the two different ways of seeing (the Oriental and the Western) into a "more inclusive, complex, humanized, and mature" vision, and by Edmund Wilson, who concludes that the conflict between these two cultures is never resolved because Kipling, unwilling to face one, "does not dramatize any fundamental conflict," Said writes:

> There is an alternative to these two views, I believe, that is more accurate about and sensitive to the actualities of late-nineteenth-century British India as Kipling, and others, saw them. The conflict between Kim's colonial service and loyalty to his Indian companions is unresolved not because Kipling could not face it, but because for Kipling *there was no conflict;* one purpose of the novel is in fact to show the absence of conflict once Kim is cured of his doubts, the lama of his longing for the River, and India of a few upstarts and foreign agents. That there *might have been* a conflict had Kipling considered India as unhappily subservient to imperialism, we can have no doubt, but he did not: for him it was India's best destiny to be ruled by England. . . . It is crucial to remember that there were no appreciable deterrents to the imperialist world-view Kipling held. . . . My point in this contrapuntal reading is to emphasize and highlight the disjunctions, not to play them down. (*CI*, 145–46)

In other words, despite the collapsing of the great distance between Britain and its colonies registered in Austen's earlier narrative in the intervening century, the natives of these colonies—the actual lives under British rule—continue at the turn of the century to remain invisible to the inhabitants of the imperial metropolis. Alternatively, to reverse the emphasis—and it is the nuance of this reversal I want to foreground[5]—the metropolis has virtually no consciousness of its "Other," the fact that there *is* an "Other" that irremediably belongs to it. To invoke the language of ontology I have deliberately used in referring to Austen's perception of what constitutes being, in the eyes of the British these human beings remain devoid of substance: they are beings who are nonbeings. This thematization, then—this emphatic reembodiment, as it were—of the nothingness to which the certainty of British truth has reduced the "denizens" of the colonies is precisely what Said intends in this first phase of the structure of *Culture and Imperialism*. By his unrelenting contrapuntal attention to the margins, to the structures of attitude and reference, of Austen's and Kipling's representative novels, Said discloses that the opposition between the Being of the British and the nonbeing of the colonies' indigenes permeated the body of the cultural discourse—from Austen, through Dickens, Thackeray, and Meredith, to Conrad and Kipling—of nineteenth-century Britain right down to the capillaries. More important for my purposes, he also reveals the profound extent to which this deeply inscribed perspective—this being *inside* the colonial-imperial nation—kept British nationalism immune to disturbance from the outside: to the immediacy of the violence of imperialist practice in the colonies and to the human suffering this predatory violence entailed.

* * *

As Said moves into the second phase of his genealogy of modern Western (imperial) civilization, from his analysis of nineteenth-century (Victorian) to twentieth-century Modernist cultural production, he emphasizes the paradox of the fulfillment of the logical economy of the imperialist narrative: its end. Analogous to Heidegger's epochal disclosure that the imperial metaphysical philosophy of the (Western) ontotheological tradition had come to its end (to its fulfillment and demise) in technological modernity—had made visible the nothing (*das Nichts*) that its objective truth could not finally accommodate to the totality[6]—Said's disclosure in this second phase of *Culture and Imperialism* focuses on the radically contradictory consequence of the West's annulment of and indifference to the being of the "Other," which had been the necessary logical and practical imperative for the formation of civilization, that is, Occidental imperialism. Specifically, he shows that, as in the case of the discourse of Orientalism, the logic of British imperialism self-destructs in the Modernist period, at the very moment when, as the example of Kipling testifies, it proclaims its universal triumph. That is, although its fundamental purpose had from the beginning been to annul the very *be-ing* of the "Other," it ends in precipitating the "Other" as a force that destabilizes the homeland and the confident collective national consciousness on which the British imperial project depended.

Historically, Said shows, the e-mergence of the destabilizing "Other" was instigated by the binarist dynamics of imperialism, above all, its crude indifference to and indeed arrogant contempt for the different culture(s) of the indigenous people beyond the periphery of the metropolitan culture; its deracination of deeply rooted native populations; and, as in the case of the Great Mutiny of 1857, the swift, relentless, efficient, and brutal calling "to most strict account" those recalcitrant indigents who resisted this culture-shattering process. But it is not only the historical resistance of the colonized peoples that Said invokes. After all, as his reading of Kipling's *Kim* makes clear, even a massively significant insurrection such as the mutiny could be accommodated to the triumphalist national discourse of imperialism to keep the historical reality of the colonized peoples at bay, that is, to render its violent depredations remote from the consciousness of the British people. In addressing this aggressive imperial history, Said overdetermines the momentum of the dislocations necessarily incumbent on the imperial project's violence, which took the form of an increasing migration, first of the threatening *image* of the Britain's colonial "Others" and then of their actual *bodies,* into the metropolitan world, a momentum of coming near from afar—of *visitation,* as it were—that jarred the complacency and certitude of national solidarity into deep anxiety. In other words, the structural process of Said's genealogy recounts a history of the imperial consciousness that at the beginning is more or less blind to its repressed "Other" but, in its maturation and through the necessary dislocations and outraged resistance against its violent effects, gradually and imperceptibly precipitates its "Other"—its idea of the "Other"—into manifest and disturbing visibility and immediacy.

"A Note on Modernism" concludes chapter 2, appropriately entitled "Consolidated Vision" and containing Said's analyses of *Mansfield Park* and *Kim.* A casual reading (abetted by its title) might suggest that this brief section is an inconsequential sidelight or digression. Understood in the context I have provided, however, it turns out to be the very center, the pivotal moment of argument, where Said renders explicit the relationship between Austen's and Kipling's novels (as well as Verdi's *Aïda,* and Camus's *L'Étranger*), on the one hand, and the postcolonial literary and critical texts that follow, on the other. Recalling the euphoric triumphalism of the "hundreds" of empire-oriented novels, epitomized by Kipling's *Kim,* published at the height of the European imperial project (which seemed indifferent to the "disenchantment," or what Lukacs called "ironic disillusion," of the fin de siècle realist novel [*CI,* 187]), Said diagnoses a profound transformation in the tonality of the Modernist novel:

> As against this optimism, affirmation, and serene confidence, Conrad's narratives [for Said, the Modernist novel's epitome]—to which I have often referred because more than anyone else he tackled the subtle cultural reinforcements and manifestations of empire—radiate an extreme, unsettling anxiety: they react to the triumph of empire the way Hirschman says that romantics responded to the triumph of an interest-centered view of the world. Conrad's tales and novels in one sense reproduce the aggressive contours of the high imperialist understanding, but in another sense they are infected with the easily recognizable, ironic awareness of the post-realist modernist sensibility. Conrad, Forster,

Malraux, T. E. Lawrence take narrative form from the triumphalist experience of imperialism into the extremes of self-consciousness, discontinuity, self-referentiality, and corrosive irony, whose formal patterns we have come to recognize as the hallmarks of modernist culture, a culture that also embraces the major work of Joyce, T. S. Eliot, Proust, Mann, and Yeats. I would like to suggest that many of the most prominent characteristics of modernist culture, which we have tended to derive from purely internal dynamics in Western society and culture, include a response to the external pressures on culture from the *imperium*. (*CI*, 188)

This extraordinarily resonant passage bears lingering over for its pertinence to what I have been saying about the structural dynamics of *Culture and Imperialism*. First, Said, unlike the New Critics, who defined Modernist art for a whole generation of students and largely restricted its parameters to the West, identifies the rise of this "new" art with the emergence of a pervasive anxiety, not simply in the English consciousness, but in the mind of Europe (and America) as well, at the end of the nineteenth century—the very moment of imperialism's alleged triumph. And it is clear from the preceding context that Said attributes this pervasive Western anxiety not simply to the depredations of imperialist practice per se but to the massive deracinations, global in scope, of the colonized indigenes. These deracinations inevitably provoked sporadic but geographically widespread reactions, precipitating the indigenes' hitherto invisible being into a general visibility no longer repressible by Europeans. This is why, in his readings of Austen and Kipling, Said repeatedly emphasizes the British colonial project's sense of certainty, of natural rightness. It is the global (totalizing) imperial project itself, he implies, that eventually precipitated the very resistance it wanted to contain or defuse.

Second, in identifying Conrad's novels with the "post-realist modernist sensibility," Said underscores what I have said earlier about the structure of *Culture and Imperialism*: that the object of his analysis is not, as it is in Marx and others, the economic or political orientation of British imperialist practice. For Said, that kind of critical analysis has all been done without much consequence; indeed, as was true of Marx, it was sometimes complicit with the imperial project. Rather, he focuses on cultural production, for it is cultural production that not only informs the imperial project but also, and above all, produces the metropolitan structures of attitude and reference that take the actual conditions produced by imperialism in both worlds to be natural—the way things really are. But this is to overgenerally characterize the point Said makes about Modernist culture in the previously quoted passage and throughout his book. According to Said, it was not simply culture but rather the novel—specifically, the realistic novel—that, to invoke Gramsci (who is a massive presence in Said's discourse), produced the "spontaneous consent"[7] that nineteenth-century imperial culture needed to carry out its narrative project. In speaking of "the realistic" novel, Said means of course the ostensibly objective narrative art that was inaugurated in the eighteenth century by writers such as Daniel Defoe and Henry Fielding and, in consonance with the rise of empirical science, "perfected" in the nineteenth century: the narrative art that, in the process of realizing (or rationalizing) the world, obscured by effacing, just as did Jane Austen and Rudyard Kipling, precisely the differential realities it was representing.[8] In other words, in invoking Conrad's representative "post-realist modernist sensibility," Said intends to identify the historical moment when, in the wake of the dislocations precipitated by the depredations of imperialism, metropolitan Europe became not simply conscious of the colonial "Other" but aware of its existence as a pervasive, threatening "presence *within* Europe." In the paragraph following the passage I have been analyzing, Said powerfully conveys this anxiety-provoking presence of what had hitherto been innocuously remote:

> In Mann's great fable of the alliance between creativity and disease—*Death in Venice*—the plague that infects Europe is Asiatic in origin; the combination of dread and promise, of degeneration and desire, so effectively rendered by Aschenbach's psychology is Mann's way of suggesting, I believe, that Europe, its art, mind, monuments, is no longer invulnerable, no longer able to ignore its ties to its overseas domains. Similarly, Joyce, for whom the Irish nationalist and intellectual Stephen Dedalus is ironically fortified not by Irish Catholic comrades but by the wandering Jew Leopold Bloom, whose exoticism and cosmopolitan skills undercut the morbid solemnity of Stephen's rebellion. Like the fascinating inverts of Proust's novel, Bloom testifies to a new presence within Europe, a presence rather strikingly described in terms unmistakably taken from the exotic annals of overseas discovery, conquest, vision. Only now instead of being *out there,* they are *here,* as troubling as the primitive rhythms of the *Sacre du printemps* or the African icons in Picasso's art. (*CP,* 188)[9]

This profoundly troubling awareness is what Said foregrounds in "A Note on Modernism." Unlike the realistic novelists of the nineteenth century, from Austen to Kipling, the Modernists—Joseph Conrad, E. M. Forster, Joyce, Mann, Proust, André Gide, among many others—had become acutely conscious of this "new presence." To the Modernists the empire's "Others" are no longer remote: "instead of being *out there,* they are *here.*" Their consciousness has become, as in the telling case of Thomas Mann, "infected" by a deep anxiety about this now present—and contagious—but hitherto remote and invisible multitudinous "Others" of the empire. Alternatively, we might say without forcing Said's rhetoric that the empire's "Others" impinge on the

Modernist metropolitan artistic consciousness as an anxiety precipitated by the alienated peoples of the colonized world, who now appear as apparitions, as (to borrow a metaphor I have used elsewhere) specters that haunt their discourses.[10] Antigua, Said takes pains to emphasize, did not haunt Austen's consciousness, nor did India haunt Kipling's. But now, at the end of the imperial age, Africa haunts Conrad's very being; India haunts E. M. Forster's, the Arabian world haunts T. E. Lawrence's, Indochina haunts Malraux's. Nor is this metaphorics of ghostly visitation inappropriate, for in referring to an incorporeal reality, a reality devoid of being, it mirrors the nothing that the end of the Western metaphysical tradition has precipitated against itself to haunt the "peace" of its empire: the age of the world picture or, what is the same thing, the Pax Metaphysica.

This is not to say that the emergence of the Modernist novel at this epochal moment of European history suddenly initiates an oppositional cultural momentum against the dominant imperial culture or, for that matter, takes up the cause of Europe's colonized "Other." On the contrary, the Modernists' response to the anxiety-provoking reality of the empire's "Other" was not ameliorative: "When European culture finally began to take account of imperial 'delusions and discoveries'—in Benita Parry's fine phrase for the Anglo-Indian encounter—it did so not oppositionally but ironically, and with a desperate attempt at a new inclusiveness" (CI, 89). As Said insistently reminds us, the Modernists responded to this haunting anxiety by spatializing and thus suppressing the history that instigated it, that is, by accommodating this disruptive history to a self-referential, autotelic microcosmic aesthetic form, a circular ironic form that, in I. A. Richards's famous formulation, would be "immune from irony,"[11] that is, from worldly criticism. To put it more specifically, the Modernists internalized into an inclusive and transcendental whole the historical dynamics—the dislocations and fragmentations—of the imperial world that had shockingly precipitated the nonbeingness of its "Other" as a "disease" that threatened to infect Europe.[12] Discussing the Modernists' means for dealing with "the" ironic sense of how vulnerable Europe was, and how—in Conrad's great phrase—"this also has been one of the dark places of the earth," Said writes,

> A new encyclopedic form became necessary, one that had three distinctive features. First was a circularity of structure, inclusive and open at the same time: *Ulysses, Heart of Darkness, A la recherche, The Waste Land, Cantos, To the Lighthouse.* Second was a novelty based almost entirely on the reformulation of old, even outdated fragments drawn self-consciously from disparate locations, sources, cultures: the hallmark of modernist form is the strange juxtaposi-

tion of comic and tragic, high and low, commonplace and exotic, familiar and alien, whose most ingenious resolution is Joyce's fusing of the *Odyssey* with the Wandering Jew, advertising and Virgil (or Dante), perfect symmetry and the salesman's catalogue. Third is the irony of a form that draws attention to itself as substituting art and its creations for the once-possible synthesis of the world empires. When you can no longer assume that Britannia will rule the waves forever, you have to reconceive reality as something that can be held together by you the artist, in history rather than in geography. Spatiality becomes, ironically, the characteristic of an aesthetic rather than of politic domination, as more and more regions—from India to Africa to the Caribbean—challenge the classical empires and their cultures. (*CI*, 189–90)

This illuminating passage about the Modernist imagination—which in one brief stroke renders the New Critics' history of Modernism an obsolete fiction—reveals the difference between Said's global understanding of the Modernist text and that of the Eurocentric New Critics, whose formalist legacy was a Modernist art stripped of any connection to the historical world. From Said's secular perspective, the formalist structures these Modernists articulated were in large part intended to annul anxiety of the emergence of the empire's "Others." They were, then, despite the assumption of distance from history, "worldly texts," tethered to the dislocating historical realities from which they wanted to escape. The Modernists, including writers, painters, sculptors, and their theorists, were aware that the Western subject, insofar as it had been leveled and quantified by nineteenth-century instrumentalist thinking—the "interest-centered view of the world," as Said puts it—was a momentum that threatened the humanity of humankind. Their response, however, was not to foreground the complicity of instrumental thinking (and the realist narrative) with the ravages of imperialism but to advance a critique of interest that ended in the projection of subjective worlds (formalist microcosms) that were compensatory alternatives to the world constructed by the instrumentalist truth discourse of interest. Said is sympathetic with the Modernists' anti-instrumentalism. Nonetheless, insofar as this momentum remained unaware of or indifferent to the complicity between instrumentalism/capitalism and the global imperial project—for example, the absolute dependency of the industrial metropolis on the raw materials of the colonies—it is profoundly limited. Even more important, in the very act of creating these compensatory alternative subjective worlds— worlds characterized by an inclusive, ever-expanding circular structure, the integration of geographic and historical fragments, and a self-reflexive irony that was immune to the free play of criticism—Modernists were in fact reproducing the Eurocentric imperial world.

Nevertheless, Said's contrapuntal critical consciousness does not over-determine the resolution of the dislocations that instigated their peculiar anxiety—the accommodation of the contradictory dislocations of imperialism into an inclusive formal whole. Rather, Said reveals the willful, virtually hysterical effort to annul the anxiety of imperialism's "Others," an effort that betrays the force of the "Other" in the very process of repressing it. In other words, Said's representation of the Modernists' deeply troubled awareness of the empire's "Other" at the end of the imperial itinerary, or more precisely, the impingement of the being of this "Other"—its hitherto nonbeing—on their anxious consciousness, discloses the presence of this "Other" as general disembodied image, a specter, echoing and modifying Marx, haunting Europe.[13] The bodies of these "Others" of the empire remain geographically remote from the metropolis, as was true in the case of Jane Austen's *Mansfield Park,* but now their collective specter has drawn menacingly near. This, I suggest, is the point Said makes in "A Note on Modernism."

* * *

If we take Said's marginal "Note on Modernism" as a focal point, then, what follows is a third, "postcolonial" phase in the structure of *Culture and Imperialism,* one that, in its development of the pivotal awakening of the Modernist's consciousness of the empire's spectral "Other," brings the totalizing logic of imperialism to its end—to its fulfillment and demise. To clarify this paradoxical culminating moment of Said's—and empire's—itinerary, I want to return to the essential and necessary logic underlying the British (and the Western, i.e., liberal democratic/capitalist) empire's comportment toward its colonial "Others." As Said repeatedly reminds us, the British expansionist momentum, especially in the wake of the rise of capitalism, differed significantly from other historical imperial projects—not simply Asian but also European, such as those of the Romans and, in modern times, of the Spanish, the Portuguese, and the Belgians. The latter were all brutal interventions motivated by rapacity and greed, whereas British imperialism was represented as ameliorative and "incorporative." In his brilliant reading of Conrad's *Heart of Darkness,* which, as I tentatively observed in chapter 3, inaugurates his contrapuntal critical project, Said writes:

> Recall that Marlow contrasts Roman colonizers with their modern counterparts in an oddly perceptive way, illuminating the special mix of power, ideological energy, and practical attitude characterizing European imperialism. The ancient Romans, he says, were "no colonists; their administration was merely a squeeze and nothing more." Such people conquered and did little else. By

contrast, "what saves us is efficiency—the devotion to efficiency," unlike the Romans, who relied on brute force, which is scarcely more than "an accident arising from the weakness of others."

> "Today, however, the conquest of the earth, which mostly means the taking it away from those who have a different complexion or slightly flatter noses than ourselves, is not a pretty thing when you look into it too much. What redeems it is the idea only. An idea at the back of it; not a sentimental pretense but an idea; and an unselfish belief in the idea—something you can set up, and bow down before, and offer a sacrifice to. . . ."

In his account of his great river journey, Marlow extends the point to mark a distinction between Belgian rapacity and (by implication) British rationality in the conduct of imperialism.

Salvation in this context is an interesting notion. It sets "us" off from the damned, despised Romans and Belgians, whose greed radiates no benefits onto either their consciences or the lands and bodies of their subjects. "We" are saved because first of all we needn't look directly at the results of what we do; we are ringed by and ring ourselves with the practice of efficiency, by which land and people are put to use completely, the territory and its inhabitants are totally incorporated by our rule, which in turn totally incorporates us as we respond efficiently to its exigencies. Further, through Marlow, Conrad speaks of redemption, a step in a sense beyond salvation. If salvation saves us, saves time and money, and also saves us from the ruin of mere short-term conquest, then redemption extends salvation further still. Redemption is found in the self-justifying practice of an idea or mission over time, in a structure that completely encircles and is revered by you, even though you set up the structure in the first place, ironically enough, and no longer study it closely because you take it for granted.

Thus Conrad encapsulates two quite different but intimately related aspects of imperialism: the idea that is based on the power to take over territory, an idea utterly clear in its force and unmistakable consequences; and the practice that essentially disguises or obscures this by developing a justificatory regime of self-aggrandizing, self-originating authority interposed between the victim of imperialism and its perpetrator. (*CI,* 68–69; emphasis added)

In speaking of "incorporation" Said means, I think, an attitude toward the "Others" of empire, analogous to liberal capitalist democracy's and orthodox Marxism's (and for that matter, humanism's) relationship to the subaltern classes. Grounded in a metaphysically informed understanding of temporality, that is, a Western or Eurocentric interpretation of history that assumes its universality, a history that views the cultures of the periphery as "backward" or "underdeveloped" or "prepolitical," this attitude or comportment accommodates the foreign bodies to the metropolitan body—brings "them" into "our" orbit—but, as Foucault says of the "de-viants" of the liberal nation-state, with the purpose of disciplining or re-forming their "erratic" ("immature") energies into "useful and docile [modern] bodies" to serve the metropolitan culture. According to Said, this incorporative logical historical economy, in which the aliens are intended to eventually take their "proper" (subaltern) place in the larger determinative whole, was the essential source of Western imperialism's inordinate historical strength. It also was or eventually and necessarily turned out to be its essential weakness, its Achilles heel, as the sequel culminating in the section of *Culture and Imperialism* aptly entitled "The Voyage In and the Emergence of Opposition" persuasively testifies.

This Saidian perspective on the modern West's interpretation of history (particularly as it pertained to the relationship between the dominant West and the subaltern East) was fully developed by the postnationalist theorists of postcolonialism associated with the historians of the India-based Subaltern Studies Group—Ranajit Guha, Gyanendra Pandey, Shahid Amin, Ashis Nandy, Gautam Bhadra, Partha Chatterjee, Dipesh Chakrabarty, and others.[14] As I noted in chapter 1, most postcolonial theorists and critics, especially Indian (including many of those Said influenced), adopted this Western or Eurocentric concept of history, whether in its democratic capitalist or Marxist or generally humanist allotrope, and in assuming its universalism left the hegemony of metropolitan Britain intact. This was especially true of the nationalist natives of the Third World (e.g., leaders such as Jawaharlal Nehru and Mohandas Gandhi and Indian historians such as Sumit Sarkar). The Subaltern Studies Group constituted a significant exception to this rule. At the outset, it is true, they committed themselves in some degree to the incorporative or accommodational Marxist view of history (the "'histories-from-below' approach pioneered in English historiography by Christopher Hill, E. P. Thompson, and others"),[15] which, as did the capitalist version, represented the various Indian cultures according to its "uneven development thesis," the "not yet" of a "stagist" view of history. Later, however, under the influence of the poststructuralists' critique of essentialism and identitarianism, most notably that of Heidegger and Foucault and of Gramsci and Said, they rejected this "progressivist," teleological, or in Chakrabarty's term, "historicist" interpretation in favor of a radically secular understanding of history, one that was nonfoundational ("grounded" in difference), anti-identitarian, antihumanist, and not least, antinationalist and that posited the singularity of cultures. I quote from the concluding chapter ("Reason and the Critique of Historicism") of Dipesh Chakrabarty's aptly titled *Provincializing Europe* at some length to suggest the remarkable continuity not only between Said's and Chakrabarty's postcolonial, secular understanding of history but also between Said's understanding and that of Heidegger, Foucault, and other poststructuralists; in short, the continuity among Said's contrapuntal analysis, Heidegger's hermeneutic circle (*Wiederholung,* "repetition"; *Auseinandersetzung,* "antagonistic dialogue"), and Foucault's genealogy, all of which, in opposition to the (Western) metaphysical principle of principles, understand difference to be prior to and necessary for the possibility of identity and not the other way around:

> To provincialize Europe in historical thought is to struggle to hold in a state of permanent tension a dialogue between two contradictory points of view. On one side is the indispensable and universal narrative of capitalism—History 1, as I have called it. This narrative both gives us a critique of capitalist imperialism and affords elusive but necessarily energizing glimpses of the Enlightenment promise of an abstract, universal but never-to-be-realized humanity. Without such elusive glimpses . . . there is no political modernity. On the other side is thought about diverse ways of being human, the infinite incommensurabilities through which we struggle—perennially, precariously, but unavoidably—to "world the earth" in order to live within our different senses of ontic belonging. These are the struggles that become—when in contact with capital—the History 2s that in practice always modify and interrupt the totalizing thrusts of History 1.
>
> Although this book is not committed to either Marx or Heidegger in any doctrinaire or dogmatic sense, the spirit of their thinking and their guiding concepts preside over the two poles of thought that direct the movements of this book. . . . Marx and Heidegger represent for me two contradictory but profoundly connected tendencies that coexist within modern European social thought. One is the analytical heritage, the practice of abstraction that helps us to universalize. We need universals to produce critical readings of social injustices. Yet the universal and the analytical produce forms of thought that ultimately evacuate the place of the local. [Chakrabarty's notion of universal is, I take it, what Heidegger means, in his account of hermeneutic circularity, by the "presuppositions" or "forestructures" that enable inquiry but that, in being put at risk by the inquirer, are deconstructed by the differential dynamics of temporality] . . . Such thought fundamentally tends to sever the relationship between thought and modes of human belonging. The other European heritage is the hermeneutic tradition that tends to reinstitute within thought itself this relationship between thought and dwelling. My attempt in this book has been to write some very particular ways of being-in-the-world—I call them Bengali only in a provisional manner—into some of the universal, abstract, and European categories of capitalist/political modernity. For me provincialing Europe has been a question of how we create conjoined and disjunctive genealogies for European categories of political modernity as we contemplate the necessarily fragmentary histories of human belonging that never constitute one or a whole.[16]

I am suggesting, then, that the incorporative or accommodational logical imperatives of British or Western democratic/capitalist imperialism, despite its motive and practice of exploitation, *necessarily* entailed and precipitated not simply the dis-location and un-homing of the colonial natives but also a momentum that eventually—precisely at the historical moment when the logic of imperial practice reached fulfillment—bore witness to a massive, multimotivated, figurative and literal migration of the empire's "Others" into the metropolis, a migration that in the end, to use Chakrabarty's term, profoundly and decisively provincialized Great Britain. That is, the migration disrupted the binary logic informing the very idea of the British empire and a coherent British national identity and transformed the metropolis—the concentered and concentering city that measures the value of its peripheral "Others"—into a site of potential contestation. In the pivotal period of Modernism, then, the empire's "Others" impinged on the British consciousness as a threatening disembodied general image; now, in the postmodern or postcolonial period, the empire's spectral "Others" impinge in a *bodily* form.

To counter the potential political threat of this now embodied specter, the dominant metropolitan culture was compelled to resort to a far more sophisticated and desperate strategy of incorporation or accommodation, one that was intended to "educate" the migrants into the virtues of British culture. As Said's student and later colleague Gauri Viswanathan has observed in *Masks of Conquest,* the study of the canonical British literary tradition was inaugurated in India long before it was institutionalized in Britain.[17] Insofar as this education was addressed to the deracinated victims of imperialism's cruel, exploitative logic and practice, it was inevitable that, despite the intention of pacification, this multitude of the unhomed would produce oppositional thinkers who would, using the very instruments that the metropolis afforded them, become the organic consciousness of their fellow mutilated migrants. Said refers to these when he speaks of "one fairly discrete aspect of this powerful impingement—that is, the work of intellectuals from the colonial or peripheral regions who wrote in an 'imperial' language, who felt themselves organically related to the mass of resistance to empire, and who set themselves the revisionist, critical task of dealing frontally with the metropolitan culture, using the techniques, discourse, and weapons of scholarship and criticism once reserved exclusively for the European" (*CI,* 243). It should now be obvious that this contradictory "voyage in," imperialist logic's unforeseen yet inevitable precipitation of its own shadow, is what leads Said to introduce those great nomadic postcolonial intellectuals—C. L. R. James, George Antonius, Ranajit Guha, S. H. Alatas, Frantz Fanon, Albert Memmi, and many others—at this culminating postmodern stage of the imperial project. Like Said himself, these intellectuals have produced contrapuntal readings of the Western imperial tradition's enabling texts, thereby bearing witness to the self-destruction of the logic and practice of Western imperialism, of both the Pax Metaphysica and the Pax Europa, and inaugurating, however tentatively, the project of thinking positively the victimized beings that the West's imperial understanding of being has perennially relegated to the status not simply of the underdeveloped but of nonbeing. "The voyage in," Said writes, invoking the dialectics of Western metaphysics/history,

> constitutes an especially interesting variety of hybrid cultural work. And that it exists at all is a sign of adversarial internationalization in an age of continued imperial structures. No longer does the *Logos* dwell exclusively, as it were, in London and Paris. No longer does history run unilaterally, as Hegel [and Marx] believed, from east to west, or from south to north, becoming more sophisticated and developed, less primitive and backward as it goes; instead, the weapons of criticism have become *a part of the historical legacy of empire,* in which the separation and exclusions of "divide and rule" are erased and surprising new configurations spring up. (*CI*, 145; emphasis added)[18]

* * *

In his inaugural interrogation of Joseph Conrad's *Heart of Darkness*—where he distinguishes between the rapacity of Roman (and Belgian) imperialism and a British imperialism that obscured its violence by "developing a justificatory regime of self-aggrandizing, self-originating authority interposed between the victim of imperialism and its perpetrator," Edward Said concludes: "We would completely miss the tremendous power of this argument if we were merely to lift it out of *Heart of Darkness,* like a message out of a bottle. Conrad's argument is inscribed right in the very form of narrative as he inherited it and as he practiced it. *Without empire, I would go so far as saying, there is no European novel as we know it, and indeed if we study the impulses giving rise to it, we shall see the far from accidental convergence between the patterns of narrative authority constitutive of the novel on the one hand, and, on the other, a complex ideological configuration underlying the tendency to imperialism*" (*CI*, 70; emphasis added). Before considering the profoundly revelatory "conclusion" to his contrapuntal reading of the paradoxical history of the relationship imperial Europe has had with its colonial "Others," I want to return to the notion of narrativity that he underscores in this passage and that the structural dynamics of *Culture and Imperialism* interrogates, silently but insistently and powerfully—a narrativity, more specifically, that has played a prominent polyvalent role in determining Western history at its multiple sites.

Since the novel's identification with imperialism pervades his book—indeed, lies at the heart of it—we can safely claim that narrative has a special but rarely remarked meaning for Said at this point in his career, and it is associated with what I have in this chapter been attempting to say about the paradoxical structural dynamics of *Culture and Imperialism*. This meaning, I suggest, derives from the poststructuralist theory that he is often but erroneously claimed to have eschewed. For Said, therefore, *narrative* is not the aesthetic counter-term that the literary and critical discourses of the Western tradition have employed up until the moment of the poststructuralist revolution. Rather, he sees the word as having an ontological resonance. That is, he uses it to mean a way of thinking (representation) coeval with the founding of the idea of the West and the kind of civilization it has produced. More specifically, he means that mode of representation first articulated in Aristotle's *Poetics* and institutionalized by Horace's *Ars Poetica,* a mode of storytelling that Aristotle and his Roman followers understood as the literary/cultural counterpart or mirror image (microcosm) of their metaphysical interpretation of being (the macrocosm).

Metaphysical perception—the perception of being from after or above its temporal disseminations (*physis*)—implies an "unmoved mover," a Logos that constitutes the origin of an organic temporal itinerary that eventually comes to its destined and totalizing end. In other words, it implies a story in which the end is there from the beginning as a presence determining—giving (circular) shape to, imposing structure on—the temporal process, the differential and differentializing dynamics of being, ultimately, the nothingness that finally cannot be shaped, that is, spatialized or structured.[19] Similarly, as Aristotle suggests in the *Poetics* (and as Nietzsche argues in *The Birth of Tragedy* against the "Apollonian" tradition), a work of literary art, specifically tragedy (i.e., a representation of human action), merits the name only when it is endowed with a plot: a beginning, middle, and end. Implicit in the late Greeks' formulation of narrative, as in their metaphysical interpretation of being, the end, understood as both termination and goal of a temporal process, is there from the very beginning, a presence determining the structure or, rather, willfully structuralizing the historicity of the singular human events that are being represented by the narrator. From a poststructuralist perspective, the most pertinent aspect of both paradigms is the selective process that determines what is included and excluded in the story, that is, the imperial binary logic that not only privileges identity over difference, the one over the many, or, to invoke the ontological rhetoric I have been using in this book, Being over nothingness (nonbeing) but also enables the privileged term to demonize the minority term.

It is just this fundamentally Western concept of narrative, I suggest, that Edward Said interrogates in pointing to the complicity between culture and imperialism. By *culture* he means the indissoluble and regulated relay or continuum of representational discursive practices that constitute the "justificatory regime of self-aggrandizing self-originating authority interposed between the victim of imperialism and its perpetrator." In Said's discourse, however, as the previously quoted passage about Conrad's *Heart of Darkness* makes clear, it is epitomized by the novel form. In other words, he gives to the novel, especially in its eighteenth- and nineteenth-century realist form, privileged status in his critique of imperialism precisely because more than any other form of modern cultural production, it is the absolute precipitate of imperialist metaphysical thinking.

As is well known, Said explicitly expressed impatience with, if not outright hostility to, certain aspects of poststructuralist theory, above all, its overdetermination of an "unworldly textuality":

> From being a bold interventionary movement across lines of specialization, American literary theory of the later seventies had retreated into the labyrinth of "textuality," dragging along with it the most recent apostles of European revolutionary textuality—Derrida and Foucault—whose trans-Atlantic canonization and domestication they themselves seemed sadly enough to be encouraging. It is not too much to say that American or even European literary theory now explicitly accepts the principle of noninterference, and that its peculiar mode of appropriating its subject matter . . . is *not* to appropriate anything that is worldly, circumstantial, or socially contaminated. "Textuality" is the somewhat mystical and disinfected subject matter of literary theory.
>
> Textuality has therefore become the exact antithesis and displacement of what might be called history. Textuality is considered to take place, yes, but by the same token it does not take place anywhere or anytime in particular. It is produced, but by no one and at no time.[20]

Unfortunately a multitude of Said's "worldly" followers, both postcolonialists and cultural critics, have misconstrued this impatience as a rejection of poststructuralism rather than an effort to reestablish the original balance between theory and practice—*an understanding of their indissoluble relationality*—which his reference to the original moment of theory as "a bold interventionary movement across lines of specialization" testifies to have been his intent. As a consequence, the now "triumphant" postcolonialism and cultural criticism (I do not include the Subaltern Studies postcolonial theorists among them) understand themselves in binary opposition to poststructuralist theory, especially with the latter's overdetermination of an ontological critique of the Western philosophical tradition, to the detriment of the power and authority of the oppositional criticism Said so much wanted to bring into being.

As I have shown in chapter 3, in analyzing the rhetoric he uses to characterize the discourse of Orientalism, this ontological register—this critique of the Western metaphysical tradition—is everywhere implicit in Said's historical analysis of the relationship between cultural production and the practice of imperialism. This should be clear from his insistent disparagement and even abhorrence of the self-identical subject and of the identitarian (i.e., sectarian) politics, not least the nationalism to which it gave rise. Even clearer evidence, however, appears in *Culture and Imperialism,* throughout which Said invokes the rhetoric of the metaphysical tradition in the process of disclosing the complicity of the novel and imperialism. This invocation occurs most notably in his constant reference to the binarist metaphorics of the circle—center and periphery (metropolis and provinces)—the essential diagram (structure) of the metaphysical interpretation of being and of thinking *meta ta physika*. In *Orientalism,* admittedly, in keeping with his commitment to the worldliness of criticism, Said subordinates the metaphysical provenance of this system of metaphorics to his contrapuntal critique of culture and imperialism, but the former is nonetheless there, informing the latter. Indeed, it is the presence of this provenance that confers such extraordinary depth and force on his disclosure of the complicity between the narrative of Western culture (the novel) and the narrative of Western imperialism and on the positive possibilities this disclosure liberates. And this, I want to emphasize, is a matter not simply of the content of *Culture and Imperialism* but of its (antinarrative) structure.

To establish this, it will be necessary, however briefly, to make explicit what Said, in overdetermining worldly praxis, takes for granted (because, since *Beginnings,* he assumes it to be by this time self-evident) in his identification of narrative and the history of Western imperialism. The structure of the narrative, he implies, is simply another version of the diagram of the circle understood in terms of the binary opposition between center and periphery. We must not forget the essential disclosure made by the poststructuralist interrogation of Western thought: that narrative structure, Western storytelling, whether cultural or historical, involves the representation of time—the differences that temporality disseminates—in terms of linearity, a representation that produces the illusion that time's radicality is being given its rightful due. If this linearity, however, is understood in terms of beginning-middle-end, in which the end is always present from the beginning or origin, determining the temporal process, it becomes evident that this representational process

is circular and plenary (totalizing and self-confirming): re-presentation. Another way of saying this, one that has not been adequately articulated but
constitutes the essence of the content *and* structure of Said's book, is that
this new, postmodern historical awareness of the circularity of the linear
representation of temporality also entails a symptomatic awareness of the
limits of the totalizing narrative paradigm. It brings to our attention, as the
Subaltern Studies Group has done with great force, not simply the imperial
will to power informing the linear representation's teleology but also those
differential phenomena of being that would contradict its totalizing, origin-
oriented logic were their singularity allowed to *be*.

Let me reconstellate my earlier remarks about Heidegger's own contrapuntal representation of the history of Western thinking into this context. According to Heidegger (and however implicitly, many other poststructuralists),
it may be recalled, the philosophical tradition inaugurated in late Greek and
especially Roman antiquity has come to its end in what he calls modernity,
or as he appropriately puts this, following the spatializing, representational,
or territorializing directives of metaphysical thought, the age of the world
picture.[21] By this he means that the narrative movement precipitated by the
logic that introduced the very idea of Western civilization has come full
circle, to closure. Having fulfilled all the possibilities in thought and practice
latent at its origin, it cannot be developed any further. It has become plenary.
Heidegger points out, however, that with this historical totalization—and
here we should keep in mind the antistructural structure of Said's *Culture
and Imperialism*—the Western philosophical tradition has come to its end
in a second sense. The fulfillment or globalization of the spatializing logical
economy of the Western metaphysics tradition in modernity—the moment
when this imperial logic has finally transformed and domesticated (colonized) the temporal/differential dynamics of being into a world picture—
brings it (and the idea of the West) to its demise or, more precisely, to its
self-de-struction. In what sense? In the sense that its coming to its end
discloses that which its logic cannot finally contain, that which its idea of
development cannot rationalize and accommodate. It is at this moment of
fulfillment that another reality emerges: the reality to which the (teleo)logic
of Western metaphysical thinking, insofar as it understands itself in terms
of measurable and quantifiable objects, is necessarily blind.

Because metaphysical thinking—and here we should keep in mind the
historical itinerary of the British consciousness of the empire's "Other" as Said
traces it from Austen through Kipling to Conrad and the Modernists—thinks
being only in terms of "beings," it cannot acknowledge this other reality (Heidegger calls this reality the nothing [*das Nichts*]) as belonging to—as being

of—Being. Nevertheless, Heidegger remarks, even the casual but necessary invocation of the nothing in the everyday discourse of post-Enlightenment science—its structures of attitude and reference, as it were—discloses its living reality in the very act of identifying itself:

> This trinity [of the truth discourse of modern science]—relation to the world, attitude, and irruption [of Man as measure]—in this radical unity brings a luminous simplicity and aptness of Dasein to scientific existence. If we are to take explicit possession of the Dasein illuminated in this way for ourselves, then we must say:
>
> That to which the relation to the world refers are beings themselves—and nothing besides.
>
> That from which every attitude takes its guidance are beings themselves—and nothing further.
>
> That with which the scientific confirmation in the irruption occurs are beings themselves—and beyond that nothing.
>
> But what is remarkable is that, precisely in the way scientific man secures to himself what is most properly his, *he speaks of something different.* What should be examined are beings only, and besides that—nothing; beings alone, and further—nothing; solely beings, and beyond that—nothing.
>
> What about this nothing? Is it an accident that we talk this way automatically? Is it only a manner of speaking—and nothing besides?[22]

The scientific attitude toward the nothing that Heidegger is rendering explicit, we might say, is a premodern one, like, say, Jane Austen's attitude toward the slaves of Antigua. In the age of the world picture, which has brought the logic of Western science to its self-destructive limits and in so doing precipitated anxiety about its truth, scientific man, such as, say, the European Modernists Said cites, has been compelled to demonize the nothing: "The nothing—what else can it be for science but an outrage and a phantasm? If science is right, then only one thing is sure: science wishes to know nothing of the nothing. Ultimately this is the scientifically rigorous conception of the nothing. We know it, the nothing, in that we wish to know nothing about it" (WIM, 96).

In his (and the early poststructuralists') thinking of the nothing, Heidegger overdetermines the ontological register. Nevertheless, I have been trying to make explicit the tacit ontological ground of Said's disclosure of the complicity of narrative art with the imperialist practice of the West, thereby suggesting in part that the end of logocentric Western philosophy, the end of Western culture, and the end of Western imperialism are indissolubly, however unevenly, related events and occur more or less simultaneously in postmodernity. In addition, I have been suggesting that this continuum of "ends" has disclosed or decolonized an analogous indissoluble relay of "Others," from the ontological nothing (*différance,* the unpresentable, the lack, the absent cause, and so on), through the more concrete and "practical" deviants of the modern nation-state, to the international migrants or nomads—those, like the nothing, with whom the West hitherto would have nothing to do—who now, in what I am calling the postmodern age of globalization, have come to haunt the truth and practice of Western (imperial) civilization.

Not least, as will become clear momentarily, I have been trying to suggest that this multisituated coming-to-the-end of the Western tradition has borne witness to the emergence, at least symptomatically, of a kind of art and thought that no longer imagines and thinks according to the imperial imperatives of narrative, from the beginning or the end, but, attuned to the imperatives of the question, instead operates in the in-between. It is no coincidence that, as Heidegger, Derrida, and Foucault have shown, postmodern poetry is represented symptomatically by "madmen" such as Hölderlin, Trakl, Nerval, and Artaud; art, by "madmen" such as Goya and van Gogh; and thought, by "madmen" such as Nietzsche. As Foucault puts it in *Madness and Civilization,* the work of all these men "opens a void, a moment of silence, a question without answer, provokes a breach without reconciliation where the world is forced to question itself."[23] Nor is it coincidental that the postmodern novel, like poststructuralist theory, is characterized by its resistance to narrative—endings, resolutions, denouements, closures—and, through this resistance to the idea of a determinative origin, intimates precisely the kind of reality with which Western narrative, like Western philosophical inquiry, would increasingly have nothing to do. Unlike the confident realists of the imperialist nineteenth century, who were on the whole oblivious to this reality (and thus complicit with imperial terror), and the anxious Modernists invoked by Said, who shrank back from it, postmodern novelists such as Sartre, Beckett, Borges, Calvino, Pynchon, Coover, Acker, and DeLillo acknowledge the nothing—the "unpresentable," or "the sublime," as Lyotard puts it (a little too sanguinely, but reminiscent of Said's meditations on beginnings); in fact, they "bear witness to it," against the "terror" enabled by "the nostalgia of the whole and the one," by the logic that, on the analogy of metaphysics, Lyotard appropriately calls "metanarrative":

> The postmodern would be that which, in the modern, puts forward the unpresentable in presentation itself; that which denies itself the solace of good forms, the consensus of a taste which would make it possible to share collectively the nostalgia for the unattainable; that which searches for new presentations, not in

order to enjoy them but in order to impart a stronger sense of the unpresentable. A postmodern artist or writer is in the position of a philosopher: the text he writes, the work he produces are not in principle governed by preestablished rules, and they cannot be judged according to a determining judgment, by applying familiar categories to the text or the work. These rules and categories are what the work of art itself is looking for. The artist and the writer, then, are working without rules in order to formulate the rules of what *will have been done.* Hence the fact that work and text have the characters of an *event.*[24]

With respect to the generally neglected structure of *Culture and Imperialism,* this detour into its ontological underpinnings lets us understand it as an antistructural structure, a gradual but inexorable antinarrative or contrapuntal process that dis-integrates the traditional Western novel and discursive treatise, their binarist logic, and the imperial interpretive presuppositions to which these gave rise. In so doing, the structure *enacts* the historical content of Said's text: the incremental self-destruction of the narrative-oriented structure of the "integral" history of modern Western imperialism and the binarist logic (the "us" and "them") on which it depended. Said puts this relay between structure and content provisionally in terms of his disclosure of the paradox incumbent on the fulfillment of Western imperialism's narrative logic and practice—the precipitation of a new kind of resistance to imperialism emanating from the inevitable "voyage in" that the empire's "Others" make to the metropolis.

Pointing to the ultimate complicity of European intellectuals on the left—a complicity that was in part the consequence of their universalism, that is, the metaphysical perspective informing their vestigial Eurocentrism, disciplinarity, and identity—Said asks: "how has the liberationist anti-imperialism tried to break this shackling unity?" And he answers:

> First, by *a new integrative or contrapuntal orientation* in history that sees Western and non-Western experience *as belonging together* because they are connected by imperialism. Second, by an imaginative, even utopian vision which reconceives emancipatory (*as opposed to confining*) theory and performance. Third, by an investment neither in new authorities, doctrines, and encoded orthodoxies, nor in established institutions and causes, *but in a particular sort of nomadic, migratory and anti-narrative energy.* (*CI,* 279; emphasis added)

This passage, as my emphases are intended to show, exemplifies the indissoluble relay among the ontological, the narrative (cultural), the interpretive, and the imperial practices that informs the structure and content of *Culture and Imperialism.* More specifically, it recapitulates the multiple decenterings precipitated by the coming to its end of the Western tradition: the metaphysical interpretation of being, the self-identical subject, (meta)narrative, integral national identity (nationalist culture), and the global imperial project (the precipitation of a massive and diverse global population of unhomed migrants), all of which can be subsumed under the rubric of the decentering of metanarrative. Furthermore, it tentatively posits the positive possibilities of this relay of decenterings that constitute the essential occasion of this historical in-between world, this interregnum between the imperialist age and an age to come. It is to these decenterings and the positive—contrapuntal—possibilities precipitated by the logical economy of Western thinking/history I want finally to (re)turn.

* * *

At the terminal and decentering point of *Culture and Imperialism,* in a movingly eloquent—I am tempted to say grace-filled—passage where he summarizes the imperial history he has contrapuntally rehearsed earlier, Said foregrounds the tremendously paradoxical consequence for global humanity emerging from the fulfillment of the Western imperial project:

> Surely it is one of the unhappiest characteristics of the age to have produced more refugees, migrants, displaced persons, and exiles than ever before in history, most of them as an accompaniment to and, ironically enough, as *afterthoughts* of great post-colonial and imperial conflicts. As the struggle for independence produced new states and new boundaries, it also produced homeless wanderers, nomads, vagrants, unassimilated to the emerging structures of institutional power, rejected by the established order for their intransigence and obdurate rebelliousness. And insofar as these people exist *between* the old and the new, *between* the old empire and the new state, their condition articulates the tension, irresolution, and the contradictions in the overlapping territories shown on the cultural map of imperialism. (*CI,* 332; emphasis added)

As the structure of *Culture and Imperialism* compels us to realize, one should not simply read this passage as a description of the way the depredations of imperialism momentously transformed global demographics, precipitating a vast and heterogeneous global population of displaced, unhomed and stateless émigrés. One should also recognize that its author—an organic intellectual, in Gramsci's term[25]—is someone who, like the late "Others" of the empire who voyaged in to the metropolis in the wake of its logic's implosion, is organically attuned to the misery of the unhomed multitude and has intuited a different way of perceiving that is commensurate with, indissolubly related to, their mutilated condition.

This indissoluble continuity between the displaced or exilic organic thinker and the deracinated subjects of his contrapuntal discourse is overtly but carefully developed in what follows, as both the structural analogy with the previous paragraph and the key repetitions suggest.

> There is a great difference . . . between the optimistic mobility, the intellec-
> tual liveliness, and the "logic of daring" described by the various theoreticians
> on whose work I have drawn [esp. Gilles Deleuze, Félix Guattari, and Paul
> Virilio] and the massive dislocations, waste, misery, and horrors endured in
> our century's migrations and mutilated lives. Yet it is no exaggeration to say
> that liberation as an intellectual mission, born in the resistance and opposi-
> tion to the confinements and ravages of imperialism, has now shifted from
> the settled, established, and domesticated dynamics of culture *to its unhoused,
> decentered, and exilic energies, energies whose incarnation today is the migrant,
> and whose consciousness is that of the intellectual and artist in exile,* the political
> figure *between* domains, *between* forms, *between* homes, and *between* languages.
> From this perspective then all things are indeed counter, original, spare, strange.
> From this perspective also, one can see "the complete consort dancing together"
> contrapuntally. And while it would be the rankest Panglossian dishonesty to say
> that the bravura performances of the intellectual exile and the miseries of the
> displaced person or refugee are the same, it is possible, I think, to regard the
> intellectual as first distilling then articulating the predicaments that disfigure
> modernity—mass deportation, imprisonment, population transfer, collective
> dispossession, and forced immigrations. (*CI,* 332–33; emphasis added)[26]

When, here and elsewhere, Said invokes the exilic condition in referring to the oppositional intellectual that the opening close of the imperial Western tradi-tion precipitates, we should not read him, as all too many postcolonial critics have done, as limiting the meaning of the appositive "the political figure" to the site of imperialism or colonialism proper. As his further qualification of the intellectual's exilic condition ("between forms, between homes, and between languages") emphatically suggests, the politics of this political figure is far more inclusive than that. It is a polyvalent politics, a politics that is simultane-ously ontological, epistemological, linguistic, cultural, and political.

At the risk of seeming to privilege the ontological register that Said mini-mizes to affirm the worldliness of the text, let me once more consider Hei-degger's thesis about the end of philosophy in the postimperial context that Said diagnoses in the previously quoted passage. In his essay on the great modern German poet Georg Trakl, "Language in the Poem," Heidegger in-vokes the alienated poet/thinker that the reduction of being to world picture by the fulfillment of the logic of metaphysics has precipitated against itself. He calls this decentered and exilic poet/thinker *die Abgeschiedene,* "the one apart,"[27] or rather, "a-part," wandering in the interregnum, between worlds (the spatialized world coming to its end and the world to come). This figure is, alternatively, the "ghostly" (*geistlich*) stranger who, alienated from his or her homeland by the triumph of instrumental language, exists "at the fringe of the technically-economically oriented world of modern man," where, attuned to the silence—the unsayable—that the imperial saying of Western modernity has precipitated as its self-destructive contradiction, the *Abgeschiedene* hopes to embody "it" in a (contrapuntal?) language commensurate with its haunting unpresentability (LP, 196–97).

This is not to say that Heidegger's *Abgeschiedene* is the counterpart of Said's political figure living between forms, homes, and languages. As almost always—and at great cost—Heidegger's diagnosis of the Western interregnum overdetermines the ontological site of the continuum of being: the sheer act of thinking. Rather, the point is that Said overcomes the disabling disciplinary limits of Heidegger's and the early poststructuralists' critique of Western modernity, wherein they restrict not only Western imperialism to the thought of being or language but also their postmodern disclosure of the West's "Other" to "the nothing" (Heidegger), the "unpresentable" (Lyotard), "différance" (Derrida), "aporia" (de Man), or "absent Real" (Lacan). Said, that is, understands, first, the Western representation of being as an indissoluble relay of imperialisms extending from the ontological site through the cultural (narrative) site to the site of imperial practice proper and, second, the contradictions precipitated by the West's coming to its end as an indissoluble relay of its "Others" extending from the nothing or unpresentable through the antinarrative to the massive number of greatly diverse unhoused, unhomed migrants or nomads who now bodily haunt the West's hitherto hardly challengeable global hegemony. Understood in this way, then, Said's overcoming renders *Culture and Imperialism* commensurate to the actual conditions of the historical interregnum, to their both oppositional and projective imperatives.

Said powerfully articulates these revolutionary projective possibilities in passages immediately following those I have been discussing. But before turning to those possibilities, I want to consider the previously quoted passage a bit more to attend to his telling qualifying distinction between the multitude of unhomed and stateless migrants and the organic exilic intellectual or artist who is their "consciousness." Here and throughout the book—indeed, his entire oeuvre—Said makes every effort to represent the "Others" of the empire (to which they are nonexistent or simply "afterthoughts") as real, as corporal: living human beings whose victimization by imperialism has entailed the infliction of inordinate pain and suffering on their bodies and souls. Equally important, the intellectuals and artists to whom he is referring are in one way or another mutilated precipitates of the imperial crucible's scorching fires.

From this "damaged" perspective, as Said reiterates (using Gerard Manley Hopkins's phrase), "all things are indeed counter, original, spare, strange." That is, their perspective enabled them to distill and then to articulate "the predicaments that disfigure modernity—mass deportation, imprisonment, population transfer, collective dispossession, and forced immigrations"; it enabled the victimized "Others" of empire, hitherto nonbeings (as in Jane Austen and Kipling) or at best specters (as in Conrad, Mann, and Forster), to retrieve the historical corporeality that imperialism has denied them. Unfortunately, this organically felt empathy with these mutilated "Others" is largely missing in the now huge archive of postcolonial or postimperial criticism. Indeed, in abstracting and institutionalizing the corporeal and spiritual pain and suffering of the empire's victims, this archive (e.g., Negri and Hardt's *Empire,* with its retrogressive universalist perspective) has gone so far as to glibly represent the vast population whose lives have been mutilated by the depredations of empire as an abstract "multitude" that will somehow automatically usher in a new global communism.[28]

As I have suggested in analyzing the antistructural structure of *Culture and Imperialism,* Said's corporealization of the ontological spectrality of the empire's "Others" lies at the heart of his insight into the global postimperial age, and one must register this fact if one is to understand his revolutionary version of the task that the oppositional exilic intellectual faces in the interregnum: the liberating potentialities for resistance that he or she, as a deracinated and nomadic spectral body precipitated by the ravages of imperialism, embodies against the now delegitimated and historically anachronistic authority of the still-powerful Western imperial project.[29]

In thematizing the nothing precipitated by the fulfillment of Western modernity's imperial instrumentalist thought, Heidegger pursued an intention neither diagnostic nor nihilist. His purpose, rather, was to *think* the nothing that modernity "wished to have nothing to do with" *positively.* In this sense it was, like his *Destruktion* of the Western philosophical tradition, intended to be both de-structive and pro-jective. His project, that is, did not simply aim at the liberation—the decolonization, as it were—of the nothingness or (to him the same thing) the radical temporality of being that the imperial thought of Western modernity had reduced and confined to structure; it further sought to think the nothing's positive potentialities. His abiding question was this: what would a thinking be like were it to take as its point of departure the nothing that had come increasingly to haunt the imperial metaphysical interpretation of being? Similarly, for Said, the project of the intellectual in the interregnum—"the political figure between domains, between forms, between homes, and between languages"—is to think the positive possibilities of the unhomed no-bodies to which the imperial West has reduced the historical bodies of a vast portion of global humanity.

It is thus significant that, in inaugurating this project, that is, in pursuing the directives suggested by the coming to its end of imperialism, Said invokes another (post)modern intellectual exile, Theodor Adorno (who at the rise of Nazism had fled from Germany to the United States but was never able to *settle* there), referring specifically and pointedly to his *Minima Moralia: Reflections from a Damaged Life.* "'The past life of émigrés is, as we know, annulled,' says Adorno in *Minima Moralia.* . . . Why? 'Because anything that is not reified, cannot be counted and measured, ceases to exist' or, as he says later, is consigned to mere 'background.'" These collaborative sentences about the émigré nicely summarize what I have been saying about the ontological/ cultural/biopolitical register of Said's discourse—about the polyvalent nothing that has been released by the coming to its end of the Western regime of truth that represents being (including human being) in terms of quantifiable and measurable objects. But this condition, however profoundly violated, is not a purely negative one. The émigré, who has been "consigned to mere 'background,'" may not be present and visible, a part of the gaze of those (like the Jane Austen of *Mansfield Park)* who stand at center stage in the Western narrative. To the organic contrapuntal exilic consciousness, however, he or she is, as were the slaves in Antigua, nevertheless hauntingly *there,* "always," in T. S. Eliot's words, "flickering at the corner of my eye."[30] And it is this eccentric spectral *thereness* that inaugurates the liberatory process of thinking the spectrality of the émigré corporeally and positively:

> Although the disabling aspects of this fate are manifest, its virtues or possibilities are worth exploring. Thus the émigré's consciousness—a mind of winter, in Wallace Stevens' phrase [stripped of identity]—discovers in its marginality that "a gaze averted from the beaten track, a hatred of brutality, a search for fresh concepts not yet encompassed by the general pattern, is the last hope of thought." Adorno's general pattern is what in another place he calls the "administered world" or, insofar as the irresistible dominants in culture are concerned, "the consciousness industry." There is then not just the negative advantage of refuge in the émigré's eccentricity; there is also the positive benefit of challenging the system, describing it in language unavailable to those it has already subdued.[31]

To give precision to this crucial insight, Said then goes on to quote Adorno: "*In an intellectual hierarchy which constantly makes everyone answerable, unanswerability alone can call the hierarchy directly by its right name.* The circulation sphere, whose stigmata are borne by intellectual outsiders, opens a last refuge to the mind that it barters away, at the very moment when refuge no longer exists. He who offers for sale something unique that no one wants to buy, represents, even against his will, freedom from exchange" (*CI*, 333; emphasis added).

To Said, Adorno's reflections on the émigré's damaged life are "too privatized," too "obdurately subjective," and thus yield only "minimal opportunities" for liberation. Nevertheless, when these reflections are reconstellated into the imperial context, as Said does here, at the end of his contrapuntal reading of the history of the relationship between Western culture and imperialism, their positive significance for the present global occasion—what I have been calling the interregnum—becomes forcefully manifest. On the one hand, in invoking Adorno's characterization of modernity as an "intellectual hierarchy" (i.e., the imperial regime of truth) that "constantly makes everyone answerable," Said is referring to the polyvalent and totalizing Western narrative—ontological, cultural (the novel), and political—that, as he has shown in the content and (anti-)structure of *Culture and Imperialism*, had hitherto imposed its hegemony on humanity but was coming to its end in late modernity. In emphasizing Adorno's imperative that in such a world, "unanswerability alone can call the hierarchy by its name," on the other hand, he is referring to the unhomed migrant, to the exilic intellectual and ultimately, insofar as he or she distills and articulates the disfiguring predicaments of modernity, to the masses of unhomed victims of empire. For Said, that is, Adorno's imperative of refusal means the strategic acceptance by the empire's "Others" of the ontological, cultural, and political status—their nonbeing or, to use the metaphorics I have appropriated from his characterization of the "voyage in," their identityless spectrality, in all these senses—attributed to them by the polyvalent imperial (meta)narrative not passively but in an active corporeal way.[32] Their polyvalent oppositional discourse and the resistance it would enable, Said implies, will not take the form of direct encounter with the infinitely more formidable oppressors, since such resistance would be tantamount to being answerable to the dictates of the forwarding narrative juggernaut of the West. Rather, as he says, it will be "anti-narrativist" and "unregimented" (*CI*, 334)—nomadic, invisible, errant—a "war machine," in Deleuze and Guattari's terms, that would molecularize the inordinate power inhering in the concentered and totalized linear/circular discourse and practice of the West. An example of this can be found in the antimetaphysical, antinarrative, and antiforwarding military strategy of the Vietnamese insurgents, born from the knowledge of the imperial West's Achilles' heel, that de-centered, disintegrated, defused, and finally defeated both the imperial cultural and military armies of the United States nearly a half-century ago.[33]

By attending to its neglected structure, I have been trying to show that Edward Said's *Cultural and Imperialism* is the precipitate—the distilled and articulated contradictory fulfillment—of the Western imperialist project. As such it is more than just a (worldly) text that bears inexorable witness—brings from the margins to center stage—to that which has been insistently repressed in the history of Western thinking, culture, and sociopolitical practice: the polyvalent "no-thing" that from the beginning and increasingly has haunted the Western imperial project until the postmodern age, when, largely because of the instantaneous globalization of space and time, this hitherto abstracted polyvalent nothing manifests itself as a corporeal specter. I mean by this last a potential force of resistance that no longer needs to resort to the kind of identity-oriented resistance demanded by the monolithic (binarist) narrative of imperialism but, enabled by the exposure of this powerful machine's weakness, its intrinsic inability to deal with what refuses to be answerable to its identity and end-oriented directionality, turns the very phantasmic nothingness to which it has been relegated against its perpetrator.

Ultimately, the positive possibilities of thinking the corporealized nothing that Said retrieves and to which he bears witness are more than simply a matter of resistance, a negative molecularizing gesture. As his projection of the exilic intellectual as one who, from the perspective of being "between domains, between forms, between homes, and between languages," can perceive the "'complete consort dancing together' contrapuntally," suggests, these possibilities are also the foundation, however tentative, for an antiutopian utopian vision (one much like the heretical vision of Aimé Césaire in his *Cahier d'un retour* or that of the exiled Puritan William Slothrop in Thomas Pynchon's *Gravity's Rainbow,* quoted as two of this chapter's epigraphs) of a diversified, hybrid humanity, a multitude of singularities, now living not according to the dehumanizing imperative of an enclosed system that privileges white over black, the Elect over the Preterite, but harmoniously together in a globalized, borderless, and utterly secularized world:

> No one today is purely *one* thing. Labels like Indian, or woman, or Muslim, or American are not more than starting points, which if followed into actual experience for only a moment are quickly left behind. Imperialism consolidated the mixture of cultures and identities on a global scale. But its worst and most paradoxical gift was to allow people to believe that they were only, mainly, exclusively white, or Black, or Western, or Oriental. Yet just as human beings make their own history, they also make their cultures and ethnic identities. No one can deny the persisting continuities of long traditions, sustained habitations, national languages, and cultural geographies, but there seems no reason except fear and prejudice to keep insisting on their separation and distinctiveness, as

if that was all human life was about. Survival in fact is about connections between things; in Eliot's phrase, reality cannot be deprived of "the other echoes
[that] inhabit the garden." It is more rewarding—and more difficult—to think
concretely and sympathetically, contrapuntally, about others than only about
"us." But this also means not trying to rule others, not trying to classify them or
put them in hierarchies, above all, not constantly reiterating how "our" culture
or country is number one (or *not* number one, for that matter). For the intellectual there is quite enough of value to do without *that*. (*CI*, 336)[34]

In the last analysis, the antistructural, contrapuntal structure of Said's heretical *Culture and Imperialism* is intended to articulate not so much a new
form of resistance as this profoundly paradoxical "utopian" vision distilled
from the horrendous predicaments disfiguring modernity, that is, from the
global shatter caused by the fulfillment—the coming to its end, the self–destruction—of the logic and practice of Western imperialism. At any rate, it
is this metamorphosis of the mutilated lives of imperialism's multitudinous
victims into a "'complete consort dancing together' contrapuntally"—this
hopeful vision incumbent on the refusal to be answerable to the narrative
imperatives of empire—that constitutes Edward Said's gracious legacy to our
postimperial occasion in the interregnum, indeed, the legacy of all those
corporeal specters *of* empire who have undertaken the voyage in to the metropolis. The embodiment of this heretical vision is, as he everywhere asserts,
the most difficult of all tasks, not impossible. But after Said, there is no turning away from its haunting imperatives.

Coda

In *Culture and Imperialism*, as I have shown, Edward Said bears decisive
witness to the disintegration of the nationalist state (the metropolis) that
instigated and fed the imperial project and to the simultaneous emergence
of the unhomed, stateless multitude following the end of imperialism as the
fundamental, global reality of the postmodern occasion. Having distilled the
spectral politics inhering in and precipitated by the antinarrative structure of
Said's genealogy of modern imperialism, I would be remiss not to constellate,
however briefly, the resonant, indeed, epochal historical irony he dramatizes
through this genealogy into a deeper historical background than the more
or less modern one to which I have thus far been alluding, a background on
which Deleuze and Guattari's "Treatise on Nomadolgy" (from which Said
has drawn) has relied but, as Said notes, in a way both highly abstracted and
marked by "bravura." I am referring to the long narrative history of the West
that begins with the founding of the very idea of Europe in late Greek and

especially Roman antiquity, when the West defined itself as *civilization* by privileging its sedentary way of life over the wandering life of the peripheral nomadic tribes, the history that, as its cultural discourse everywhere testifies, defined and determined the West's imperial relationship to the peoples at its periphery until its self-destruction in postmodernity.

Consonant with its inaugurating metaphysical representation of being, which spatialized, structured, or territorialized its radical temporality—the difference time always already disseminates—and projected this structure in the figure of the centered circle or, more precisely, of the center and the periphery, the West as West was constituted in classical antiquity (specifically, in Rome)[35] when it defined itself in terms of its progression from a condition of random kinesis to that of stasis, from a perpetual migrancy that was limited to necessity—biological reproduction or what Hannah Arendt, following Marx, has called "man's metabolism with nature"[36]—through a stabilizing tilling of the earth (agriculture: the cultivation of the *agrios,* the wilderness or wildness), to the establishment of the polis, the human, that is, the civilized or metropolitan, city (the city that measures) populated by citizens who modeled their individual identifies on the planting, cultivation, and fructification of the agricultural process. Henceforth, the West came to represent its "Other" according to the dictates of this binary logic, which privileged the sedentary/cultivated life (*bios*), which it represented as human, over the nomadic life (*zoe*), which it identified as inhuman, animal or barbaric. In turn, and according to its organic narrative logic, this representation justified the West's conquest and colonization of its peripheral "Others" in the name of bringing them and the narrative to closure—the peace (*pax*) and its fruits—that their erratic and savage energies could not otherwise achieve. Eventually this epochal sociopolitical binarist construction, like its metaphysics, became naturalized, that is, so deeply inscribed in the Western consciousness that it came to appear to most as the truth of the way things are.

To reinvoke Edward Said's apt phrase, these "structures of attitude and reference" pervade the history of the cultural and sociopolitical discourse of the West from its origins right up to the present occasion. The imperial Romans, for example, called the people living beyond the periphery of metropolitan Rome, whether the Scythians in the East or the Hibernians in the West, *silvestres* (from *silva,* "woods"), a word that to them meant simultaneously "forest dweller" and "savage." (The fact that the Latin word *colon,* from which "colony" and "colonialism" derive, means both planter/farmer—cultivator—and settler of the forest shows how deeply this opposition between the sedentary and nomadic life was embedded in the Roman mind.)

As Peter Hulme has shown, during the age of exploration, which ushered in modern colonialism, the first European visitors to the "New World" universally justified their appropriation and settlement of the Native Americans' land by invoking precisely this age-old opposition:

> The strategies of colonial discourse were directed in the first place at demonstrating a separation between the desired land and its native inhabitants. Baffled at the complex but effective native system of food production, the English seem to have latched on to the one (minority) facet of behaviour that they thought they recognized—mobility, and argued on that basis an absence of *proper* connection between the land and its first inhabitants. . . .

Francis Jennings has traced the path of the key phrase in this argument. In 1612 the Jesuit missionary Pierre Biard, describing Canadian Amerindians wrote:

> Thus four thousand Indians at most roam through, rather than occupy, these vast stretches of inland territory and seashore. For they are a nomadic people living in the forests and scattered over wide spaces as is natural for those who live by hunting and fishing. . . .

In 1625 Samuel Purchas wrote of the Virginia Algonquian:

> so bad people, having little of Humanitie but shape, ignorant of Civilitie, of Arts, of Religion; more brutish then the beasts they hunt, more wild and unmanly then that unmanned wild Countrey which they range rather than ininhabite.

And in 1629 in New England John Winthrop assimilated Purchas's point to the legal argument of *vacuum domicilium* by which the Indian had "natural" but not "civil" rights over the land because they had not "subdued" it. To Jenning's evidence could be added two earlier pieces, Robert Johnson's neat condensation of the bestial and nomadic in the patronizing pastoral description of the natives as "lost and scattered sheep"; and Robert Gray's more sophisticated argument:

> Some affirme, and it is likely to be true, that these Sauages have no particular proprietie in any part or parcell of that Countrey, but only a general residencie there, as wild beasts haue in the forrest, for they range and wander up and down the Countrey, without any law or government, being led only by their owne lusts and sensualitie, ther is no *meum & tuum* amongest them: so that if the whole lands should bee taken from them, there is not a man that can complaine of any particular wrong done unto him.[37]

Fundamental to the discourse of the Puritans, who founded the identity of America in characterizing their providentially ordained mission as an "errand in the wilderness," this inscribed binary *as structure of attitude and reference* also pervades the cultural and political discourse of the United States throughout the period of westward expansion, beginning with the occupation of Indian lands immediately west of the East Coast settlements, extending through the phase of Indian removal, to the conquest and settlement of the Far West. It informs, for example, the culture-producing Leatherstocking novels of James Fenimore Cooper, in which the rationale of appropriation is massively and naturally represented as the colonists' "settlement" and "betterment" or "improvement" of the wilderness that the "forest-dwelling," "vagabond" natives left "unattended" and "unimproved";[38] it informs as well, and not least, Francis Parkman's encyclopedic histories of the French and Indian Wars, culminating in the defeat of Pontiac. Referring to the "fertile" and "teeming" opulence of the so-called New World and the "wretched tribes of the forest" or, similarly, the "wandering tribes," this eloquent, representative mid-nineteenth-century American historian writes:

> One vast, continuous forest shadowed the fertile soil, covering the land as the grass covers a garden lawn, sweeping over hill and hollow in endless undulation, burying mountains in verdure, and mantling brooks and rivers from the light of day. Green intervals dotted with browsing deer, and broad plains alive with buffalo, broke the sameness of the woodland scenery. Unnumbered rivers seamed the forest with their devious windings. Vast lakes washed its boundaries, where the Indian voyager, in birch canoe, could descry no land beyond the world of waters. Yet this prolific wilderness, teeming with waste fertility, was but a hunting-ground and a battle-field to a few fierce hordes of savages. Here and there, in some rich meadow opened to the sun, the Indian squaws turned the black mould with their rude implements of bone or iron, and sowed their scanty stores of maize and beans. Human labor drew no other tribute from that exhaustless soil.[39]

Said is not unaware of this deeply backgrounded Eurocentric trope of Western colonial history. Indeed, he frequently alludes to it, especially in *The Question of Palestine,* where he shows that the early Zionists, deliberately following the Western model, especially that of the "American pioneer spirit," justified their right to occupy Palestine by representing the land as *"terra nullius,"* implying that the Palestinian inhabitants were nonbeings, that is, not inhabitants but something like nomads, indifferent to or incapable of improving the land:

> What concerns me a great deal more is the *strength* of the process of diffusion whose main focus was the Zionist colonization of Palestine, its successes, its feats, its remarkable institutions; just as today the strength of Israeli information is its admiring self-regard and the celebration of its "pioneering" spirit,

which Americans in particular have found it very easy to identify with. An intrinsic aspect of diffusive strength has been its systematic repression of the Arab reality in Palestine. Most accounts of the kibbutz, for example, leave out the facts that even before the state of Israel came into being (and of course after), Arabs were never admitted as members, that cheap (Arab or Oriental Jewish) hired labor is essential to kibbutz functioning, that "socialist" kibbutzim were and are established on land confiscated from the Arabs. Rather than attempt in advance to answer charges that might be made about Zionist policy toward the Arab natives in Palestine, Zionist spokesmen simply said nothing about them. In the case of the kibbutz, therefore, the institution appeared to grow and prosper more or less spontaneously in an uninhabited land, where enterprising Jewish immigrants hit upon the otherwise quite remarkable social unit which was the kibbutz.[40]

Of course, the metaphors that this rhetoric used to privilege the sedentary over the nomadic life—clearing, improvement, and settlement over wilderness, fallowness, and the wandering life—gradually disappeared in the cultural and political discourse of the West as the imperialism of overt conquest transformed into an indirect economic imperialism. Nevertheless, they remained embedded as "white metaphors"[41] in the distinction between developed and un- or under-developed nations that came to saturate the discourse of modern Western nation-states. They remained, that is, until, to borrow a phrase from Herman Melville, the "extraordinary emergency"[42] that Edward Said has documented in his genealogy of the present postcolonial global occasion.

Understood in this more deeply backgrounded historical context, Said's *Culture and Imperialism* assumes epochal stature insofar as his contrapuntal reading of the history of modern Western cultural production decisively discloses the spectral counterhistory endemic to and contradictorily emerging from the narrative logic of this very history. I mean his witness, from the perspective of being in-between, to the gradual but inexorable emergence of the migrant, the émigré, the unhomed, the nomad—precisely the state of (human) being that the West had perennially identified and annulled as nonbeing—as a massive, visible, corporeal, and menacing presence, not simply to delegitimate its binarist truth discourse and the murderous planetary cultural and sociopolitical hegemony to which this imperial truth discourse gave rise, but also, in so doing, to announce symptomatically the imperative to think this massive anti-imperialist nomadic presence positively.

The "end" of Said's genealogy of imperialism in *Culture and Imperialism*, in other words, can be said to bear witness that Western civilization in all its manifestations has come full circle, not in the sense of a temporal process whose end confirms the beginning/origin (i.e., the truth of this binary between sedentary and nomadic peoples), but rather as a repetition (*Wiederholung*), in Heidegger's sense of the hermeneutic circle, in which the end produces a difference that deconstructs the inaugural binary of the beginning.[43] In coming full circle, that is, Western history, like the Western philosophy, Western culture, and Western imperialism with which it is complicit, returns us to its beginning. But insofar as it has precipitated on a global scale the nomad as the exemplary figure in postmodernity, this return has, at least in theory, decisively reversed the binary that initially identified the West as the West in opposition to the *terra incognita* or *terra nullius* beyond its periphery. To reiterate, "the end of philosophy"—the transformation (reduction) of being to territorialized world picture—has decolonized temporality, the nothingness of being, the differences that time always already disseminates, colonized and mutilated by metaphysical thinking, and has instigated the poststructuralist revolution in thought. Similarly, the "end" of the imperialist process has decolonized the mutilated multitude of differential "Others" and rendered their nomadic status the symptom of a potential political revolution that is adequate to the human condition in the age of globalization. A symptom, I emphasize; not by any means a reality.

At the "end" of *Culture and Imperialism,* which is in fact a beginning—an annunciation of the interregnum—Said, recall, writes that "liberation as an intellectual mission . . . has now shifted from the settled, established, and domesticated dynamics of culture to its unhoused, decentered, and exilic energies, energies whose incarnation today is the migrant." This, he is careful to say, means that the new, "unassimilated" nomads, who now constitute a vast, diverse, and hybrid global population "between the old and the new, between the old empire and the new state," remain by and large the mutilated victims of imperialism or, at best, its specters: bitter, angry, intransigent, sporadically rebellious, but ineffectual as a means of fulfilling the promise of global liberation and the renewal of the human community activated by the reversal of the binary opposition between the sedentary and the nomadic. This impotence, moreover, arises largely because their mutilated nomadic condition and its positive global possibilities have not, despite the massive theoretical archive they have produced, been adequately theorized. In *Culture and Imperialism* Edward Said, following his own directive, distills and then articulates "the predicaments that disfigure modernity," brings to center stage the mutilated bodies and minds of the vast, multiply positioned migrant humanity that the Western sedentary city and its imperial juggernaut has marginalized—and this also means women: those members of humanity whom the dominant sedentary (Western) male has, throughout Western history, insistently identified as nomadic. In so doing, Said, this "political figure between forms, between homes, and between *languages*" (like Frantz Fanon, C. L. R. James, Albert Memmi, S. A. Alatas, George Antonius, Amilcar Cabral, George Lamming, Aimé Césaire, Ngugi wa Thiong'o, and the other organic intellectuals who made the "voyage in"), has gone remarkably far to fulfill this unthought promise, that is, to bring to conscious visibility those erratic "unhoused, decentered, and exilic energies . . . whose incarnation today is the migrant." Edward Said's legacy to our benighted globalized world, then, is this "new humanist" witness (to invoke Fanon)[44] to the massive and irreversible reversal of the foundational trope that has determined the West's imperialist structures of attitude and reference to and practice on the bodies of its "Others"—the discrimination that renders a certain constituency of humanity "human" and another "inhuman." In the following chapter I attempt to think this new humanism as Said (ambiguously) elaborates it in his posthumously published *Humanism and Democratic Criticism*.

5. Edward Said's Humanism and American Exceptionalism after 9/11/01

An Interrogation

In the *Prison Notebooks* Gramsci says, "The starting-point of critical elaboration is the consciousness of what one really is, and is 'knowing thyself' as a product of the historical process to date, which has deposited in you an infinity of traces without leaving an inventory." The only available English translation inexplicably leaves Gramsci's comment at that, whereas in fact Gramsci's Italian text concludes by adding, "therefore it is imperative at the outset to compile such an inventory."
—Edward Said, *Orientalism*

The historical sense gives rise to three uses that oppose and correspond to the Platonic modalities of history. The first is parodic, directed against reality, and opposes the theme of history as reminiscence or recognition; the second is dissociative, directed against identity, and opposes history given as continuity or representative of a tradition; the third is sacrificial, directed against truth, and opposes history as knowledge. They imply a use of history that severs its connection to memory, its metaphysical and anthropological model, and constructs a counter-memory—a transformation of history into a totally different form of time.
—Michel Foucault, "Nietzsche, Genealogy, History"

Edward Said's posthumously published *Humanism and Democratic Criticism* is a deeply problematic book. Whatever his intention (was it to underscore his legacy in the face of his imminent death or simply another "raid on the inarticulate / With shabby equipment always deteriorating / In the general mess of imprecision of feeling"?),[1] it will be and indeed seems already to have been understood by his legion of followers as a last will and testament to his lifelong commitment to the democratizing dynamics of humanist inquiry.[2]

This understanding rests on an interpretation that astonishingly relegates to oblivion the half-century of history following the catastrophe of World War I, which bore persuasive witness to the disclosure of Western humanism's complicity with the depredations of the rule of Man: the self-identical subject, technology, patriarchy, nationalism, racism, and imperialism. This disclosure, moreover, has been articulated, in however exaggerated a form, by Western poststructuralist thinkers from Martin Heidegger; through Jacques Derrida, Jacques Lacan, Jean-François Lyotard, Philippe Lacoue-Labarthe, and certain French feminists; to Louis Althusser, Michel Foucault, Gilles Deleuze and Felix Guattari, and Gayatri Spivak, among many others.[3] This is not to say that this tacit burial of poststructuralist theory should be attributed to Said's posthumously published "defense" of humanism and humanist studies. It is instead to suggest that whatever his reasons, Said's refusal to encounter this resonant history, or rather his apparent cavalier indifference to it, has produced two unfortunate results. (1) It has obfuscated the meaning of the very term Said wanted to redeem and thus inadvertently rendered his last book the object of contestation between those traditional liberal humanist who have always accommodated difference to the *anthropologos* and those posthumanists who, by deconstructing the humanist tradition, have been attempting to develop a different understanding of humanity (and the *studia humanitatis*), one that acknowledges its historical contingency—its freedom from both external and internalized transcendentals—or, in Said's terms, its radical "secularity." (2) In an equally important and related way, Said's dismissal of the history of the poststructuralist critique of humanism has also blurred the symptomatic directives for the critique of American-style democracy, the very critique his recuperated humanism is intended to undertake, precipitated by what he reiteratively characterizes as the epochal "changed political atmosphere" that "has overtaken the United States and, to varying degrees, the rest of the world" following "the events of September 11, 2001,"[4] by which I take him to mean the George W. Bush administration's unleashing of the "war on terror"—which was always latent in the exceptionality ethos of American democracy. This, according to a certain reading of the poststructuralist movement at large, is the polyvalent global violence that brings to its end (in both senses of the word) the otherwise incorporative or accommodational logical economy of Enlightenment or humanist modernity and thus calls for a radical revision not simply of what the humanist tradition has taken to be human but also of the idea of humanism as a mode of inquiry into being *in all its manifestations*.

* * *

In the first of *Humanism and Democratic Criticism*'s five chapters, Said writes:

> I should stress again that I am treating this subject not in order to produce a history of humanism, nor an exploration of all its possible meanings, and certainly not a thoroughgoing examination of its metaphysical relationship to a prior Being in the manner of Heidegger's "Letter on Humanism." What concerns me is humanism as a useable praxis for intellectuals and academics who want to know what they are doing, what they are committed to as scholars, and who want also to connect these principles to the world in which they live as citizens. (*HDC*, 6)

Bracketing for now the problematic nature of Said's typical overdetermination of praxis at the apparent expense of theory (which could easily be interpreted as putting them in a binary opposition that privileges the former over the latter), we are compelled by his all too brief reference to Heidegger's extraordinarily influential "Letter on Humanism"—which instigated the poststructuralist critique of Western humanism—to retrieve what Heidegger's inaugural "examination [of humanism's] metaphysical relationship to a prior Being" disclosed about it. The essence of this disclosure is contained in the following striking genealogy of the word (quoted earlier, in another context, in chapter 2) from the "Letter," responding to Jean Beaufret's question, "Comment redonner un sens au mot 'Humanisme'?" (How can we restore meaning to the word "Humanism"?).

> *Humanitas,* explicitly so called, was first considered and striven for in the age of the Roman Republic. *Homo humanus* was opposed to *homo barbarus. Homo humanus* here means the Romans, who exalted and honored Roman *virtus* through the "embodiment" of the *paideia* [education/culture] taken over from the Greeks. These were the Greeks of the Hellenistic age, whose culture was acquired in the schools of philosophy. It was concerned with *eruditio et institutio in bonas artes* [scholarship and training in good conduct]. *Paideia* thus understood was translated as *humanitas.* The genuine *romanitas* of *homo romanus* consisted in such *humanitas.* We encounter the first humanism in Rome: it therefore remains in essence a specifically Roman phenomenon, which emerges from the encounter of Roman civilization with the culture of late Greek civilization. The so-called Renaissance of the fourteenth and fifteenth centuries in Italy is a *renascentia romanitatis.* Because *romanitas* is what matters, it is concerned with *humanitas* and therefore with the Greek *paideia.* But Greek civilization is always seen in its later form and this itself is seen from a Roman point of view. The *homo romanus* of the Renaissance also stands in opposition to *homo barbarus.* But now the in-humane is the supposed barbarism of gothic Scholasticism in the Middle Ages. Therefore a *studium humanitatis,* which in

a certain way reaches back to the ancients and thus also becomes a revival of Greek civilization, always adheres to the historically understood humanism. For Germans this is apparent in the humanism of the eighteenth century supported by Winckelmann, Goethe, and Schiller.[5] On the other hand, Hölderlin does not belong to "humanism," precisely because he thought the destiny of man's essence in a *more original* way than humanism. (emphasis added)[6]

I cannot in this limited space unpack this remarkably resonant genealogy of the meaning of humanism, a genealogy that, we must remember, despite the massive campaign by contemporary traditional humanists to obfuscate it, was written following the disintegration of Europe during World War II[7] and that, to reiterate, inaugurated the poststructuralist interrogation of the discourse and practice of humanism conducted by Derrida, Lacan, Lyotard, Althusser, Foucault, and others. It will suffice to point out, against Said's implication, that Heidegger understood humanism not simply as a disciplinary category but also as a historically constructed category at once ontological, educational/cultural, moral, and insofar as the former reproduces the metropolitan/imperial citizen, political. As the hierarchical binary between Roman/human and barbarism makes clear, Heidegger viewed humanism, no less than the theism from which it has always disassociated itself, as a metaphysical mode of inquiry—the perception of the multiple phenomena of being (temporality, the subject, the ecos, languages, genders, races, cultures) from an Archimedean fixed vantage point (*meta*)—that enabled the spatialization, coercion, or accommodation of temporal difference to the prior transcendental principle of identity (the *anthropologos*). It was thus in essence a polyvalent *imperial* mode of inquiry that, despite its Enlightenment strategy of disciplinary compartmentalization, assumed the various sites of temporal being to be an indissoluble if historically uneven continuum subject to its knowability and colonization by Man, the naturalized transcendental Logos.

Heidegger's genealogy of humanism in his "Letter" is admittedly too brief to warrant the ideological weight I am giving it. But if we recall and reconstellate the philologically enabled distinction he makes between the *originative* thinking of the Greeks (especially the pre-Socratics) and the *derivative* humanist thinking of the Romans in the great but neglected *Parmenides* lectures he gave during World War II (1942–43), my point about the paradoxical continuity between Roman/humanist ontology (thinking) and Roman/Western imperialism proper becomes powerfully manifest. I quote from the *Parmenides* at some length to suggest the salience of this genealogy of humanism not only to Heidegger's later thought, after *Being and Time*, but also to the "posthumanist" thought of the poststructuralists, particularly that of the Michel Foucault who influenced Edward Said, which disclosed the complicity of the supposed disinterestedness of humanist inquiry (knowledge) with political coercion (power):

> The essential domain which prevails for the deployment of the Roman *"falsum"* [the antithesis of *veritas,* "truth"] is that of the *"imperium"* and of the "imperial." We take these words in their strict and original sense. *"Imperium"* means "command" [*Befehl*]. . . . In passing through French, *befehlen* [which originally meant "to entrust"] became "to command"; more precisely, it became the Roman *imperare—im-perare* = to install, to take preliminary measures, that is, *prae-cipere,* to occupy in advance and by so doing to have the "possessed" as domain [*Gebiet*], to dominate over it. The *imperium* is the domain that founds itself on the basis of the order [*Gebot*], and under whose dominion the others are subject. . . .
>
> To commanding as the essential foundation of sovereignty belongs "being on high" [*Obensein*]. That is only possible through constant surmounting in relation to others, who are thus the inferiors. In the surmounting, in turn, resides the constant ability to oversee [super-vise and dominate, *Übersehen-können*]. We say "to oversee something," which means "to master it" [*beherrschen*]. To this commanding view, which carries with it surmounting, belongs the always-being-on-the-lookout. That is the form of all action that oversees, but that holds to itself, in Roman the *actio* of the *actus.* The commanding overseeing is the dominating vision which is expressed in the often cited phrase of Caesar: *veni, vidi, vici*—I came, I *oversaw* [*übersah*], I conquered. Victory is already nothing but the consequence of the Caesarian gaze that dominates [*Übersehens*] and the seeing [*Sehens*] which has the character of *actio.* The essence of the *imperium* reposes in the *actio* of constant action. The imperial *action* of the constant surmounting over others implies that the others, in the case where they raise themselves to a comparable or even identical height of command, will be brought down—in Roman: *fallere* (participle: *falsum*).[8]

The *Parmenides* lectures, however, do more than just disclose the general complicity between Western metaphysical thinking and imperialism. In a philological analysis that prefigures Foucault's seminal distinction between the overt use of power and that which appropriates knowledge to coercive purposes—and, not incidentally, Said's differentiation, following Joseph Conrad in *Heart of Darkness,* between a primitive imperialism of brute force and a rational one that is redeemed by an "idea" worth serving[9]—they also make explicit the indissoluble relationship between the modern allotrope of the Western metaphysical interpretation of being (the anthropological) and modern imperialism, which, unlike the rapacious non-European or nonhumanist forms, colonizes and administers its "Others" in the name of universal peace, as in the Pax Romana, the Pax Britannica, and the Pax Americana:

The "bringing-to-fall" can be accomplished in a "direct" assault [*Ansturm*] and an overthrowing [*Niederwerfen*: literally "throwing down"]. But the other can also be brought to fall by being outflanked [*Um-gehen*] and tripped up from behind. The "bringing-to-fall" is now the way of deceptive circumvention [*Hinter-gehen*]. . . . Considered from the outside, going behind the back is a complicated, circumstantial and thus mediate "bringing-to-fall" as opposed to an immediate overthrowing. In this way, what is brought-to-fall becomes not thereby annihilated but in a certain manner redressed within the boundaries which are staked out by the dominators. This "staking out" [*Abstecken*] is called in Roman: *pango*, whence the word *pax*, peace. This, thought imperially, is the firmly established condition of what has been brought to fall. *In truth, the bringing-to-fall in the sense of deception and outflanking is not the mediate and derived imperial* actio *but the imperial* actio *proper. It is not in war, but in the* fallere *of deceptive outflanking and its appropriation to the service of dominion that the proper "great" trait of the imperial reveals itself.* . . . In the Roman *fallere*— to bring-to-fall—as a going around resides deceit; the *falsum* is the insidiously deceptive: "the false."

What happens when the Greek *pseudos* [the counterterm to *aletheia*, "un-concealment"] is thought in the sense of Roman *falsum*? The Greek *pseudos* as what dissimulates and thereby also deceives is now no longer experienced and interpreted in terms of concealment, but from the basis of deception. The Greek *pseudos*, through its translation into the Roman *falsum* [as with the Greek *aletheia*, through its translation into *veritas*], is *trans*ferred into the imperial Roman domain of the bringing-to-fall. (*P,* 60 [41])

This Heideggerian critique of traditional Western humanism overdetermines the latter's ontological (metaphysical) foundation, but it also, against the spatialization and the post-Enlightenment compartmentalization that divided the knowledge of being into disciplines, perceives humanism's complicity with cultural and political imperialism. More specifically, as is suggested by Heidegger's distinction between an imperialism of overthrowing (force) and one of indirection—the inscription of imperial power relations by means of the humanistic discourse of truth—it discloses the means by which traditional humanism has been able to transcend the limitations of imperial power's overt use (its vulnerability to insurrection) by internalizing the systematics of coercion through knowledge production (the truth that is incumbent on ostensibly disinterested inquiry).

The distance from this genealogy of traditional humanism to that of the poststructuralists is not great. Despite his insistent reservations about Heidegger's residual metaphysics, Jacques Derrida continues and indeed amplifies Heidegger's genealogical critique of humanism (without identifying Rome as the West's origin), shifting the historical focus from antiquity to modernity—

Kant and Hegel and even Sartre, Husserl, and Heidegger himself. In "The Ends of Man," for example, he writes:

> Any questioning of humanism that does not first catch up with the archeological radicalness of the questions sketched by Heidegger, and does not make use of the information he provides concerning the genesis of the concept and the value man (the reedition of the Greek *paideia* in Roman culture, the Christianizing of the Latin *humanitas,* the rebirth of Hellenism in the fourteenth and eighteenth centuries, etc.), any metahumanist position that does not place itself within the opening of these questions remains historically regional, periodic, and peripheral, juridically secondary and dependent, whatever interest and necessity it might retain as such.[10]

Equally important, Derrida radicalizes his critique of humanistic Man by denying the human subject even the vestigial remains of a self-present identity. Indeed, his essential purpose in this grounding-breaking essay—much like Said's insistent deconstruction of the collective "we" (against "them") adopted by Orientalists in their representation of the Orient—is to deconstruct the universal "we" adopted by Europeans, even by those critics of humanism, such as Husserl and Heidegger, who would free humanity from the bondage of self-identical or anthropological Man:

> To the extent that it describes the structures of human-reality, phenomenological ontology is a philosophical anthropology. Whatever the breaks marked by this Hegelian-Husserlian-Heideggerian anthropology as concerns the classical anthropologies, there is an uninterrupted metaphysical familiarity with that which, so naturally, links the *we* of the philosopher to "we men," to the *we* in the horizon of humanity. Although the theme of history is quite present in the discourse of the period, there is little practice of the history of concepts. For example, the history of the concept of man is never examined. Everything occurs as if the sign "man" had no origin, no historical, cultural, or linguistic limit. (EM, 116)

In "The Ends of Man" (and elsewhere in his early work), Derrida, like Heidegger, overdetermines the sites of thinking (rather than practice) on the continuum of being—the ontological, the epistemological, and the linguistic—at the expense of the "worldly." It should not be overlooked, however, as it too often has been, that in this essay Derrida addresses the same question about the viability of humanism that Beaufret posed to Heidegger in the mid-1940s. This time, however, as Derrida underscores in his preliminary remarks about the colloquium in New York where it was read, the question arises in the context of America's brutal intervention in Vietnam in the name of the "free world," that is, with an acute awareness of the spectral political contradiction that haunts the alleged benignity of the world of humanist democracy. Referring to the fact that the 1968 international colloquium on humanism is being sponsored by a Western humanist nation, he says:

> If I permit myself to recall this obvious fact, it is because a colloquium which has chosen *anthropos,* the discourse of anthropos, philosophical anthropology, as its theme, must feel bearing down on its borders the insistent weight of this difference, which is of an entirely other order than that of the internal or intra-philosophical differences of opinion which could be freely exchanged here. Beyond these borders, what I will call the philosophical *mirage* would consist as much in perceiving philosophy—a more or less constituted and adult philosophy—as in perceiving the desert. For this other space is neither philosophical nor desert-like, that is, barren. If I recall this obvious fact, it is also for another reason: the anxious and busy multiplication of colloquia in the West is doubtless an effect of that difference which I just said bears down, with mute, growing and menacing pressure, on the enclosure of Western collocation. The latter doubtless makes an effort to interiorize this difference, to master it, if we may put it thus, by affecting itself with it. The interest in the universality of the anthropos is doubtless a sign of this effort. (EM, 113)

One could easily continue retrieving the sustained history of the poststructuralist genealogical critique of Western humanism that Said would all too hastily forget in his project to recuperate the dignity and worth of the humanist tradition. This would include recalling the variously sited anti- or posthumanisms of Paul de Man, Jean-François Lyotard, Hélène Cixous, Philippe Lacoue-Labarthe, Gayatri Spivak, and not least, Louis Althusser, specifically Althusser's identification of humanism, and above all humanist education, as an ideological state apparatus that interpellates the human subject, that is, reduces him or her to a "subjected subject" who serves the dominant democratic capitalist culture.[11] I will, however, bring this retrieval to an abrupt yet I hope resonant close by juxtaposing two passages where Foucault addresses the question of humanism: his decisive genealogy of Jeremy Bentham's "humane" if not precisely humanist panopticism (which, as I have shown in chapter 2, derives from Heidegger's genealogy of humanism, the visualist metaphysics of anthropologism)[12] and his famous indictment of Enlightenment humanism in "Revolutionary Action 'Until Now.'" I do this at some length not only to recall Said's great debt to this French poststructuralist, particularly to his *Surveiller et punir* (which Said's disciples are now discounting), but also and especially to underscore the inherent polyvalency of poststructuralist critical practice, which Said, who tends to identify it as "theory" rather than praxis— the binary opposite of politics—thus seeks to deny:

The Panopticon . . . must be understood as a *generalizable model* of functioning; a way of defining power relations in terms of the everyday life of men. No
doubt Bentham presents it as a particular institution, closed in upon itself.
Utopias, perfectly closed in upon themselves, are common enough. . . . But the
Panopticon must not be understood as a dream building: it is the *diagram* of a
mechanism of power reduced to *its ideal form;* its functioning, abstracted from
any obstacle, resistance or friction, must be represented as a *pure architectural
and optical system:* it is in fact a *figure* of political technology that may and must
be detached from any specific use.

It is polyvalent in its application; it serves to reform prisoners, but also to
treat patients, to instruct school children, to confine the insane, to supervise
workers, to put beggars and idlers to work. It is a *type* of location of bodies in
space, of distribution of individuals in relation to one another, of hierarchical
organization, of disposition of centers and channels of power, of definition of
the instruments and modes of intervention of power, which can be implemented
in hospitals, workshops, schools, prisons. Whenever one is dealing with a multiplicity of individuals on whom a task or a particular form of behaviour must
be imposed, the panoptic *scheme* may be used. It is—necessary modifications
apart—applicable "to all establishments whatsoever, in which within a space
not too large, to be covered or commanded by buildings, a number of persons
are meant to be kept under inspection."[13]

By humanism I mean the totality of discourse through which Western man
is told: "Even though you don't exercise power, you can still be a ruler. Better
yet, the more you deny yourself the exercise of power, the more you submit
to those in power, then the more this increases your sovereignty." Humanism
invented a whole series of subjected sovereignties: the soul (ruling the body,
but subjected to God), consciousness (sovereign in a context of judgment, but
subject to the necessities of truth), the individual (a titular control of personal
rights subjected to the laws of nature and society), basic freedom (sovereign
within, but accepting the demands of an outside world and "aligned with destiny"). In short, humanism is everything in Western civilization that restricts
the *desire for power:* it prohibits the desire for power and excludes the possibility
of power being seized. The theory of the subject [in the double (Althusserian)
sense of the word] is at the heart of humanism and this is why our culture has
tenaciously rejected anything that could weaken its hold on us.[14]

The poststructuralists symptomatically recognized that the meta-physics
of the metaphysical tradition manifested itself as a relay of representations
extending from the theoretical (ontology, epistemology, ecology, linguistics)
to the practical (society, culture, and politics). Nonetheless, they remained
by and large disablingly captive to the disciplinary (divide-and-conquer)
logic that had its origins in Aristotle but was given its greatest force by the

rise of humanism, science, and democracy during the Enlightenment. It was, indeed, this vestigial disciplinarity of the early poststructuralists (Heidegger, who overdetermined the ontological critique of humanism; Derrida and de Man, who overemphasized the ontolinguistic critique of humanism; and not least the latters' American followers, who reduced the political potential of deconstruction to an antiformalist formalist literary aestheticism) that instigated the politically oriented momentum to put praxis in something like a binary opposition to theory. In so doing, it prepared the ground for its demise, or at any rate, for the present increasingly vocal annunciations of "the end of theory," in favor of a variety of disciplinary, praxis-oriented, and too often identitarian approaches: cultural criticism, neo-Marxism, feminism, gay criticism or minority studies, and postcolonial criticism. Not incidentally, this momentum, enabled by its inaugural theorists' unfortunate failure to fully perceive the potential for polyvalent political praxes inhering in poststructuralist theory (or was it a failure of nerve in the face of what was seen?), was synecdochically represented, if not initiated, by Said's essay "Reflections on American 'Left' Literary Criticism." Again, this liberating—but in hindsight, curiously limiting—essay was first delivered at the *boundary 2* conference "The Question of Textuality," held at Binghamton in 1978, a little more than a decade after the 1966 "Structuralist Controversy" conference that introduced deconstruction to America by way of Derrida's antihumanist "Structure, Sign and Play in the Discourse of the Human Sciences." Invoking the conflict between the new "theoretical opposition to the old nationalist literary traditions institutionalized in the academy" and "those old traditions fighting back with appeals to humanism" that emerged in the American academy in the 1970s, Said writes:

> I am . . . concerned . . . with the "Left" side of the controversy, and my real beginning point is a pair of observations about what the Left has not produced. Consider, first, that in American literary studies there has not in the past quarter century been enough work of major historical scholarship that can be called "revisionist." . . . For there to be effective interpretation in what is, after all is said and done, a historical discipline, there must also be effective history [Nietzsche's term], effective archival work, effective involvement in the actual material of history. Certainly the individual work of literature exists to a considerable extent by virtue of its formal structures, and it articulates itself by means of a formal energy, intention, capacity, or will. But it does not exist only by those, nor can it be apprehended and understood only formally. And yet for the most part literary studies have been dominated, even in their Marxist variety, by a relative absence of the historical dimension. Historical research on the Left had been neutralized by the notion that interpretation is

based ultimately on method or rhetoric, as if either of those two defined the separate competency and dignity of the literary theorist. Moreover, the whole concern with oppositional knowledge (that is, a knowledge that exists essentially to challenge and change received ideas, entrenched institutions, questionable values) has succumbed to the passivity of ahistorical refinement upon what is already given, acceptable, and above all already defined. . . .

The second observation is the other side of the coin, that literary studies on the Left, far from producing work to challenge or revise prevailing values, institutions, and definitions, have in fact gone too long a way in confirming them. (167–68)[15]

There is no gainsaying Said's judgment. Indeed, I would include in this criticism the disciplinary penchant of the various American "Lefts"—destructionist, deconstructionist, feminist, neo-Marxist, genealogist—to compete with one another in the academic marketplace, as in the debate between Derrida and Foucault over the meaning of madness or Jameson's Marxist criticism of the poststructuralism of Lyotard's analysis of the postmodern condition. That is, they continued *to practice an identitarian politics* at the expense of the collaborative antifoundationalist (antihumanist) project announced by the advent of an understanding of the traditional disciplinary "fields" of knowledge that perceived them as groundless and as an indissoluble continuum.

We need not, however, address these various historically emergent antifoundationalist Lefts, including Said's, according to the imperatives of their conflicting perspectives, as the residual adherence to the disciplines has compelled too many oppositional intellectuals to do. If, however, we attend as well to what these Lefts have in common, not least the rejection of a transcendental principle, that is, *a radical secularism,* a somewhat different story emerges. From this *interested* perspective—from this being-in-the-midst—we can readily see that each theoretical orientation, as I have suggested in my invocation of Heidegger, Derrida, and Foucault, is in varying degrees symptomatically, if not consciously, attuned to the sites of knowledge adjacent to the chosen site of its inquiry. More tellingly, we can also perceive that the process of the historical development of poststructuralist thinking at large—from Heidegger to Lacan to Derrida to Lyotard to Kristeva to Spivak to Althusser to Foucault to Jameson to Raymond Williams to Laclau and Mouffe, and, I would add, to Edward Said and the legion of postcolonial critics, including the Subaltern Studies group, he had influenced—bears witness to an irrepressible, however uneven, symptomatic momentum on the part of the marginalized sites to thwart the disciplinarity of the leading critical intellectuals by infiltrating themselves, like Derrida's revenants, into his or her privileged site of inquiry.

Indeed, despite Edward Said's insistent disclaimer, this enabling itinerary of poststructuralist history is epitomized by the itinerary of his oppositional criticism, the itinerary that culminates in his great book *Culture and Imperialism*. First, as I have shown, this book once and for all broke the hold that the disciplines of economics and politics—the Marxist base/superstructure model—had previously held on the critique of Western imperialism, doing so by foregrounding the role that cultural production had hitherto played in the political domination of the West's "Others." Furthermore, if only symptomatically, it disclosed the role that metaphysical ontology (the panoptic or center/periphery model that informs Said's "anti-Eurocentric" discourse) and its literary allotrope, the novel, has always played in this degrading Western colonial practice. In a remarkable echo of Heidegger's neglected differentiation between a primitive and a modern imperial practice, as well as of Foucault's differentiation between the ancien régime and the Enlightenment, Said writes:

> Thus Conrad encapsulates two quite different but intimately related aspects of imperialism: the idea that is based on the power to take over territory, an idea utterly clear in its force and unmistakable consequences; and the practice that essentially disguises or obfuscates this by developing a justificatory regime of self-aggrandizing, self-originating authority interposed between the victim of imperialism and its perpetrator.
>
> We would completely miss the tremendous power of this argument if we were merely to lift it out of *Heart of Darkness*, like a message out of a bottle. Conrad's argument is inscribed right in the very form of narrative as he inherited it and as he practiced it. Without empire, I would go so far as saying, there is no European novel as we know it, and indeed if we study the impulses giving rise to it, we shall see the far from accidental convergence between the patterns of narrative authority constitutive of the novel on the one hand, and on the other, a complex ideological configuration underlying the tendency to imperialism. (*CI*, 69–70)

The relay could not be more clear: a Eurocentric justificatory regime (theory), the European novel, European culture, and European imperialism (practice). However much Said and his adherents repeatedly binarized poststructuralist theory and oppositional politics, his critical practice, as well as that of "post-theory" criticism at large, adheres to the transdisciplinary imperatives that the original poststructuralist deconstruction of the metaphysics identified with the origins of the West at least symptomatically disclosed to the secular imagination, if it did not itself adequately practice them. A closer reading of Said's previously discussed essay on American left-oriented criticism will justify this claim. In other words, here at least, it is not post-structuralist theory as such that renders its adherents' criticism unworldly; it is, rather, the failure, whether from blindness or abuse, of its theorists and practitioners to fulfill its worldly possibilities.[16]

* * *

Specifically what is it, according to Said, about poststructuralist criticism that renders it unworldly and politically impotent? Following from his famous essays in *The World, the Text, and the Critic,* especially the one on American leftist criticism and "Criticism between Culture and System," Said attributes this failure at the outset of *Humanism and Democratic Criticism* to poststructuralism's "antihumanism":

> During the 1960s and 1970s the advent of French theory in the humanistic departments of American and English universities had brought about a severe if not crippling defeat of what was considered traditional humanism by the forces of structuralism and post-structuralism, both of which professed the death of man-the-author and asserted the preeminence of antihumanist systems such as those found in the work of Lévi-Strauss, Foucault himself, and Roland Barthes. The sovereignty of the subject—to use the technical phrase for what Enlightenment thought did with Descartes's notion of the *cogito,* which was to make it the center of all human knowledge and hence capable of essentializing thought in itself—was challenged by what Foucault and Lévi-Strauss carried forward from the work of thinkers such as Marx, Freud, Nietzsche, and the linguist Ferdinand de Saussure. This group of pioneers showed, in effect, that the existence of systems of thinking and perceiving transcended the powers of individual subjects, individual humans who were inside those systems (systems such as Freud's "unconscious" or Marx's "capital") and therefore had no power over them, only the choice to either use or be used by them. This of course flatly contradicts the core of humanistic thought, and hence the individual *cogito* was displaced, or demoted, to the status of illusory autonomy or fiction. (*HDC,* 9–10)

Said's extraordinary telescoped characterization of the advent of critical theory in the 1960s and 1970s offers us a curious yet persistent reversal, one drawn to our attention by his rather arbitrary *equation* of structuralism and its practitioners (Saussure, Lévi-Strauss, Barthes) with poststructuralism and its practitioners (Foucault and the Barthes who became one). On the one hand, he identifies poststructuralist theory with *system,* that is, a form of essentialism (identity) that subsumes singularities (difference: the "sovereign subject," "man-the-author"), particularly the singularity of human being, to its *telos,* whereas poststructuralism's adherents have insistently represented it as antisystemic and antiessentialist, free of transcendental categories, whether external or internal to man—that is, to appropriate Said, as a radically secular (if not worldly) critical practice. On the other hand, he identifies humanism with radical secularism, an antisystemic, antiessentialist mode of inquiry that acknowledges the singularity and sovereignty of the subject and his or her freedom to choose, whereas the traditional Western humanists have largely represented humanism as a *universal* mode of being that subsumes the singularity of human beings to an internalized transcendental category, Man or Mankind, a representation that has enabled the poststructuralists to perceive the alleged freedom of this humanist man as "illusionary autonomy or fiction."

Of course, as Said has insistently observed, the early poststructuralists overdetermined the systematics of discourse—the "unconscious," "language," "capital," or "disciplinarity"—and overmethodologized their theory, all of which rendered their work "unworldly," "jargon-ridden," "ahistorical," indeed, impotent in the face of, if not complicit with, the very institutions of power they were theoretically opposing. This seems to have been often willfully deliberate, as in the case of Paul de Man and the American literary critics his (and Derrida's) deconstruction influenced. In general, however, it can be argued, as I have been suggesting, that this unworldliness and political impotence resulted from their failure to explicitly realize the symptomatic worldliness of their theory. To put this less pejoratively, it resulted from their quite justifiable early and inaugural emphasis on the inordinate difficulty of breaking free from the constraints of a discourse of knowledge production and its institutions—schools, the media, the culture industry, and so on—that pervasively represented themselves as disinterested, humane, and democratic and, as Foucault observed, saturated the Western body politic right down to its capillaries. Indeed, this is precisely what Said said much later in his summary of Foucault's life work after his death:

His great critical contribution was to dissolve the anthropological models of identity and subject-hood underlying research in the humanistic and social sciences. Instead of seeing everything in culture and society as ultimately ema-nating either from a sort of unchanging Cartesian ego, or a heroic solitary artist, Foucault proposed the much juster notion that all work, like social life itself, is collective. [One hears here an echo of Vico's notion that humans make their own history.] The principal task therefore is to circumvent or break down the ideological biases that prevent us from saying that what enables a doctor to practice or a historian to write history is not mainly a set of individual gifts, but an ability to follows rules that are taken for granted as an unconscious a priori by all professionals. More than anyone before him Foucault specified rules for these rules, and, even more impressively, he showed how over long periods of time the rules became epistemological enforcers of what (as well as how) people thought, lived, and spoke. *If he was less interested in how rules could be changed, it was perhaps because as a first discoverer of their enormous detailed power he wanted everyone to beware of what disciplines, discourses,* epistemes *and statements were* really all about, without illusions.[17]

This condition of modernity, which I claim goes far to explain the post-structuralists' prioratization of discourse, was movingly articulated long ago by Theodor Adorno in his analyses of the minimalized potential for human agency afforded by the "administered society" (to which I have referred in chapter 3) and by Raymond Williams, both worldly thinkers with whom Said identified. In *Marxism and Literature,* for example, Williams employs Althusser's poststructuralist dismantling of the Marxists' disciplinary base/superstructure model to reconstellate Antonio Gramsci's concept of hegemony into his polyvalent diagnosis of modernity, that is, modern Western culture:

> The concept of hegemony often, in practice, resembles these definitions [of ideology], but it is distinct in its refusal to equate consciousness with the articulate formal system which can be and ordinarily is abstracted as "ideology." It of course does not exclude the articulate and formal meanings, values and beliefs which a dominant class develops and propagates. But it does not equate these with consciousness, or rather it does not reduce consciousness to them. *Instead it sees the relations of domination and subordination, in their forms as practical consciousness, as in effect a saturation of the whole process of living—not only of political and economic activity, not only of manifest social activity, but of the whole substance of lived identities and relationships, to such a depth that the pressures and limits of what can ultimately be seen as a specific economic, political, and cultural system seems to most of us the pressures and limits of simple experience and common sense.* Hegemony is then not only the articulate upper level of "ideology," nor are its forms of control only those ordinarily seen as "manipulation" or "indoctrination." It is a whole body of practices and expectations, over the whole of living: our sense and assignments of energy, our shaping perceptions of ourselves and our world. It is a lived system of meanings and values—constitutive and constituting—which as they are experienced as practices appear as reciprocally confirming. *It thus constitutes a sense of reality for most people in the society, a sense of absolute because experienced reality beyond which it is very difficult for most members of the society to move, in most areas of their lives.* It is, that is to say, in the strongest sense a "culture," but a culture which has also to be seen as the lived dominance and subordination of particular classes.[18]

There are, as many critics in the past have testified, crucial differences among these various postmodern articulations of the extraordinary difficulty of agency in post-Enlightenment modernity. Given the history of commentary and criticism about theory, a history that has insistently tended to remain disciplinary, competitive, sectarian, and discriminating, however, my purpose throughout this book has been to show what these various diagnoses of modernity have in common, to show, that is, that in some symptomatic global sense they were manifestations of a tentative *collaborative* effort by intellectuals in various disciplines to diagnose the malady of the modern—liberal democratic—*épistémè* in such a way as to overcome the limitations of the traditional (Marxist) left, which, in challenging the hegemony of democratic capitalism, employed the same logic of power relations (and concept of history) as its opponent. I mean by this last the *épistémè* that since the Enlightenment had been represented by the dominant culture in the Western, especially the Anglo-American, world as the apogee of humankind's historical struggle for freedom.

Perhaps, as Said implies, the poststructuralists were too pessimistic about the possibilities of human agency, but given the pervasively acknowledged inscription of the knowledge/power nexus in the body of Western society, Said—and those who represent *Humanism and Democratic Criticism* as his *Summum*—is too optimistic about these possibilities. Be that as it may, the representation of poststructuralist theory as such as a determinism is simply an oversimplification. If it is acknowledged that poststructuralist theory is radically antimetaphysical, it will be seen that its fundamental intention is to de-*construct* or de-*structure* the (polyvalent) structuring or territorializing (and identitarian) operations of thinking *meta ta physika* in order to liberate or decolonized the differential dynamics of being, including the nonidentical self, that such thinking would subsume to its overtly coercive or, as in the case of its democratic allotrope, accommodational or incorporative totalizing will to power. As R. Radhakrishnan has said in an otherwise appreciative recent essay on Said's humanism,

> *Humanism and Democratic Criticism* teems with passages where Said celebrates the self-reflexive, de-stabilizing, and protean play of language in literary and aesthetic works, but in all these references he is thinking of literary language that to him is organic to experience, not the "language" of theory that to him is occlusive of worldliness and experience. It would appear then this non-essentialist play of literary language and aesthetic elaboration is essential. Not an ontological thinker and not a philosopher, Said chooses not to do battle with essentialism *per se,* but with identitarian historical modes of living and being that are underwritten by essentialism, in particular, nationalism.

Why then does Said, who believes in, or would like to believe in, the epistemological assailability of humanism, not take poststructuralism to heart (poststructuralism whose very life breath is the "death of essentialism") or for that matter, Heidegger's "Letter on Humanism" which Said rightly identifies as "a thoroughgoing examination of its [humanism's] metaphysical relationship to a prior Being," but only to say, as a consequence, that "what really concerns me is humanism as a useable praxis for intellectuals and academics"? Would not the epistemological deconstruction of humanism be perfectly compatible with Said's critical praxis?[19]

It is not to poststructuralist theory as such that Said's severe criticism applies; it is, rather, to its abuses. As I have noted, Said often, if inconsistently, points to this in passing.

What, then, of the humanism that Said seeks to recuperate from the critique of the poststructuralists? Here, again, we enter a rather murky terrain, already signaled by his intention to bypass the "history of humanism," an "exploration of all its possible meanings," and "its metaphysical relationship to a prior Being" in favor of offering a humanism that is "a useable praxis for [contemporary] intellectuals and academics who want to know what they are doing, what they are committed to as scholars, and who want also to connect these principles to the world in which they live as citizens." All too cognizant of the centrality—and power—of the critique of anthropologism in the poststructuralist interrogation of Western modernity, Said does not by any means ignore this criticism of humanism and the *studia humanitatis*. Echoing, in a more historically specific context, the poststructuralists, he urges us to recall "that antihumanism took hold on the United States intellectual scene partly because of widespread revulsion with the Vietnam War [In France it was the "events of May '68"]. Part of that revulsion was the emergence of a resistance movement to racism, imperialism generally, and the dry-as-dust academic humanities that had for years represented an unpolitical, unworldly, and oblivious (sometimes manipulative) attitude to the present, all the while adamantly extolling the virtues of the past, the untouchability of the canon, and the superiority of 'how we use to do it.'" This superiority, according to Said, was the stance these elitist traditional humanities adopted to ward off "the disquieting appearance on the intellectual and academic scene of such things as women's, ethnic, gay, cultural, and postcolonial studies, and, above all, . . . a loss of interest in and the vitiation of the core idea of the humanities" (*HDC*, 13). Alluding, no doubt, to Allan Bloom's crude jeremiad against this invasion, Said concludes, "The centrality of the great literary texts was now threatened not only by popular culture but by the heterogeneity of upstart or insurgent philosophy, politics, linguistics, psychoanalysis, and anthropology."

Nonetheless, rather than attribute these disabling limitations—the essential-ism or universalism, elitism, nostalgia, unworldliness, and in the context of its crisis, the indirect reactionary sociopolitics to which the poststructuralists bore witness—to the idea of humanism as such, Said attributes them to the abuse of humanism by its modern practitioners, who range from Matthew Arnold, Irving Babbitt, Paul Elmer More, and T. S. Eliot to Allan Bloom, Dinesh D'Souza, and Roger Kimball:

> But it is worth insisting, in this [the American context] as well as other cases, that attacking the abuses of something is not the same as dismissing or entirely destroying that thing. So, in my opinion, it has been the abuse of humanism that discredits some of humanism's practitioners without discrediting humanism itself. Yet in the past four of five years, an enormous outpouring of books and articles has, in a vast overreaction to this purported or attempted antihuman-ism—which in most cases was an often idealistic critique of humanism's misuses in politics and public policy, many of which were in regard to non-European people and immigrants—gone on to diagnose such lugubrious improbabilities as the death of literature or the failure of humanism to respond robustly enough to the new challenges. (*HDC*, 13)

This way of articulating "humanism's sphere" presents a problem not simply because it is consonant with much of the critique of humanism made by the "antihumanist" poststructuralists, as the previous quotations from Heidegger, Derrida and especially Foucault testify. (I will return to this agreement later.) Equally important, the account compels us to ask about the nature of the earlier and allegedly more authentic humanism that this "bad," antihistoricist modern humanism—which Said often ambiguously calls "classic Eurocentric humanist thought" (*HDC*, 43)—abuses, even as it denies the reader a clear account of this abused essence of humanism, since Said has decided not to proffer a history of the word's meaning. As R. Radhakrishnan puts this problem, in commenting on Said's belief "that 'it is possible to be critical of humanism' in the name of humanism" (*HDC*, 10):

> I must confess that my response to a passage like this—and the book from which it is taken abounds with such passages—is truly ambivalent: on the one hand I respect the clarity of intention that shines through the language, but on the other hand, I am troubled and disappointed by a certain short-handedness in the mode of argumentation. It reads to me as though Said, having decided what his beliefs and intentions are, is really not interested in demonstrating how these beliefs and intentions are defensible historically as well as theoretically. This is just another way of saying that Said ends up paying a price for his political transparency: lack of sustained argumentation and definitional clarity. I am quite amazed by the ease that characterizes Said's claim that "it is possible to be

critical of humanism" in the name of humanism. Is this a proleptic gesture, an empirical claim, a counter-empirical claim, a theoretical guarantee? What does "belief" mean in the context of the received histories of humanism? (It must also be stated here that the harsh critics of humanism are not just high theorists but also a range of subaltern constituencies including critical race theorists, leaders of the "new nigger" movement, and others who are not interested in any kind of critical-remedial relationship with humanism, even if it is prepared to learn from such egregious and costly blunders such as colonialism and Eurocentrism.) I realize that what drives Said's rhetoric is that very imperative that Said valued so much in Raymond Williams: the search for alternatives, and resources of hope. But "in the name of what" are these to be realized?[20]

In the process of his critique of the classic humanism of Babbitt to Bloom, Said does of course refer to and identify with humanists from the Renaissance to modernity—Erasmus, Rabelais, Coli di Rienzi, Aretino, Montaigne, Thomas More, Vico, Leo Spitzer, Erich Auerbach, Ralph Waldo Emerson, and Richard Poirier, among others. Throughout his book, however, he never addresses these earlier figures in a way that clearly indicates them to collectively constitute a humanist tradition that has been abused by the modern humanists against whom he directs his severe criticism. For example, after invoking the Renaissance humanists Erasmus, Rabelais, and More as ancestors of this "good" humanism (without discriminating among their markedly different visions of humanity), he indicts other well-known Renaissance humanists, as well as those Americans who celebrated the "Founding Fathers," as precursors of the modern Eurocentric humanists who have abused humanism. Invoking Walter Benjamin's famous dictum "every document of civilization is also a document of barbarism," Said goes on to write that humanism

> is being required to take account of what, in its high Protestant mode [probably the Arnoldian tradition], it had either repressed or deliberately ignored. New historians of the classical humanism of the early Renaissance . . . have at last begun to examine the circumstance in which iconic figures like Petrarch and Boccaccio lauded the "human" and yet were not even stirred into opposition to the Mediterranean slave trade. And after decades of celebrating the American "founding fathers" and heroic national figures, there is at last some attention being paid to their dubious connections to slavery, the elimination of the Native Americans, and the exploitation of nonlandowning, nonmale populations. There is a straight line between these once-occluded figures in the carpet and Frantz Fanon's comments that "the Graeco-Roman statue [of humanism] is crumbling in the colonies." (*HDC*, 46–47)

In *Humanism and Democratic Criticism*, the humanists of the past who seem to offer the kind of humanism Said champions against the "classical" abusers of humanism are, as his previous work suggests, Giambattista Vico, Leo Spitzer, and Erich Auerbach. And this is because they have the philological method in common. I will return to Said's effort to retrieve philology into the present occasion, a philology, as he wryly notes, that modern critics consider to be "just about the least with it, least sexy, and most unmodern of any of the branches of learning associated with humanism" (*HDC*, 57). Here I want to comment on Said's well-known admiration for Auerbach's magisterial work *Mimesis: The Representation of Reality in Western Literature,* more specifically, to consider what, above all else, Said admires about Auerbach's masterpiece. This is obviously no easy task. There is first of all Auerbach's extraordinary erudition: his command of the Romance languages; his enormously broad and deep knowledge of the European literary tradition from Homer to Virginia Woolf and of the theological/philosophical, cultural (the tension between Hellenic and Judaic influences), and historical or worldly conditions out of which this literature emerged; his humane attitude toward its various representations of reality; the acute discriminations his careful philological orientation enabled; and his visibly heroic effort to render the humanistic project productive of new knowledge, an act of repetition rather than of recollection. These are, however, to some degree subsumed by the resonant insights about Europe and European humanism suggested by Auerbach's exile from his native country during World War II, as seen in Said's repeated appropriation of the lines from Victor of St. Hugo that Auerbach cites "as a model for anyone—man *and* woman—wishing to transcend the restraints of imperial or national or provincial limits" (CI, 335):

> It is therefore, a source of great virtue for the practiced mind to learn, bit by bit, first to change about in visible and transitory things, so that afterwards it may be able to leave them behind altogether. The person who finds his homeland sweet is still a tender beginner; he to whom every soil is as his native one is already strong; but he is perfect to whom the entire world is as a foreign place. The tender soul has fixed his love on one spot in the world; the strong person has extended his love to all places; the perfect man has extinguished his.[21]

Said's (controversial) reading of Hugo of St. Victor seems to imply that Auerbach's humanism (and his philological method) is, unlike the "classical humanism" of modernity Said excoriates, a *radical* secularism. The classical humanists, on the one hand, represent themselves and humanity, taken as a universal collective, to be at the center of and therefore at home amid the otherwise anxiety-provoking variousness of all the phenomena of earthly being, on the analogy of God and his Creation in Christian theology. Their humanism is, in other words, a naturalized supernaturalism. The exilic Auerbach, on the other hand, perceives himself (and humanity) as uncentered or decentered, a cosmic exile "to whom the entire world is as a foreign place." In short, whereas the classical humanism of the moderns is a secularism, but a secularism that is informed by a principle of presence (or identity), Auerbach's, Said seems to imply, is a secularism that refuses that temptation of "otherworldly" transcendentals. For Auerbach, to be human is always to be *in* but at the same time *estranged* or *alienated from* the world. As Said says of the view of humanity informing the humanism of Vico, Auerbach's great humanist predecessor, it is a "tragic" condition but for that very reason (as I will later show more fully) always open-ended and humanly enriching.[22]

But is this ultimately true of Auerbach's humanism? Despite the complexities one encounters in addressing this question, Auerbach's writing provides ample evidence suggesting otherwise. His humanism is indeed secular, as Said shows, but is it radically secular in the previous sense? One of the consistent limitations of the enabling distinction Said makes between unworldly and worldly literary criticism, between theological and secular approaches to literary texts, is that it fails by and large to clearly point out that the humanism of the Renaissance (as Heidegger observed and the enormous influence of metropolitan Rome in the theological and secular history of the West up to T. S. Eliot—about which Said has nothing to say—testifies) was precisely a secularism that modeled its vision of the world on that of Christian theology. That is, it substituted the *anthropologos* for the *theologos* and internalized the external transcendental of Christianity. The vision of these Renaissance humanists was limited not simply, as Said says of Boccaccio, by their Eurocentrism but also by their indissolubly related anthropocentrism. In this context one first of all thinks of Renaissance humanists such as Tomasso Campanella, who, following the Roman architect Vitruvius, imagined the circular City of the Sun (1633) and the highly disciplined life that such a utopia entailed (the same could be said of More's Utopia). One also thinks of those disciplinary circular cities envisioned and enacted by the humanists of the Renaissance and of the later Enlightenment—from Filarete (1400–1469), Giocondo (ca. 1435–1515), Cataneo (?-1569), Cerceau the Elder (1500–1584), and Daniel Speckle (1536–89) through Vauban (1633–1707) to Claude-Nicholas Ledoux (whose Arc-et-Senans and Chaux [1774–79] were, according to Michel Foucault, the precursors to Jeremy Bentham's Panopticon, the disciplinary city of the Enlightenment, and Baron Haussmann's Paris).[23]

This confusing failure is, in fact, symptomatically revealed by Aamir Mufti, one of Said's most reliable commentators, in his introduction to a recent special issue of *boundary 2* published shortly before the appearance of *Humanism and Democratic Criticism*. The issue focuses on the legacy of Said's work as it pertains to secularism "at a time when the world of humanistic knowledge was [under the pressure of "postmodernism"] coming to be shaken to its core, its basic assumptions about the possibilities of knowledge seemingly washed away." Here Mufti strategically—but true to Said's *actual* critical practice, as we have seen in his critique of Ernest Renan's natural supernaturalism— pointedly reverses Said's normal usage, "secular criticism," referring to it as "critical secularism." Mufti emphasizes the importance of this reversal by using the revised phrase as the title of the special issue, doing so to disclose a more authentic meaning inhering in, if not to rationalize the ambiguity of, Said's general references to secular criticism.

> As a number of commentators have pointed out in recent years, Said's use of the term *secular* involves a displacement of its usual significations. Secular criticism in Said's reckoning is, first of all, a practice of unbelief; it is directed, however, not simply at the objects of religious piety but at secular "beliefs" as well, and, at its most ambitious, at all those moments at which thought and culture become frozen, congealed, thing-like, and self-enclosed—hence the significance to him of Lukacs's notion of reification. At no point is *secular* used in his work in simple opposition to the religious per se. Above all, his concern has been with domi- nation through the classification and management of cultures, and of human collectivities, into mutually distinct and immutable entities, be they nations, properly speaking, or civilizations or ethnicities. To the great modern system for the classification of cultures Said gave the name Orientalism and viewed the hierarchies of this system as marking the presence of a "reconstructed religious impulse, a naturalized supernaturalism" . . . . Secular criticism thus struggles above all with the imposition of national (or civilizational) molds over social and cultural life, against all unmediated and absolute claims of membership in a national (or civilizational) community. This catachrestic use of the term *secular* carries the implication that energies of nationalism in its very broadest sense are thoroughly religious in nature, in a sense that has nothing whatever to do with whether or not an organized religion or a certain canonized popular religious life plays any role, symbolic or organizing, in this or that nationalism. In this sense, the secularism implied in secular criticism is a *critical secularism,* as I am calling it here, a constant unsettling and an ongoing and never-ending effort at critique, rather than a once-and-for-all declaration of the overcoming of the religious, theological, or transcendental impulse.[24]

Mufti's clarification of Said's secularism is acute—and much welcomed— in its acknowledgment and indeed affirmation of the indissoluble relation- ships among modern Western metaphysics, nationalist culture, and imperial politics (a naturalized supernaturalism).[25] I do not cite this passage to fault it. I cite it, rather, to point to Mufti's visible anxiety over the very real possibility, enabled by the uncertainty of the term's meaning—an uncertainty exacerbated by its use in *Humanism and Democratic Criticism*—that the classical humanists Said criticizes will interpret his privileged references to secularism or worldliness as an *accommodational* metaphysical perspective on the differential phenomena of being that in the end vindicates their universalism, identitarianism, and Eurocentricism, that is, will leave these references vulnerable to the kind of poststructuralist critique of humanism I have previously invoked.

To return to Auerbach, Said obscures his failure to radicalize his exile from "Europe"—to acknowledge the decentering he suffered under the Nazi regime as an unhoming not simply from his German homeland but also from the at-homeness of a humanist tradition whose securalism or worldliness was subsumed by a synthesizing principle of presence (or identity). Auerbach's humanism was extraordinarily productive of new knowledge, as Said everywhere shows, not least in the chapter on Auerbach in *Humanism and Democratic Criticism*. In the end, however (by which I mean at the base), there was always the *anthropologos* that accommodated this superstructural new—this otherwise singular—knowledge to itself and, as Said himself admits in passing (HDC, 95–96),[26] to the Europe, indeed, as Vassilis Lambropoulos has powerfully argued, to the Judeo-Christian (as opposed to Greek) Europe, that imagined it.[27] No matter the gradual shifting of emphasis from the center to the periphery, from identity to difference, from unity to multiplicity; it is this anthropological/Eurocentric base that determines Auerbach's inquiry, whether in the early Dante book, *Mimesis,* or the late "Philology and Weltliteratur," where, as Said notes, Auerbach, facing the post–World War II "dissolution of the educational and professional institutions in which he had been trained, and the emergence of 'new' non-European literatures and languages," comes to feel that the Goethean (humanist) global synthesis has "become invalid or untenable" (*HDC,* 95).

This failure—and its disabling consequences—becomes patently evident in Auerbach's analysis of medieval figural interpretation and this exegetical method's role in the establishment and unitary history of the representation of reality in the Western world. In "Figura"[28] and throughout *Mimesis,* Auerbach focuses entirely on the positive contributions enabled, via Judeo-Christian figural interpretation, by the epochal collapse of the elitist classical *Stiltrennung* (separation of styles) into the *sermo humilis,* not least giving back to the lowly a history that the classical age had denied them. This brilliant philological insight into European history was, as Said observes, one of Auerbach's most important contributions to modern scholarship. What Auerbach's humanistic insight apparently does not allow him to see in this providentially determined exegetical method, however, is the highly restrictive economy and polyvalent will to power over difference of its promise-fulfillment structure, its teleo-logic: the often monomaniacal or ludicrously single-minded will of its practitioners, parodied playfully by Cervantes and mercilessly by Voltaire, to reduce the singular events of the Old Testament into utter conformity with the events, present and future, of the New Testament, and beyond that, the events of the historical world, not least in its imperial Roman dispensation, into the prophetic totality envisioned by Christianity.

It should be remembered, moreover, that figural interpretation was not simply a matter of ontological and cultural representation; it was also one of morality and sociopolitics, that is, a hegemonic truth discourse—a "textual attitude," in Said's phrase—that saturated the European body politic from the time of St. Augustine to the Renaissance. In the medieval era figural inter-pretation was complicit with the crusades against Islam and the depredations of the Holy Roman Empire, to name the most obvious instances. With the Reformation and the rise of Protestantism, especially the American Calvinist variety, this same figural exegesis was appropriated to the colonization of the "New World," rendering it complicit first with the New England "Israelites'" divinely ordained "errand in the wilderness" (prefigured, in precisely the Auerbachian sense, by the Israelites of the Old Testament), which justified the extermination of the "lowly" ("savage," "diabolic," "bestial") Native Ameri-cans,[29] and then, following the rise of American democracy, with the "as-similation" of the "lowly" immigrants to the dominant Anglo-Protestant core culture.[30] Relatedly and closer to Said's worldly project, particularly in *The Question Concerning Palestine*, as I noted in chapter 4, the European Zionists from the beginning sought to justify their right to return to Palestine, their representation of the Palestinian Arabs as nonbeings and their land as empty (*terra nullius*), their settlements and "improvements," and their systematic ex-pulsion or containment of the area's "nomadic" inhabitants by appealing not simply to the justificatory regime informing European imperialism, which Said emphasizes, but also to the American allotrope of European Christian figural history. I am referring to the systematic prefigurative or typological exegetical method that justified the Puritans' divinely ordained "errand in the wilderness" and that in its secularized form came to be embodied in the American pioneer spirit under the aegis of "Manifest Destiny." Indeed, Said alludes to this appeal insistently, if always indirectly, when, in discussing the effort the Zionists made to "mitigate the presence of large numbers of na-tives on a desired land" by convincing themselves and the West "that these natives did not exist"[31]—that the land was, "like the view of America as an empty land held by the Puritans" (*QP,* 68), a *terra nullius*—he identifies this tactic with the "'pioneering spirit,' which Americans in particular found it very easy to identify with" (*QP*, 21).

Despite his lengthy treatment of Auerbach's analysis of the *figura* and the history of its influence on the representation of reality, Said, like his mentor, says nothing about this dark sociopolitical side of figural interpretation as he praises Auerbach for perceiving within this Judeo-Christian interpretation the "*human . . . will*," not God, as the maker of "the whole of human history":

> One last and quite difficult aspect of *figura* needs pointing out here. Auerbach contends that the very concept of *figura* also functions as a middle term between the literal-historical dimension and, for the Christian author, the world of truth, *veritas*. So rather than conveying only an inert meaning for an episode or character in the past, in its second and more interesting sense *figura* is the intellectual and spiritual energy that does the actual connecting between past and present, history and Christian truth. . . . Thus for all the complexity of his argument and the minuteness of the often arcane evidence he represents, Auerbach, I believe, is bringing us back to what is an essential Christian doctrine for believers but also a crucial element of *human* intellectual power and will. In this he follows Vico, who looks at the whole of human history and says, "mind made all this," an affirmation that audaciously reaffirms, but also to some degree undercuts, the religious dimension that gives credit to the divine. (*HDC*, 103)

Earlier in *Humanism* Said underscores the "destructive" consequences of leaping hastily from the singular "to mobilized collective selves": these leaps "lead to what Lukacs used to call *totalities, unknowable existentially* [because transcendental] *but powerfully mobilizing*." As do all metaphysical systems— whether theological (such as that of figural interpretation) or secular (such as that of anthropology, to which Lukacs refers)—"they possess great force exactly because they are corporate and can stand in unjustifiably for action that is supposed to be careful, measured, and humane. 'Our view,' said Mrs. Albright [as U.S. secretary of state], 'is that the sanctions are worth it,' 'it' being the killing and destruction of numberless civilians genocidally dispatched by a phrase" (*HDC*, 80–81). Given his lifelong effort to support the Palestinian cause against the systemic force of Zionism, it is surprising that Said does not perceive the analogy between this historical instance of inhumane repression justified by the "reality" produced by the Zionist totality and the inhumane repressiveness that characterized the history of medieval and Reformation Europe and America.

According to Said, Auerbach and Vico audaciously reaffirm the human mind over God's as the maker of history. When, however, his exposition of Auerbach's insights is reconstellated into the *historical world* that figural interpretation authorized, one is compelled to ask just how man's mind differs from God's if the history man willfully projects in the name of his truth is a figural (or in Derrida's terms, "preformational") history,[32] a "naturalized supernatural history," to use Said's own pejorative phrase, that ruthlessly dedifferentiates singularity or differentiates only to more efficiently dedifferentiate and discipline singularity?

Nor does Said say anything about the dark side of figural interpretation's precipitation of the lowly into history. His summary of Auerbach's account is, in fact, an unequivocal encomium not simply to the brilliance of the latter's philological reading of the Judeo-Christian exegetical tradition but to the aspect of Judeo-Christian history that, in breaking the hegemony of the classical separation of styles in favor of the low style, prepared the way for the rise of realism, secularism, humanism, and presumably democracy:

> Christianity shatters the classical balance between high and low styles, just as Jesus' life destroys the separation between the sublime and the everyday. What is set in motion as a result is the search for a new literary pact between writer and reader, a new synthesis or mingling between style and interpretation that will be adequate to the disturbing volatility of worldly events in the much grander setting opened up by Christ's historical presence. To this end, St. Augustine's enormous accomplishment, linked as he was to the classical world by his education, was to be the first to realize that classical antiquity had been superseded by a different world requiring a new *sermo humilis*, "a low style such as would properly only be applicable to comedy, but which now reaches out far beyond its original domain, and encroaches upon the deepest and highest, the sublime and the eternal." The problem then becomes how to relate the discursive, sequential events of human history to each other within the new figural dispensation that has triumphed conclusively over its predecessor, and then to find a language adequate to such a task, once, after the fall of the Roman Empire, Latin was no longer the lingua franca of Europe. (*HDC*, 106–7)

Given that Said more than anyone else taught us to perceive the violence toward the "Other" latent in "the textual attitude"—the preference for "the schematic authority of a text to the disorientations of direct encounters with the human"[33]—it is ironic that he should, in the process of admiring imaginative human possibilities of figural interpretation, overlook the carnage justified by the story of the creation and end of the world fabricated by the Christian biblical exegetes and eventually inscribed in the mind of Europe (and, in its Protestant mode, of America).

Auerbach's philological humanist scholarship indeed manifests a far greater tolerance of otherness than do the mandarin or nationalist classical humanists and the policy experts they have spawned. Despite this—and Said's concluding assertion that the author of *Mimesis* "offers no system" (*HDC*, 117)—Auerbach's humanism is motivated, if only vestigially, by the same yearning for synthesis and the restricted economy (of closure) that Said is criticizing.[34] However foreign the world became for Auerbach in his cruel exile, I do not think he finally achieved the strength to "extinguish his love" of all places, not least the Western humanist homeland, to enable him, in Said's words, to "grasp human experience and its written records in all their diversity and particularity" (*CI*, 335). At least that is how I read the last sentences of Auerbach's epilogue to *Mimesis*, after he has revealed that he wrote it in exile in Istanbul during the war: "I hope that my study will reach its readers—both my friends of former years, if they are still alive, as well as all the others for whom it was intended. And may it contribute to bringing together again those whose love for our western history has serenely persevered."[35] Like the Virgil and the Dante he loved—and the diasporic Israelites of the Old Testament—he felt as if he were a member of a "saving remnant" that would bear the relic of the shattered "City" of the incarnate Logos across the seas of historical crisis to replant it in a "new time and world."[36]

* * *

None of this, to repeat, is to say that Said, like Auerbach, fails to escape the blindnesses of classical humanism or, in Kant's term, the "anthropological attitude." It is to say, rather, that his effort to define humanism by avoiding its genealogy and symptomatically putting it into a binary opposition with poststructuralism renders its meaning ambivalent and thus subject to abuse by precisely those classical humanists he severely criticizes. On the contrary, I think that in Said's *practice*—when, that is, he interprets worldly literary texts or events of the contemporary historical occasion—he comes as close as has any intellectual in the past half-century to overcoming these blindnesses, to fulfilling the transdisciplinary imperatives of an uncentered mode of inquiry, call it whatever one will. Such a mode of inquiry (1) acknowledges the finitude, contingency, "thrownness," and "uncanniness"—the "not-at-homeness"—of the human condition; (2) perceives the knowledge of being neither as spatial categories—territorialized domains, regions, provinces, or realms to be conquered—nor as disciplinary compartments that render the task of such conquest more efficient but rather as a temporal continuum whose dynamics ultimately ward off containment and closure; and thus (3) understands human agency as an activity that privileges the Question over the Answer, the comportment that lets the singularity of being in all its manifestations, from difference as such to the various peoples of the world, *be* over that which would master and exploit its singular energies.

In *Humanism and Democratic Criticism* (and elsewhere), Said invokes not Auerbach's philology but Giambattista Vico's as the exemplary practice of humanist inquiry, a gesture of retrieval that he makes palatable to a contemporary audience by provocatively—and tellingly—identifying this "least with-it, least sexy, and most unmodern of any of the branches of learning associated with humanism" with Friedrich Nietzsche, "the most radical and intellectually audacious of all Western thinkers during the past 150 years" (*HDC*, 56).

> In Europe, Giambattista Vico's *New Science* (1744) launches an interpretive revolution based upon a kind of philological heroism whose results are to reveal, as Nietzsche was to put it a century and a half later, that the truth concerning human history is "a mobile army of metaphors and metonyms" whose meaning is to be unceasingly decoded by acts of reading and interpretation grounded in the shapes of words as bearers of reality, a reality hidden, misleading, resistant, and difficult. The science of reading, in other words, is paramount for humanist knowledge. (*HDC*, 58)

Bracketing for the moment the fact that Nietzsche profoundly and fundamentally influenced the poststructuralists—Heidegger, Derrida, Lyotard, Althusser, Deleuze, and not least Foucault—and that the famous quotation to which Said refers was often the point of departure for their variously sited deconstructive interpretive practices, let us examine more closely what it is about Vico's philology that Said would retrieve and, beyond that, about the nature of Said's understanding of what it means to be human, and what this understanding demands of the humanist vis-à-vis his or her scholarly and worldly practice. Following the directives suggested by Nietzsche's remark about language, Said finds Vico's philological method of reading to involve two "crucial motions" that he calls "reception" and "resistance" (*HDC*, 61)— and later, as we shall see, "belonging and detachment" (*HDC* 76).

The first motion involves

> submitting oneself knowledgeably to texts and treating them provisionally at first as discrete objects (since this is how they are initially encountered); moving then, by dint of expanding and elucidating the often obscure or invisible frameworks in which they exist, to their historical situations and the way in which certain structures of attitude, feeling, and rhetoric get entangled with some currents, some historical and social formulations of their context. . . .
>
> Thus a close reading of a literary text—novel, poem, essay, or drama, say— in effect will gradually locate the text in its time as part of a whole network of relationships whose outlines and influence play an informing role *in* the text.

And I think it is important to say that for the humanist, the act of reading is the act therefore of first putting oneself in the position of the author, for whom writing is a series of decisions and choices expressed in words. It need hardly be said that no author is completely sovereign or above the time, place, and circumstances of his or her life, so that these, too, must be understood if one is to put oneself in the author's position sympathetically. Thus to read an author like Conrad, for example, is first of all to read his work as if with the eye of Conrad himself, which is to try to understand each word, each metaphor, each sentence as something consciously chosen by Conrad in preference to any number of other possibilities. (*HDC,* 61–62)

On the surface, this encomium to close receptive reading—later enhanced by Said's characterization of it as "heroic" (*HDC,* 67)—could paradoxically be interpreted as mistaking carefulness for a willful, logocentric or metaphysical effort to impose a telos, a principle of presence, a center, on the text's differential dynamics, even texts, such as Laurence Sterne's or Thomas Pynchon's, that deliberately eschew closure. This possible reading is, in fact, enhanced by Said's invocation of the following passage from Leo Spitzer as "the best formulation of it." The scholar-humanist-reader, Spitzer says, must

work from the surface to the "inward life-center" of the work of art: first observing details about the superficial appearance of the particular work . . . ; then, grouping these details and seeking to integrate them into a creative principle which may have been present in the soul of the artist; and, finally, making the return trip to all the other groups of observations in order to find whether the "inward form" one had tentatively constructed gives an account of the whole. The scholar will surely be able to state, after three or four of these "fro voyages," whether he has found the life-giving center, the sun of the solar system [which Said says Spitzer regards as "the work's compositional principle"]. (qtd. in *HDC,* 64–65)

This interpretation, however, overlooks Said's overly casual but crucial allusion to Raymond Williams's analysis of the "structures of feeling," those deeply inscribed lived meanings that are hidden within the truth discourse of modern Western societies. Unlike ideology, we recall, this truth discourse—hegemony—

is a whole body of practices and expectations [developed by the dominant culture], over the whole of living: our senses and assignments of energy, our shaping perceptions of ourselves and our world. It is a lived system of meanings and value—constitutive and constituting—which as they are experienced as practices appear as reciprocally confirming. It thus constitutes a sense of reality for most people in society, a sense of absolute because experienced reality beyond which it is very difficult for most members of the society to move, in most areas of their lives.[37]

This allusion to Williams, which also harks back to Nietzsche's revelation that truth is a mobile army of metaphors and metonyms (and to Derrida's discussion of veridical language in "White Mythology"),[38] prepares the way for the second movement of philological reading, resistance. After asserting the worldliness of the reader and the text he encounters, Said writes:

> It can be said that two situations are in play: that of the humanist reader in the present and that of the text in its [historically established] framework. Each requires careful analysis, *each inhabits a local and wider historical framework,* and each must solicit relentless questioning by the humanist. The literary text derives, true enough, from the assumed privacy and solitude of the individual writer, but the tension between the privileged location and the social location of the writer is ever present, whether the writer is a historian like Henry Adams, a relatively isolated poet like Emily Dickinson, or a renowned man of letters like Henry James. (*HDC,* 74–75; emphasis added)

At the risk of oversimplifying, in this dense and resonant passage Said is, as my emphasis suggests, describing a position of reading that is paradoxically both passive and active, inside and outside, native and alien, local and foreign, familiar and estranged. Unlike the active receptivity of the New Critics or the passive receptivity—the disinterestedness—of the traditionalist humanists, both of whom assume a certain at-homeness in their world and thus inadvertently either unworld the text or render it complicit with the identity of the "local," Said characterizes a position of reading from a radically "exilic" or "border" perspective that enables such a "humanistic reader" both to feelingly understand the text's worldly meaning and to perceive its author's blindnesses.

Said cautions "against going from the 'private *ijtihad,*' or close reading, to the wide horizon too quickly, too abruptly and unreflectingly" (*HDC,* 75), but it is nevertheless the essential imperative of the kind of humanism he espouses:

> A reader is in a place, in a school or university, in a work place, or in a specific country at a particular time, situation, and so forth. But these are not passive frameworks. In the process of widening the humanistic horizon, its achievements of insight and understanding, the framework must be actively understood, constructed, and interpreted. *And this is what resistance is: the ability to differentiate between what is directly given and what may be withheld, whether because one's own circumstances as a humanist specialist may confine one to a limited space beyond which one can't venture or because one is indoctrinated to*

recognize only what one has been educated to see or because only policy experts
are presumed to be entitled to speak about the economy, health services, or foreign
and military policies, issues of urgent concern to the humanist as a citizen. (HDC,
75–76; emphasis added)

In applying this humanist imperative to the ominously reactionary contemporary American context, Said overdetermines this second motion of
philological reading, no doubt because it is historically—that is, in the context
of the long hegemony of the nation-state (and behind that of the principle
of identity)—the most difficult to undertake:

> Yes, we need to keep coming back to the words and structure in the books we
> read, but, just as these words were themselves taken by the poet from the world
> and evoked from out of silence in the forceful ways without which no creation
> is possible, readers must extend their readings out into the various worlds each
> one of us resides in. It is especially appropriate for the contemporary humanist
> to cultivate that sense of multiple worlds and complex interacting traditions,
> that inevitable combination I've mentioned of belonging and detachment, re-
> ception and resistance. The task of the humanist is not just to occupy a position
> or place, not simply to belong somewhere, but rather to be both insider and
> outsider to the circulating ideas and values that are at issue in our society or
> someone else's society or the society of the other. (HDC, 76)

Following this identification of the humanist critic with the ambulant or
desedentarized exilic consciousness,[39] Said goes on to offer the example of the
"great Jewish thinkers" whom Isaac Deutscher collectively and oxymoroni-
cally called the "non-Jewish Jew"—"Spinoza, chief among them, as well as
Freud, Heine, and Deutscher himself"—who "were in, and at the same time
renounced, their tradition, preserving the original tie by submitting it to the
corrosive questioning that took them well beyond it, sometimes banishing
them from community in the process." In pursuit of this directive, Said concludes: "Not many of us can or would want to aspire to such a dialectically
fraught, so sensitively located a class of individuals, but it would be illuminating to see in such a destiny the crystallized role of the American humanist,
the non-humanist humanist as it were" (HDC, 77; emphasis added).

The itinerary of Said's argument in behalf of the "return of philology," in
short, culminates in the precipitation of the exilic consciousness (the be-
longingness of belonging and not belonging to a particular place) and its
identification with the paradoxical nonhumanist humanist. Given this itinerary, what does Said imply about the meaning of the human in the word
humanism? Obviously, in overdetermining the notion of exile *from* a place
or a location—being both inside and outside, belonging and not belonging,

at the same time—Said means primarily that to be truly human, as well as a humanist, one must inhabit a geographic/cultural or worldly space (e.g., a nation) and at the same time remain *outside* it, conscious of, able to *see*, the differential imperatives of worldly spaces outside the periphery of its vision, or as Althusser would put it, its "problematic." This implies rejecting any form of nationalism grounded in a transcendental or biological (filial) principle of presence or identity—and its binary, us-against-them logic—as a construction produced by the dominant culture that justifies violence against the "Other."[40] When Said writes about the exilic consciousness, however, he clearly means "place," "position," or "location" also to be metaphors for the ontological concept of identity: the self-present self. Thus being truly human and humanist means not just being an exile from a national homeland but also being both present and unpresent to one's self. Being human and a humanist is to dwell, *always,* in both the familiarized world and the uncanny that is ontologically prior to it—what Heidegger long ago called *die Unheimlichkeit* of the not-at-home. This always being-in-the midst (*interesse*), to put it negatively, is a situation that disables the will to power inhering in any metaphysical/identitarian comportment toward being such as the "classical humanism" Said criticizes, a comportment that, in assuming a telos, privileges the answer over the question in inquiry. To put it positively, it is a situation that, despite the "tragic" it entails, acknowledges being's anxiety-provoking open-endedness (at all its sites) and thus privileges the question over the answer; that is, it *enables human agency* in the radical sense of this phrase. This, in effect, is what Said says of the philological project of Vico's *New Science*:

> Despite the progress, despite the certainty and truth of later knowledge, Vico, I believe, takes the tragic view that human knowledge is permanently undermined by the "indefinite nature of the human mind." . . . One can acquire philosophy and knowledge, it is true, but the basically unsatisfactory fallibility (rather than constant improvement) of the human mind persists nonetheless. So there is always something radically incomplete, insufficient, provisional, disputable, and arguable about humanistic knowledge that Vico never loses sight of and that . . . gives the whole idea of humanism a tragic flaw that is constitutive to it and cannot be removed. This flaw can be remedied and mitigated by the disciplines of philological learning and philosophical understanding . . . , but it can never be superseded. Another way of putting this is to say that the subjective element in humanistic knowledge and practice has to be recognized and in some way reckoned with since there is no use in trying to make a neutral mathematical science out of it. (*HDC,* 12)

In thus acknowledging the tragic—that there is "always something radically incomplete, insufficient, provisional, disputable, and arguable about humanistic knowledge"—Said is on the one hand criticizing a Western ontological and universalist representation of the human that envisions human being (*anthropos*) as the center—and as the fixed and certain measure (Logos)—of being and, more immediately, that perceives this central or metropolitan Man as endemic to the West, as opposed to all other modes of human thought and practice at its periphery. It is a deeply inscribed, socially constructed view of human being that, on the analogy of God and his Creation, assumes Man, specifically Western Man, to be the lord and master of being (over "all that he surveys"), as when Daniel Defoe, recapitulating synecdochically the "glorious" history of Britain at the transition from theology to anthropology, represents his protagonist's relationship to the island world he inhabits (the continuum between self, family, nation, and family of nations) after he has "settled," "enclosed," and "improved"—"colonized"—its being:

> What a Table was here spread for me in a Wilderness, where I saw nothing at first but to perish for Hunger.
>
> It would have made a Stoick smile to have seen, me and my little Family sit down to Dinner; there was my Majesty the Prince and Lord of the whole Island; I had the Lives of all my Subjects at my absolute Command. I could hang, draw, give Liberty, and take it away, and no Rebels among all my Subjects.[41]

This humanism is in short an anthropo-logy: the arrogant view of (Western) humanity and the humanist, concealed beneath the façade of a benign sovereign free will, that the poststructuralists, from Heidegger to Foucault, rejected, having seen, each in his or her own way, how the will to power inhering in the panoptic—transcendental secular—perspective of traditional humanism enabled depredations to thinking, to the psyche, and to sexual, racial, and ethnic relations. It is also, not incidentally, this metropolitan humanism that postcolonial theorists influenced by poststructuralism, such as Guha, Chakrabarty, and Chatterjee, as well as Third World activists such as Frantz Fanon, C. L. R. James, and Aimé Césaire, rejected for the violence its understanding of the human inflicted on the different cultures of their worlds.

On the other hand, in acknowledging with Vico the "tragic" as an inescapable ontological condition—a condition of uncertainty that, despite its power to "remedy" or "mitigate," cannot be "superseded"—Said is affirming a humanity and humanism that, to put it generally, understands itself not as sovereign subject or lord and master but, given the "advantage" of its consciousness over other beings, as caretaker of being in all its manifestations.

This more specifically takes two forms. (1) It is a humanity and humanism that is interested in the sense of that adjective's etymology—*inter esse;* to be in the midst—and acts in the world *care*fully (as opposed to calculatively, which is the imperative of metaphysics and the epistemology of the answer), that is, according to the ethical imperatives inhering in the tragic human condition, the condition of being in between—always inside and outside the "world," both "ek-sistent and in-sistent," as Heidegger, following Nietzsche, put the human condition at the beginning of the poststructuralist revolution. (2) Further, it is a humanity that excludes no one in the community of humanity, as the image on the book jacket of *Humanism and Democratic Criticism* suggests, an image no doubt intended to echo the lines Said frequently quoted from Aimé Césaire's *Cahier d'un retour*: "and no race has a monopoly on beauty, on intelligence, on strength / and there is room for everyone at the convocation of / conquest."[42]

The acceptance of this radically "tragic" view of human being (and knowledge), the identityless identity of men and women, and the decision to think and act the ethical imperative of care for which the tragic human condition calls: all this is what Said means in identifying the exilic thinker—the insider/outsider—as the nonhumanist humanist. As I have been suggesting in thus invoking the genealogical discourse of the Nietzschean tradition, this relay among the tragic view, the identityless identity of human beings, and the care-ful ethics these entail is also, however inadequately thought or announced, the legacy of the poststructuralist theory that has rejected the hegemonic concept and practice of humanism or affirmed a "posthumanist" humanism.

Said, of course, distanced himself from the poststructuralists and their "antihumanism" not too long after his highly theoretical meditation on beginnings, and this distance is maintained even less ambiguously throughout *Humanism and Democratic Criticism.* Elsewhere I have singled out three basic and related aspects of poststructuralist theory and practice that he severely criticizes: (1) in restricting its interpretive/critical focus to the site of textuality, it slighted the worldliness of the texts and, in so doing, remained complicit with the disciplinarity and professionalism that is fundamental to the knowledge/power relations of modernity; (2) in substituting one form of totalizing system for that of the humanism it attacks, it thus, like its antagonist, annulled the possibility of human agency; (3) in insisting on the fundamental undecidability of all (worldly) texts, it ended in a political quietism.[43] These were indeed disabling limitations of the early poststructuralists and especially of their followers in American literary criticism. As I have been suggesting, however, they are not endemic to the ontology of poststructuralism, which is, to reiterate, radically antifoundational. Poststructuralist theory reversed the metaphysical principle of principles: that identity is the condition for the possibility of difference. That is, it rejected both the metaphysical interpretation of being (and its dream of peace), whether theological or anthropological, that has informed the history of Western civilization and, in so doing, the assumption that a principle of presence inheres in being, including human being. It thus retrieved the ontological priority of the question from a hegemonic humanist discourse that privileged the answer. In other words, whereas metaphysical thinking, even its "democratic" modern allotrope, which favored the human individual against the human collective, was ultimately deterministic, the poststructuralist inversion of the identity/difference principle—its affirmation that difference is the condition for the possibility of identity, in which case identity comes to be understood as a construction always subject to change—enabled a radical notion of free will or human agency. The limitations of poststructuralism were not theoretical but practical. On the one hand, they were historically determined. First, these limitations resulted primarily from the early recognition of the extent to which the principle that privileges identity over difference (and the "white" metaphors, including those of seeing and grasping, endemic to it) saturated the Western languages of humanist knowledge production and rendered agency extremely difficult. Second, this saturation initially and quite naturally constrained early poststructuralist critical inquiry to the disciplines of ontology and epistemology, that is, to the site of language or textuality, at the expense of the other, "more practical" sites on the continuum of being. On the other hand, as I argued over a decade ago, these limitations resulted from the co-optation of poststructuralist theory, above all Derridian deconstruction, by American literary critics who either misunderstood the emancipatory thrust of its overdetermination of the "play of *différance*" or willfully discounted it in favor of systematizing an anti–New Critical aesthetic formalism.[44]

This misconceived restriction of poststructuralist theory to a disciplinary antiformalist formalism eventually instigated more politically oriented critics to explore the worldliness of texts. Henceforth feminists adapted the poststructuralist critique of logocentrism to their critique of patriarchy as phallocentrism, and in a far more contentious way, Louis Althusser (following Gramsci) revised the base/superstructure model of orthodox Marxism to enable both his own critique of the cultural "problematic" of modern capitalism and Michel Foucault's genealogical critique of the modern disciplinary society (panopticism), both of which, as in the case of all the earlier poststructuralist practices, interrogated the ontological primacy of vision. Unfortunately these various practices consciously competed with one another for authority, remained in some degree disciplinary, and therefore were articulated as systems or methods, as Said never fails to remind us.

If we attend, however, not to the rhetoric of competition or sectarianism but to the commonality of the (anti)foundational ground of these various poststructuralist critical practices, we can see at least the possibility that they constitute a momentum, however incremental, uneven, and erratic, of development during which poststructuralist theory *symptomatically* metamorphosed from a disciplinary to a transdisciplinary—and potentially collaborative—antiessentialist outlook that perceives being as an indissoluble, if historically uneven, continuum from the ontological to the social to the political, from the "less" to the "more" worldly sites. Seen in this way, Said's critique of Western Orientalism, for example, does not constitute a radical departure from Foucault's poststructuralist antihumanism. Rather, as I have argued in chapter 3, it extends the latter's Nietzschean genealogy of the panopticism of the Enlightenment nation-state. That is, it opens up the representation of the *internal* "Others" by the dominant (bourgeois capitalist) culture of the modern nation-state as deviants (nonhuman) to be accommodated to its humanist hierarchical power structure through humanist knowledge production (the regime of truth), to include the panoptic Western nation-state's colonization of its *external* "Others" (the various cultures of the East) through the same regime of humanist knowledge production. Indeed, this possibility will be underscored if, as I have done in chapter 3, we interpret Said's pervasive use of the spatial metaphorics of ontological discourse—most notably vision and object (panoptics), center and periphery (or margin), and civility and savagery—to express his decisively delegitimating insights into the discourse of Orientalism as having been assimilated into the more overtly worldly sites he rightly overdetermines.

Despite Said's reiterated criticism of Foucault's "theoretical overtotalization" of power,[45] it could be said that in collapsing the disciplinary boundaries among (Western) language, the nation-state, and the worlds outside the West—or alternatively, in perceiving the discourse of hegemony, nationalism, and empire as an indissoluble continuum, however uneven at particular historical moments—Said comes closer than any other modern oppositional intellectual to fulfilling the transdisciplinary and agency-oriented imperatives for the emancipatory thinking and acting demanded by the de-centering of the Logos of the *anthropos*. Indeed, it could be said that Said's lifelong endeavor was in some sense to think the new understanding of humanism, humanist inquiry, and the humanities to which his poststructuralist predecessors were blinded by the very disciplinary structure they had called into question, a radically secular humanism that was appropriate to the change of terrain prompted by the coming to its end—the gradual self–de-struction— of Western imperial thinking and practice and the ensuing precipitation into spectral being of its nonbeing "Others." One of the great ironies of his last book, *Humanism and Democratic Criticism,* is that in the very process of announcing this new humanism, or posthumanism, Said obfuscates its lineaments by distancing himself from the revolution of which he was the most distinguished heir.

* * *

In a fundamental way the lectures constituting *Humanism and Democratic Criticism* were intended to provide directives enabling us to understand and deal with the events of 9/11, which Said felt were epochal in their radical defamiliarization of the world previously organized by the West. More specifically, his retrieval and reevaluation of humanism was meant to provide directives for resisting the George W. Bush administration's contempt for history, its extremist response to the attacks on the World Trade Center and the Pentagon, and its arrogant effort to impose American-style democracies in the Middle East by force, a policy that threatens to render the "clash of civilizations" thesis of Orientalists such as Bernard Lewis and American policy experts such as Samuel P. Huntington a self-fulfilling prophecy: "I think the moment has come, for me at least, to reconsider, re-examine and reformulate the relevance of humanism as we head into a new millennium with so many circumstances undergoing enough dramatic change to transform the setting entirely" (*HDC,* 6). Given the sense of finality informing this statement of intent, one might say that for Said, the events of 9/11 and the Bush administration's response constitute the culmination of an imperial global history presided over by the West that has, in Althusser's resonant Marxist terms, inadvertently but necessarily produced a radical "change of terrain"; specifically, it precipitated into corporeal presence the hitherto geographically and psychologically remote specter—the West's (colonized) "Other"—that, according to Said, has come increasingly to haunt the Western metropolis.[46]

The significance of this epochal estrangement of the global terrain is, needless to say, too complex for easy determination, but Said's diagnosis of the devastating legacy of imperialism at the end of *Culture and Imperialism* provides us, as I have shown, with a suggestive context and productive directives for rethinking humanism and the humanities:

> Surely it is one of the unhappiest characteristics of the age to have produced
> more refugees, migrants, displaced persons, and exiles than ever before in

history, most of them as an accompaniment to and, ironically enough, as after-thoughts of the great post-colonial and imperial conflicts. As the struggle for independence produced new states and new boundaries, it also produced home-less wanderers, nomads, and vagrants, unassimilated to the emerging structures of institutional power, rejected by the established order for their intransigence and obdurate rebelliousness. *And insofar as these people exist between the old and the new, between the old empire and the new state,* their condition articulates the tensions, irresolutions, and contradictions in the overlapping territories shown on the cultural map of imperialism. (*CI,* 332; emphasis added)

As I read this culminating moment of a book that traces the itinerary of the West's colonized "Others" in terms of an increasing psychological and then corporeal impingement on both the metropolitan consciousness and met-ropolitan space, Said is positing a history of Western imperialism in which its binarist logic, in the process of fulfilling its possibilities, self–de-structs. Not unlike the "end of philosophy" and its precipitation of the nothing (*das Nichts*) that Heidegger announced with the coming into being of the tech-nological age of the world picture, this end of imperialism not only discloses the illegitimacy of the West's traditional representation of what it means to be human but also brings into corporeal proximity the spectral nonbeings that have always haunted this Western humanist logic.

Imperialism's "coming to its end" means first of all, as Said makes clear by reiterating the in-between status of this vast population of migrants, that the late postimperial occasion is an interregnum, a time in which the "old world"—*in all its modes of thought and practice*—is dying while a new, post-nationalist/postimperialist world is struggling to be born. More important, however, it means that in the wake of the self-destruction of Western impe-rialism and its binary logic, a multitude of human beings to whom the West had hitherto denied the status of humanity (and history)—"the multitude," in Negri and Hardt's version[47]—are symptomatically demanding not to be accommodated to the "Manhood" they had been denied by the imperial West but, as Frantz Fanon put it, a "new humanism," a new understanding of what it means to be human that is not tethered to an anthropological and Eurocentric principle of presence. Or to again invoke Said's identification of philology with humanism and of the humanist intellectual as one who exists both inside and outside the text and the world, they demand an all-inclusive humanism that is always already in-between, exilic, tragic, questioning, and careful. Following the previously quoted passage from *Culture and Imperial-ism,* Said, we may recall, adds this:

> There is a great difference, however, between the optimistic mobility, the intel-lectual liveliness, and "the logic of daring" described by the various theoreti-

cians on whose work I have drawn, and the massive dislocations, waste, misery, and horrors endured in our century's migrations and mutilated lives. Yet it is no exaggeration to say that liberation as an intellectual mission, born in the resistance and opposition to the confinements and ravages of imperialism, *has shifted from the settled, established, and domesticated dynamics of culture to its unhoused, decentered, and exilic energies,* energies whose incarnation today is the migrant, and whose consciousness is that of the intellectual and artist in exile, *the political figure between domains, between forms, between homes, and between languages.* From this perspective then all things are indeed counter, original, spare, strange. From this perspective also, one can see "the complete consort dancing together" contrapuntally. And while it would be the rankest Panglossian dishonesty to say that the bravura performances of the intellectual exile and miseries of the displaced person or refugee are the same, it is possible, I think, to regard the intellectual as first distilling then articulating the predicaments that disfigure modernity—mass deportation, imprisonment, population transfer, collective dispossession, and forced immigration (*CI*, 332–33; emphasis added)

Here Said is addressing the peculiar question of liberation instigated by the implosion of imperialism and the epochal shift of "liberation as an intellectual mission" from "the settled, established, and domesticated dynamics of culture to the unhoused, decentered, and exilic energies whose incarnation today is the migrant." Clearly, however, if we reconstellate this passage from *Culture and Imperialism* into the context of his posthumously published book, it does more than just anticipate his definition of philology, humanism, and the humanities in the latter. In emphasizing the exilic intellectual's status as the "political figure between domains, between forms, between homes, and between languages," it also tells us, more clearly than *Humanism and Democratic Criticism* does, what he means by the human, humanism, and the humanities. For it is obvious here, in a way it is not in the latter, that this being "in-between" is one that does not exist only at sites of culture and sociopolitics but extends from the ontological and epistemological sites—thinking as such—through the site of language, to those other, more obviously worldly sites that Said, no doubt rightly, overdetermines. That is, far from rejecting the essence of poststructuralist theory, this Saidian being "in-between" tacitly incorporates it and extends its horizon beyond the disciplinary sites to which its practitioners have tended to restrict it.

In defining humanism in *Humanism and Democratic Criticism*, Said muffles this crucial insight into the uneven continuum of being, not least the role that ontological interpretation—metaphysical inquiry/thinking—has always and increasingly played in the Western imperial project, including the production of the displacements and dispossessions constituting "the predicaments that disfigure modernity." It is this, I suggest, that renders his last book, however suggestive, finally inadequate to the imperatives for thought and action precipitated by the terrain that 9/11 changed: the Bush administration's announcement of America's "war on terror," and its tacit invocation of a state of emergency that threatens to unleash global chaos and destroy what little democracy exists in the United States. For it is not only safeguarding American economic interests or securing America's political authority that motivates these drastic metropolitan measures. However important these are, they are themselves informed by "the American way of life" that began to take shape with the Puritans' providentially ordained "errand in the wilderness," that is, the ontologically grounded exceptionalism that not only privileged a "new" America over the "Old World" but also justified and even demanded an imperial frontier—a threatening wilderness (or enemy)—the struggle against which would always rejuvenate America, preclude it from decaying or reverting, as had the Old World, to one form of barbarism or another. After the Puritan theocracy's demise and the humanist American Revolution, including the framing of the Constitution, this divinely ordained "missionary" errand became the secular doctrine of Manifest Destiny, which resulted in the removal of indigenous populations; the imperial Mexican War; the Indian wars, which eventuated in the virtual genocide of the Native Americans; and, at the end of the century, when the continental frontier had been closed, in the imperial Spanish-American War under presidents McKinley and Theodore Roosevelt.

As the documented history of twentieth-century America amply testifies— not least in the wake of World War II and the emergence of the cold war—this deeply inscribed ontological-cultural-political paradigm of the geographical frontier had by this time become a metaphor (the "wilderness" of the world) but continued to inform American global policy. During the Vietnam War, however, specifically when it became dramatically clear that the United States was destroying the land, the culture, and the people of a Southeast Asian country struggling to free itself from colonial rule in order to "save Vietnam for the free [humanist] world," this deep ontologically grounded structure of the American character (or rather of the dominant Anglo-Protestant core culture) and its predatory violence emerged to visibility. In consequence, America's Anglo-Protestant exceptionalist national identity began to unravel, as the polyvalent U.S. protest movement symptomatically attests. Significantly, further symptomatic evidence appeared with the emergence of antihumanist poststructuralism, as is suggested by the previously quoted comments Derrida made at the 1968 symposium in New York. To counter this unraveling, the dominant culture in America (i.e., the political elite, the corporate world, and the media) and its intellectual deputies (e.g., William Bennett, Lynn Cheney, Allan Bloom, Roger Kimball, Hilton Kramer, and Samuel Huntington, among many other traditional humanists) mounted a massive campaign in the name of the humanist ethos, seeking to use "the best that has been thought and said about the world," in Matthew Arnold's terms, to "forget Vietnam" or, as George H. W. Bush put the healthy debate over the American national identity, to "kick the Vietnam syndrome."[48]

Beginning after the humiliating defeat of the United States in Southeast Asia and extending through the implosion of the Soviet Union, this amnesiac initiative, the dominant culture's frantic will to recuperate the ontological origins of the American exceptionalist identity, was brought to fruition by the "surgical defeat" of Saddam Hussein's army in the First Gulf War, a culmination to which the imperial Project for the New American Century (PNAC)—its envisioning of a global Pax Americana—bears telling witness.[49] Al Qaeda's polyvalently symbolic attacks on the World Trade Center and the Pentagon sealed the Pandora's box opened by the anti–Vietnam War protest movement and the advent of poststructuralism in the United States. Subsequently, I submit, the Bush administration—an alliance of neoconservative "humanists" and Anglo-Protestants—announced its global "war on terror" (and, tacitly, a state of emergency), invaded Afghanistan, dissimulated about Saddam Hussein's weapons of mass destruction, invaded Iraq, and began to impose capitalist-style democracies on Islamic countries as much in the name of this deeply backgrounded—hegemonic—ontological American exceptionalist ethos as in that of the more overtly worldly—and visible—interests that Said and too many of his followers privilege in their criticism.

These, admittedly, are large generalizations that cannot be documented within the limits of this chapter.[50] Perhaps, however, their viability can find support in a brief but pointed reference to the exemplary post-9/11 global projections made by one of the most visible humanist intellectual deputies of the dominant culture in America, Samuel P. Huntington. An influential policy expert, Huntington wrote *The Clash of Civilizations* (whose thesis Said shredded on several occasions)[51] and a recent diagnosis of the post-9/11 era, *Who Are We? Challenges to America's National Identity* (2004).[52] As its title implies, the latter book manifests the acute nationalist anxiety provoked by emerging internal symptoms that threaten to disintegrate the civilizational unity of America and directly invokes the foundational history of this unity that he uses to justify his extraordinary elitist projection of America's global future. Indeed, this book is especially noteworthy because its very structure is modeled on the "American jeremiad," the ritualized crisis discourse inaugurated by the Puritans at the outset of American history to perennially recuperate a disintegrating unity and rejuvenate its divinely ordained exceptionalist errand, which, as Sacvan Bercovitch has brilliantly shown, became fundamental to the hegemonic discourse of a secularized United States.[53]

Though Huntington's book was instigated by the events of September 11, not least by the nationalist fervor they mobilized, its real point of departure, as the inordinate amount of space he devotes to it testifies, lies in his acute anxiety (and that of his class—the duplicitous "we" in the title) over what he calls in his first chapter "the crisis of national identity." According to Huntington, this crisis was precipitated by the momentum of dissent inaugurated in the decade of the Vietnam War, the democratic initiative of which he tellingly refers to as "deconstructing America," tying that to "the rise of subnational identities" in a rhetoric that suggests the complicity of an emergent (foreign) deconstructionist theory (and apparently practice) with alien internal cultural forces that were denationalizing America:

> The deconstructionists promoted programs to enhance the status and influence of subnational racial, ethnic, and cultural groups. They encouraged immigrants to maintain their birth country cultures, granted them legal privileges denied to native-born Americans, and denounced the idea of Americanization as un-American. They pushed the rewriting of history syllabi and textbooks so as to refer to the "peoples" of the United States in place of the single people of the Constitution. They urged supplementing or substituting for national history the history of subnational groups. They downgraded the centrality of English in American life and pushed bilingual education and linguistic diversity. They advocated legal recognition of group rights and racial preferences over the individual rights central to the American Creed. They justified their actions by theories of multiculturalism and the idea that diversity rather than unity or community should be America's overriding value. The combined effect of these efforts was to promote the deconstruction of the American national identity that had been gradually created over three centuries and the ascendance of subnational identities. (*WAW*, 142)

Having identified the source of anxiety, Huntington goes on according to the structural imperatives of the American jeremiad. First he recalls the glorious historical origins of the American national identity in the Puritans' divinely ordained exceptionalist "errand in the wilderness," a recollection, not incidentally, he articulates in a rhetoric that affiliates the imperialism of the Word of God (the *theologos*) with that of colonialism (the settlements that justified the expropriation of the "nomadic" Native Americans' land):

> The settling of America was, of course, a result of economic and other motives, as well as religious ones. Quakers and Methodists settled in Pennsylva-

nia. Catholics established a beachhead in Maryland. Religious intensity was undoubtedly greatest among the Puritans, especially in Massachusetts. They took the lead in defining their settlement based on "a Covenant with God" to create "a city on the hill" as a model for all the world, and people of the other Protestant faiths soon also came to see themselves and America in a similar way. In the seventeenth and eighteenth centuries, Americans defined their mission in the New World in biblical terms. They were a "chosen people," on an "errand in the wilderness," creating "the new Israel" or the "new Jerusalem" in what was clearly "the promised land." America was the site of a "new Heaven and a new earth, the home of justice," God's country. The settlement of America was vested, as Sacvan Bercovitch puts it, "with all the emotional, spiritual, and intellectual appeal of a religious quest." This sense of holy mission was easily expanded into millenarian themes of America as "the redeemer nation" and "the visionary republic." (*WAW*, 142)[54]

Second, to underscore the founding and enabling character of this origin, Huntington reminds his readers of the several "Great Awakenings," analogous to and deriving from the Puritans' jeremiads, that have periodically irrupted into American history to mobilize, reunify, and regenerate the American national identity in times of crisis.

Countering the thesis, insistently affirmed by Said, that America is an immigrant and therefore a radically multicultural society, Huntington locates the origins of the American national identity not in the founding of the American creed (the juridical and governmental tenets of constitutional democracy) or in the immigrations it enables but in the settler Puritans' commitment to the "Covenant with God" and their divinely ordained mission. Following the inexorable imperatives of this origin, he thus identifies the "Anglo-Protestant culture" as the "core culture" of America. It is this "Anglo-Protestant core culture," according to Huntington, that constitutes the essence of the American national identity and that has been put into crisis by the "deconstruction of America" and the emergence of what he vulgarly calls "subnational cultures" to prominence since the 1960s. It is this Anglo-Protestant core culture, this "civilizational" national identity—and its *ontologically ordained exceptionalist global mission*—that his jeremiad *Who Are We?* seeks to recuperate. As this post-9/11 American humanist—his text never indicates that he is a practicing Protestant—summarily puts this reactionary jeremiadic project of recuperation and rejuvenation (by violence) in his preface:

All societies face recurring threats to their existence, to which they eventually succumb. Yet some societies, even when so threatened, are also capable of postponing their demise by halting and reversing the processes of decline and renewing their vitality. I believe that America can do that and that Americans should recommit themselves to the Anglo-Protestant culture, traditions, and values that for three centuries and a half have been embraced by Americans of all races, ethnicities, and religions and that have been the source of their liberty, unity, power, prosperity, and moral leadership as forces for good in the world. (*WAW,* xvii)

To return, after this detour to the events of September 11 that have altered the terrain of our knowledge about the world at large and that instigated Huntington's jeremiad, we can now understand the role al Qaeda plays in the global scenario he projects in *Who Are We?*—and by extension, the role that the American exceptionalist discourse he is recuperating, if not his particular appropriation of it, is playing in the Bush administration's foreign policy in the Middle East in particular and in the global arena in general. In the discourse of the American jeremiad, the difficult experience of the wilderness functioned as a *necessary* evil that both threatened the well-being of the civilized community—produced anxiety—and thereby renewed its members' commitment to the "Covenant" and their communal energy. (This is also the function of the secular frontier myth of the development of the American national identity as advanced by the American historian, Frederick Jackson Turner.)[55] Similarly, following the demise of the cold war, by which time the concept of the frontier had metamorphosed into a general metaphor, the anxiety instigated by the loss of a frontier/enemy, which was always a necessary ingredient in the myth of American exceptionalism and its power to sustain the unity of the American identity, was relieved by al Qaeda's attacks on American soil and the focalization of an emergent "militant Islam" as "America's" new global adversary. This paradoxical relief is, in fact, articulated by Huntington at the climax of his jeremiadic narrative of America's role in the post-9/11 world. "At the end of the twentieth century," he writes in a section tellingly entitled "The Search for an Enemy,"

> democracy was left without a significant secular ideological rival, and the United States was left without a peer competitor. Among American foreign policy elites, the results were euphoria, pride, arrogance—and uncertainty. The absence of an ideological threat [his policy-making term for the traditional frontier is "fault line"] produced an absence of purpose. . . . The ideal enemy for America would be ideologically hostile, racially and culturally different, and militarily strong enough to pose a credible threat to America. The foreign policy debates of the 1990s were largely over who might be such an enemy. (*WAW,* 262)

After rehearsing all the possibilities imagined by these anxious policy experts, Huntington concludes in a language all too reminiscent of the terrible banality of the policy experts who conducted the Vietnam War from the Pentagon: "And on September 11, 2001, Osama bin Laden ended America's search. The attacks on New York and Washington followed by the wars with Afghanistan and Iraq and the more diffuse 'war on terrorism' makes militant Islam America's first enemy of the twenty-first century" (*WAW*, 263).

With these attacks on American soil by "militant Islam," Huntington's earlier annunciation of "the clash of civilizations"—his grotesque reduction of the great variety of cultures within the West and the East to a Manichaean model—is brought to what can only be called its paranoid fulfillment. "American identity," he writes, "began a new phase with the new century. Its salience and substance in this phase are being shaped by America's new vulnerability to external attack and by a new turn to religion, a Great Awakening in America" (*WAW*, 336). In keeping with the inexorably reductive structural logic of the American jeremiad, in other words, Huntington invokes the civilizational threat that "militant Islam" poses to America not simply to mobilize the disparate constituencies of the nation but to recuperate and rejuvenate the "Anglo-Protestant core culture," which, he affirms against the claims of the "American creed," has been the defining characteristic of the American national identity, the etymon of America's greatness, and the abiding justification of its "benign" errand in the wilderness. As in the case of the American jeremiad, but now on a global scale, perpetual war—waged in the name not simply of "homeland security" and the Pax Americana but, as his insistent emphasis on the ontological register makes manifest, of the American understanding of what it means to be truly human—must, he implies, necessarily be America's and the world's future. This deeply backgrounded, polyvalent American exceptionalism, at whose deepest level lies a "civil religion" or "secular theology" that determines the meaning of the human, is, mutatis mutandis, the vision that has justified the Bush administration's *thinking* and *practice* in its relationship to a global "militant" or "extremist" Islam.

The perception of the global future as a clash of civilizations, enabled by the events of 9/11, could become a world-devastating, species-annihilating, self-fulfilling prophecy, and its corollary, "homeland security," a permanent state of exception that could destroy democracy in America in the name of saving it. This paranoid vision has radically estranged the terrain of the knowledge about the world, or to put it in the American context Said emphasizes, has dislocated the traditional humanist perspective on the world that humanity inhabits and rendered its members exiles, "between domains, between forms, between homes, between languages." If this is the case, if this paranoid American vision is, as I Said's practice indicates, informed not simply by an economic or a political or cultural economy but also by an ontological and epistemological economy—an economy that determines the meaning of what a human being *is* and how he or she ought to comport his or her self toward being at large—then a humanism that does not examine its genealogy in the way the early poststructuralists (Heidegger, Derrida, Lyotard, Foucault) did will remain inadequate, despite its advances over the latter, to the tasks of resisting the American juggernaut's momentum toward cataclysm and of envisioning a global configuration of humanity in which, as Said so beautifully puts it, "'the whole consort dances together' contrapuntally."

Again, this is by no means to privilege the early poststructuralists over Said. That would be a retrogressive initiative. It is to say, rather, that *Humanism and Democratic Criticism,* however heuristic its directives concerning opposition in America, cannot have the status that so many of his friends and disciples have given it, that of a final statement, a *Summum,* an *apologia pro vita sua.* Despite its decisive criticism of the inhumanity of various "traditional" or "classical" humanistic practices, it troubles but ultimately does not challenge the ontologically grounded meaning of humanism that, in claiming its liberation from the arbitrary authority of the theological principle of presence, the Word of God, enabled a "liberal humanist" perspective that accommodated the "Other"—difference, individuality, agency—to its invisible *anthropologos,* "enabled" them to take their "proper" place within the circle of which the Word of (Western, now American) Man is the center. For, to invoke the passage from Gramsci on the imperatives of "knowing oneself" (quoted as one of the epigraphs to this chapter), the implications of which Said has virtually given us to think, this deeply inscribed dehumanizing ontological understanding of the human is also a trace—indeed, one of the most fatally determinative—of the "infinity of traces" that "the historical process to date" has deposited in us "without leaving an inventory."

Said may in practice reject traditional Western humanism, but in *Humanism and Democratic Criticism,* by inventorying the traces that have disfigured modernity, he finally leaves this trace—the accommodational tolerance of traditional humanism—intact. And tolerant humanism is certainly not "'the whole consort dancing together' contrapuntally." As Said's critical secular practice suggests, for that contrapuntal vision of global humanity we need a definition of human being that demotes Man from the status of sovereign subject, the lord and master over all he surveys, to render humanity—the *anthropos logon echon* (the being not endowed with the Word but *burdened* by words, by the capability of undecidable speech)—the responsible caretaker of a mute being in all its infinite singularity, variety, and mystery.

6. Edward Said's Mount Hermon and Mine

A Forwarding Remembrance and a Coda

> But at my back I always hear
> Times winged chariot hurrying near.
> —Andrew Marvell, "To His Coy Mistress"

> It is perfectly true, as philosophers say, that a life must be understood backwards. But they forget the other proposition, that it must be lived forwards. And if one thinks over that proposition, it becomes more and more evident that life can never really be understood in time simply because at no particular moment can I find the necessary resting-place from which to understand it—backwards.
> —Søren Kierkegaard, *Journals*

If I remember correctly, my first more or less direct contact with Edward Said came about when I wrote to ask him for a contribution to a symposium on postmodernism, the inaugural issue of *boundary 2*, the "journal of postmodern literature" that my friend, the novelist Robert Kroetsch, and I had imagined into being during the harrowing year I spent as a Fulbright Professor of American literature at the University of Athens. This was in 1969–70, when the ruthless military dictatorship that had staged a coup d'état in 1967 against an emergent democracy in the name of *isichia kai taxis* (quiet and order)—the mandate of right-wing Greece set in place by the Truman Doctrine in the nation's post–civil war period—was at the peak of its power, thanks largely, once again, to the shameful though predictable support of the U.S. government under the Nixon administration. At that time the New Criticism's imperative to closure was still determining the form and content of scholarly and critical writing in America, even though its authority was disintegrating under the pressure of the excesses of America's brutal conduct of its war against the Vietnamese people and, at home, against the civil rights movement.

I had read and admired Edward's early work on Conrad and some of the essays that eventually were incorporated in *Beginnings* and felt instinctively not simply an intellectual affiliation but also a curiously unspecifiable spiritual kinship that the following years have not abated but rather deepened and somewhat clarified. So when the time came to decide who in the American academy might be responsive to our effort to launch the first journal of literary criticism to venture across the boundary established by Modernism—in hindsight, one could say, to explore the postmodern, a word that at the time had little status and no consistent meaning—I was certain that Edward was one of them.

I don't remember whether Edward assented to the viability of the term; I have the feeling that he was uncomfortable with it, if not altogether hostile. Be that as it may, I do remember that shortly after I wrote him, he called me at home one evening to accept the invitation and to suggest two possibilities: an essay on the French "structuralist" thinker Michel Foucault, who at that time was barely known in the United States, especially in the literary critical community (it would be five more years before the French publication of *Surveiller et punir* and two more before its translation into English as *Discipline and Punish*), or one on the relative cultural power of "strong languages," such as French and English, and "weak languages" such Arabic. Since I knew something about Foucault, I chose the first option, not realizing then that what Edward was talking about in the second was to become, by way of the "worldliness" of Vico's and Auerbach's philological investigations he explores in *Beginnings* (1975), the point of departure of his great book *Orientalism* (1978)—or rather, that the two options he proposed, mediated by the publication of Foucault's *Surveiller et punir*, would eventually coalesce in that great inaugural work. (The essay he wrote for the first issue of *boundary 2* was "Michel Foucault as an Intellectual Imagination," and it was incorporated into the chapter of *Beginnings* entitled "*Abecedarium Culturae*: Absence, Writing, Statement, Discourse, Archeology, Structuralism.")

As I remember it, that telephone conversation was curiously formal. He was professional at first, polite but very serious—indeed, severe—and somewhat distant, but as we talked about the purposes of the journal, he began to modulate that tone, which I took to be a gesture of solidarity with our project and an invitation to shed formalities. Acting on this not entirely accurate interpretation, I called him "Ed" at some point and was politely but decisively informed that he preferred being called "Edward." This to me inexplicable gesture was surprising, on the verge of disconcerting, and I found it difficult after that to recuperate a place in the dialogue. In effect it brought our conversation to a close. This enigmatic gesture of concealment is what I remember most vividly of this first encounter, and it has determined my comportment in his presence ever since. Only now, in the process of reading his memoirs—learning of the definitive role that the name Edward, by which he was addressed by his tenderly loving yet severely critical mother, both Palestinian and American, soft and austere, giving and demanding, siren and nemesis at the same time, played in splitting him into the two selves he's been ever since—have I come to sense the meaning of that abrupt retreat.

But I begin this reminiscence here not because I want to remember what I remembered about that telephone conversation in the next few years. On the contrary, I begin here to remember something Edward said to me that I did not register completely at the time because the embarrassment I felt at my vulgar intrusion had taken the edge off its coincidental interest, something that began to loom increasingly larger for me as I came to know him and his thinking better but that disclosed itself as an enigma I am compelled to talk about after having read his memoirs. What I learned that evening in the fall of 1970 was that almost twenty years before, between the fall of 1951 and the spring of 1953, Edward had been a student at Mount Hermon, a preparatory school for boys in Massachusetts, during the two years I taught there after a year of graduate work at Columbia University. I don't recall his saying much about his experience there. I do remember that he said he didn't take any courses with me but was aware of my presence—or rather, of the persona that the students had imposed on me: a too serious, forbidding, and if I remember correctly, intimidating intellectual who for that reason and because of my olive, foreign skin was out of place in that collegial prep-school environment and whom, for some inexplicable reason, maybe because of my non-Anglo-Saxon surname, they called "Chico."

My next direct encounter with Edward occurred on a winter evening in 1975, again in the form of an unexpected telephone call from him, this time as a member of the Columbia University English department's hiring committee. My student Paul Bové had applied for a job at the university, and Edward, who apparently had read and liked some of his dissertation, "Destructive Hermeneutics" ("the first 'deconstructive' dissertation accepted by an American university," as one literary historian has put it), and wary of Columbia's penchant for determining "first rateness" by the candidate's institutional pedigree, had decided to ask me for my candid opinion of Paul's qualifications and promise as a teacher, critic, and scholar. I assured him that this young man was endowed with a brilliant critical mind—the best that I had encountered among my students up to that time—and ferociously but carefully engaged in the politics of literature (I may have referred to him as an exemplary "worldly critic" in anticipation of Edward's later usage), and I predicted that one day his critical voice would be heard. I also informed him that it was Paul who had alerted me to the publication of *Beginnings* and recommended that I read it in its entirety. In the process of this conversation, during which I did not make the mistake I had made in our first, I intuited that Edward had become truly interested in Paul and that he would support his candidacy despite the odds against his venerable department's hiring someone from a public graduate school that, to make matters worse, was not more than five years old. And that endeared him to my irredeemably class-conscious heart. Near the close of this telephone conversation, Edward changed the subject, reminding me again (having apparently forgotten that he had told be before) that he had attended Mount Hermon during the years I taught there. I had not forgotten this curious coincidence, but neither had I thought terribly much about it. Now, thanks to his attunement to—or was it a sense of affiliation with?—Paul Bové, it had, in some degree at least, become an active current in the river of my memory. After that, and especially after Paul had become Edward's colleague and friend, whenever Edward's name attracted my attention, I often wondered about those two years he spent in the neighborhood of my first turbulent years as a teacher and not least what it would have been like to have had Edward in one of my renegade English classes.

I finally met Edward after Paul and his wife, Carol, had moved to Columbia, where I often visited them at their apartment on Clermont Avenue, between 116th Street and Riverside Drive. Since then, I've had several opportunities to talk with him, including the one in Binghamton in 1978 provided by *boundary 2*'s sponsorship of the symposium entitled "The Problems of Reading in Contemporary American Criticism," which assessed the state of theory a little over a decade after the famous Johns Hopkins conference on structuralism (1966) at which Jacques Derrida delivered his groundbreaking essay "Structure, Sign, and Play in the Discourse of the Human Sciences." This was the symposium at which Edward first delivered the equally groundbreaking essay "Reflections on Recent American 'Left' Criticism," which as I see it marked the beginning of the end for deconstruction's hegemony in America. Strangely, none of these meetings became the occasion for anything more than the reiteration of our coincidental years at Mount Hermon. Perhaps the circumstances of these meetings precluded that possibility. As I recall them, broaching the issue was always there in my consciousness, but not strong enough to warrant intruding. That was probably because, to me, the Edward Said I was talking with was not the biographical Edward Said—the young Palestinian boy who, for whatever reason, had been sent by his parents to this isolated New England boarding school founded at the beginning of the twentieth century by a couple of fire-breathing evangelical ministers ferociously committed to the Puritan work ethic. He was, rather, the Edward Said of *Orientalism,* the Palestinian-American who through the sheer force of his humane intelligence and awesome historical sense was leading both a resistant American academy and the even more resistant American media into recognizing the not so promising land of American-style globalism. That is, I didn't think that his years at Mount Hermon were important to him.

My recent reading of his memoir, *Out of Place,* disabused me of that perception. What surprised me about that quietly intense and deeply moving book, instigated by his discovery that he had been afflicted by an incurable disease, was that he devotes virtually an entire chapter, one that to me at least is its climax, to his exilic two years at Mount Hermon. On the basis of the Said I had come to know—the politically engaged Palestinian-American scholar and activist of *Beginnings, Orientalism, The Question of Palestine, The World, the Text, and the Critic,* and *Culture and Imperialism*—I expected his years as a graduate student at Harvard and Princeton to be the decisive moment of his formative adolescent life. It was, after all, there that he first encountered the revolutionary work of the great modern comparativist scholars whose names recur everywhere in his writing like base motifs in a sonata: Leo Spitzer, Theodor Adorno, Antonio Gramsci, and the dislocated migrant Erich Auerbach. But to my surprise, that was not the case. In *Out of Place* these institutions are treated almost as an afterthought. Certainly Edward makes no effort to connect the comparativist approach—that which decisively broke down the traditional disciplinary and canonical study of literature and inaugurated the transdisciplinary or global approach he was to adopt—with the thematics of exile, of what I, following Heidegger, have been calling the *Abgeschiedene,* the stranger who is apart from but a part of his or her homeland. What I found, on the contrary, was the story of a sensitive but extremely disoriented teenage Arab boy whose philo-American father, with the reluctant consent of his mother, had torn him out of an exilic context that had at least become safely familiar (the Cairo-Lebanon circuit) and dropped him into a geographically isolated and culturally alien northeastern American environment. This was the Mount Hermon School for Boys in Bernardston, a small, virtually homogeneous Yankee village on the Connecticut River between Brattleboro, Vermont, and Greenfield, Massachusetts, where the fates, in their random indifference to the intentions of those they single out to insert their tentacles, had at the very same time dropped me in the fall of 1951, after my year of graduate study at Columbia:

We returned to New York [from Madison, Wisconsin] via the Milwaukee Road Railroad and a TWA flight from Midway Airport, and the day after Labor Day finally found ourselves on a train leaving Grand Central Station bound for Mount Hermon. The only part of the long journey on the White River Junction train [the same train that a few days before had brought me to Mount Hermon from the Claremont Junction station ten miles west of my parents' house in Newport, New Hampshire] that I remember was our arrival at the tiny, excessively rural Massachusetts station, where a lone taxicab was waiting to take us the final couple of miles to the school. We barely had an hour together, since my parents were to take the return train to New York. When we had found my room, and my parents had had a brief meeting alone with the headmaster, my mother spent fifteen minutes helping me to unpack and make the bed (my unknown roommate was already neatly installed). Then they rapidly departed, leaving me standing with a lump in my throat at the entrance to my imposing dormitory building, Crossley Hall, as they disappeared from view. The void that suddenly surrounded me and that I knew I had to endure for the one academic year I was to be at Mount Hermon [it turned out to be two] seemed unbearable, but I also knew that I had to return to my room to recover some sense of my mother's recent presence—her smell, a trace of her hands, even perhaps a message.

A blond and blue-eyed youth of my own age was there to greet me. "Hi. I'm your roommate, Bob Salisbury," he said pleasantly, leaving me no opportunity to recuperate some of my mother's disappearing aura and I realized that I had now definitively arrived.[1]

To me, Mount Hermon was barely a memory. So much time and transformative experience had intervened that the two years of the life I began to live simultaneously with Edward in that doubly remote place, where, to borrow his ironic flat Americanism, we had both "definitively arrived," had virtually faded out of my consciousness. In reading these opening lines of Edward's bitterly poignant story, however, that forgotten and maybe repressed world suddenly burst forth into my consciousness as if it were a withered flower that suddenly comes to life, though now it was inhabited and charged by the specter of the young Palestinian exile who was there in the same space, but not there for me. And it is this spectral presence haunting my renewed remembrance of the years I taught at Mount Hermon that has triggered this reminiscence.

Though after fifty years my memory of Mount Hermon is not as distinct as Edward's, his vivid account of the school in *Out of Place* has precipitated a retrieval of this forgotten time (taking retrieval in the sense of the differential same that Heidegger gives to the word "*Wiederholung*"). It has, in other words, enabled me to return to that distant past and to know it for the first time. Specifically, this retrieval not only confirms in general much of what

Edward found repelling and painfully alien and alienating about the school but also has enabled me to recall another aspect of that long-past world to which Edward was apparently blind as a fifteen-year-old boy and, as far as I can tell from what he says about it from the perspective of the present, always remained so. This latter aspect was a marginal but excitingly emergent and still visible initiative in American intellectual life that not only redeemed my two years in that otherwise suffocating white, upper-middle-class, and proper Protestant educational environment but also instigated a momentum of thinking about the American world Mount Hermon represented that eventually became fundamental to my comportment toward being in all its manifestations.

* * *

For Edward, Mount Hermon was from beginning to end "altogether alienating and desolate" (226) as both a geographical and a cultural space, not only a natural setting utterly foreign to the Middle Eastern landscape and climate in which he had grown up, but also and above all a cultural milieu whose alien style and mores made him feel more acutely out of place than ever before. As far as one can tell from his memoirs, there were only two redeeming exceptions to the uncongeniality of this alien environment. One was the music of the school organist, Carleton L'Hommedieu, which inspired Edward to return to the piano. ("L'Hommy," as Said tells us the students called him, was a "cadaverously thin" aesthete who nevertheless "played a robust prelude and postlude" [232] at the chapel services that students and faculty alike were required to attend four times a week. To me he was a peripheral figure, remote in his prim demeanor from the messiness of the world I knew. As they did for Edward, however, his renderings of Bach, whom I was just then discovering by way of the new Pablo Casals recordings of the Prades Bach Festival, redeemed those deadly pietistic convocations.) The other, which I initially found difficult to understand, was the course he took with Jack Baldwin, one of my senior colleagues in the English department. According to Edward, this course, which included a month-long close reading of Shakespeare's *Macbeth,* was truly transformative:

> For literally the first time in my life a subject was opened up for me by a teacher in a way that I immediately and excitedly responded to. What had previously been repressed and stifled in academic study [at Victoria College (VC) in Cairo]—repressed in order that thorough and correct answers be given to satisfy a standardized syllabus and a routinized exam designed essentially to show off powers of retention, not critical or imaginative faculties—was awak-

ened, and the complicated process of intellectual discovery (and self-discovery) has never stopped since. The fact that I was never at home or at least at Mount Hermon, out of place in nearly every way, gave me the incentive to find my territory, not socially but intellectually. (231)

But these oases in a desert landscape could not redeem the rigidly codified and highly disciplinary life—the "Americanness"—Edward encountered at Mount Hermon. This not quite elitist New England preparatory school for boys (the brother school of Northfield Academy for Girls, located directly across the Connecticut River) was founded by the famous American evangelist Dwight L. Moody in the late nineteenth century in the name of "the dignity of manual labor." The school's Protestant work ethic was inculcated in the students by ten hours a week of mandatory labor on the farm and in the laundry, the kitchen, the dining hall, and so on (Edward's first task, assigned to him in the name of the "dignity of manual labor," was "to pick the eyes out of potatoes" [226]); this commitment to the work ethic became the signature of a Mount Hermon education.

What immediately struck the young Palestinian—and became a fundamental aspect of his relation to the school—was the utter hypocrisy of the American discourse and practice that pervaded the Mount Hermon world:

> At Hermon, the going currency was "common or shared values," care and concern for the students, interest in such intangibles as leadership and good citizenship, words of encouragement, admonishment, praise administered with a kind of fastidiousness I never dreamed of in VC, where war was a constant feature of daily life, with no palliatives either offered by the authorities or accepted by us, the students. Judgment in the United States was constant but concealed under a teasing fabric of rolling words and phrases, all of them in the end borne up by the unassailable moral authority of the teachers. (229)

It was, not incidentally, his extreme consciousness of the power of the homogenizing American discourse pervading Mount Hermon culture that compelled Edward to abhor the name Ed, the diminutive that had virtually brought our first conversation to a close: "To my increasing sadness, by early December 1951, I had become Americanized as 'Ed Said' to everyone except [Jeff] Brieger [a student from Germany], whose unbridled irony and polyglot wit seemed more precious to me every day, as more and more of my past seemed to slip away, worn away slowly but ineluctably by the American modalities of our routinized days and evenings" (237).

In this retrospective rhetoric, especially when read in the context of the moral pieties of the educational institution, founded in the name of "the dignity of manual labor," into which the young Arab had been exiled, one cannot help but hear the genealogical discourse of Michel Foucault, who, following Max Weber, traced the disciplinary society's strategy of reformation and normalization back to the emergent Protestant work ethic and its obsession with detail, above all in America. As always in his relationship to Foucault, however, Edward extends this early intuition into the leveling effect of Mount Hermon's hypocritical educational ideals to encompass a wider, global ideological horizon. For that early memory of this intuition, probably activated by his awareness of the indissoluble relationship between the exceptionalist Puritan doctrine of election and the work ethic, also and perhaps above all included an intuition into the American prejudice against Third World foreigners concealed behind the patronizing language of liberal educational institutions: the racist assumption that in no endeavor—academics, sports, leadership—could an Arab possibly achieve the excellence of which the American boy is intrinsically capable. Immediately following the passage referring to the pervasive judgmental gaze concealed behind Mount Hermon's care for the student self, he writes:

> I also soon learned that you could never really find out why or on what basis you were judged, as I was, inadequate for the role or status that relatively objective indicators like grades, scores, or match victories entitled you to. While I was at Mount Hermon I was never appointed a floor officer, table head, a member of the student council, or valedictorian . . . and salutatorian . . . although I had the qualifications. And I never knew why. But I soon discovered that I would have to be on guard against authority and that I needed to develop some mechanism or drive not to be discouraged by what I took to be efforts to silence or deflect me from being who I am rather than becoming who they wanted me to be. In the process I began a lifelong struggle and attempt to demystify the capriciousness and hypocrisy of a power whose authority depended absolutely on its ideological self-image as a moral agent, acting in good faith and with unimpeachable intentions. (229–30)

In the final pages of the chapter Edward returns to this awareness of the racist ethnocentrism underlying the vaunted liberality of the Mount Hermon ethos, recalling, in terms that *should not be taken, as they have been, as narcissistic self-absorption,* his last days at the school. By this time he had become acutely aware that he "remained a kind of *lusus naturae,* a peculiar odd boy out," who, despite his high achievements in sports and academics, "seemed incapable of achieving the moral status—I can think of no other word to describe it—that the school's general approval could bestow on me. I was known as someone with a powerful brain and unusual past, but I was not fully a part of the school's corporate life. Something was missing. Something, I was to discover, that was called 'the right attitude.'" As he puts it to emphasize the Puritan origins of this difference, he had also come to realize that "there was something chosen about [his American peers], an aura, that I clearly lacked" (247). Nevertheless, he was astonished when he learned, quite late, that the administration had denied him the title of salutatorian, even though he placed academically either first or second in the graduating class, granting the honor instead to someone below him in rank ("six or seventh")—and to make matters worse, he learned of the slight from the very student, Fred Fisher, whom the administration had chosen over him. "I felt I was entitled to such a graduation honor and had been denied it, but in some strange yet peculiarly fitting way I knew I should *not* have been given it. . . . Unlike Fisher I was not a leader, nor a good citizen, nor pious, nor just all-round acceptable. I realized I was to remain the outsider, no matter what I did" (248). It was at this profoundly ironic moment in his youth and in this essentially homogenized American space when Edward's insistent feeling of being out of place at Mount Hermon coalesced into a conscious recognition of the racial prejudice that informs and debilitates the discourse of American democracy. It was also at this dislocating moment in this complacently immutable place when he became an American "Arab" in an alien white world, the one a-part of/from the homeland that has characterized his nomadic being and practice as a teacher, scholar and public figure ever since:

> It was . . . at this point that I felt that coming from a part of the world that seemed to be in a state of chaotic transformation became the symbol of what was out of place about me. Hermon School was primarily white: there were a handful of black students, mostly gifted athletes and one rather brilliant musician and intellect, Randy Payton, but the faculty was entirely white. . . . Until the Fisher-graduation episode I felt myself to be colorless, but that forced me to see myself as marginal, non-American, alienated, marked, just when the politics of the Arab world began to play a greater and greater role in American life. I sat through the tedious graduation ceremonies in my cap and gown with an indifference that bordered on hostility: this was *their* event, not mine, even though I was unexpectedly given a biology prize for, I firmly believe, consolation. (249)

* * *

Edward's observations about the supervisory, normalizing, and racially prejudicial ethos informing the liberal and accommodational educational discourse and practice he encountered as a student at Mount Hermon remarkably echo my own experience as a beginning teacher at that school. Older than Edward when I came to Mount Hermon in the fall of 1951—he was fifteen; I was twenty-five—I was no doubt capable of discriminations that his youth did not allow. I had been exposed to the dark side of American exceptionalism during World War II and was therefore more conscious of its duplicity. As a first-generation Greek-American soldier, I had experienced the humiliating sting of ethnic and class prejudice, never having been allowed to forget my lowly foreigner status, especially by the largely white, middle-class, and all-American officer class. (It is time to demolish the myth constructed by Hollywood—and, despite the disclosures of the Vietnam War, perpetuated to this day in films such as *Saving Private Ryan*—that World War II was won by an inordinately patriotic and self-sacrificing American army of assimilated Jews, Italians, Germans, Frenchmen, Poles, Swedes, etc.) In addition, having been taken prisoner of war during the last desperate German assault against the American army at St. Vith in Belgium (the Battle of the Bulge), I had also borne appalled witness to the Allies' gratuitous firebombing of Dresden, which had incinerated 130,000 civilians in one night-and-day raid and left this venerable open city, devoid of military significance, in charred ruins (I now believe the Dresden attack, like the atomic bombing of Hiroshima and the indiscriminate B-52 bombing of North Vietnam, to have constituted mass murder in its utter indifference to human life).

I had also graduated from Wesleyan University in Middletown, Connecticut, and had just finished my M.A. course work at Columbia University under the so-called G.I. Bill of Rights, which, like the Marshall Plan to rebuild Europe, I much later came to realize was in fact a cold-war strategy designed to accommodate to the new global economy the symptomatic class and racial consciousness that the war had precipitated in the mass of second-generation immigrants who had largely fought it. These inside outsiders formed the class that the dominant American culture, epitomized by the tremendously influential "General Education in a Free Society" (better known as the "Harvard Red Book") commissioned by the cold-warrior president of Harvard James Bryant Conant (1945), viewed as fertile ground for Communist propaganda. At both of these schools, though in different ways, I had felt the alienating effects of class, ethnic, and racial prejudice, of America's instrumentalist ethos, and of the cold-war ideology, all of which permeated the nation's institutions of higher education in that sadly benighted time. At Wesleyan I had encountered an oppressively elitist and male-oriented environment that, as it continues doing today, hid behind a publicity-produced image of liberality and humane learning. It was an environment epitomized by a powerful, institutionally sanctioned fraternity system that, besides barring women from its rolls, tacitly excluded Jews and admitted the few token blacks, Asians, and students from working-class immigrant families like myself on a quota system. The minority we made up, for example, was consigned to an "eating club" that was the signature of our alien and inferior social status. At

Columbia I had borne witness not only to the cynical exploitation of the inordinately large number of M.A. students it admitted—all my classes, except one seminar, were large lecture courses conducted in amphitheaters that sat over one hundred students and precluded the possibility of any contact with the distinguished professors who taught them, all vocal exponents of the great humanist tradition (Mark Van Doren, Lionel Trilling, Marjorie Nicholson, William York Tindall, and Gilbert Highet)—but also to an institution that, in its selective hiring policies and authorization of guest speakers, was accommodating itself to the political imperatives of an emergent McCarthyism. During my year there, several leftist scholars and writers—most notably, I recall, the novelist Howard Fast—were forbidden to speak on campus. In 1968, during the Vietnam War, when the students at Columbia rose up to protest the university administration's crassly racist decision to build a gymnasium in Morningside Heights Park adjacent to Harlem and its statist sponsorship of the U.S. government's Institute of Defense Analysis (IDA), I was not taken by surprise. Nor was I surprised when the administration called in the New York Police Department and then sanctioned the officers' brutal suppression of the student uprising. Indeed, given that Columbia had consistently betrayed the idea of the university and free inquiry in favor of the imperatives of the "military-industrial complex" (which Clark Kerr, at the University of California at Berkeley, was celebrating as "the knowledge industry") and the national security state, I wondered why all this had not happened long before.

This is not to say that I came to Mount Hermon in full consciousness of my alienation from America. This feeling of not being at home in these educational spaces was symptomatic. In fact, I lived those years torn between the desire to become "Americanized," as so many sons and daughters of immigrant families were then doing, to escape the painful stigma of my "grease-ball" otherness and the desire to resist the powerful attraction of this "American dream." To my later shame, I had eventually joined a fraternity at Wesleyan (Sigma Chi), even though I did it more for social survival than out of solidarity with the system; probably because way down deep I found that kind of fraternity superficial and repellently unfraternal, I never became one of the "brothers." In addition, though I detested Columbia, I willfully and gradually replaced my working-class image—long hair, pegged pants, steel-rimmed glasses, and small-town ghettoized provincialism—with the "Ivy League look": short hair, gray flannels, horn-rimmed glasses, buttondown oxford shirt, rep tie, tweed sports jacket, and a cosmopolitan manner that I felt, if I did not then know, ill-suited my essential identity as a member of an ethnic and working-class minority.

Despite these gestures toward accommodating myself to the dictates of the American way of life, however, the dislocating experience of the war and the five ensuing years in an alien educational environment was too fundamental to be entirely effaced. When I came to Mount Hermon, I brought to this first venture in teaching an inordinate idealism that had been instigated by my dislocating experience during the war, especially by that formative and traumatic moment, which I later identified as "Dostoyevskian," when I was taken prisoner in the Battle of the Bulge. Our division, the youthful and inexperienced 106th (it was also, coincidentally the unit to which Kurt Vonnegut, whose *Slaughterhouse Five* gave notoriety to the Dresden bombing, belonged), which had recently been transported across the Channel to replace the seasoned Second Division in the Ardennes Forest, had been annihilated by the massive German counterattack in Belgium during the winter of 1944. (I think now, against the official history of the Battle of the Bulge, that we were sent in as cannon fodder to draw the German army into the vulnerable pocket that was the beginning of the end of the war). My unit, the 423d Regiment, had disintegrated in the initial German assault, and afterward I had found myself in the company of four other demoralized young soldiers seeking to find a larger unit to join in the rear. On the second day of this interminably horrific quest, we came under a barrage of eighty-eight-millimeter artillery fire and sought refuge in an abandoned garbage pit on a hillside that stank with rotting sauerkraut. Not long afterward, however, when German soldiers began firing their Schmeizers over our heads and calling in English, "Hands up, Amerikaners," we realized to our terror that we had been trapped. There was nothing we could do but surrender. When one of my unknown comrades cried out, "I don't want to die!" whatever will to resist we had evaporated, and we rose from our crouching position, almost simultaneously, our hands over our heads and our clothes reeking with the stench of slimy and decaying food. In that nightmarish moment, the horror of which I have never been able to erase, I waited with tightly closed eyes for what seemed an eternity and with a kind of desperate resignation for the bullet that would end my life—a life that had barely begun. But it didn't explode in my head. Something else did, something utterly foreign to my prior sense of self: a promise that, if I survived the war, I would dedicate my spared life in whatever way I could to resist injustice and the power that feeds on it. I reiterated this amorphous promise to myself at the time of the Dresden bombing, when, in its aftermath, the German authorities assigned the surviving prisoners of war in the area the horrendous task of searching the rubble for the bodies of the dead and loading them into horse-drawn wagons for mass burial. That, of course, was a wildly melodramatic vow, and as I now look back at it, I laugh at my presumptuous naïveté (though the inexorable fact remains: I have borne that vow, albeit modified by my more mature awareness of the duplicity within the liberal ideal that celebrates the ameliorative power of individual initiative, like a chalice throughout my life, however ineptly I have carried out its holy imperatives).

At the time I came to Mount Hermon, however, the sense of calling I had suddenly acquired during the war was still too strong to be overpowered by this more mature knowledge about the way power works in modern liberal democratic societies. Its force had marginalized, if not subdued, the realities about American education that had been disclosed to me at Wesleyan and Columbia, and it had predisposed me to perceive this new environment, about which I knew as little as Edward had on his arrival, as a space of potential. So, unlike Edward, I entered it with the sense of excitement that often accompanies an inaugural moment of a young man's life.

But it was not long before my naïve idealism ran up against the solid and unmovable reality of the Mount Hermon educational environment. Indeed, my first intuition of this disabling reality and of being out of place in it came on the day I arrived, when I was greeted at the train station at Bernardston by Jack Baldwin, the teacher in the English department and coach of the varsity golf team whom Edward singles out in his memoir as the one teacher who had a positive transformative influence in his intellectual development. Baldwin had been assigned the task of showing me the campus and installing me in the dormitory, Hazel Hall (next door to Crossley, Edward's dormitory), where I would spend the next two years of my life. That greeting remains indelibly inscribed in my mind. As I got off the train, I was hailed from a distance by a stocky man in his early fifties, whose attire—a baseball cap, an oversized woolen sweater, baggy chinos, and sneakers—was incommensurate to what I had expected of a preparatory school teacher (later I came to think it was his deliberate way of differentiating his down-to-earth versatility from the supercilious demeanor and narrow perspective of the "intellectuals" he disliked). "Hi! Hi, Bill Spanos." As he approached to shake my hand and introduce himself, he told me that he could tell from my grim "scholarly appearance" that I was the person for whom he was looking from the moment I stepped off the train, doing so in a tone that, despite my predisposition to be grateful for this cordial demonstration of hospitality, I couldn't help suspect was mocking me. Edward's evaluation notwithstanding, this "well-rounded" man, who really didn't like literature or liked it only as a humanistic amateur, eventually became for me one of the several symbols of everything that I found repellent and dislocating at Mount Hermon.

I have but a dim recollection of the Mount Hermon English department, of which I was a decidedly junior member and to which, and as with all the English departments I have since joined, I never quite belonged. This was no doubt to be expected, since I willfully set out in the ensuing years to obliterate the detestable memory of its rigid hierarchical structure, of which I was at the absolute bottom; the undeviatingly standardized—and normalizing— canonical courses we were assigned to teach; and the supervisory gaze that hovered over us in and out of the classroom. I remember only three of a faculty of about eight: Jack Baldwin, whom Edward mentions, and Gale Bennett and Louis Smith, whom he does not.

I remember Bennett because he was the morally authoritarian master of Hazel Hall, where I lived and served as the third floor's faculty supervisor, and decidedly preferred sports to literature. By some point in my second year I had established a rapport with several bright student floor leaders. To break the deadly monotony of the nightly routine—study until ten and then lights out and silence—I would invite them to my room to listen to the American classical music I was then, thanks to a visit to Tanglewood, beginning to listen to: Copland, Harris, Sessions, Ives, Schuman, and Bernstein. At a certain point, Bennett then called me into his office to tell me that I should cease holding these nightly gatherings because rumor had it that they involved homosexuality. (I did not tell him they did not, though they didn't, nor did I terminate the practice.)

I remember Smith because he was the marionette chairman of the English department, whose primary aim, both in the organization of its program and in his comportment toward his faculty, was to ensure the department's quantitative success, which he understood as high scores on the students' college entrance examinations and high enrollment in prestigious Ivy League colleges. There was to be no deviation from the standardized canonical cur- riculum, which, like the Mount Hermon community as a whole, had virtually nothing (but really everything) to do with the historical world in which we lived—the United States' rapid and ominous transformation into a national security state committed to the global "defense" of the "free world" had by this time "secured" Greece for the "free world" by its massive financial and military aid to the fascist government in the Greek Civil War and had pre- cipitated the Korean War. Chafing under the constraints of this worldless educational regime, which was enforced by prescribed texts for each course, I often tried to break its deadly monotony by opening our discussions, some- times forcefully, to these programmatically excluded worldly issues, all cir- culating around the election of Dwight Eisenhower over Adlai Stevenson and the irreversible establishment of American cold-war policy. Invariably this initiative was reported to Mr. Smith, who would then call me into his office to reprimand me for my errancy. With the exception of three or four students, as I recall, most of those attending the freshman and sophomore courses to which I was limited were impatient with or even hostile to my effort to historicize these mandated texts, to render them, in Edward's later terminology, "worldly."

I particularly remember one of these students, a German boy (though I don't recall his name), because while I was teaching John Steinbeck's novel *The Moon Is Down,* one of the few prescribed texts I felt worthy of inclusion in the syllabus, I mentioned that I had survived the firebombing of Dresden, and to my great surprise I learned from him that he too lived through that terrible event. In his memoirs Edward speaks lovingly of a certain ironic German student, Gottfried Brieger, a recent immigrant who, along with Edward, was one of the very few members of the Mount Hermon "community," students and faculty alike, who recognized the founder, D. L. Moody, as a "charlatan" and who refused assent to the school's dominant mythology of "the dignity of manual labor": "The only other dissenter was Jeff Brieger, who cornered me in the Browsing Room and said, 'Mais c'est dégoutant,' pointing at one of the many hagiographical studies [of Moody] we were meant to read" (234). I now wonder whether Edward's Brieger was that German boy who had suffered the Dresden bombing with me. I have often wondered, too, how Edward would have responded had he enrolled in one of my "errant" classes.

Just as Edward soon came to find himself in the company of a small group of dissenters from the Mount Hermon "way" (mostly foreigners), so too did I as a teacher. Not long into that first fall semester, I became acutely aware of the homogeneity of the Mount Hermon community, both students and faculty; the worldlessness of the Mount Hermon world, which, as Edward eloquently puts it, "limited the complex intercourse of daily life to an unreflective minimum in which memory had no role" (233); and the disciplinary and normalizing dynamics of its presiding work ethic. Much as he did, I sought refuge from that life and my own sense of isolation among a small group of unmarried outsiders, particularly Bill Burney and Fred Podaril. (Later, as will be seen, three other faculty members eventually became in a certain sense even more important to me than these.)

Burney, a graduate of the University of Iowa who had come to Mount Hermon at the same time as I, was a quiet, soft-spoken, but extraordinarily articulate and creative young man of my age, whose studied mild-mannered and highly ethereal demeanor (which sometimes exasperated me) belied a deep intensity, one aspect of which was a profound contempt for what he called the spirit-destroying vulgarity of the anti-intellectual utilitarianism that concealed itself behind Mount Hermon's ethos of humanism and the work ethic. It was he who introduced me to the poetry of Wallace Stevens; to English folk ballads, which he sang for me, accompanied by his guitar, late at night after the boys were in bed; and to the black walnut pancakes that became a staple of my Sunday morning breakfast for a long time after. Podaril, a refugee from German-occupied Czechoslovakia who had come to Mount Hermon as a teacher of German several years before, was the antithetical counterpart of Bill Burney. A portly, down-to-earth, acerbic Rabelaisian cynic, he despised the hypocrisy of the Mount Hermon ethos and the historical weightlessness of the community over which it presided, and he studiously absented himself from the social rituals that it mandated, preferring to cook his own meals and to kayak on the Connecticut River or escape to a nearby farm owned by some Czech friends whenever he could. He deliberately avoided his Mount Hermon colleagues and often startled me by his expression of utter contempt for the American students he taught— "those little mindless bastards"—though from what I gathered from students and faculty alike he was a superb teacher.

In this particular company of dissenters from the Mount Hermon norm, I was enabled to identify more specifically—and sooner than Edward did—my initially vague and amorphous intuition into the disciplinary and normalizing ends that were the real agenda of what Edward calls the "shared or common values," the benignly humane rhetoric, and the prescribed communal rituals that characterized the "Mount Hermon way." I will not rehearse here all the specific manifestations of this duplicitous corporate agenda—the communal meals and their rituals; the compulsory supervision of the students' extracurricular activities, such as the asexual dances at Northfield; the undeviating time tables that we were required to enforce; the athletic teams that we were assigned regardless of our wishes and competence (though I played varsity football and baseball in high school and was a member of the track team at Wesleyan, I was condemned to coach junior-varsity basketball at Mount Hermon); and so on. They would only duplicate from my teacher's perspective what Edward says about them as a student in his memoirs. Here, for a reason that will momentarily become clear, I will refer to only one of these: the midweek noon (and for the students, Sunday) convocations that both faculty and students were required to attend. For Edward, who abhorred them, these convocations, invariably conducted by chosen faculty, were

> dreadful, pietistic, non-denominational (I disliked that form of vacillation in particular) full of homilies, advice, how-to-live. Ordinary observations were

encoded into Moodyesque sturdy Christianity in which words like "service" and "labor" acquired magical (but finally unspecifiable) meaning, to be repeated and intoned as what gave our lives "moral purpose." There had been nothing of that at VC; now it was a full load of the stuff. And no beatings, or bullying prefects. We were all Hermon boys, six hundred of us marching on after Moody and Ira Sankey, his faithful sidekick. (234)

For my colleagues and I, sitting in a balcony at the back of the hall and above the students—overseers of the errant rout, the panoptic guardians of the word of Dwight Moody, as I would now put it—these convocations were just as deadly. I was indignant at being compelled to attend and profoundly uneasy about the supervisory role we had to play. Above all, like Edward, I found the sermons of which I was a captive audience both excruciatingly boring and repellent. These talks we were compelled to hear were really sermons about "the good life" that the rigors of a Mount Hermon education (including its work ethic) would guarantee. Invariably delivered in either the orotund or occasionally the fire-and-brimstone pulpit style and with the complacent self-certainty of their truth, they were filled with the pious platitudes of a New England Protestant tradition that had been emptied of historical content. Nonetheless, I couldn't help feel that in some invisible way "the good life" extolled in these pious platitudes circulating around the self-evidence of service and labor was paradoxically historical insofar as it was distinctly essentialist, white, Protestant, patriarchal, and American and that these banalities had something to do with the formation of a society that preferred duty over the existential self, Dwight Eisenhower over Adlai Stevenson, and the national security state over the quest for global justice that the defeat of German and Japanese totalitarianism had made a possibility.

One significant aspect of this feeling is worth recalling here because of its surprising absence from Edward's memoirs. It apparently did not occur to Edward, despite his acute consciousness of his Third World status, that the student bodies of both Mount Hermon and its sister institution, the Northfield Academy, included a fairly large number of students whose parents managed the Latin American banana plantations of the United Fruit Company. This was the American company that ruthlessly exploited the labor of the indigenous people in those vulnerable countries, and thanks to its inordinate lobbying power, largely determined the United States' neocolonialist foreign policy in Latin America, specifically, its strategic installation and support of dictatorial regimes. It struck me as hypocrisy or, given Mount Hermon's universalist unworldliness, more likely ideological blindness that neither the administration nor the faculty in general seemed to indicate any uneasiness about this dubious connection with such an extreme example of the rapacity of American capitalism.

To give some sense of my state of mind at this time (and, at the risk of some embarrassment, of the style in which I expressed it), let me quote from letters I wrote to Bill Burney after he had left Mount Hermon (letters he recently returned to me after going through his files at the time of his retirement from the English department of Southeastern Connecticut State University):

Have you discovered the elixir that transforms apterix into the albatross? It's somewhere in the alembic. Continue to stir. For me? Mud. (6/25/52)

Rubendall [the headmaster] ascends out of the bottomless pit occasionally to frighten my tomorrows. And he does. But I must go back. Purge and Purify or fail and fall. (7/11/52)

Rube rubs ruthlessly across my apathetic imagination like a dirty finger. (7/23/52)

The time cometh and Dr. Rubendall's fair nordic heart looms like Urizen's Specter about to divide the eternal world and I grow cold inside remembering his heavenly host Smith Baldwin Bennett Burdick on their merry-go-round horses with the Golden Rules Books in their hands waving them tyrannically in inevitable victory. Yes. I go to fight the hordes of heaven alone without Burney without Angevin without a great deal of courage. Only words words words ineffectual Satanic words against the omnipotence of his life view. (7/28/52)

One day spills over into another like Mount Hermon personalities with only an occasional flash vision of an earlier and creative age in the seven thousand eternities that have whimpered out of my existence arising primarily out of a few positive imagimoments with Patricia whom I love hopelessly and who loves me hopelessly because her father and mother and sister cannot or are unwilling to understand me believing sincerely and forcefully that I cannot make her happy, not possessing the drive motivated by faith in the American Democratic system and that I am racially inferior, possessing skin pigment a shade darker than heaven know what and this simple and conventional prejudice . . . has me pinned and wriggling on the wall and blinded my inner eye. (9/6/52)

The Seven Storey Mountain and its fire graced only by your phonograph and Bach. Faces are Gorgonic and the old cliches ring like tolling bells in Donne's "Devotions." . . . Hayes wins and we must teach reading instead of literature. And create machines instead of men. The ogre reigns in his senility and the heirs wait greedily to stonify the unstonified. Bach's grace. And Fred. Nothing more. (9/12/52)

And then "Hi! Hi! Brooklyn in the 7th, 2 to 1, Campanella on 3rd, Hodges on 1rst, Robinson at bat, 2 and 2 count, one out"—Immovable Gorgon-faced, deep

parallel lines chiseled out by that God he worships. Omniscient and omnivo-
rous throwing his darkness on what is by nature lighted. And the ogre that
mouths his sickeningly sweet indeeds as though they were determined by the
First Cause. (11/12/52)

Lectured to the Literary Society on Blake and Shaw before the vacation. A part-
ing assault on Mount Hermon's sterility. Ineffectual. One cannot communicate
with the dead. (4/10/53)

In my second year, after having been exposed by a couple of recent Union
Theological Seminary graduates (about whom I will speak later) to the Christian existential—specifically Kierkegaardian—thought that was then in its in-
fancy in the United States, I began to teach the canonical texts prescribed for
my English courses (and occasionally unauthorized pieces such as "Professor
Sea Gull," Joseph Mitchell's wonderful portrait of the madly deconstructive
bohemian Joseph Ferdinand Gould in *McSorley's Wonderful Saloon*) from the
radically heretical perspective of the extraordinary Kierkegaardian dictum
that "we think backward, but live forward." Not satisfied by such a limited
audience, however—and, I must confess, because I had decided by then that
I had had my fill of the Mount Hermon ethos and was ready to return to
graduate school—I began looking for a wider, more public venue and found
it in the convocation. After all, these undeviatingly sterile (and sterilizing)
gatherings of the Mount Hermon community, or rather the leveling and
public-producing effects of their uniform Moodyesque form and content,
had come to epitomize for me the essence of a Mount Hermon education's
various practical manifestations. Sometime in early spring I therefore vol-
unteered to give a talk at one of those compulsory midweek convocations
with the intention of exposing the structure of that deadly institution and its
disciplinary and normalizing imperatives, if not of undermining them. To
this end I chose to deliver my talk not in the form of the usual platitudinous
homiletic abstractions that were force-fed to the students but as a simple,
enigmatic fairy tale devoid of commentary (I later used the word "sacramental" to characterize it) but replete with hidden allusions to Kierkegaard
and the writers I was then reading—Blake, Shaw, Donne, Herbert, Eliot, and
Yeats, for example. I will spare my reader the burden of my retelling this story.
It will suffice to say that it involves a beautiful young princess who awakens
from a mental sleep induced by a comely and mighty king who, in providing her with all the pleasures she could imagine, had come, unknown to her,
to possess her body and mind; this awakening is instigated by a nameless
voice that increasingly haunts the very real reality of the pleasure world in
which the king has immersed her, until this anxiety shatters that world and

its comfortable coordinates. I will quote a few lines from the conclusion of a draft I found in a journal I kept at that long-ago time to convey the style in which I chose to tell this fairy tale (and, to be candid, to expose myself to the embarrassment of its excessively romantic prose):

> She rushed into the room. There, at her feet, on a magnificent blood-red carpet lay a broken doll—the body, dressed in sable, on its stomach, its severed head several feet away, facing the stained-glass casement and bathed in a pool of blood-red light. She put her hand to her lips to stifle a cry of horror. Then she remembered the star's words about the king, and like a flash of light in the dark her life before this night appeared to her as in a vision. And she understood. She picked up the head and looked deeply into its eyes. And she saw nothing. And in that nothing her quest began.
>
> Oh, kingly doll you fed me lies
> You froze my heart and sealed my eyes.
> But now the spell you cast is dead
> And from your world my heart has fled
> To forests deep on eagle's wing it flies
> Where in the shade of night the lone one cries
> Somewhere my new-born heart and his shall meet
> And as one living heart they'll ever after beat.

The student congregation's response to my fairy tale surprised me. After the initial commotion precipitated by its utterly unexpected form and style, the auditorium became increasing silent, which I sensed, with a degree of elation, as a sign of deep engagement in the subversive symbolism of my story, however well they understood it. At the same time, the response of the Mount Hermon faculty as a whole was predictable. It immediately made quite a stir among them, which reverberated throughout the campus for several days after. One group of the faculty accused me of acting in "bad taste" and being inappropriately "obscurantist"; another, of violating the venerable tradition of the Mount Hermon convocation. I especially remember the obligatory conversation I had after my talk with the headmaster, Howard Rubendall, about whom Edward writes with some degree of sympathy, though I can't help detect a faint tone of irony in his characterization of this stately and imposing man—fair, blond, tall, always stylishly dressed—a curiously contradictory combination of churchman and public relations expert. (He was, I think, a graduate of Union Theological Seminary before it became identified with Christian existentialism.) At any rate, he informed me, in his always overly cordial and hearty yet discomforting manner, that my convocation talk was "imaginative," which I took to be his way both of avoiding reference to its content and of letting me know that imagination was not what the Mount Hermon convocation was all about. The only faculty members who expressed enthusiasm were Jim Whyte, the college pastor, who also taught courses in philosophy; John Angevin, who taught history (I think); and David Jewell, who taught the social sciences. These were all recent graduates of Union Theological Seminary, which was then, under the aegis of Van Dusen, Tillich, and Niebuhr, coming under the influence of the Christian existentialism of Continental theologians such as Rudolf Bultmann, Karl Barth, and the Jewish thinker Martin Buber. Indeed, in the following days these young faculty members, attuned to the impact my convocation talk had made on the student body, asked their classes to write commentaries on it. Their interpretations were wildly erratic, but as Jim Whyte told me, most not only appreciated the refreshing difference from the tired fare to which they had been accustomed but also recognized that there "was something rotten in the state of Denmark."

Edward says nothing about this event, which was intended to undermine the complacent Mount Hermon ethos, the very ethos that made him feel alien there. Indeed, in referring to the Moodyesque tenor that pervaded the tradition of the Mount Hermon convocation, he says that "not one teacher or student expressed the slightest doubt that Moody was worthy of the highest admiration." In the process of reading his memoirs, especially about his intense revulsion and resistance to the sermons' unrelenting "dreadful" moral pieties that were "repeated and intoned as what gave our lives 'moral purpose,'" it inevitably occurred to me to imagine him in that audience and, perhaps, one of those students who were assigned to write about it later in the week and to wonder with deep fascination what his response to my parable had been. Did he, as his unequivocating disdain for the moral pieties of these obligatory convocations might suggest, simply tune out from the beginning? Or was it, as my rereading of the extant draft now seems all too easily to allow, simply another version of the same to this brilliant, precocious, and alienated young Arab?

* * *

My profound interest in Edward's silence about my talk fifty years later is not intended to suggest hurt feelings or bruised pride. I note this significant omission for a larger purpose, one that concerns history and memory, particularly an aspect of American intellectual, social, and political history at that moment and its fate under the aegis of the amnesiac Western memory, which in so many ways has been the supreme theme of my intellectual work. In order to make all this clear, however, I need to put this absence in terms of a fundamental and to me telling difference between Edward's experience at Mount Hermon and mine. For Edward, it was essentially the lack of any redeeming momentum at Mount Hermon that precipitated the redemptive intellectual identity that was to determine his future work. For me, I now realize thanks to Edward's memoirs, it was the presence of such a momentum, however peripheral and inadequately practiced by its proponents, that not only redeemed my two otherwise benighted years at Mount Hermon but inaugurated a transformation of my sense of calling, indeed, of my relationship to being, and that eventually coalesced to "shape" the identity that has determined my intellectual labor ever since. This momentum was the Christian—specifically, Kierkegaardian—existentialism thought and practiced by the three previously mentioned recent Union Theological Seminary graduates, Whyte, Angevin, and above all Jewell. The difference, then, was this marginal but exciting momentum, about which Edward says nothing in his remembrance of Mount Hermon.

It is, of course, understandable that a fifteen-year-old Arab boy, recently arrived in the United States from the Middle East, might not have seen the intellectual significance of Kierkegaardian existentialism for that contemporary American occasion. But it comes as somewhat of a surprise to me that he did not register some recognition of this significance many significantly historical years later, when he wrote these memoirs. He does, in fact, refer to one of these mentors and to Kierkegaard when he recalls the relief he experienced at being spared the repetition in his second year of the "literalist and, I must say, fundamentalist" material of the "simple-minded class [on the Old Testament] (doubtless an idea of Dr. Moody) designed to make us pious" that he had studied his first year:

> Were it not that my record was so good I'd have had the same Bible teacher (Chester something) in my senior year, with the New Testament as our text, but instead I was allowed to take the alternative Bible IV given by the school chaplain and co-swimming coach Reverend Whyte, known to all as Friar Tuck for his portliness, red hair, and all-around good humor. I was seventeen, but thanks to his openness and total absence of dogmatism we had a superb reading course in classical philosophy, from Plato and Aristotle, through the Enlightenment to Kierkegaard. (245)

As the deflecting interpolations imply, however, these were passing references and suggest little awareness, either then or, more important, when he wrote his memoirs, of their symbolic importance for the intellectual life not only of Mount Hermon but of America in the 1950s.

Coming to Mount Hermon from the suffocating liberal humanist environment of Columbia University, which was accommodating itself to the anticommunist cold-war consensus both administratively and academically, I welcomed this Kierkegaardian initiative as if it were an oasis in a cultural desert. Thanks to the prodding of David Mize, a fellow alien at Wesleyan from St. Louis, I had read an edition of selections from Kierkegaard's *Journals*—the first translation of his work into English (edited and translated by Alexander Dru and published in 1939)—as an undergraduate in 1948. I found its fierce thinking voice revelatory in the context of the blandly canonical way most of my professors were representing the literature we were reading. Because I was in the thrall of William Blake and Bernard Shaw, however (my master's thesis topic at Columbia), I had not had a chance to read Kierkegaard beyond this inaugural introduction. It was only after I got to know John Angevin, Jim Whyte, and especially David Jewell and his beautiful, tremendously intelligent, and caring wife, Steffe (Elaine Steffenroot)—these latter came to encapsulate the essence of what I now believe it means to be human—that Kierkegaard, particularly the Kierkegaard who proposes dread as the necessary condition of a forwarding life in time, became a looming if baffling presence in my consciousness and began to inform my sense of calling as a teacher. I especially remember and treasure the occasional evenings after the Mount Hermon world closed down when I walked over to Crossley Hall for coffee and cake and those astonishing conversations with David and sometimes Steffe, where we discussed this brooding hunchback misfit, the invisible intellectual match to and opponent of Hegel, the prime exponent of thinking "backward" and, proleptically, the leveled European world that Hegel's philosophical memory (*Er-innerung*) was then producing in Europe in the form of "the crowd." Those extraordinary conversations, and the books I devoured in consequence (*The Present Age, Fear and Trembling, Either/Or,* and *Concluding Unscientific Postscript*), increasingly alienated the world as I had hitherto perceived it, transforming its sedimented commonness into something "rich and strange" not only in the personal and aesthetic senses but also, though to a lesser extent, in the social sense. It was these intense informal nocturnal conversations with the Jewells that led me to feel, for the first time, that I was a unique individual, not simply the predictable cipher—a lowly working-class Greek—that the ethnocentric and class-structured world in which I had grown up had led me to believe I was.

But this exposure to Kierkegaard was not simply a matter of personal transformation. After coming to know the Jewells, I began to realize that their "Kierkegaardian" perspective was shared among a segment, however minuscule and marginal, within the Mount Hermon community. That led me to perceive it as an emergent pedagogical momentum that had a broader historical context. I eventually realized that the common educational background of Whyte, Angevin, and Jewell was no coincidence; all were recent graduates of Union Theological Seminary, which was located across from Columbia University on Broadway. Unlike Columbia and its complacent and unquestioning satisfaction with the great European humanist tradition (as its vaunted and inordinately influential "World Civilization" testifies), Union, I discovered, was proffering to this postwar generation of Protestant theological students a radically different education, one in which the question rather than the answer was paramount. It was a demythologized and ecumenical Christianity, evolving under the influence of Kierkegaard and such contemporary European theologians as Bultmann, Barth, Fritz Buri, Tillich (who had fled Nazi Germany and come to Union), Gabriel Marcel, Nikolay Berdyayev, Martin Buber, and the great anti-Nazi activist minister Dietrich Bonhoeffer. Moreover, it was deeply responsive to the radicalized Heideggerian existentialist momentum that had emerged during World War II largely in opposition to the totalitarian worldview of the German Nazis and Italian Fascists, which some of existentialism's proponents—Sartre, Merleau-Ponty, Beauvoir, Camus—saw in some sense as the fulfillment of the logical economy of the Western philosophical tradition. Under the influence of these former Union seminarians, in other words, I came, symptomatically if not completely consciously, to see that this small contingency of Christian existentialists at Mount Hermon was a microcosm of a larger marginal intellectual community and the harbinger of an American momentum of thought that was, in essence, not only antimetaphysical but anti-"Western" and more specifically anti-"American."

Although it was, as I recall, primarily this intellectual initiative to which I was immediately attracted in my encounter with these former Union seminarians, I also became aware of its sociopolitical allotrope. They had, after all, chosen the classroom rather than the pulpit, which would have guaranteed at least a more uniform Christian audience. To be candid, however, it was not this consideration that provoked my awareness so much as my colleagues' accounts of the unusual activist callings that a number of their fellow students had chosen, callings that had taken them into the black ghettos of America's cities, the Black Belt of the South, and the cruel world of the Mexican migrants in the Southwest. I remember George Todd, for example, with little diminishment of the awe and admiration I felt then. He was a close Union friend of David Jewell, who had invited him to Hermon around Christmastime in 1952. Todd described his life as a minister of a church that he and several of his colleagues had established in an abandoned storefront in Spanish Harlem as a means of engaging the impoverished and desperate inhabitants of this notorious ghetto in opulent New York in a consciousness-raising dialogue. (This dialogic educational practice in the heart of American darkness, I then felt, was not simply another version of the patronizing liberal pedagogy that accommodated the oppressed into the dominant "democratic" culture's circle; I felt it to be symptomatic of something positively different, which I was not then equipped to understand fully. Only now do I see that it was proleptic—indeed, the precursor to Paulo Freire's revolutionary "cointentional" "pedagogy of the oppressed" [*conscientização*], by means of which the silenced colonized have been enabled to speak for themselves.)

At that time in my life, this was as far as I could take my sense of the larger national significance of the Union Theological Seminary enclave I encountered at Mount Hermon. That changed when I read Edward's memoirs, which—especially his omission of reference to what I have been calling this marginal Kierkegaardian momentum—helped me to retrieve that time and suddenly enabled me to extend this symptomatic insight into the national context to include the intellectual and social history of modern America that was then yet to unfold. That is, his striking omission, for whatever reason, allowed me to realize from the vantage point of the present global post-cold-war occasion what has been strategically obliterated by the custodians of the American historical memory, including the fundamentalist and reactionary Christian Right, which has utterly co-opted the religious initiative in America. What I for the first time now saw and knew about my Mount Hermon, thanks to Edward's version of his, was that the Kierkegaardian thought and practice of my Union colleagues at Mount Hermon—and my own clumsy efforts to assimilate them to my sense of self—was symptomatic of an extremely significant inaugural and potentially transformative intellectual momentum emanating largely, though not exclusively, from the emergent Christian existentialist persuasion of Union Theological Seminary. I now saw that, first of all, they reflected Union's introduction of Continental existentialist thought to the intellectual life of America, thus enabling the formation of a radical coalition of dissident members of the various religious denominations (including Protestants, Catholics, and Jews) and creating a matrix for the later reception of an even more consciously political poststructuralist thought that includes Edward Said's. As such, especially with respect to people such as George Todd and David Jewell (who in the early 1960s relocated to Texas to minister to the ethnic migrants who were being ruthlessly exploited by the white American landowning farmers), they typified Union's inauguration of a momentum for national sociopolitical resistance against the dominant liberal capitalist culture, one that included the protestation of the inhumanity of racial discrimination in America and the mind-debilitating and world-threatening cold-war consensus, including U.S. imperialist foreign policy in Latin America and (though less prominently) Korea.

This emergent Christian existentialism arising at Union and other affiliated Protestant seminaries, such as Yale Divinity School, Drew University, and the University of Chicago School of Theology, many of whose faculty were trained at or were inspired by Union, was an emergent momentum of thinking and practice that ten years later, in the 1960s, flowered not only into a powerful oppositional intellectual and moral force—I think of Nathan Scott Jr., Stanley Romaine Hopper, and Will Herberg, for example—but also, though asymmetrically, into a practical initiative in America. This religiously motivated initiative, perhaps most visibly represented by the former cold warrior William Sloan Coffin, John Muste, and the Catholic activist Father Daniel Berrigan, influenced, if it did not spearhead, the protest movement against the United States' arbitrary intervention in Vietnam, where a native people was struggling to gain national independence from a long and brutalizing European colonial occupation, and particularly against America's horrendously destructive conduct of the war, in which, in the name of the "free" (and Christian) world, the people of Vietnam were indiscriminately reduced by the logic of "cost efficiency" to the "body count." It was also this same Christian existentialism that influenced the leadership of the nonmilitant black (and white) civil rights movement, as is manifestly clear in all Martin Luther King's speeches, especially "A Time to Break Silence," in which he links the civil rights movement to the Vietnam War. In its most recent phase, after the existentialist momentum was seen to rely too heavily on the individual self, this Union momentum underwent a transformation that came to be called "liberation theology." As the work of Paulo Freire and Enrique Dussel, among others, bears witness, this newer religious perspective has played and continues to play an important role in postcolonial Latin America.

What I want to underscore, precisely because it came as a shock of recognition as I read Edward's account of his two years at Mount Hermon, is that the history I have too briefly recalled here has been virtually effaced by the triumphalist historical revisionism that followed the collapse of the Soviet Empire and the proclamation by the deputies of American liberal capitalist/technological culture of "the end of history" and the advent of "the New World Order." As I have observed, this revisionism has been aided and abetted by the fundamentalist Christian right, which, as its coverage by the media makes clear, has achieved hegemonic status in the domain of religious thought and practice in the United States—that is, has annulled the value of religious thinking in an utterly secularized world. The Left, of course, has noted this amnesia of the American cultural memory, but, as in

my and Edward's cases, it is attempting to counter the latter's representation of the contemporary global occasion by retrieving a history that, as did
both Edward and I, omits from consideration what I have been calling the
Kierkegaardian momentum, which played a decisive role in the anti–Vietnam
War and civil rights movements. This, it now occurs to me, is unfortunate, in
part because that history's exclusive preoccupation with the secular domain
of sociopolitics leaves it indifferent to what my Mount Hermon colleagues
inadequately referred to as "the spiritual" but what I, following Heidegger, call
the "being" of being—a reasonable translation given that Heidegger, along
with Kierkegaard, was a fundamental source for the theology of Bultmann,
Tillich, the Niebuhrs (Reinhold and Richard), and other Christian existentialists of that time. In so doing, furthermore, this Left discourse mounts
its resistance in the very language of the ontologic that has informed this
devastating history even as its discourse circulates in an unthought way
around this "Other" of the truth of materiality. In invoking the spiritual in
their critique of American cold-war policy and its particular hot wars—the
Greek Civil War, the Korean War, the Guatemalan Civil War, the Vietnam
War—and of the United States' perennial support of brutal dictatorships
everywhere in the world, but especially in Latin America, these American
Christian existentialists were symptomatically and presciently intuiting an
imperial European/American ontologic, call it pragmatic, technological, or
capitalistic, that was polyvalent in its practical application. However inadequately, in other words, they sensed it as an ontologic that had as its end
the reduction of the Other of quantitative matter to the disposable same,
not only at the site of being as such, but all along the continuum of being,
from the subject, to nature (the *ecos*), to the social "deviant," and finally to
other cultures. (I claim this to be their legacy to the discourse and practice
of opposition in the 1960s, despite the fact that, because they perceived the
Stalinist communism of the Soviet Union as more threatening to this "spirit"
than was the capitalism of the United States, a few of these theologians—
Reinhold Niebuhr, for example—participated in cold-war policy.) Is not this
the testimony of postmodern thought as a whole, insofar as it would decolonize the being—the "nothing" (Heidegger), the "*différance*" (Derrida), the
"*différend*" (Lyotard), the "rhizome" (Deleuze and Guattari), and so on—that
the imperial metaphysical logic of the West has colonized? Is this not also
the testimony of Edward Said himself, whose lifelong project as someone
out of place—a nobody, as he insistently notes, from the perspective of the
Mount Hermon ethos and, since then, of the West's truth of Being—has been
not only to disclose the plight of the deterritorialized of the earth but also,
more recently, to render the very placelessness of these "denizens" a space

of positive resistance against "citizenry" as that term is understood in the new, American global order? If there is any single motif that subsumes the last thirty years' various oppositional discourses, whether philosophical, cultural, or sociopolitical, it is the indefinite but very real notion of some other reality that, try as the custodians of the truth might to annul "it," always returns to haunt this global truth. After reading Edward's memoirs, I now realize that what those Union seminarians at Mount Hermon were trying to articulate in the name of the word *spirit* was an early and symptomatic manifestation of this repressed nothing—this other, "spectral" reality—with which the dominant truth will, at all costs, have nothing to do.

Let me reiterate. In focusing my own reminiscences on Edward's omission of reference to this marginal Kierkegaardian momentum at Mount Hermon, my intention has not been to criticize his blindness. It would be presumptuous, at least, to expect a high-school student from the Middle East with virtually no knowledge about American culture to perceive this marginal momentum, let alone register it as a synecdoche of an emergent oppositional momentum in that culture. Nor should one expect the Edward who writes this memoir about his formative years fifty years ago—the expatriated Palestinian scholar and critic who has devoted his life to the analysis of "Orientalism," the West's perennial will to colonize and appropriate the Middle East—to give prominence to such a spatially and temporally distanced momentum. On the contrary, it is precisely the absence of reference to this momentum in his memoirs that has triggered the shock of recognition that has enabled me not only to remember a part of my life I had long forgotten but also to know it for the first time: to realize that it was this brief moment in my distant past that, despite its negativity, inscribed the idea that eventually transformed my sense of self and calling and made me, for good or ill, the intellectual I am. And for this I am grateful to Edward. Whatever *Out of Place* has meant to all the others who have read this wonderful book, to me it speaks with such poignant intimacy that I can't help but take it as a gift. To invoke the language that has inadvertently emerged in the process of writing my own reminiscence of Mount Hermon, it has stirred the dormant ghost of that past into life.

Coda

By the beginning of the spring semester of 1953, I had had enough of the debilitating banalities of the Mount Hermon ethos. Bill Burney, my closest friend, had left to undertake graduate work in English at the University of Iowa (or was it Yale?), and David Jewell had announced that he would be leaving Mount Hermon to pursue further graduate studies at Union and Columbia Teachers College. Compelled by the force of the estrangement precipitated by that Kierkegaardian momentum, I decided it was time for me, too, to return to graduate school. I applied for and received a teaching assistantship at Cornell, where I spent the next year working toward my doctorate. There, unfortunately, I encountered more or less the same educational world I had left behind at Columbia. In the meantime, I had met and fallen in love with Margaret Prince, who was a sophomore at Barnard, and at the end of that year we were married by David Jewell in one of the chapels of Union Theological Seminary. Since our financial situation was a matter of making ends meet, we decided once again to postpone my doctoral work until she had finished college. I instead took what turned out to be an excruciatingly mindless position as writer and editor for the annual edition of the *Encyclopedia Americana,* the only aspect of which I enjoyed was my friendship with Murray Greene, one of the senior editors who was studying contemporary philosophy in the evenings at the New School for Social Research and, as I recall, was translating (with Theodore Kisiel) Werner Marx's *Heidegger and the Tradition* (1971).

We spent two and a half grim years living in New York, the first few months in a seedy "residential hotel" called Reldnass Hall, on the edge of Morningside Heights and Harlem, then on 114th Street, and finally on 158th Street and Riverside Drive, in a Jewish neighborhood where the Greenes lived—coincidentally, it was also the setting of Tom Buchanan's extramarital rendezvous in F. Scott Fitzgerald's *Great Gatsby.* They were redeemed by our friendship with the Jewells, however, who bridged the otherwise immeasurable intellectual gap between the Mount Hermon that had instigated my will to leave it and the deadly hack work I was doing for the encyclopedia. Our first daughter, Maria, was born in the winter of 1955, and later that year, after hearing that the University of Wisconsin English department had awarded me an assistantship, we packed our minimal belongings into a broken-down Chevrolet and drove out to Madison to begin again.

Like Columbia and Cornell, Wisconsin's English department in 1956 was traditional: though it offered a few courses in American literature, for example, it frowned upon dissertations in that area. Nevertheless, a number of professors were there (Merritt Hughes, the Milton scholar; Ricardo Quintana, an eighteenth-century scholar; Ruth Wallerstein, a sixteenth-century scholar; and Paul Wiley, who studied English Modernism) whose traditionalism was eccentric and thus more tolerant of the new existentialist heresy. This group included above all Richard Hoffman, who taught a course on the intellectual foundations of modernity that included a unit on existential thought; the very young Karl Kroeber, who indelibly introduced me to the comparativist approach of Erich Auerbach (a fundamental presence in Edward Said's work) in a tremendously provocative course on the history of the novel from Petronius to Woolf; and in the philosophy department, Richard Kaelin, who was teaching the Continental philosophers, including Sartre and Heidegger. Among my graduate-student acquaintances, there were Richard Wasson, who became my closest friend, and at a slightly greater remove, Joseph Riddel, who wrote his dissertation with Hoffman on the poetry of Wallace Stevens, both of whom, though in quite different ways, I acknowledge for the intensity and brilliance of their errant intellectualism, which always pushed the traditional fare we were getting in our classes beyond the boundaries into the space that years later came to be called postmodern.

During my four years at Wisconsin, I was still thinking within the framework of Christian existentialism, as my dissertation, "The Christian Tradition in Modern British Verse Drama: The Poetics of Sacramental Time," clearly suggests. In it I extracted the plays of T. S. Eliot from the New Critical context in which they had been hitherto embedded and reconstellated them into the Kierkegaardian context. In the process, however, and thanks to courses with Hoffman and Kroeber and, above all, to the violent dialogues with Wasson (I would now call them, after Heidegger, *Auseinandersetzungen*), I began to realize that the concept of differential time I was trying to retrieve from the New Critic's will to accommodate it to the eternal and identical whole was more radical than the Kierkegaardian time I had brought with me to Wisconsin from Mount Hermon. That realization marked the beginning not of my forgetting of the Kierkegaardian momentum I had discovered in a remote corner of Mount Hermon but of its transformation into the spectral force that, like time's winged chariot, has haunted my work ever since.

Appendix: September 11, 2006

Early one day, in March or April of 2002—it was around eight in the morning, while I was still in bed—I received a telephone call from Edward, who said that he had read my memoir and liked it a lot. But he also wanted to let me know, in his engaging, bantering way, that I was demanding too much of him in being surprised that the Kierkegaardian/existentialist agenda of several of his younger Mount Hermon teachers had not affected him, that it was unreasonable of me to expect a teenaged Arab boy just arrived from the Middle East to be engaged by what I understood as a philosophical initiative that redeemed the school's otherwise deadly Protestant work ethic. As a corrective to my invocation of certain Christian existentialists as providing a

philosophical and moral groundwork in the United States for the future protest movement against the Vietnam War, he also informed me that a number
of these intellectuals, most notably Reinhold Niebuhr, were cold warriors,
and in this light he recommended my reading Frances Stoner Saunders's
book *Who Paid the Piper: The CIA and the Cultural Cold War* (1999). Only
at the end of our conversation did he tell me that he would be pleased if I
would join him at Mount Hermon in June, where, for some unfathomable
reason, given his severe criticism of the school in his memoir, the current
administration had asked him to give that year's commencement address. I
accepted his invitation enthusiastically, anticipating an extended conversation
about a hitherto forgotten but formative time in both our lives.

In an e-mail note on May 19, 2002, following up on our earlier telephone
conversation, I wrote Edward the following:

> Dear Edward,
> Last night, as I was flipping through the TV channels, I came across C-Span,
> which was reproducing a speech given on April 2, 2002, on "American Security"
> by David Horowitz, the ultra-right wing president of the Society of American
> Popular Culture. I'm sure you know this man's politics and style, so I need not
> comment on what he had to say about the "perilous threat" to the good and
> noble and freedom-loving American people that the fanatic Arab/Islamic world
> poses. What I think is worth mentioning, should you have missed this appall-
> ingly vulgar C-Span program, is Horowitz's astonishing representation of the
> "university left" as a "fifth column" that must be eradicated. As I listened to his
> incredibly monolithic diatribe against the Palestinians—I was tempted to say
> "Ahabian" but didn't because that would give a certain tragic dignity to his rav-
> ings, which, in fact, were an obscene mockery of Ahab's monomania—I realized
> that at a certain point in his speech, he would invoke your work as symptomatic
> of this threat. And indeed he did. At the climactic moment—I'm pretty sure it
> was strategic—he not only attacked your person as a Palestinian fanatic, but also
> undertook a pointed and sustained vilification of your book on Orientalism. He
> said that this subversive book had resulted in the destruction of the American
> academic institutions that heretofore had produced disinterested scholars who
> produced "objective research" about the Middle East for the government of the
> United States. Thanks to the influence of your book and the visibility it gave
> you, these academic institutions had been reorganized to produce researchers
> in foreign affairs who are in fact anti-American—actually he said "they hate
> America"—and were mostly Arabs. And this, in large part, was, I think, what
> he meant when he informed his responsive audience that academia in the U.S.
> is "a fifth column" that should be eradicated. The speech literally made me sick
> to my stomach, and so I had to turn it off. But I couldn't turn off the despair I
> felt at the grotesquely chauvinistic way the media conglomerates represent what

is going on in the world—their utter blindness, cynical or strategic, to a global occasion that any sane person can see is a matter of life and death for millions of people, if not the planet at large—and their tacit silencing of the kind of human and reasonable dissent that has always characterized your work.

Anyway . . . This occasion has also given me the opportunity to write and ask you about your health. The last time I heard from you, you said that in April you were going in for a different kind of therapy. I hope with all my heart it has had a positive effect. We need you. . . . [Here I inform Edward of my own poor health.]

Finally, are you going to Mount Hermon to deliver your graduation address? And, if you are, would you kindly send me the date and time? All things being equal—and if you don't mind—I would like to attend that event, both to get a chance to see and talk with you in THAT context, and to remember Mount Hermon, which, after all is said and done, was curiously formative for me.

My warmest regards, Edward,

Bill

On May 23 Edward responded ominously, yet with his typical perseverance:

Dear Bill,

I'm just coming out of the first cycle of a horrendously complicated and rigorous protocol that will go on through October. I won't bother you with the details, but I can write and read, and have no energy now to do much else. I was concerned about your health and heart but feel reassured by your tone and absence of any bad findings. Horowitz sells my books for me: of course I never reply but Orientalism helped me educate my children rather well and it is still selling and still in print in each of the 35 languages into which it has been translated. Latest is Ukrainian. But I will do the Hermon graduation; it is to be on Sunday morning June 2 at 11, although Ueller the president wants us there at 9, god only knows why. We're spending the night of the first with friends in the Berkshires and will drive up past Greenfield at the crack of dawn! Please let me know if you'll come and if you'd stay for lunch; I'll get them to invite you. Let me know.

Fondest, all best,

Edward

On May 28 I accepted Edward's invitation to join him:

Dear Edward,

O.K. I'm planning to drive out to Greenfield, Mass. or Brattleboro, Vt. on Friday (It's unlikely that I'll be able to find a room in the vicinity of Bernardston), and to come to the graduation ceremonies at Mount Hermon early the next morning. I say planning, because my body (or is it my mind?) vacillates between down and up like a yo-yo. I've been feeling pretty good these last few days, but I can't be sure it will last. In other words, if I don't show up, it will be because the yo-yo is down. I'm hoping hard it will be up. Being at Mount Hermon on that particular occasion would be for me something like an epochal moment.

My best,
Bill

On May 30, Edward sent me the following note confirming what I had been anticipating. It was the last e-mail he would send me:

Bill,
I'm crushed, I was at the hospital yesterday since over Mem day I developed a very high fever, chills, shaking, etc. I now have pneumonia and my state is very fragile. My doctor has grounded me till August at least, a crushing blow, but since I've had three life-threatening pneumonias in the last three months, it's pretty ominous and has discouraged me for the first time since I began treatment 8 years ago. My immune system is not functional and am kept alive by daily injections of neutrophils, three antibiotics, a sulfa drug and gatorade. I'm to stay at home for the next few days and then very little exertion after that for two months. I haven't told Mt Hermon yet but since I have written the speech I'm going to propose that my son goes and read it for me. He's a fabulous 30 yr old, a lawyer and human rights and asylum and anti-death penalty activist, but have no idea if they'll accept. All my other commitments for June and July here and abroad have had to go too but I feel the worst about Hermon, partly too because I was so anxious to see you there. I can't say anymore, best,
Edward

Needless to say, I was profoundly disturbed by this turn and equally disappointed that my deeply anticipated conversation with Edward in that mutually resonant context would not transpire.

Shortly before Edward's son, Wadie, delivered his father's address to the graduating students at Mount Hermon, Edward's secretary sent me at his request a copy of it. I quote the last two paragraphs to proffer another instance not only of Edward Said's remarkable generosity in the face of his vilification by the deputies of the American government but also of his humane and recalcitrantly optimistic vision of a future world in which everyone on earth is admitted—a final witness that Said purposefully puts in the mouth of a black man:

Finally, despite the great self-sufficiency of our country, its enormous power, geographic range, the variety of its people and history, we must never forget that its real essence is that it remains a heterogeneous society of former immigrants, not the home of a homogeneous master race. Being American means being a hundred other things as well since the world has come here, left its marks bad as in the events of 9/11, good as in contributions of immigrants like Einstein and Charlie Chaplin, as well as children of transported slaves like Toni Morrison and W. E. B. Dubois and stamped our society with their traces. No identity is pure, everyone counter, original, spare, strange, as the English poet Gerard Manly Hopkins put it, and this is a source of joy and richness of attitude, and shouldn't be a way of shutting the Other out. We are all Others in the final analysis. This is what makes America unique, not the fact that we have left behind the history of our backgrounds and have emerged, as if from a gigantic cookie-cutter, cut from the same mold. Human history is not a competition to dominate and be what is frequently called the best. It is rather a vast interweaving of human lives, interacting in all sorts of unforeseen and unseen ways, which it is our destiny to understand and cherish since America is the best vantage point to actually see history being made. Too often in America we use the word "history" as a synonym for oblivion, as in the dismissive phrase "you're history." Just the opposite I'd say: awareness of history assures us of our humanity, guarantees our life as a republic, ensures our identity not as a combative "us" ready for war against an equally combative "them," but as an essential part of the human march toward emancipation and enlightenment. We still have a very long way to go.

Let me close by quoting some marvelous lines about the high drama of what is before us as makers of the human narrative, lines written by the great twentieth-century Caribbean-French poet Aimé Césaire:

> but the work of man is only just beginning
> and it remains to man to conquer all
> the violence entrenched in the recesses of his passion
>
> and no race possesses the monopoly of beauty,
> of intelligence, of force, and there
> is a place for all at the rendezvous
> of victory

On September 25 of the next year, I received a late-night call from my *boundary 2* colleague Paul Bové, informing me of Edward's death. I was profoundly shaken by the news, not only because the Western world, especially America, had lost its conscience, and the West's "Others," one of their most enabling consciousnesses, but also because, as I hope this book has made amply clear, he was a presence in my intellectual and moral life.

In the end, his untimely passing from the fraught contemporary scene cannot obliterate his memory, despite the craven efforts of his neoconservative enemies to do so. We are assured of this by his great contribution to our knowledge of the benighted world we now inhabit under the aegis of America's Ahabian gaze and its prosthetic military juggernaut, his luminous polyvalent directives for changing it or, to put it in terms of the polyphonic music of Said's beloved Johann Sebastian Bach, for transforming the "clash of civilizations" precipitated by the long imperial history culminating in America's univocal global hegemony into a humane "'whole consort dancing together' contrapuntally."

Notes

Chapter 1: Edward W. Said and the Poststructuralists

1. For example, though not strictly speaking a neoconservative, the reviewer of Said's posthumously published *On Late Style: Music and Literature against the Grain* (New York: Pantheon, 2006), Edward Rothstein, marginalizes Said's focus on the open-endedness of the late style by focusing his review on Said's commentary on Jean Genet's solidarity with the Palestinian cause in 1970, thus implicating Said with terrorism: "'I defend the Palestinians whole heartedly and automatically,' Genet writes, 'They are in the right because I love them.' He recalls the brotherly kisses he bestowed on a fellow guerrilla in Jordan in 1970: 'The one they embraced would be leaving that night, cross the Jordan River to plant bombs in Palestine and often would not return.'

"But wouldn't a 'late style' have some sense of irony about this romanticization of violence? Or some notion about precisely what these light, sparkling, open figures were intending? Wouldn't it require being more attuned to the precise character of the contradictions so warmly embraced? Doesn't late style require some scrupulous self-reflection, some sense of how earlier perceptions might themselves require revisiting and revising? Wouldn't something similar have helped Said's own late style?" (*New York Times Book Review,* July 16, 2006, p. 19).

2. Statement of Stanley Kurtz before the Subcommittee on Select Education, Committee on Education and the Workforce, U.S. House of Representatives, http://edworkforce. house.gov/hearings/108/sd/titlevi61903/kurtz.htm.

3. I am referring to several of those who were privy to the lectures that became *Humanism and Democratic Criticism* and spoke to this matter in the special issue of *boundary 2* (31, no. 2 [Summer 2004]) edited by Aamir Mufti and entitled *Secular Criticism* and to several of those who contributed to the volume edited by Homi Bhabha and W. T. J. Mitchell and entitled *Edward Said: Continuing the Conversation* (Chicago: University of Chicago Press, 2005), which commemorated Said's death.

4. Timothy Brennan, *Wars of Position: The Cultural Politics of Left and Right* (New York: Columbia University Press, 2006), 98. Later in that book (101), Brennan identifies

poststructuralist theory's "splic[ing] together" of the "racial and political" other, "as though they were the same thing"—a splicing that, he claims, "was simply unacceptable to Said"— with "the Heideggerian turn." Brennan's book was published after Said's *Humanism and Democratic Criticism.*

5. Paul A. Bové, "Continuing the Conversation," in *Edward Said: Continuing the Conversation,* 41.

6. Said, *On Late Style,* 7.

7. For a brilliant critique of Said's contradictory distinction between a "bad," ontologically "essentialist" humanism and a "good," "essential" humanism, see R. Radhakrishnan's essay "Edward Said's Literary Humanism" (*Cultural Critique* 67 [Fall 2007]: 24–25): "Does Said really believe that he can hold on to the good vibes and connotations of the mere adjective 'essential,' while at the same time cast himself as an uncompromising antagonist of 'essentialism' as a philosophical-theoretical-epistemological position? . . . *Humanism and Democratic Criticism* teems with passages where Said celebrates the self-reflexive, de-stabilizing, and protean play of language in literary and aesthetic works, but in all these references he is thinking of literary language that to him is organic to experience, not the 'language' of theory that to him is occlusive of worldliness and experience. It would appear then this non-essentialist play of literary language and aesthetic elaboration is essential. Not an ontological thinker and not a philosopher, Said chooses not to do battle with essentialism *per se,* but with identitarian historical modes of living and being that are underwritten by essentialism, in particular, nationalism.

"Why then does Said, who believes in, or would like to believe in, the epistemological assailability of humanism, not take poststructuralism to heart (poststructuralism whose very life breath is the 'death of essentialism'); or for that matter, Heidegger's 'Letter on Humanism' which Said rightly identifies as 'a thoroughgoing examination of its [humanism's] metaphysical relationship to a prior Being,' but only to say, as a consequence, that 'what really concerns me is humanism as a useable praxis for intellectuals and academics?' Would not the epistemological deconstruction of humanism be perfectly compatible with Said's critical text?"

8. Aamir R. Mufti, "Secular Criticism: A Reintroduction for Perilous Times," in *Secular Criticism,* a special issue of *boundary 2* (31, no. 2 [Summer 2004]: 1–2). In this piece Mufti focuses on the legacy of Edward Said. The list of names he cites as postmodernists is curiously eclectic, but I believe they are subsumed by "continental [European] theory" (as opposed to Said's American milieu), of which poststructuralism is a dimension.

9. Brennan, *Wars of Position,* 98–99.

10. Michel Foucault, *The Order of Things: An Archaeology of the Human Sciences* (New York: Vintage, 1973; French orig., *Les Mots et les choses* [Paris: Gallimard, 1966]). See especially the sections in chapter 9 ("Man and His Double") in which Foucault writes of "the analytic of finitude" and the three doubles, "the empirical and the transcendental," "the cogito and the unthought," and "the retreat and return of the origin" (312–35).

11. Edward Said, *Beginnings: Intention and Method* (New York: Basic, 1975), 327 (emphasis added). Further references to this work will be abbreviated to *B* and appear parenthetically.

12. For an amplification of this crucial Heideggerian understanding of human being (*Dasein*), one that closely resembles the inseparable "doubles" cited in note 10, see Wil-

liam V. Spanos, *Heidegger and Criticism: Retrieving the Cultural Politics of Destruction* (Minneapolis: University of Minnesota Press, 1993), 112–13.

13. For a notable exception to this marked tendency of postcolonial criticism, see Abdirahman A. Hussein, *Edward Said: Criticism and Society* (London: Verso, 2002), which devotes two long introductory chapters to Said's *Beginnings*.

14. See the chapter entitled "The Ontological Origins of Occidental Imperialism: Thinking the *Meta* of Metaphysics," in William V. Spanos, *America's Shadow: An Anatomy of Empire* (Minneapolis: University of Minnesota Press, 2000), 1–63.

15. Martin Heidegger, *Parmenides*, trans. André Schuwer and Richard Rojcewicz (Bloomington: University of Indiana Press, 1992), 45.

16. A significant exception to this generalization is R. Radhakrishnan. See especially the essays "Toward an Effective Intellectual: Foucault and Gramsci" and "Ethnic Identity and Poststructuralist Differance," in *Diasporic Mediations: Between Home and Location* (Minneapolis: University of Minnesota Press, 1996) 27–61 and 62–79.

17. Louis Althusser, "From *Capital* to Marx's Philosophy," in Althusser and Étienne Balibar, *Reading "Capital"* (London: Verso, 1979), 13–69, esp. 18–28. See also William V. Spanos, "Althusser's Problematic in the Context of the Vietnam War: Towards a Spectral Politics," *Rethinking Marxism* 10 (Fall 1998): 1–21; repr., Spanos, *American Exceptionalism in the Age of Globalization: The Specter of Vietnam* (Albany: SUNY Press, 2006).

18. Michel Foucault, *Discipline and Punish,* trans. Alan Sheridan (New York: Pantheon, 1977), 205 (emphases added).

19. For influential examples of the pervasive charge of poststructuralist theory's complicity with the dominant institutions of power, see Fredric Jameson, *Postmodernism; or The Cultural Logic of Late Capitalism* (Durham, N.C.: Duke University Press, 1991); Michael Hardt and Antonio Negri, *Empire* (Cambridge, Mass.: Harvard University Press, 2000); and Brennan, *Wars of Position.*

20. Jacques Derrida, *Positions,* trans. Alan Bass (London: Athlone, 1972); Derrida, *Specters of Marx: The State of the Debt, the Work of Mourning, and the New International,* trans. Peggy Kamuf (London: Routledge, 1994); Gayatri Spivak, translator's preface, in Jacques Derrida, *Of Grammatology* (Baltimore, Md.: Johns Hopkins University Press, 1976), ix–xc.

21. Derrida, *Specters of Marx*, 13, 10.

22. Aijaz Ahmad, *In Theory: Classes, Nation, Literature* (London: Verso, 1992), 176–77. Further references will be abbreviated to *IT* and appear parenthetically.

23. Said, as I have noted, is always equivocal on this crucial question. But there is as much evidence, invariably indirect, for this view of his relationship with poststructuralism as there is against it. One example of such evidence, which has to be taken seriously because it came just when Said was making the difficult Conradian effort to reconcile his literary and political selves, appears in a written interview with the editors of *Diacritics* conducted in 1976, the year before the publication of *Orientalism*: "The focus of interest in Orientalism for me has been the partnership between a discursive and archival textuality and worldly power, one as an index and refraction of the other. As a systematic discourse Orientalism is written knowledge, but because it is in the world and directly about the world, it is *more* than knowledge: it is *power*. . . . From such Baconian realizations it is not difficult to see, for example, that most knowledge of something gets into texts according

to historical laws, social and economic forces, worldly circumstances which make for important and urgent study. Particularly to a literary critic today, who because of his or her institutional marginality seems content with being a commentator from the outside on what transpires in the world. Our interpretive worldly wisdom has been applied, in a sense, to everything except ourselves; we are brilliant at deconstructing the mystifications of a text, at elucidating the blindnesses of a critical method, *but we have seemed unable to apply these techniques to the very life of texts in the world, their materiality, their capacity for the production of misery or liberation, their monumentality as Foucault has spoken of it. As a result we are mesmerized by the text, and convinced that a text is only a text, without realizing how saying that, such a narrow view is not only naïve, it is blind"* (*Power, Politics, and Culture: Interviews with Edward W. Said* [New York: Pantheon, 2001], 26 [emphasis added]).

24. Martin Heidegger, *Being and Time,* trans. John Macquarrie and Edward Robinson (New York: CSM, 1962), 44; emphasis in original.

25. Edward W. Said, *Culture and Imperialism* (New York: Knopf, 1993), 332.

26. Edward W. Said and Jean Mohr, *After the Last Sky,* new ed. (New York: Columbia University Press, 1999), 11.

27. James Clifford, "On *Orientalism," The Predicament of Culture: Twentieth-Century Ethnography, Literature, and Art* (Cambridge, Mass.: Harvard University Press, 1988), 255–77.

28. Edward W. Said, *Orientalism* (New York: Vintage, 1979), 122; further references will be abbreviated to *O* and appear parenthetically.

29. For a brilliant analysis of the German Enlightenment university—its identification of the anthropologos, the university, humanistic culture, and nation—see Bill Readings, *The University in Ruins* (Cambridge, Mass.: Harvard University Press, 1996), 54–69.

30. Louis Althusser, "Ideology and Ideological State Apparatuses (Notes towards an Investigation)," in *Lenin and Marx and Other Essays,* trans. Ben Brewster (New York: Monthly Review, 1971), 181–82. Althusser's reference to "bad subjects" is crucial to Gramsci's distinction between the functioning of civil society and that of political society in liberal capitalist societies. They are the subjects who, in refusing their "spontaneous consent" to the hegemonic truth of civil society call forth the otherwise invisible repressive apparatuses of political society, thus disclosing the violence latent in bourgeois capitalist nations. See Gramsci, *Selections from the Prison Notebooks,* ed. and trans. Quintin Hoare and Geoffrey Nowell Smith (New York: International, 1991), 12.

31. The intriguing question of priority in this respect is dramatized by the fact that Althusser's essay was first published in *La Pensée* in 1970, and Hoare and Smith's translation was published only a year later. Williams's exposition of Gramsci's concept of hegemony appeared in his book *Marxism and Literature* (Oxford: Oxford University Press, 1977).

32. Williams, *Marxism and Literature,* 109–10 (emphasis added).

33. Clifford, "On *Orientalism," 258.*

Chapter 2: Heidegger, Foucault, and the "Empire of the Gaze"

1. Francis Fukuyama, *The End of History and the Last Man* (New York: Free Press, 1993). See also Richard Haass, *The Reluctant Sheriff: The United States after the Cold War*

(New York: Council on Foreign Relations, 1997). More recent variations include Samuel P. Huntington, *Who Are We? Challenges to the American National Identity* (New York: Simon and Schuster, 2004); Niall Ferguson, *Colosssus: The Rise and Fall of the American Empire* (New York: Peguin, 2004); and Michael Mandelbaum, *The Case of Goliath: How America Acts as the World's Government in the Twenty-First Century* (New York: Public Affairs, 2005).

2. On the *Auseinandersetzung* as intimate strife, see Martin Heidegger, *Introduction to Metaphysics,* trans. Ralph Manheim (New Haven, Conn.: Yale University Press, 1959), 62.

3. Martin Heidegger, "The Rectorate 1933/34: Facts and Thoughts," trans. Karsten Harries, *Review of Metaphysics* 38, no. 3 (Mar. 1985): 498.

4. See Martin Bernal, *Black Athena: The Asiatic Roots of Classical Civilization* (New Brunswick, N.J.: Rutgers University Press, 1987), 1–2. As I will suggest in chapter 3, one of the most serious lacks, given his imperative to historicize, in Said's genealogy of Western Orientalism is his failure, despite his awareness of Bernal's revisionary history, to perceive the determining role (imperial) Rome played in the formation of the official cultural identity of the West.

5. Martin Heidegger, "On the Essence of Truth," trans. John Sallis, in *Basic Writings,* rev. ed., ed. David Farrell Krell (New York: Harper and Row, 1993), 118.

6. Martin Heidegger, "The Origin of the Work of Art," trans. Albert Hofstadter, in *Basic Writings,* 149 (final emphasis added).

7. Martin Heidegger, *Being and Time,* trans. John Macquarrie and Edward Robinson (New York: CSM, 1962), 43.

8. Some suggestion of the crudeness of Victor Farias's anecdotal approach to the question of Heidegger's complicity with Nazism is suggested by his reductive attribution of Heidegger's "massive reservations about the so-called 'Latin' or 'Roman'" to "a radical xenophobia" that is "typical of a [German] tradition for which Abraham a Sancta Clara was exemplary" (*Heidegger and Nazism,* trans. Paul Burrill and Gabriel R. Ricci [Philadelphia: Temple University Press, 1989], 223)]. Abraham a Sancta Clara was a seventeenth-century German monk whose virulent anti-Semitism, according to Farias, was a decisive influence on Heidegger throughout his life.

9. I derive the word *errant* from Heidegger's discussion of errancy in "On the Essence of Truth," *Basic Writings,* 132–35, and use it throughout this book with the ironic intention of thematizing its etymology: from the Latin *errare,* "to wander without direction," that is, "to stray from the *ratio.*"

10. Jacques Derrida, "Structure, Sign, and Play in the Discourse of the Human Sciences," *Writing and Difference,* trans. Alan Bass (Chicago: University of Chicago Press, 1978), 279.

11. Martin Heidegger, "Letter on Humanism," trans. Frank A. Capuzzi, *Basic Writings,* 224. This is admittedly a problematic genealogy whose extreme generality exacerbates its controversial character. The two aspects of its content that will be challenged by humanists in the Arnoldian tradition are (1) its differentiation between the cultures of classical Greece and Rome, which since the Renaissance have been invariably—and wrongly—elided to the "Greco-Roman" age or simply "antiquity"; and especially (2) its location of the origins of modern humanism in Rome, rather than Greece, where it has been located since the revival of classical Greek studies inaugurated by Winckelmann in Germany at

the end of the eighteenth century. I cannot address these issues in this limited space. For an extended qualified defense of Heidegger's genealogy, one that also introduces Martin Bernal's location of the origins of the modern humanist representation of Western history in the "Aryan model" constructed by the German classicists of the eighteenth and early nineteenth centuries, see chapter 2, "Culture and Colonization: The Imperial Imperatives of the Centered Circle," in William V. Spanos, *America's Shadow: An Anatomy of Empire* (Minneapolis: University of Minnesota Press, 2000), 64–125. I will return to Bernal's controversial genealogy in chapter 3, where I take up Edward Said's contradictory invocation of Bernal to articulate a different genealogy of Orientalism.

12. As I have shown in *America's Shadow,* this binarist system of naturalized ("white") metaphors, based on the assumed superiority of those who cultivated the earth on which they dwelled over those "nomadic" or "wandering" tribes that did not, has pervaded the discursive history of European and American imperialism up to the very present, as the binary between "developed" and "underdeveloped" nations testifies. And, by way of Gilles Deleuze and Félix Guattari's *Thousand Plateaus: Capitalism and Schizophrenia,* trans. Brian Massumi (Minneapolis: University of Minnesota Press, 1987), it has become a prominent topic of postcolonial criticism. See, for example, Peter Hulme, *Colonial Encounters: Europe and the Native Caribbean, 1492–1797* (London: Methuen, 1986); Mary Louise Pratt, *Imperial Eyes: Travel Writing and Transculturation* (London: Routledge, 1992); and not least, Edward W. Said, *The Question of Palestine* (New York: New York Times Books, 1979), and *Culture and Imperialism* (New York: Knopf, 1993). What is missing from, and thus disabling to, these commentaries is the Roman provenance of this metaphorics. A notable exception is Richard Waswo, *The Founding Legend of Western Civilization: From Virgil to Vietnam* (Hanover, N.H.: Wesleyan University Press, 1997).

13. As I have shown more fully in *The End of Education: Toward Posthumanism* (Minneapolis: University of Minnesota Press, 1993), the Roman rhetoric that represents the disciplinary violence of education and the sociopolitical violence of colonialism in terms of "culture" and the establishment of "universal peace" informs the discourse and practice of imperialist projects throughout the history of the Occident. I am referring first of all to those projects sanctioned by the theologos mediated by the Roman imperial model: for example, the projects of the Holy Roman emperors and, from a different, Calvinist, representation of the theologos, of the American Puritans (see Sacvan Bercovitch, *The American Jeremiad* [Madison: University of Wisconsin Press, 1978], and my essay "De-struction and the Critique of Ideology," in *Repetitions: The Postmodern Occasion in Literature and Culture* [Baton Rouge: Louisiana State University Press, 1987], 282–84). I am furthermore referring to those projects justified on anthropological grounds—the projects of Napoleonic France, Victorian England, and less overtly (until the post-9/11 era), the modern United States.

14. According to the historian Arno J. Mayer in *Why Did the Heavens Not Darken? The "Final Solution" in History* (New York: Pantheon, 1988), the anti-Semitism of the Nazis and the German elite on whose approbation they initially relied was integrally related but subordinated to their "crusade" against the Bolshevists (whom they called "judeobolshevists"). It is Mayer's central thesis that the decision to exterminate the Jews—"judeocide," or the "Final Solution"—was made only after the disastrous failure of "Operation Barbarossa" in the East.

15. Éliane Escoubas, "Heidegger, la question romaine, la question impériale: Autour du 'Tournant,'" in *Heidegger: Questions ouvertes,* ed. Eliane Escoubas (Paris: Editions Osiris, 1988), 173–88.

16. Martin Heidegger, *Parmenides,* vol. 54 of *Gesamtsausgabe* (Frankfurt am Main: Vittorio Klostermann, 1982), 67. My translation. English-language trans., André Schuwer and Richard Rojcewicz (Bloomington: Indiana University Press, 1992). Further citations will appear parenthetically and include both paginations.

17. Louis Althusser, "Ideology and Ideological State Apparatuses (Notes towards an Investigation)," *Lenin and Philosophy and Other Essays,* trans. Ben Brewster (New York: Monthly Review Press, 1971), 180–81. Behind Althusser's formulation of the subjected subject of capitalism is, of course, Lacan's formulation of the subject of post-Freudian psychoanalysis; ahead of Althusser is Foucault's formulation of the subject of the disciplinary society and Said's account of the Orientalized subject. Is it exorbitant to say that Heidegger's formulation of the subject of humanism stands as the point of departure for this chain?

18. Martin Heidegger, "The Question concerning Technology," *The Question concerning Technology and Other Essays,* trans. William Lovitt (New York: Harper and Row, 1977), 17–21. Just as Heidegger's understanding of the subject anticipates Althusser's interpellated subject, so also his understanding of "enframing" (*Ge-stell*) anticipates Althusser's "problematic," especially as its implications for sight are articulated in "From *Capital* to Marx's Philosophy," in Althusser and Étienne Balibar, *Reading "Capital"* (London: Verso, 1970), 24–28. See also William V. Spanos, "Althusser's 'Problematic' in the Context of the Vietnam War: Towards a Spectral Politics," *Rethinking Marxism* 1 (Fall 1998): 1–21; repr. in *American Exceptionalism in the Age of Globalization: The Specter of Vietnam* (Albany, N.Y.: SUNY Press, 2008).

19. Michel Foucault, *Discipline and Punish: The Birth of the Prison,* trans. Alan Sheridan (New York: Pantheon, 1977), 31. Further citations will be abbreviated to *DP* and appear parenthetically.

20. See Richard Ohmann's analysis of the memoranda that make up the Pentagon Papers in *English in America: A Radical View of the Profession* (New York: Oxford University Press, 1976), 190–206. See also Spanos, *The End of Education,* 181–84.

21. Heidegger, "Letter on Humanism," 219–20. It is impossible to determine what Heidegger means by Marx's attainment of "an essential dimension of history." His differentiation between Marx's understanding of alienation and Hegel's, however, and more significantly, his dissociation of Marx's history from the history represented by metaphysics, suggest that he interprets it in a way that cuts against the grain of the essentialism of "Marxism," which is to say, in the terms that have more recently become fundamental to the neo-Marxist critique of "vulgar" Marxism's "economism."

22. Michel Foucault, "Theatrum Philosophicum," *Language, Counter-Memory, Practice: Selected Essays and Interviews,* ed. Donald F. Bouchard, trans. Bouchard and Sherry Simon (Ithaca, N.Y.: Cornell University Press, 1977), 168, 170.

23. Michel Foucault, "Final Interview," *Raritan* 5, no. 1 (Summer 1985): 8–9.

24. This important essay first appeared in *Homage à Jean Hyppolite* (Paris: Presses Universitaires de France, 1971), five years after *Les Mots et les choses* (1966; English-language title, *The Order of Things*) and two years after *L'Archéologie du savoir* (1970; English-lan-

guage title, *The Archaeology of Knowledge*). Though Foucault invokes Nietzsche's critique of the Origin in *Les Mots*, it is not until the Nietzsche essay that the implications of this critical genealogy are fully worked out. This suggests that it constitutes the beginning of Foucault's transformation from his "archaeological" mode of inquiry into the "genealogical" one that informs *Surveiller et punir* (1975). This then implies that his reading of Heidegger, which, recall, was "a philosophical shock" enabling him to understand Nietzsche for the first time, occurred around that year.

25. This situation has been somewhat modified by the publication of Alan Milchman and Alan Rosenberg, eds., *Heidegger and Foucault* (Minneapolis: University of Minnesota Press, 2003).

26. Michel Foucault, "Nietzsche, Genealogy, History," *Language, Counter-Memory, Practice,* 152. The paradox that this "Egyptianism" is also an "Apollonianism" should not be overlooked.

27. Michel Foucault, *Surveiller et punir: Naissance de la prison* (Paris: Editions Gallimard, 1975). As Alan Sheridan renders it in his English translation, *Discipline and Punish: The Birth of the Prison* (New York: Pantheon, 1977; hereafter cited parenthetically as *DP*), the title obscures the crucial relationship between visual perception and power and thus diverts the reader from making the connection between the metaphysical tradition (and the cultural apparatuses to which it has given rise) and sociopolitical power; that is, from noticing the affiliative relationship between Foucault's and Heidegger's anti-ocularcentric discourses—a discourse shared by Edward Said, as I will show by thematizing the rhetoric of vision, of surveying, of the eye's gaze, in his analysis of Orientalism.

28. Michel Foucault, "Truth and Power," *Power/Knowledge: Selected Interviews and Other Writings, 1972–1977,* ed. Colin Gordon (New York: Pantheon, 1980), 112.

29. For an influential example of the distortion that results from limiting Foucault's genealogy of the panoptic gaze to the post-Enlightenment and his critique to empirical science, see Martin Jay's unsympathetic essay "In the Empire of the Gaze: Foucault's Denigration of Vision in Twentieth-Century French Thought," in *Foucault: A Critical Reader,* ed. David Couzens Hoy (Oxford: Basil Blackwell, 1986). Jay limits the context of Foucault's analysis of the gaze to the modern French interrogation of visualism and the origins of this French initiative to Bergson's critique of science as the "spatialization of time" (*durée réelle*). It thus obscures the affinities of Foucault's "denigration of vision" with Heidegger's and the larger (historical) context this chapter thematizes: that which understands the ideological continuity between the "objectivity" of empirical science and the "disinterestedness" of "lyrical" humanism. Jay widens the context of this modern denigration of visual perception in his magisterial but deeply flawed *Downcast Eyes: The Denigration of Vision in Twentieth-Century Thought* (Berkeley: University of California Press, 1993).

30. William V. Spanos, "Postmodern Literature and Its Occasion: Retrieving the Preterite Middle," *Repetitions,* 200–205. On the one hand, Foucault refers to the circular fortresses that Sebastien Le Preste de Vauban built for Louis XIV in *Surveiller and punir* but dismisses them as an architectural geometry intended to facilitate the observation of "external space" (*DP,* 172). On the other hand, he invokes the Rousseauian Claude-Nicholas Ledoux's circular salt works at Arc-et-Senans as a precursor to Jeremy Bentham's Panopticon: "The perfect disciplinary apparatus would make it possible for a single gaze to

see everything constantly. A central point would be both the source of light illuminating everything, and a locus of convergence for everything that must be known: a perfect eye that nothing could escape and a centre towards which all gazes would be turned. This is what Ledoux had imagined when he built Arc-et Scnans" (*DP*, 173–74; see also Foucault, "The Eye of Power," *Power/Knowledge*, 147–48). What Foucault fails to recognize in emphasizing the "epistemic break" occurring in the Enlightenment is that his description and analysis of the function of Ledoux's Arc-et-Senans applies *mutatis mutandis* to, say, Tommaso Campanella's circular utopian "City of the Sun," modeled on the orderly circular macrocosm and governed from the center by the Platonic "Metaphysician" (also called "Sun" on the analogy with its planetary counterpart in the Copernican astronomy); see Campanella, *La Città del sole: Dialogo poetico/The City of the Sun*, bilingual ed., trans. Daniel J. Bonno (Berkeley: University of California Press, 1981), 26–30. The point I am making about the relationship between the circle—the perennial image of beauty and perfection *and* power—is inadvertently made by at least two contemporary humanists who have written on the history of the circular city: E. A. Gutkind, *International History of City Development*, 8 vols., vol. 5, *Urban Development in Western Europe: France and Belgium* (New York: Free Press, 1970); and Norman J. Johnston, *Cities in the Round* (Seattle: University of Washington Press, 1983). Both, but especially Johnston, interpret the military/disciplinary uses to which the circular/utopian model was increasingly put after the Renaissance as a tragic betrayal of the utopian ideal envisaged by Plato and, above all, the Renaissance humanists, in which the circular city is represented as the worldly manifestation of eternal cosmic beauty, whereas all the evidence, including that of their own texts, points to them as the historically specific fulfillment of the latent power that theorists of the circular city, both utopian and practicing architects and engineers, had from the beginning recognized in this totalizing geometry of beauty. See, for example, Johnston, *Cities in the Round*, 45. See also Rudolph Wittkower, *Architectural Principles in the Age of Humanism* (London: Alec Tiranti, 1952), 15. For an interesting study (influenced generally by Foucault) on the relationship between Vauban's fortresses and the literature of eighteenth-century France, see Joan Dejean, *Literary Fortifications: Rousseau, Laclos, Sade* (Princeton, N.J.: Princeton University Press, 1984).

31. The discourse of Vitruvius provides one of the first articulations of the imperial use to which the concept of the geographical center of the world has been and is put: "Such being nature's arrangement of the universe, and all these nations being allotted temperaments which are lacking in due moderation, the truly perfect territory, situated under the middle of the heaven, and having on each side the entire extent of the world and its countries, is that which is occupied by the Roman people. . . . Italy presents ground of praise for its temperate and unsurpassed [climate]. . . . Thus the divine mind has allotted to the city of the Roman people an excellent and temperate region in order to rule the world" (*The Ten Books of Architecture*, 6.1, 10–12). See Claude Nicolet, *Space, Geography, and Politics in the Early Roman Empire* (Ann Arbor: University of Michigan Press, 1991), 194. Foucault cites this enabling text in an interview entitled "Space, Knowledge, and Power," in *The Foucault Reader*, ed. Paul Rabinow (New York: Pantheon, 1984), but characteristically minimizes without denying any influence it might have had in the articulation of a relay between spatial and political economies: "In discussing Rome, one sees that the problem revolves around Vitruvius. Vitruvius was reinterpreted from

the sixteenth century on, but one can find in the sixteenth century—and no doubt in the Middle Ages as well—many considerations of the same order as Vitruvius; if you consider them as *reflections upon.* The treatises on politics, on the art of government, on the manner of good government, did not generally include chapters or analyses devoted to the organization of cities or to architecture. The *Republic* of Jean Bodin does not contain extended discussion of the role of architecture, whereas the police treatises of the eighteenth century are full of them" (240).

32. This architectural and city-planning tradition—and the ideology informing its commitment to the radial circular schema—is discernible in the geometry of Baron Haussmann's Paris. See David H. Pickney, *Napoleon III and the Rebuilding of Paris* (Princeton, N.J.: Princeton University Press, 1958). Walter Benjamin's *Arcades Project,* trans. Howard Eiland and Kevin McLaughlin (Cambridge, Mass.: Belknap, 1999), can be profitably read in the context of this architectural tradition.

33. Campanella, *Città del sole,* 54/55.

34. Although Foucault does not acknowledge it, the immediate source of his phrase is no doubt Jean-Paul Sartre's discussion of *le regard* (the look), which, like Medusa's eye, transforms the threatening and (because ultimately unknowable) unpredictable Other into stone. See *Being and Nothingness: An Essay in Phenomenological Ontology,* trans. Hazel Barnes (New York: Citadel, 1964), 406; Sartre's extended phenomenological account of the look can be found on 228–78. For one of Sartre's many fictional and dramatic instances of the look, see the Dr. Rogé/Achilles entry in *Nausea,* trans. Lloyd Alexander (New York: New Directions, 1964), 92–96. Ultimately, of course, as Foucault seems to be aware, the specific image goes back to the commonplace visual depiction of God's all-seeing eye looking down on the vainly concealed sinner in Renaissance and especially Puritan emblem books. See, for example, Geoffrey Whitney, *A Choice of Emblems* (Leyden, 1586), 229.

35. From Foucault's demystified perspective, as from Heidegger's, the term *Enlightenment* assumes an ironic significance. The emphasis on the spatializing eye, which in fact deliberately forgets or conceals temporal being for the sake of power over "it," becomes not simply a blindness but a blinding insight. For a similar critique of the Enlightenment, see Max Horkheimer and Theodor Adorno, *Dialectic of the Enlightenment,* trans. John Cumming (New York: Herder and Herder, 1972).

36. Marjorie Hope Nicolson, the celebrated humanist literary historian, says nothing of this "new knowledge of man" in her celebratory account of the rise of the technology of optics in *Newton Demands the Muse: Newton's Optics and the Eighteenth Century Poets* (Princeton, N.J.: Princeton University Press, 1946).

37. Max Weber, *The Protestant Ethic and the Spirit of Capitalism,* trans. Talcott Parsons (New York: Scribner's, 1958), 104–5.

38. This Calvinist ontology, which compels the accommodation of the smallest detail to the inscrutable providential design of God, was not, as Foucault seems to imply, restricted to the space of the nation. It was applied also to global space. This is evident in the colonial discourse of Elizabethan and Augustan Britain, as Daniel Defoe's *Robinson Crusoe* bears synecdochic witness. More important for the purposes of this book, it is further evident in the American Puritans' errand in the ("New World") wilderness; in that project's secularized counterpart, the post-Revolutionary imperial discourse of Manifest Destiny; and most recently, as I will show in the last chapter, in the ruling American elite's

post-9/11 appeal to the "Anglo-Protestant core culture" in behalf of America's victory in the "clash of civilizations." See especially Samuel P. Huntington, *Who Are We? The Challenges to America's National Identity* (New York: Simon and Schuster, 2004), 59–80.

39. Though Foucault is referring here specifically to Jean Baptiste de La Salle's "dream of the ideal classroom" in *Conduite des écoles chrétiennes* (B.N. Ms. 11759), it is clear that the reference is intended to apply to other disciplinary institutions as well.

40. According to Foucault, "the power of the Norm appears" when the emergent disciplines combine with "other powers—Law, the Word (*Parole*), and the Text, Tradition"—and with surveillance to become fundamental to the pedagogical economy of power in modern society: "The Normal is established as a principle of coercion in teaching with the introduction of a standardized education and the establishment of the *écoles normales* [teacher-training colleges]. . . . Like surveillance and with it, normalization becomes one of the great instruments of power at the end of the classical age" (*DP*, 184; see also 192).

41. See, however, note 30 to this chapter.

42. See Robert Marzec, *An Ecological and Postcolonial Study of Literature: From Daniel Defoe to Salman Rushdie* (New York: Palgrave, 2007). Using Gilles Deleuze and Félix Guatarri's treatise on "nomadology" in *A Thousand Plateaus* as a point of departure, Marzec has productively explored the momentous literary, cultural, and sociopolitical effects of the decisive demographic transformation precipitated by the British enclosure movement in the period of the Enlightenment.

43. Using Bentham's own words, Foucault underscores the polyvalency of this panoptic schema: "It is a way of obtaining from power 'in hitherto unexampled quantity,' 'a great and new instrument of government. . . ; its great excellence consists in the great strength it is capable of giving to *any* institution it may be thought proper to apply it to'" (Bentham, 66). See also *DP*, 206–7). Despite his references to technology and machinery, moreover, Foucault is not finally limiting the polyvalency of the spatial/visual diagram to scientific uses. That he is also, however marginally, thinking the uses to which it has been and can be put by "poetic" humanists becomes clear in an interview entitled "The Eye of Power," which followed the publication of *Surveiller et punir*. In this interview, he identifies Bentham's "liberal scientific" (technological) project with Rousseau's liberal "lyrical" project: the pedagogy of "self-fulfillment" (152). The affiliative relation between Rousseau and Bentham to which Foucault points is also suggested by the fact that Claude-Nicholas Ledoux, the eighteenth-century French architect whose circular manufactory, Arc-et-Senans, prefigured Bentham's Panopticon, was an avowed Rousseauist. See Spanos, "Postmodern Literature and Its Occasion," 203–5; see also Joan Dejean, "*Julie* and *Émile*: 'Studia la Matematica,'" *Literary Fortifications*, 112–90.

44. Foucault, "Nietzsche, Genealogy, History," 100.

45. Though Foucault, following Bentham, emphasizes the domestic sociopolitical scene in *Discipline and Punish*, he is not unaware of the panoptic mechanism's applicability to imperial theory and practice. See, for example, his references to the Napoleonic empire in *DP*: "'Discipline must be made national,' Guibert said. 'The state that I will depict will have a simple, reliable, easily controlled administration. It will resemble those huge machines, which by quite uncomplicated means produce great effects; the strength of this state will spring from its own strength, its prosperity from its own prosperity. Time, which destroys all, will increase its power. It will disprove that vulgar prejudice by which

we are made to imagine that empires are subjected to an imperious law of decline and ruin.' . . . The Napoleonic regime was not far off and with it the form of state that was to survive it and, we must not forget, the foundations of which were laid not only by jurists, but also by soldiers, not only councillors of state, but also junior officers, not only men of the courts, but also the men of the camps. The Roman reference that accompanied this formation certainly bears with it this double index: citizens and legionaries, law and manoeuvres" (168–69).

46. Foucault, "Nietzsche, Genealogy, History," 161.

47. Hannah Arendt, *The Life of the Mind,* ed. Mary McCarthy (New York: Harcourt Brace, 1978), 3–4.

48. Heidegger, "The Question Concerning Technology," 15–19.

49. Martin Heidegger, "What Is Metaphysics?," in *Basic Writings,* 95–96.

50. Martin Heidegger, "Language in the Poem: A Discussion on Georg Trakl's Poetic Work," *On the Way to Language,* trans. Peter D. Hertz (New York: Harper and Row, 1971), 172.

51. "Madness here does not mean a mind filled with senseless delusion. The madman's mind senses—senses in fact as no one else does. Even so, he does not have the sense of the others. He is of another mind. The departed one is a man apart, a madman, because he has taken this way in another direction" (Heidegger, "Language in the Poem," 173).

52. Martin Heidegger, "Hölderlin and the Essence of Poetry," trans. Douglas Scott, *Existence and Being,* ed. Werner Brock (Chicago: Henry Regnery, 1949), 289.

53. Martin Heidegger, "What Are Poets For?" *Poetry, Language, Thought,* trans. and ed. Richard Hofstadter (New York: Harper and Row, 1971), 91.

54. Foucault returns to the way madness haunts the hegemony of reason in modernity in *The Order of Things*: "And precisely when this language emerges in all its nudity, yet at the same time eludes all signification as if it were a vast empty despotic system, when Desire reigns in the wild state, as if the rigour of its rule had levelled all opposition, when Death dominates every psychological function and stands above it as its unique and devastating form—then we recognize madness in its present form, madness as it is posited in the modern experience, as its truth and its alterity. In this figure, which is at once empirical and yet foreign to (and in) all the we can experience, our consciousness no longer finds—as it did in the sixteenth century—the trace of another world; it no longer observes the wandering of a straying reason; it sees welling up that which is, perilously, nearest to us—as if, suddenly, the very hollowness of our existence is outlined in relief; the finitude upon the basis of which we are, and think, and know, is suddenly there before us: an existence at once real and impossible, thought that we cannot think, an object for our knowledge that always eludes it" (375). See also Foucault's remarks on the "human double," the "'cogito' and the unthought," in his analysis of "the analytic of finitude" (322–28).

55. Michel Foucault, *Madness and Civilization: A History of Insanity in the Age of Reason* (New York: Vintage, 1988), 278.

56. Heidegger, "Origin of the Work of Art," 173–75.

57. Foucault, *Madness and Civilization,* 288 (emphasis added).

58. Michel Foucault, *The History of Sexuality, Volume 1: An Introduction,* trans. Robert Hurley (New York: Pantheon, 1978), 10. For Foucault's generalization of the "repressive

hypothesis" to include sociopolitical sites other than the sexual, that is, his recognition of its polyvalency, see also "Truth and Power," 109–33.

59. For a succinct account of Foucault's understanding of the repressive hypothesis, see Hubert L. Dreyfuss and Paul Rabinow, *Michel Foucault: Beyond Structuralism and Hermeneutics* (Chicago: University of Chicago Press, 1982), 129–30.

60. Foucault, "Truth and Power," 119.

61. See also Derrida, "Structure, Sign, and Play," 279.

62. Should the convergence I am suggesting sound like a perverse imposition on Foucault's texts, let me retrieve a largely overlooked dimension of his genealogy of European modernity that, though he subordinates it to his immediate focus on the emergent technologies of discipline (the discourse of detail, the table, the examination, anatomy, and so on), nevertheless informs them through and through. I am referring to what Foucault calls "the Roman reference" (briefly remarked previously in my citation of the military camp as a source of the panoptic diagram): the fact that the age of the Enlightenment modeled its cultural, military, and sociopolitical self-image on Roman (not Greek) antiquity. "One should not forget," Foucault writes in invoking the representative example of the "pyramidal" supervisory structure of the French Jesuit colleges, "that, generally speaking, the Roman model, at the Enlightenment, played a dual role; in its republican aspect, it was the very embodiment of liberty; in its military aspect, it was the ideal schema of discipline. The Rome of the eighteenth century and of the Revolution was the Rome of the Senate, but it was also that of the legion; it was the Rome of the Forum, but it was also that of the camps" (*DP*, 146).

63. Martin Heidegger, "A Dialogue on Language (between a Japanese and an Inquirer)," *On the Way to Language*, 15. See also Heidegger, "The End of Philosophy and the Task of Thinking," *Basic Writings*, where he writes: "The end of philosophy proves to be the triumph of the manipulable arrangement of a scientific-technological world and of the social order proper to this world. The end of philosophy means the beginning of the world civilization based upon Western European thinking" (377).

64. Michel Foucault, "Questions on Geography," *Power/Knowledge*, 69 (emphasis added). The parallel between this genealogy of the discourse of geography and Heidegger's should not be overlooked. As I have suggested elsewhere, the interlocutors' comment that this discourse "grew up in the shadow of the military" is very likely a reference to the complicity of the Roman or Romanized Greek geographies—those of Pliny, Strabo, Diodorus Siculus, and so on—with the Roman imperial project. See Spanos, "Culture and Colonization," 64–125. See also Nicolet, *Space, Geography, and Politics*.

Chapter 3: Orientalism

1. Michel Foucault, "The History of Sexuality" (interview with Lucette Finas), *Power/Knowledge: Selected Interviews and Other Writings, 1972–1977*, ed. Colin Gordon (New York: Pantheon, 1980), 184.

2. Michel Foucault, "Truth and Power" (interview with Alessandro Fontana and Pasquale Pasquino), *Power/Knowledge*, 112–13. See also "The History of Sexuality," 84–85. In an interview on *Beginnings* that Said gave to *Diacritics* in 1976, while he was still working on *Orientalism*, he speaks of the moment, following the Arab-Israeli War of 1967, when

he came to feel the need to relate his two selves—the American literary academician and the politically motivated Palestinian Arab exile. In the process of speaking to this difficult issue of his two worlds—"the ivory tower concerns of technical criticism" and "the world of politics, power, domination, and struggle"—Said says there "are links between [them] which I for one am beginning to exploit in my own work" and then goes on to invoke Foucault (after having criticized Derrida for the unworldliness of his textual emphasis): "What is the ongoing life of a dependent or colonial people but the imposition on a people of a powerful and duplicitous system (discourse) of the sort that Foucault has studied in his work?" (*Power, Politics, and Culture: Interviews with Edward W. Said*, ed. Gauri Viswanathan [New York: Pantheon, 2001], 16). This teasing reference to Foucault's "work" is inconclusive, of course, but I suggest that it is directed specifically to *Surveiller et punir*, which was published by Gallimard in France in 1975, a year before the interview.

3. For an amplified account of this inaugural and founding divide between West and East, Occident and Orient, see William V. Spanos, "Culture and Colonization: The Imperial Imperatives of the Centered Circle," chapter 2 of *America's Shadow: An Anatomy of Empire* (Minneapolis: University of Minnesota Press, 2000), 64–125. As I will show, a fundamental difference between Edward Said's version of this founding moment and mine resides in this: following the directives of Heidegger's powerful argument about the inaugural role metropolitan Rome played in forming the Occidental identity, I locate this moment in Rome's appropriation and reduction of originative Greek thinking to a calculative thinking appropriate to its imperial project. Unlike Heidegger (and Foucault), Said pays no attention to Rome's inordinate influence on Western identity. Instead, he locates this founding moment in Greece (as far back as Homer's *Iliad*). Curiously, in *Culture and Imperialism* Said invokes Martin Bernal's *Black Athena* to show that the "authoritative" interpretation of the origins of the Occident was established in the nineteenth century by German Orientalists and that Greece was in fact a "multicultural culture." But he does not read Bernal's epochal revision back into the origins of the Occident: "Studies such as Martin Bernal's *Black Athena* and Eric Hobsbawm and Terence Ranger's *The Invention of Tradition* have accentuated the extraordinary influence of today's anxieties and agendas on the pure (even purged) images we construct of a privileged, genealogically useful past, a past in which we exclude unwanted elements, vestiges, narratives. Thus according to Bernal, whereas Greek civilization was known originally to have roots in Egyptian, Semitic, and various other southern and eastern cultures, it was redesigned as "Aryan" during the course of the nineteenth-century, its Semitic and African roots either actively purged or hidden from view. Since Greek writers themselves openly acknowledged their culture's hybrid past, European philologists acquired the ideological habit of passing over these embarrassing passages without comment, in the interest of Attic purity" (Edward W. Said, *Culture and Imperialism* [New York: Knopf, 1993], 15–16). This difference between my interpretation and Said's is admittedly a matter of debate, though as I will show in chapter 4, Said's omission of any reference to Rome in his account of the formation of the West's identity constitutes a serious limitation of his otherwise magisterial analysis of Western Orientalism. Whether or not the origins of the official Western identity reside in ancient Greece or Rome, this ambiguity should not obscure the main point I am making: that the identity of the Occident, which puts itself in a binary opposition to the Orient, was formed at the moment in classical antiquity when the official culture, following the

practical imperatives of the metaphysical interpretation of being, came to call that geographical space "the Occident" in opposition to its "Other."

4. When I use the term *Occident,* I do not mean to imply a monolithic entity. As Said insistently notes in *Orientalism,* there is neither a real Orient nor a real Occident. Rather, they are constructions produced hegemonically by the dominant or ruling culture of the West, creations designed to reduce the recalcitrant variety and plurality of each culture to naturalized essentialist and inescapably fixed abstractions that privilege the Occident over the Orient, the better to justify and facilitate the Occident's project of domination. It is this "official Occident"—this "naturalized supernatural" culture—to which I refer when I speak of the "Occident" in this chapter.

5. Michel Foucault, "Nietzsche, Genealogy, History," *Language, Counter-Memory, Practice: Selected Essays and Interviews,* ed. Donald F. Bouchard, trans. Bouchard and Sherry Simon (Ithaca, N.Y.: Cornell University Press, 1977), 152.

6. In Foucault's work, the precursor to this polyvalency appears in his demonstration of the relationality of grammar, natural history, and wealth in the period of the Enlightenment. See *The Order of Things* (New York: Vintage, 1973), 57. Nonetheless, it is not until *Discipline and Punish: Birth of the Prison* (New York: Pantheon, 1977) that Foucault introduces the sociopolitical function of this epistemic relationality. Further citations of the latter text will be abbreviated to *DP* and appear parenthetically.

7. As Foucault puts this in *Discipline and Punish,* "I would like to write the history of this prison, with all the political investments of the body that it gathers together in its closed architecture Why? Simply because I am interested in the past? No, if one means by that writing a history of the past in terms of the present. Yes, if one means writing the history of the present" (3–31).

8. See "Intellectuals and Power: A Conversation between Michel Foucault and Gilles Deleuze," *Language, Counter-Memory, Practice,* 204–16. Referring to Deleuze's observation that the "present revolutionary movement has created multiple centers, and not as the result of weakness or insufficiency," Foucault responds, "The question of geographical discontinuity which you raise might mean the following: as soon as we struggle against exploitation, the proletariat not only leads the struggle but also defines its targets, its methods, and the places and instruments of confrontation; and to ally oneself with the proletariat is to accept its positions, its ideology, and its motives for combat. This means total identification. But if the fight is directed against power, then all those on whom power is exercised to their detriment, all who find it intolerable, can begin the struggle on their own terrain and on the basis of their proper activity (or passivity). In engaging in a struggle that concerns their own interests, whose objectives they clearly understand and whose methods only they can determine, they enter into a revolutionary process. They naturally enter as allies of the proletariat, because power is exercised the way it is in order to maintain capitalist exploitation. They genuinely serve the cause of the proletariat by fighting in those places where they find themselves oppressed. Women, prisoners, conscripted soldiers, hospital patients, and homosexuals have now begun a specific struggle against the particularized power, the constraints and controls, that are exerted over them. Such struggles are actually involved in the revolutionary movement to the degree that they are radical, uncompromising and nonreformist, and refuse any attempt at arriving at a new disposition of the same power with, at best, a change of masters. *And*

these movements are linked to the revolutionary movement of the proletariat to the extent that they fight against controls and constraints which serve the same system of power" (216; emphasis added). See also Foucault, "Truth and Power," 126–30.

9. In analyzing the character of the discourse of Orientalism, Said invokes Nietzsche's assertion, made prominent by the poststructuralists, that the truth of language is nothing but "a mobile army of metaphors, metonyms, and anthropomorphisms—in short, a sum of human relations, which have been enhanced, transposed, and embellished poetically and rhetorically, and which after long use seem firm, canonical, and obligatory to a people: truths are illusions about which one has forgotten that this is what they are" (quoted in *O*, 203; the quotation from Nietzsche is to be found in "On Truth and Lie in an Extra-Moral Sense," in *The Portable Nietzsche*, ed. and trans. Walter Kaufmann [New York: Viking Press, 1954], 46–47. What must be added, however, is that this mobile army of metaphors circulates around the metaphor of vision, which substitutes for the ineffable knowledge of being—precisely the enabling metaphor that I overdetermine in this book.

10. With significant exceptions, I do not provide page references for these key words because they appear ubiquitously and indeed relentlessly throughout Said's text.

11. Said acknowledged his debt to Foucault's analysis of the relation between the classificatory table and disciplinary power: invoking Sylvestre de Sacy's contribution to Joseph Dacier's report on the state of Orientalist learning commissioned by Napoleon in 1802, *Tableau historique de l'érudition française*, he writes: "The importance of the *Tableau historique* for an understanding of Orientalism's inaugural phase is that it exteriorizes the form of Orientalist knowledge and its features, as it also describes the Orientalist's relationship to his subject matter. In Sacy's pages on Orientalism—as elsewhere in his writing—he speaks of his own work as having *uncovered, brought to light, rescued* a vast amount of obscure matter. Why? In order *to place it before* the student. For like all his learned contemporaries Sacy considered a learned work a positive addition to an edifice that all scholars erected together. Knowledge was essentially the *making visible* of material, and the aim of a tableau was the construction of a sort of Benthamite Panopticon. Scholarly discipline was therefore a specific technology of power: It gained for its user (and his students) tools and knowledge which (if he was a historian) had hitherto been lost" (*O*, 127).

12. As I will demonstrate in chapter 4, when Said interprets Conrad's novel *Heart of Darkness*, he significantly reverses the meaning he gives to the word *narrative* in this passage.

13. Aijaz Ahmad, *In Theory: Classes, Nations, Literature* (London: Verso, 1992), 179; further citations will be abbreviated to *IT* and appear parenthetically.

14. Joseph Conrad, *Heart of Darkness*, critical ed., 3d ed., ed. Robert Kimbrough (New York: Norton, 1988), 10. In chapter 4 I return to Conrad's (and Said's) account of Roman imperialism by invoking Tacitus's biography of Agricola, the Roman administrator of Britain in A.D. 61, in which the Roman historian offers a quite different version of Roman or at least of Agricola's imperialism.

15. Said, *Culture and Imperialism*, 69.

16. Michel Foucault, "Questions on Geography" (an interview with the editors of *Hérodote*), *Power/Knowledge*, 69.

17. Ibid., 76.

18. Edward W. Said, "Culture and Imperialism," *Power, Politics, and Culture: Interviews with Edward W. Said*, ed. Gauri Viswanathan (New York: Pantheon, 2001), 194–95 (emphasis added, except for first occurrence of *natural*). Further references will be abbreviated to CI and appear parenthetically. Originally published in *boundary 2* 20, no. 1 (Spring 1993).

19. Edward W. Said, "History, Literature, and Geography," *Reflections on Exile* (Cambridge, Mass.: Harvard University Press, 2000). Further references will be abbreviated to HLC and appear parenthetically. Originally published in *History and Literature,* ed. Hoda Gindy (Cairo: University of Cairo Press, 1995).

20. Edward W. Said, "Foucault and the Imagination of Power," *Reflections on Exile,* 239–40; originally published in *Foucault: A Critical Reader,* ed. David Couzens Hoy (Oxford: Blackwell, 1986), 149–55.

21. See Joseph Buttigieg, *The Prison Notebooks, Vol. 1*; and Spanos "Cuvier's Little Bone: Joseph Buttigieg's English Edition of Antonio Gramsci's *Prison Notebooks*," *Rethinking Marxism* 18, no. 1 (Jan. 2006): 23–36.

22. Foucault, "Truth and Power," 121.

23. With respect to Curzon's obsession with geography, Said mentions as telling an address Curzon made to the Geographical Society in 1912, while he was president of that body. Curzon announced: "An absolute revolution has occurred, not merely in the manner and methods of teaching geography, but in the estimation in which it is held by public opinion. Nowadays we regard geographical knowledge as an essential part of knowledge in general. By the aid of geography, and in no other way, do we understand the actions of great natural forces, the distribution of population, the growth of commerce, the expansion of frontiers, the development of States, the splendid achievements of human energy in various manifestations.

"We recognize geography as the handmaid of history. . . . Geography, too, is a sister science to economics and politics; and to any of us who have attempted to study geography it is known that the moment you diverge from the geographical field you find yourself crossing the frontiers of geology, zoology, anthropology, chemistry, physics, and almost all the kindred sciences. Therefore we are justified in saying that geography is one of the first and foremost of the sciences: that it is part of the equipment that is necessary for a proper conception of citizenship, and is an indispensable adjunct to the production of a public man" (qtd. in *O,* 215–16).

See also Said's discussion in *Culture and Imperialism* of Rudyard Kipling's emphasis on the geography of India—above all the relationship between mapping and administering the colony—in *Kim*.

24. Taking as absolute Said's secularist reservations about the pessimistic stance Foucault and the poststructuralists take on human agency, Timothy Brennan, as I have observed in chapter 1, identifies the poststructuralists, and presumably Foucault, with this Renan, who naturalizes the supernatural to protect his certainty from the corrosive differences of the secular world. See Brennan, "Humanism, Philology, and Imperialism," in *Wars of Position: The Cultural Politics of Left and Right* (New York: Columbia University Press, 2006), 98–99. Given Said's invocation of Foucault throughout his scathing critique of Renan's natural supernaturalism, it is not easy to see how Brennan can be so dismissively adamant about this identification.

25. For an incisive summary analysis and critique of the Orientalist as "expert," see "Edward W. Said, The Politics and Culture of Palestinian Exile," *The Pen and the Sword: Conversations with David Barsamian* (Edinburgh: AK Press, 1994), 27–28.

26. Samuel Beckett, *Watt* (New York: Grove, 1959), 43–44.

27. In a series of conversations with Tariq Ali that took place in June 1994 and were published as *Conversations with Edward Said* (London: Seagull, 2006), Said identifies the time of this turn with the Arab-Israeli War of 1967. In response to Ali's characterization of him in 1963, when he began teaching at Columbia University, as a "Dorian Gray," Said said, "I was completely a creature of an American and even a kind of upper-class WASP education, Princeton and Harvard. There were no Arab students taking English literature. All of them studied Middle Eastern things, and I had very little to do with them, or they were in the sciences. But after 1967 there was an attempt by a few Arabs who were around here to get together, mainly at first to contemplate the disaster, the enormous catastrophe of 1967. But by 1968, which for most people represents the great student revolution—one going on in Columbia, where I was. . . . But for me, I associate it not with the student revolution but the beginning of the Palestinian resistance movement in Jordan. And very soon after that, again, through friends and family—a cousin of mine, in 1970 had become a spokesperson of the Palestinian movement . . . so by 1968 was completely involved" (73–74). The fact remains that there is no *direct* evidence of this in *Orientalism*. One senses his general anger in the engaged tonality of his critique of Orientalism, but Said does not identify it with his Palestinian or exilic identity; nor, despite this oppositional stance, does he abandon the protocols of scholarly production by appealing to his exilic status, as he was later to do in "Reflections on Exile," *Granta* 13 (Winter 1984), and *Culture and Imperialism*. In part this is to reiterate that at this period, Said's sense of the "end of Orientalism," his marginality, and the particular (in-direct) form of resistance these entailed were *symptomatic,* not conscious. It is also to suggest, however, that the greatness of Said's *Orientalism* is not simply that it enabled postcolonial studies but also that it enabled a rethinking of the onto-cultural-political thinking of the West.

Chapter 4: Culture and Imperialism

1. See Edward W. Said, "The Pen and the Sword: Culture and Imperialism," *The Pen and the Sword: Conversations with David Barsamian* (Edinburgh: AK Press, 1994): "So rather than say, Jane Austen's novel [*Mansfield Park*] is really about England, I say no, it's about the Caribbean. In order to understand it you have to understand the writing of Caribbean history by other Caribbean writers. It's not just Jane Austen's view of the Caribbean that we need. We need the other views as well. I establish what I call a reading which is based on counterpoint, many voices producing a history" (71).

2. Edward W. Said, *Culture and Imperialism* (New York: Knopf, 1993), 62. Further citations will be abbreviated to *CI* and appear parenthetically.

3. As he often does in his collaborative work, Said appropriates these crucial terms from Raymond Williams (enlarging their meaning in doing so), particularly his *Marxism and Literature* (London: Oxford University Press, 1977); see the section entitled "Structures of Feeling" (128–35).

4. Enrique Dussel, *Philosophy of Liberation,* trans. Aquilina Martinez and Christine Morkovsky (Maryknoll, N.Y.: Orbis, 1985), 5–6.

5. On the surface, there appears to be little difference between these two statements. A closer examination, however, reveals that the first draws the reader's attention to the perspective of the metropolis, whereas the second draws it to the perspective of the "Other." In overdetermining the metropolitan gaze, then, the first remains vestigially Eurocentric; in overdetermining the gaze of the metropolis's "Other," the second is more authentically postcolonial. One of the great limitations of much postcolonial criticism, especially texts written in the West and by Westerners, is precisely its failure to attune itself to this nuance: to the mutilated and outraged being of the victims of imperialism.

6. Martin Heidegger, "The End of Philosophy and the Task of Thinking," in *Basic Writings,* rev. ed., ed. David Farrell Krell (San Francisco: Harper, 1993), 439–41.

7. Antonio Gramsci, *Selections from the Prison Notebooks,* ed. and trans. Quintin Hoare and Geoffrey Nowell Smith (New York: International, 1971), 12.

8. See Jean-François Lyotard, *The Postmodern Condition: A Report on Knowledge,* trans. Geoff Bennington and Brian Massumi (Minneapolis: University of Minnesota Press, 1984). "Realism," Lyotard observes, "whose only definition is that it intends to avoid the question of reality implicated in that of art, always stands somewhere between academicism and kitsch. When power assumes the name of a party, realism and its neoclassical complement triumph over the experimental avant-garde by slandering and banning it—that is, provided the 'correct' images, the 'correct' narratives, the 'correct' forms which the party requests, selects, and propagates can find a public to desire them as the appropriate remedy for the anxiety and depression that public experiences" (75). As such, realism is complicit with "terror": "Under the general demand for slackening and for appeasement, we can hear the mutterings of the desire for a return of terror, for the realization of the fantasy to seize reality. The answer is: Let us wage war on totality; let us be witnesses to the unpresentable, let us activate the differences and save the honor of the name" (82).

9. This troubled European Modernist evocation of the empire's "Other" was not restricted to literature. It was a pervasive and mutually influencing characteristic of all the arts of the time: music, painting, sculpture, architecture. One of the fundamental characteristics of paintings by Picasso, Modigliani, Wyndham Lewis, and Lyonel Feininger, for example, and of sculptures by Brancusi, Jacob Epstein, and Gaudier Brjeska, was an adaptation of the anonymous, highly stylized, and geometric forms of African (and Oriental) art, which these Modernists took to be antihuman, the end of a spontaneous will to abstraction in the face of the terror of nature, in opposition to the "realistic" European artistic tradition that, under the aegis of humanism, glibly "imitated" nature. This Modernist momentum was profoundly influenced by the German art historian Wilhelm Worringer, whose book *Abstraktion und Einfühlung* (1908) was popularized, especially in England, by the English critic and poet T. E. Hulme in his manifestos on the modernity of modern poetry (see *Speculations: Essays on Humanism and the Philosophy of Art,* ed. Herbert Read [New York: Harcourt, Brace, 1924]). In invoking Africa and the Orient, Worringer, Hulme, and the Modernist European poets and artists whose work incorporated references to these hitherto peripheral cultures did not consciously think of them in terms of the threat they posed to the imperial metropolis. Troubled by the gradual but inexorable disintegration of the classical/Christian Logos and the unity and authority of

the idea of Europe in the nineteenth century, a process they attributed to the triumph of empirical science and instrumental reason, they ostensibly sought to compensate for this decentering of the European identity—this emergence of the nothingness of being—by substituting an impersonal dehumanized art of abstraction that was self-reflexive and autotelic. Nonetheless, insofar as these Modernist artists represented the complex manner in which the cultures of Africa and the Orient comported themselves to a volatile nature as the will to abstraction, they were symptomatically perceiving the emergence of these hitherto peripheral cultures into the consciousness of Europe as continuous with the internal corrosion of the European identity.

10. See William V. Spanos, "Thinking in the Interregnum: Prolegomenon to a Spectral Politics," *America's Shadow: An Anatomy of Empire* (Minneapolis: University of Minnesota Press, 2000), 191–206, where I use the term in reference to the interregnum between the age of imperialism and the rise of postcolonialism.

11. I. A. Richards, *Principles of Literary Criticism* (London: Routledge and Kegan Paul, 1926): speaking of experiences that manifest themselves in the "poetry of exclusion" and "the poetry of inclusion," that is, Modernist, Richards writes, "The structures of these two kinds of experiences are different, and the difference is not one of subject but of the relations *inter se* of the several impulses active in the experience. A poem of the first group is built out of a set of impulses which run parallel, which have the same direction. In a poem of the second group the most obvious feature is the extraordinarily [*sic*] heterogeneity of the distinguishable impulses. But they are more than heterogeneous, they are opposed. They are such that in ordinary, non-poetic, non-imaginative experience, one or other set would be suppressed to give as it might appear freer development to the others. The difference comes out clearly if we consider how comparatively unstable poems of the first kind are. . . . Irony in this sense consists in the bringing in of the opposite, the complementary impulses; that is why poetry which is exposed to it is not of the highest order, and why irony itself is so constantly a characteristic of poetry which is" (250).

12. The analogy with Jean-François Lyotard's ontological definition of Modernism in *Postmodern Condition* should not be overlooked: "Here, then, lies the difference [from the postmodern]: modern aesthetics is an aesthetics of the sublime, though a nostalgic one. It allows the unpresentable to be put forward only as the missing contents; but the form, because of its recognizable consistency, continues to offer to the reader or viewer matter for solace and pleasure" (81).

13. Again, I have used this metaphor in *America's Shadow* to articulate the radical limits of Western imperialism's totalizing discourse and practice. Though Said does not invoke the word *specter* or the ontological resonance I am attributing to it, the rhetoric of haunting nevertheless pervades his discourse about the empire's "Other."

14. See Edward W. Said, foreword to *Selected Subaltern Studies,* ed. Ranajit Guha and Gayatri Spivak (New York: Oxford University Press, 1988), v–x. In this foreword Said emphasizes "the new history" that these postcolonial theorists were writing, one that was different from that of both the British and the Indian nationalist elite in its focus on resistance of the subalterns, the Indian peasantry and urban workers. He characterizes this new history, moreover, in such a way as to remind the reader of Foucault's Nietzschean genealogy and his own contrapuntal perspective on received historical narratives. Pointing to the lack of written documentation of the struggles of the Indian masses—to the fact that

the history of India was documented by the victors (and the Indian nationalist elite that took over this history from the colonizers)—Said writes, "Subaltern history in literal fact is a narrative missing from the official story of India. Somehow to supply the narrative, or to supplement the existing narrative with a new narrative—these are epistemological tasks of great difficulty. It requires, and indeed, receives, what in another connection Foucault had called a 'relentless erudition,' a deeply engaged search for new documents, a brilliantly resourceful re-deployment and re-interpretation of old documents" (vii–viii). The reference to Foucault may be to the opening pages of "Nietzsche, Genealogy, History," in *Language, Counter-Memory, Practice: Selected Essays and Interviews,* ed. Donald F. Bouchard, trans. Bouchard and Sherry Simon (Ithaca, N.Y.: Cornell University Press, 1977), 139–40.

15. Dipesh Chakrabarty, "A Small History of *Subaltern Studies,*" *Habitations of Modernity* (Chicago: University of Chicago Press, 2002), 7.

16. Dipesh Chakrabarty, "Reason and the Critique of Historicism," *Provincializing Europe: Postcolonial Thought and Historical Difference* (Princeton, N.J.: Princeton University Press, 2000), 254–55. See also Ranajit Guha, *Elementary Aspects of Peasant Insurgency in Colonial India* (Delhi: Oxford University Press, 1983); Partha Chatterjee, *Nationalist Thought and the Colonial World* (London: Zed, 1986) and *The Nation and Its Fragments: Colonial and Postcolonial Histories* (Princeton, N.J.: Princeton University Press, 1992); and Edward W. Said, foreword to *Selected Subaltern Studies.*

17. Gauri Viswanathan, *Masks of Conquest* (New York: Columbia University Press, 1989). See also Said, "The Pen and the Sword," 68.

18. For a reading of Said's "voyage in" narrative that supplements mine, see Bruce Robbins, "Secularism, Elitism, Progress, and Other Transgressions: On Edward Said's 'Voyage In,'" in *The Pre-Occupation of Postcolonial Studies,* ed. Fawzia Afzall-Khan and Kalpana Seshaderi-Crooks (Durham, N.C.: Duke University Press, 2000), 157–70, which addresses the issue in term of cultural capital. In this essay, Robbins counters the argument, most famously proffered by Arif Dirlik, that for "Third World intellectuals who have arrived in First World academe, postcolonial discourse is an expression not so much of agony over identity, as it often appears, but of new found power" ("The Postmodern Aura: Third World Criticism in the Age of Global Capitalism," *Critical Inquiry* 20, no. 2 [Winter 1994]: 339). Invoking Said's discussion of the "voyage in" in *Culture and Imperialism* on behalf of his argument, Robbins contrasts it with the "French model of intellectual authority" [articulated by Pierre Bourdieu in *Homo Academicus*], in which the "other" becomes an "oblate": the ventriloquized victim of his or her "elite status." "In this model," he writes, "no authority is ascribed to the place from which the mobile oblate sets out; all authority is imagined to flow from the institutional destination." In Said's "voyage in" narrative, however, the emphasis is radically redistributed: "While it does not underestimate the continuing authority of metropolitan institutions, neither does it treat the composition of cultural capital as fixed once and for all or assume that to accept it is necessarily to offer the donor unconditional loyalty in return. National origin matters; transfers from the periphery to the center do not leave the center as it was. The transnational story of upward mobility is not just a claiming of authority; it is also a redefinition of authority, a redefinition that can have many beneficiaries, for it means a recomposition as well as redistribution of cultural capital, in short, progress is by no means inevitable, but is possible" (163–64).

19. See William V. Spanos, "The Ontological Origins of Occidental Imperialism: Thinking the *Meta* of Metaphysics," *America's Shadow*, 1–63.

20. Edward W. Said, "Secular Criticism," *The World, the Text, and the Critic* (Cambridge, Mass.: Harvard University Press, 1983), 3. See also his "Reflections on American 'Left' Literary Criticism," 158–77 of the same volume, and *Culture and Imperialism*, 278–79.

21. Martin Heidegger, "The Age of the World Picture," in *The Question Concerning Technology and Other Essays,* ed. and trans. William Lovitt (New York: Harper and Row, 1977). Amplifying on his assertion that Western man, in having become "that being upon which all that is, is grounded as regards the manner of its Being and its truth," also "becomes the relational center of that which is as such," Heidegger writes: "With the word 'picture' we think first of all of a copy of something. Accordingly, the world picture would be a painting, so to speak, of what is as a whole. But 'world picture' means more than this. We mean by it the world itself, the world as such, what is, in its entirety, just as it is normative and binding for us. 'Picture' here does not mean some imitation, but rather what sounds forth in the colloquial expression, 'We get the picture' [lit., "we are in the picture"] concerning something. This means the matter stands before us exactly as it stands with it for us. 'To get into the picture' [lit., "to put oneself into the picture"] with respect to something means to set whatever is, itself, in place before oneself just in the way that it stands with it, and to have it fixedly before oneself as set up in this way. But a decisive determinant in the essence of the picture is still missing. 'We get the picture' concerning something does not mean only that what is, is set before us, is represented to us, in general, but that what is stands before us—in all that belongs to it and all that stands together in it—*as a system.* 'To get the picture' throbs with being acquainted with something, with being equipped and prepared for it. Where the world becomes picture, what is, in its entirety, is juxtaposed as that for which man is prepared and which, correspondingly, he therefore intends to bring before himself and have before himself, and consequently intends in a decisive sense to set in place before himself. Hence world picture, when understood essentially, does not mean a picture of the world but the world conceived and grasped as picture. What is, in its entirety, is now taken in such a way that it first is in being and only is in being to the extent that it is set up by man, who represents and sets forth. Wherever we have the world picture, an essential decision takes place regarding what is, in its entirety. *The Being of whatever is, is sought and found in the representedness of the latter*" (129–30; emphasis added).

22. Martin Heidegger, "What Is Metaphysics?" *Basic Writings,* 95 (emphasis added). Further citations will be abbreviated to WIM and appear parenthetically.

23. Michel Foucault, *Madness and Civilization: A History of Insanity in the Age of Reason* (New York: Vintage, 1988), 288.

24. Lyotard, *The Postmodern Condition,* 81. In 1979, when Lyotard published this book, he noted at its end that "under the general demand for the slackening and the appeasement, we can hear the mutterings of the desire for a return to terror, for the realization of the fantasy to seize reality," and then goes on to say, "The answer is: Let us wage a war on totality; let us be witnesses to the unpresentable" (82). It is worth observing in this context that the "general demand for slackening and appeasement" has become increasingly—and ominously—pronounced in the United States in the interval between the emergence of postmodern theory and practice during the Vietnam decade and the present post-9/11

moment. Besides the neoconservatives' invention of the "culture wars" and symptomatic of it, this demand is demonstrated by the American publishing industry—a crucial part of what Adorno called the "consciousness industry"—which has sustained a successful effort to marginalize postmodern fiction in favor of a return to the realistic narrative. This "slackening and appeasement," moreover, has contributed significantly to the transformation of the "mutterings of the desire for a return to terror" in the aftermath of 9/11.

25. For a brilliant analysis of Gramsci's concept of the organic intellectual, see R. Radhakrishnan, "Toward an Effective Intellectual: Foucault or Gramsci," *Diasporic Mediations: Between Home and Location* (Minneapolis: University of Minnesota Press, 1996), 46–55. Nonetheless, I question the distinction Radhakrishnan (and Gayatri Spivak) makes between what he takes to be Foucault's agency-limiting notion of the "specific intellectual" and Gramsci's agency-enabling "organic intellectual" (53), especially in his assertion that by refusing to assume an avant-guardist representational leadership, the former, unlike the latter, becomes incapable of producing "coalitional" or "historical blocs," a diversity of resistant subject positions within continuity. See also "Ethnic Identity and Poststructuralist Difference" (66–68), in the same text; and Gayatri Spivak, "Can the Subaltern Speak? in *Marxism and the Interpretation of Culture,* ed. Cary Nelson and Lawrence Grossberg (Urbana: University of Illinois Press, 1988), 271–313. This issue is too complex to argue here. I will simply quote from the passage in "Intellectuals and Power: A Conversation between Michel Foucault and Gilles Deleuze," in Michel Foucault, *Language, Counter-Memory, Practice: Selected Essays and Interviews,* ed. Donald F. Bouchard, trans. Bouchard and Sherry Simon (Ithaca, N.Y.: Cornell University Press, 1977), that I would use as my starting point were I to discuss it. Rejecting the Marxist notion of the general or representative intellectual, which models itself on the general intellectual of bourgeois capitalist society who "speaks for all humanity" and thus universalizes the great varieties of oppressions in the figure of the proletariat, Foucault and Deleuze, like Gramsci, articulate a notion of the specific intellectual who, as Deleuze says of Foucault in his relation to the inmates of prisons, "create[s] conditions that permit the prisoners themselves to speak," who, although focusing resistance at the site of each's particular condition of exploitation, is aware of the multiplicity of sites and constituencies on which and whom power is practiced. See note 8, chapter 3, where I quote at length from Foucault's conversation with Gilles Deleuze on the relationship between the specific intellectual and the specific struggles of the oppressed under the democratic capitalist regime of truth.

26. The quoted passage is from T. S. Eliot's *Four Quartets* ("Little Gidding"), *The Complete Poems and Plays, 1909–1950* (New York: Harcourt, Brace, 1952), 144.

27. Martin Heidegger, "Language in the Poem," *On the Way to Language,* trans. Peter D. Hirtz (New York: Harper and Row, 1971), 171; further references will be abbreviated to LP and appear parenthetically.

28. Antonio Negri and Michael Hardt, *Empire* (Cambridge, Mass.: Harvard University Press, 2000).

29. For a suggestive, if somewhat opaque, early (pre–*Culture and Imperialism*) meditation on Said's notion of the exilic intellectual, see Abdul R. JanMohamed, "Worldliness-without-World, Homelessness-as-Home: Toward a Definition of the Specular Border Intellectual," in *Edward Said: A Critical Reader,* ed. Michael Sprinker (Cambridge, Mass: Blackwell, 1992), 96–120. Given that Said insistently excoriates the visualism of Western

knowledge production, however, I find JanMohamed's use of the adjective *specular* to characterize the "border intellectual" troubling insofar as it implies a perspective that spatializes, fixes, brings to stand, the differential dynamics that the intellectual's predicament—homelessness—discloses to him or her.

30. Eliot, *The Family Reunion*, scene 2, *The Complete Poems and Plays*, 250.

31. Here, it should be noted, Said openly identifies the imperial dispensation (insofar as administration, as he pointedly remarks in his discussion of Conrad early in the book, is the essential characteristic that distinguished British imperialism from the rapacious variety) with Western cultural production and Western consciousness.

32. In underscoring the emergent positive possibilities of the victim's refusal to be answerable to the narrative of the dominant culture, is it possible, I wonder, that Adorno (and Said), like Maurice Blanchot, Gilles Deleuze, Giorgio Agamben, and Antonio Negri and Michael Hardt, has Herman Melville's "Bartleby the Scrivener" in mind—the "I prefer not to" that disintegrates the bourgeois capitalist worldview of the "benign" narrator-lawyer for whom Bartleby copies legal documents? See Blanchot, *The Writing of Disaster*, trans. Ann Smock (Lincoln: University of Nebraska Press, 1986), 17–21; Deleuze, "Bartleby; or, The Formula," *Essays: Critical and Clinical*, trans. Daniel W. Smith and Michael A. Greco (Minneapolis: University of Minnesota Press, 1997), 68–90; Agamben, "Bartleby, or On Contingency," *Potentialities: Collected Essays in Philosophy*, trans. Daniel Heller-Roazen (Stanford, Calif.: Stanford University Press, 2000), 243–71; and Negri and Hardt, *Empire*, 203–4.

33. See William V. Spanos, "Vietnam and the *Pax Americana*: A Genealogy of the New World Order," *America's Shadow*, 126–69; and Spanos, "*A Rumor of War*: 9/11 and the Forgetting of the Vietnam War," *boundary 2* 24 (Fall 2003): 29–66.

34. The quotation is from T. S. Eliot, "Burnt Norton," *Four Quartets*, *The Complete Poems and Plays*, 117.

35. See William V. Spanos, "Culture and Colonization: The Imperial Imperatives of the Centered Circle," *America's Shadow*, 64–125.

36. Hannah Arendt, *The Human Condition* (Chicago: University of Chicago Press, 1958), 98.

37. Peter Hulme, *Colonial Encounters: Europe and the Native Caribbean 1492–1797* (London: Methuen, 1986). For a fuller account of this nexus see Spanos, "Culture and Colonization"; and Richard Waswo, *The Founding Legend of Western Civilization: From Virgil to Vietnam* (Hanover, N.H.: Wesleyan University Press, 1997), 41–54.

38. See especially James Fenimore Cooper, *The Pioneers*, ed. James D. Wallace (Oxford: Oxford University Press, 1991). This binary opposition between the sedentary and the nomadic life lies at the heart of this inaugural American novel about the American frontier.

39. Francis Parkman, *The Conspiracy of Pontiac* (New York: Library of America, 1991), 459. This opposition saturates Parkman's racist discourse. Parkman even invokes the archaic legal term "domiciliated" (558), which John Winthrop used to justify the Massachusetts Bay Puritans' expropriation of the Native Americans' land, to distinguish the civilized white man's superior mode of life from that of the natives.

40. Edward W. Said, *The Question of Palestine* (New York: New York Times Books, 1979), 21. The relationship between this Zionist discourse and America is even more intimate

(and ironic) than Said claims. This can be seen if it is recalled that the American Puritans of the Massachusetts Bay Colony interpreted their "election" and divinely ordained "errand in the wilderness" of the "New World" (to "build a city on the hill") on the analogy of the Old Testament Israelites' exodus from captivity in Egypt and their journey into the "promised land." The American Puritans, that is, understood their "errand" in terms of what Eric Auerbach (in analyzing the hermeneutics of the patristic exegetes of the Old and New Testaments) and, later, Sacvan Bercovitch (in analyzing the hermeneutics of the American Puritan biblical exegetes) called figural interpretation: the notion that the historical events of the Old Testament prefigured those of the New Testament. What I am suggesting, in other words, is that the post-1948 Israeli Zionists resorted to the American Puritans' prefigurative or typological interpretation of Old Testament history to justify their own representation of Palestine as *terra nullius*. See Erich Auerbach, "Figura," *Scenes from the Drama of European Literature: Six Essays,* trans. Ralph Manheim (New York: Meridian, 1959), and *Mimesis: The Representation of Reality in Western Literature,* trans. Willard Trask (Princeton, N.J.: Princeton University Press, 1953), 48ff., 73–76, 156–62, 194–292, 317ff.; and Sacvan Bercovitch, *The Puritan Origins of the American Self* (New Haven, Conn.: Yale University Press, 1975), 35–71, and *The American Jeremiad* (Madison: University of Wisconsin Press, 1998). For a more ample development of Said's criticism of the Zionist representation of Palestine as a *terra nullia,* see his "Michael Walzer's *Exodus and Revolution*: A Canaanite Reading," in *Blaming the Victims: Spurious Scholarship and the Palestinian Question,* ed. Edward Said and Christopher Hitchens (London: Verso, 1988), his response to Walzer's *Exodus and Revolution* (New York: Basic Books, 1984), and the exchange between Said and Walzer published in *Grand Street* 5, no. 4 (1986): 246–59. This exchange is conveniently available in the appendix to William D. Hart's *Edward Said and the Religious Effects of Culture* (Cambridge: Cambridge University Press, 2000), 187–99.

41. Jacques Derrida, "White Mythology: Metaphor in the Text of Philosophy," *Margins of Philosophy,* trans. Alan Bass (Chicago: University of Chicago Press, 1982), 207–71.

42. Herman Melville, *Pierre; or the Ambiguities* (Evanston, Ill.: Northwestern University Press and the Newberry Library, 1971), 89.

43. See Martin Heidegger, *Being and Time,* trans. John Macquarrie and Edward Robinson (New York: SCM, 1962), 24–25, 27–28, 194–95, 363, 436–37.

44. Frantz Fanon, *The Wretched of the Earth,* trans. Constance Farrington (New York: Grove, 1963): "So, my brothers, how is it that we do not understand that we have better things to do than to follow that same Europe? That same Europe where they were never done talking of Man, and where they never stopped proclaiming they were only anxious for the welfare of Man: today we know with what sufferings humanity has paid for every one of their triumphs of the mind. . . . When I search for Man in the technique and style of Europe, I see only a succession of negations of man, and an avalanche of murders. . . . Let us decide not to imitate Europe, let us combine our muscles and our brains in a new direction. Let us try to create the whole man, whom Europe has been incapable of bringing to triumphant birth" (312–13). Fanon's "new humanism," to adapt the phrase Dipesh Chakrabarty uses to interrogate the West's universalization of its own concept of history, is intended to provincialize Europe's universalized humanism and in the process to open up an infinitely heterogeneous global humanism in which, as in Aimé Césaire's, "there is room for everyone at the rendezvous of victory."

Chapter 5: Edward Said's Humanism and American Exceptionalism after 9/11/01

1. T. S. Eliot, "East Coker," *Four Quartets, The Complete Poems and Plays, 1909–1950* (New York: Harcourt, Brace, 1952), 128.

2. A symptom of this is the collection of essays published almost immediately after Said's death under the editorship of Homi Bhabha and W. J. T. Mitchell, *Edward Said: Continuing the Conversation* (Chicago: University of Chicago Press, 2005).

3. I should point out that I use the word *poststructuralist* to refer not only to its technical meaning but also to the meaning that implicitly resonates in its etymology. Insofar as metaphysical thinking in all its varieties perceives the dynamic phenomena of being from after or above them (*meta ta physika,* or panoptically), it spatializes or more precisely *structuralizes* that which in essence—time, historicity, the nothing, alterity—cannot be finally structured. Insofar as poststructural thinking exists to delegitimize the hegemony of metaphysical (or logocentric) thinking, it is post-structuralist. Its essential function is to destructure or deconstruct the structure that the imperial metaphysical mind willfully imposed on time, historicity, the nothing, and alterity, not to annihilate it, but to release or liberate that which it has colonized, that is, enclosed and contained in a structure.

4. Edward W. Said, *Humanism and Democratic Criticism* (New York: Columbia University Press, 2003), xvi. Further citations will be abbreviated to *HDC* and appear parenthetically. For reasons that will become clear, I understand the urgency of this diagnosis of the post-9/11 occasion, which he reiterates in the book, in the light of Louis Althusser's posthumanist analysis of the epochal "change of terrain" in the "domain" of knowledge production precipitated by Marx's perception of the radically indissoluble relationality of *vision* privileged by the (capitalist) West and cultural production and politics. See Althusser, "From *Capital* to Marx's Philosophy," in Althusser and Étienne Balibar, *Reading "Capital"* (London: Verso, 1970), 24–28; see also William V. Spanos, "Althusser's Problematic in the Context of the Vietnam War: Towards a Spectral Politics," *Rethinking Marxism* 10 (Fall 1998): 1–21; repr. in revised form in Spanos, *American Exceptionalism in the Age of Globalization: The Specter of Vietnam* (Albany, N.Y.: SUNY Press, 1908).

5. It was also the model of the modern Western university—the cultural institution par excellence that reproduced the nation-state as imagined by Fichte, Schleiermacher, Kant, and others and put into practice by Wilhelm Humboldt. See Bill Readings, "The University and the Idea of Culture," *The University in Ruins* (Cambridge, Mass.: Harvard University Press, 1996), 62–70.

6. Martin Heidegger, "Letter on Humanism," trans. Frank A. Capuzzi, in *Basic Writings,* rev. ed., ed. David Farrell Krell (San Francisco: Harper and Row, 1993), 224–25.

7. For an amplification of my reading of this passage, see William V. Spanos, *Heidegger and Criticism: Retrieving the Cultural Politics of Destruction* (Minneapolis: University of Minnesota Press, 1993), 144–52. See also Philippe Lacoue-Labarthe, *Heidegger, Art, and Politics,* trans. Chris Turner (Oxford: Basil Blackwell, 1990), 95.

8. Martin Heidegger, *Parmenides,* trans. André Schuwer and Richard Rojcewicz (Bloomington: Indiana University Press, 1992), 40–41. Translation modified. Further citations will be abbreviated to *P* and appear parenthetically.

9. Edward W. Said, *Culture and Imperialism* (New York: Knopf, 1993), 69; further ci-

tations will be abbreviated to *CI* and appear parenthetically. Said makes this enabling distinction in his discussion of Marlow's differentiation between Belgian and British imperialism in Joseph Conrad's *Heart of Darkness*. One of the most serious lacks in Said's genealogy of the West's representation of its "Others" in *Orientalism, Culture and Imperialism,* and *Humanism and Democratic Criticism* is his failure to address the decisive role that imperial Rome—its calculative binarist thought, its disciplinary culture, and its imperial politics—played in the determination of the West's identity and that of the rest of the world, including the Orient. Given Said's relentless critique of Western power relations vis-à-vis the Orient (and elsewhere), it is, to say the least, surprising that none of these texts makes a substantial reference to the decisive contribution to the formation of the official identity of Europe made by the *intellectual* history inaugurated by Virgil's *Aeneid* and the "Fourth Eclogue," the latter of which was read by Christian intellectuals from St. Augustine through the Patristic biblical exegetes to Dante as a secular prefiguration of the coming of Christ (i.e., Christian Europe). This history also includes early Italian humanists such as Boccaccio, Petrach, Ficino, Campanella, Pico de la Mirandola; English and French humanists of the later Renaissance such as Erasmus, More, and Sidney, who were profoundly influenced by Virgil, Quintilian, Cicero, and Tacitus; later Modernist humanist such as Sainte-Beuve, who claimed Virgil to be the founder of the idea of Europe; T. S. Eliot, who invoked Virgil's "comprehensive vision" as the model for the new postwar Europe; and, ironically in this context, Erich Auerbach, for whom the Virgilian Dante was the harbinger of European humanism. All these writers in one way or another identified metropolitan Rome (and the Roman imperial dispensation) with the very idea of the West.

Nor does Said say anything about the equally influential juridical or political history contributing to the identity of the West (and its "Others"), which marginalized the culture and polity (the city-state) of classical Greece in favor of metropolitan, that is, imperial, Rome. I am referring to the political history beginning with the Roman Empire (the Pax Romana) and extending through the Holy Roman Empire of the medieval period to the Enlightenment, which as Foucault has reminded us, modeled itself, both in America and France, on "republican" Rome, and then to the Pax Britannica and most recently the Pax Americana.

It is difficult to determine why Said did not address this obvious history. I surmise that he symptomatically realized that to invoke it would have been tantamount to undermining his insistent commitment to the European humanist tradition. This surmise finds support in Said's invocation, in *Culture and Imperialism,* of Martin Bernal's thesis in *Black Athena*: that humanist Greece—the Greece that, according to Matthew Arnold, was characterized by "sweetness and light"—was a fabrication of the German Enlightenment humanists, who from their Orientalist perspective wished to protect an Aryan Europe from contamination by Semitic cultures, that ancient Greece was in fact a multicultural culture profoundly indebted to "black" Africa and the Semitic East and thus not qualified to be the origin of Western Orientalism. It seems, therefore, that Said's invocation of Bernal's revolutionary insight—and the prominence of Rome's intellectual and political ethos, as I have briefly summarized previously—would compel him to at least consider the possibility that Western Orientalism had its origins in imperial Rome and not, as he insists in *Orientalism,* in Greece. But surprisingly, he does not pursue this resonant insight. All of which is to say that Said's indifference to metropolitan Rome's role in the formation of the official European identity calls into question his relentless appeal to historicism against the "ahistoricism" of the poststructuralists. That is, for all his Vichian commitment to worldliness—the historicity of texts—Said is in this crucial instance not historical enough.

10. Jacques Derrida, "The Ends of Man," *Margins of Philosophy,* trans. Alan Bass (Chicago: University of Chicago Press, 1982), 128. Further citations will be abbreviated to EM and appear parenthetically.

11. Louis Althusser, "Ideology and Ideological State Apparatuses (Notes toward an Investigation)," *Lenin and Philosophy and Other Essays,* trans. Ben Brewster (New York: Monthly Review, 1971), 170ff.

12. See also, William V. Spanos, "Heidegger and Foucault: The Politics of the Commanding Gaze," in *Heidegger and Criticism,* 132–80.

13. Michel Foucault, *Discipline and Punish: The Birth of the Prison,* trans. Alan Sheridan (New York: Pantheon, 1977), 205–6.

14. Michel Foucault, "Revolutionary Action: 'Until Now,'" in *Language, Counter-Memory, Practice: Selected Essays and Interviews,* ed. Donald F. Bouchard, trans. Bouchard and Sherry Simon (Ithaca, N.Y.: Cornell University Press, 1977), 221–22.

15. Edward W. Said, "Reflections on American 'Left' Literary Criticism," *The World, the Text, and the Critic* (Cambridge, Mass.: Harvard University Press, 1983), 167–68; originally published in *The Problems of Reading in Contemporary American Criticism,* special issue, *boundary 2* 8, no. 1 (Fall 1979): 11–30; repr., in *The Question of Textuality: Strategies of Reading in Contemporary American Criticism,* ed. William V. Spanos, Paul A. Bové, and Daniel O'Hara (Bloomington: Indiana University Press, 1982).

16. Said's intervention at the *boundary 2* conference in 1978 contributed massively to turning American literary criticism away from textual analysis and toward the "worldliness" of texts. At that time, however, I read (as I still do) his severe criticism not as a rejection of deconstruction as such but as a justified condemnation of the betrayal of its revolutionary potential by Derrida's American followers in their reduction of its horizon to the site of literature and of literature to textuality (to a new New Criticism, as it were). In other words, I—and, I think, many of those who attended the conference—interpreted that effort to retrieve the worldliness of the text from textuality as an effort to fulfill the emancipatory possibilities of the deconstructive project. My reading of that moment was reflected in my essay "Retrieving Heidegger's Destruction: A Response to Barbara Johnson," in *Society for Critical Exchange Reports* 8 (Fall 1980), later expanded into "The Indifference of *Différance*: Retrieving Heidegger's Destruction," in *Heidegger and Criticism,* 81–131.

17. Edward W. Said, "Michel Foucault, 1927–1984," *Reflections on Exile and Other Essays* (Cambridge, Mass.: Harvard University Press, 2000), 196 (emphasis added); originally published in *Raritan* 4, no. 2 (Fall 1984). This, not incidentally, is the gist of Foucault's very Althusserian response (significantly made at the height of the Vietnam War) in his famous debate with Noam Chomsky in 1971 (*The Chomsky-Foucault Debate on Human Nature* [New York: Free Press, 2006]). During this conversation the moderator ironically asked why Foucault would be, as he claims he was, intensely interested in politics given his apparent refusal of the notion of a human nature and the agency that ostensibly en-

sues from it: "What I want to say is this: it is the custom, at least in European society, to consider that power is localized in the hands of the government and that it is exercised through a certain number of particular institutions, such as the administration, the police, the army, and the apparatuses of the state. . . . But I believe that political power also exercises itself through the mediation of a certain number of institutions that look as if they had nothing in common with the political power, and as if they are independent of it, while they are not. . . .

"It seems to me that the real political task in a society such as ours [I think Foucault is stressing the present historical occasion] is to criticize the workings of institutions, which appear to be both neutral and independent; to criticize and attack them in such a manner that the political violence which has always exercised itself obscurely through them will be unmasked, so that one can fight against them.

"This critique and this fight seem essential to me for different reasons: first because political power goes much deeper than one suspects; there are centers and invisible little-known points of support; its true resistance, its true solidarity is perhaps where one doesn't expect it. Probably it is insufficient to say that behind the government, behind the apparatuses of the state, there is the dominant class; one must locate the point of activity, the places and forms in which its domination is exercised. And because this domination is not simply the expression in political terms of economic exploitation, it is its instrument and, to a large extent, the condition which makes it possible; the suppression of the one is achieved through the exhaustive discernment of the other. *Well, if one fails to recognize these points of support of class power, one risks allowing them to continue to exist; and to see this class power reconstitute itself even after an apparent revolutionary process*" (40–42; emphasis added).

18. Raymond Williams, *Marxism and Literature* (New York: Oxford University Press, 1977), 109–10 (emphasis added).

19. R. Radhakrishnan, "Edward Said's Literary Humanism," *Cultural Critique* 67 (Fall 2007): 24–25.

20. Ibid., 16–17.

21. Hugo of St. Victor, *Didascalicon,* trans. Jerome Taylor (New York: Columbia University Press, 1961), qtd. by Said in *CI,* 333.

22. See pp. 380–81.

23. For a fuller account of this history, see William Spanos, *The End of Education: Toward Posthumanism* (Minneapolis: University of Minnesota Press, 1993). See also Foucault, *Discipline and Punish,* 171–77; E. A. Gutkind, *International History of City Development,* 8 vols., vol. 5, *Urban Development in Western Europe: France and Belgium* (New York: Free Press, 1970); and Norman J. Johnston, *Cities in the Round* (Seattle: University of Washington Press, 1983).

24. Aamir R. Mufti, "Critical Secularism: A Reintroduction for Perilous Times," *Critical Secularism,* ed. Aamir R. Mufti, special issue, *boundary 2* 31, no. 2 (Summer 2004): 2–3.

25. Mufti is reminding us of Said's appropriation in *Orientalism* of this phrase from M. H. Abrams, one of the most influential humanists of the pre-poststructuralist period and an opponent of critical theory, in his effort to radicalize the meaning of secularism. See Abrams, *Natural Supernaturalism: Tradition and Revolution in Romantic Literature* (New York: Norton, 1971); and Said, *Orientalism,* 114, 120–22.

26. See also Paul A. Bové, "The Last of the Latecomers (Part I): The Critical Syntheses of Erich Auerbach," *Intellectuals in Power: A Genealogy of Critical Humanism* (New York: Columbia University Press, 1985), 79–129.

27. Vassilis Lambropoulos, *The Rise of Eurocentrism: Anatomy of Interpretation* (Princeton, N.J.: Princeton University Press, 1993), 3–24, 85–91.

28. Erich Auerbach, "Figura," *Scenes from the Drama of European Literature: Six Essays* (New York: Meridian, 1959), 11–78.

29. See Sacvan Bercovitch, *The Puritan Origins of the American Self* (New Haven, Conn.: Yale University Press, 1975), and *The American Jeremiad* (Madison: University of Wisconsin Press, 1978). See also William V. Spanos, "American Exceptionalism, the Jeremiad, and the Frontier, before and after 9/11/01: From the Puritan to the New-Con Man," *American Exceptionalism*.

30. It is, as I will show shortly, precisely this elitist and repressive exegetical tradition to which, in the wake of 9/11/01, the neoconservative humanist Samuel P. Huntington appeals in *Who Are We? Challenges to the American National Identity* (New York: Simon and Schuster, 2004) when he calls for a new "Great Awakening."

31. Edward W. Said, *The Question of Palestine* (New York: New York Times Books, 1979), 19; see also 71, 77, 81, 91, 101, 150. Further references will be abbreviated to *QP* and appear parenthetically. In his introduction to the collection of interviews with Edward Said conducted by David Barsamian and entitled *The Pen and the Sword: Conversations with David Barsamian* (Edinburgh: AK Press, 1994), Eqbal Ahmad underscores the importance of this exegetical aspect of the American exceptionalist myth for Said's analysis of the deep structure informing the Zionists' justification for their return to Palestine, expropriation of the Palestinians' land, and the settlements on the West Bank. For the Zionists, he writes, following Said, "Palestine was a land without people for a people without land: a desert made to bloom by the labor of Zionist pioneers" (15). As I observed in chapter 4, this Eurocentric distinction between nomadic and sedentary cultures that justified the expropriation of land from the indigenous people of the New World became international law during the period of exploration and colonization. As Francis Jennings (in *The Invasion of America: Indians, Colonization and the Cant of Conquest* [Chapel Hill: University of North Carolina Press, 1975]) and Peter Hulme (in *Colonial Encounters: Europe and the Native Caribbean, 1492–1797* [London: Methuen, 1986]) have shown, this process of legalizing expropriation was especially enhanced by the New England Puritans. Relying on figural exegesis (their "fulfillment" of the promise of the Old Testament Israelites' exodus into the Promised Land), John Winthrop, for example, justified the Massachusetts Bay Colony's land-grabbing by appealing to "the legal argument of *vacuum domicilium* by which the Indians had 'natural' but not 'civil' rights over the land because they had not 'subdued' it" (Hulme, *Colonial Encounters*, 158).

In disclosing the myth of the American pioneer underlying the discourse and practice of Zionism in Palestine, Said (along with Eqbal) contributes significantly to our understanding of contemporary Israel's hegemonic discourse. Nevertheless, he fails to perceive the related but even deeper structure informing this Zionist discourse and the irony of its use: that it appropriates the medieval biblical exegetical method of figural interpretation (brilliantly explicated by Erich Auerbach and later, in the more pertinent American context, by Sacvan Bercovitch) that precedes and informs the secular myth of the American pioneer. That is, the Zionists appropriated the American Puritans' providentially ordained appropriation of the Old Testament Hebrew's exodus and journey to the Promised Land to justify their (genocidal) errand in the New World wilderness.

32. Jacques Derrida, "Force and Signification," *Writing and Difference,* trans. Alan Bass (Chicago: University of Chicago Press, 1978), 21.

33. Edward W. Said, *Orientalism* (New York; Vintage, 1978), 93.

34. See Bové, *Intellectuals in Power,* where he reiteratively points to Auerbach's appeal to "synthesis," thus remaining tethered to the German "mandarin" humanist tradition he was opposing.

35. Erich Auerbach, *Mimesis: The Representation of Reality in the Western World,* trans. Willard Trask (Princeton, N.J.: Princeton University Press, 1953), 557.

36. In this regard, see Harry Harootunian, "Conjunctural Traces: Said's 'Inventory,'" in *Edward Said: Continuing the Conversation*: "In the case of Erich Auerbach, we have to wonder what exactly Said had in mind in embracing a scholarly figure who spent the wartime in Turkey, once regarded the threshold of Asia and the classical boundary marking off the 'Orient' from Europe, obsessively fixed on writing an account of realist representation of the West that both reinforced the claims of cultural unity that Said's *Orientalism* sought to repudiate and quite purposefully seemed to have bracketed out the immediate environment in order to produce the text in question, *Mimesis.* . . . Auerbach's allegiance to the culture of place from which he was now estranged explains the intensity of his desire to restore to it the unity he would never have recognized had he remained in Europe. . . . For Auerbach, Turkey simply constituted the refuge of exile and offered a culture to which he neither belonged nor in which he had any really abiding interest (unlike Said's relationship to the U.S.). In fact, its very absence in his text and the negativity he associated with it (poor libraries) underscore the importance of his cultural act to rethink the unity of Europe's cultural tradition and to authenticate a singular identity between its origins and its modern present" (69–70).

37. Raymond Williams, *Marxism and Literature,* 110 (emphasis added); as the canonical literature of the humanist West shows, this difficulty applies significantly to authors.

38. Jacques Derrida, "White Mythology," *Margins of Philosophy,* 207–71.

39. The etymology of *exile* takes us back to the sedentary/nomad opposition that, as I noted at the end of chapter 4, underlies the very idea of Western civilization: from the Latin *ex* ("out") and *ul,* as in *ambulare,* "to walk" (*The Oxford Dictionary of English Etymology,* ed. C. T. Onions [Oxford: Clarendon, 1966]), 336.

40. For a powerful critique of nationalism—the exposure of the absence or lack that necessarily exists at the center of the idea of the nation—see William Connolly, *Why I Am Not a Secularist* (Minneapolis: University of Minnesota Press, 1999). Referring to John Stuart Mill's secular liberalization of Renan's famous definition of the nation in "What Is a Nation?" Connolly says that "Mill invokes the language of commonality, identity, community, same, and collective to imagine nationality, but he does not explain how tight, centered, or close identity must be to *be* identity. It is this constant combination of indispensability and uncertainty within the image of the nation that sets it up to be a condition to be remembered but never known, pursued but never present, absent but never eliminable as an end. Any regulative ideal, surely, is impossible to realize fully. But the image of the nation seems to be marked by a sense that *the density at its very center*

is both always indispensable to it and always insufficiently available. This distinctive combination in the regulative ideal of the nation makes the state particularly vulnerable to takeover attempts by constituencies who claim to embody in themselves the unity that is necessary to the nation but so far absent from it" (81). See also Arjun Appadurai, "Life after Primordialism," *Modernity at Large: Cultural Dimensions of Globalization* (Minneapolis: University of Minnesota Press, 1996), 139–57.

41. Daniel Defoe, *Robinson Crusoe,* ed. Michael Shinagel (New York: Norton, 1994), 107–8.

42. For a brilliant reading of this book jacket, see R. Radhakrishnan, "Edward Said and the Politics of Secular Humanism," 115–18.

43. See William V. Spanos, "Humanism and the *Studia Humanitatis* after 9/11," *Symplokē* 13, nos. 1–2 (2005): 238.

44. See Spanos, "Indifference of *Differance,*" 81–131.

45. Bové, *Intellectuals in Power,* 212.

46. This disclosure of the self-de-struction of the logic of imperialism—its eventual and inevitable precipitation of its spectral "Other" in corporeal form into the metropolis—is, as I have shown in chapter 4, the supreme theme of *Culture and Imperialism* in both its content and structure.

47. Besides Negri and Hardt's texts, see also Paolo Virno, *A Grammar of the Multitude,* trans. Isabella Bertoletti, James Cascaito, and Andrea Casson (New York: Semiotext[e], 2004).

48. See Spanos, *End of Education,* which documents the amnesiac history of this humanist initiative.

49. I am referring to the neoconservative think tank affiliated with the American Enterprise Institute, many of whose members hold high positions in the George W. Bush administration. Its policy document, "Rebuilding of America's Defenses," written before 9/11/01, became the model of the Bush presidency's global policies and practices, especially the invasion of Iraq, in the aftermath of 9/11 and the invasion of Afghanistan. Prominent members of the PNAC include Elliot Abrams, Jeb Bush, Dick Cheney, Paula Dobriansky, Steve Forbes, Donald Kagan, William Kristol, Norman Podhoretz, Donald Rumsfeld, and Paul Wolfowitz. See http://www.dkosopedia.com/index.php/Project_for_the_New_Century.

50. For more particular historical evidence supporting these generalizations, see Willima V. Spanos, "Vietnam and the *Pax Americana*: A Genealogy of the 'New World Order,'" *America's Shadow,* 126–69, and *American Exceptionalism.*

51. Edward W. Said, "The Clash of Definitions," *Reflections on Exile and Other Essays* (Cambridge, Mass.: Harvard University Press, 2000), 569–90. See also Said, *The Myth of 'The Clash of Civilizations,'* DVD (Media Education Foundation, 2002).

52. Huntington, *Who Are We?* Further citations will be abbreviated to *WAW* and appear parenthetically.

53. Bercovitch, *American Jeremiad*: "The American Puritan jeremiad was the ritual of a culture on an errand—which is to say, a culture based on a faith in process. Substituting teleology for hierarchy, it discarded the Old World ideal of stasis for a New World vision of the future. Its function was to create a climate of anxiety that helped release the restless 'progressivist' energies required for the success of the venture. . . . It made anxiety its end

as well as its means. Crisis was the social norm it sought to inculcate. The very concept of errand, after all, implied a state of unfulfillment. The future, though divinely assured, was never quite there, and New England's Jeremiahs set out to provide the sense of insecurity that would ensure the outcome. Denouncing or affirming, their vision fed on the distance between promise and fact" (23). It was this divinely sanctioned teleological structure that, according to Bercovitch, instigated the American future. The Puritans' "rhetoric and vision facilitated the process of colonial growth. And in sustaining that rhetoric and vision, the latter-day Jeremiahs effectually forged a powerful vehicle of middle-class ideology: a ritual of progress through consensus, a system of sacred-secular symbols for a laissez-faire creed, a 'civil religion' for a people chosen to spring fully formed into the modern world—America, the first begotten daughter of democratic capitalism, the only country that developed, from the seventeenth through the nineteenth centuries, into a wholly middle-class culture" (28–29).

54. In a move typical of his instrumentalist thinking—a calculative thinking enabled by beginning inquiry from the end he has in mind (that is, by reducing temporal history to a picture or, in the language of the policy expert, a scenario)—Huntington invokes Bercovitch's history of the American jeremiad without informing his readers that Bercovitch's statement about the Puritan settlement of America is intended to disclose the origins of the dark, violent side of the American national identity.

55. See Frederick Jackson Turner, "The Significance of the Frontier in American History," *The Frontier in American History* (New York: Dover, 1996), 37–38.

Chapter 6: *Edward Said's Mount Hermon and Mine*

1. Edward W. Said, *Out of Place* (New York: Knopf, 1999), 225. Further citations will appear parenthetically.

Index

WILLIAM V. SPANOS is Distinguished Professor of English and Comparative Literature at SUNY-Binghamton and founding editor of *boundary 2: a journal of international literature and culture*. He is also the author of several books, including *The End of Education: Toward Posthumanism, The Errant Art of Moby-Dick: The Cold War, the Canon, and the Struggle for American Literary Studies, America's Shadow: An Anatomy of Empire,* and *American Exceptionalism in the Age of Globalization: The Specter of Vietnam.*

The University of Illinois Press
is a founding member of the
Association of American University Presses.

———————————————————————

Composed in 10.5/13 Adobe Minion Pro
by Jim Proefrock
at the University of Illinois Press
Manufactured by Sheridan Books, Inc.

University of Illinois Press
1325 South Oak Street
Champaign, IL 61820-6903
www.press.uillinois.edu